*Ellen Glasgow*
*and the*
*Woman Within*

ELLEN GLASGOW

# Ellen Glasgow
# and the
# Woman Within

E. STANLY GODBOLD, JR.

*Louisiana State University Press · Baton Rouge*

"The Novel in the South." By Ellen Glasgow. Copyright 1928 by Minneapolis Star and Tribune Co., Inc. Quoted from the December 1928 issue of *Harper's Magazine* by permission of the Ellen Glasgow Estate.

"Elder and Younger Brother." By Ellen Glasgow. Quoted from the January 23, 1937, issue of *Saturday Review of Literature* by permission of *Saturday Review*.

Quotations from *The Woman Within, Letters of Ellen Glasgow*, and *A Certain Measure* are by permission of Harcourt Brace Jovanovich, Inc., and the Ellen Glasgow Estate.

*ISBN 0–8071–0040–4*
*Library of Congress Catalog Card Number 71–165068*
*Copyright © 1972 by Louisiana State University Press*
*All rights reserved*
*Manufactured in the United States of America*
*Printed by Heritage Printers, Inc.,*
*Charlotte, North Carolina*

To
Robert H. Woody

# Preface

Jn her autobiography Ellen Glasgow wrote that he who bargains for the future must play a long hazard. She played that long hazard and left a significant volume of materials of inestimable value to her biographer. Except for a few years in her early adulthood, her papers and letters were preserved, and she wrote many letters to literary friends who realized their value and saved them. Her autobiography, *The Woman Within*, which she refused to allow to be published during her lifetime, is sometimes malicious, occasionally vague and chronologically inexact, and often borders on the melodramatic; but it is always a brutally frank expression of her inner feelings toward herself and her acquaintances and a rare exercise in self-analysis by a woman intrigued by the revelations of psychology and not unfamiliar with professional psychoanalysis. Occasionally, she teased more than she revealed, and much of the autobiography was written during a time of pain and illness near the end of her life; but *The Woman Within* remains a unique document of many of the emotions that came to life in her novels and governed her often erratic relationships with people and animals.

In dealing with her novels in this biography, it has seemed advisable to emphasize only those aspects of them that touch directly upon her own life and are thus a part of her biography. Literary analyses of her novels have been attempted by Frederick P. W. McDowell in *Ellen Glasgow and the Ironic Art of Fiction* (Madison:

University of Wisconsin Press, 1960), Joan Foster Santas in *Ellen Glasgow's American Dream* (Charlottesville: The University Press of Virginia, 1965), and J. R. Raper in *Without Shelter: The Early Career of Ellen Glasgow* (Baton Rouge: Louisiana State University Press, 1971), and other such attempts are reported to be in progress. Ellen Glasgow's literary reputation was of considerable concern to her, so the contemporary reception of her work is a natural part of her biography. In an unpublished Ph.D. dissertation at Duke University, entitled "Struggle for Recognition: A Study of the Literary Reputation of Ellen Glasgow," William W. Kelly has made a careful study of both the British and American reviews of her novels and thus provided a valuable tool for the preparation of this biography. Marjorie Kinnan Rawlings began taking notes for a biography of Ellen Glasgow in 1953, but died before the end of the year. She had extensive interviews with several people who knew Ellen Glasgow well, and her notes on those interviews have contributed immeasurably to this biography.

I am indebted to a number of institutions and people who assisted in the preparation of this work. The staffs of the following libraries and institutions greeted me with courtesy and made their Glasgow materials available for my examination: the American Academy of Arts and Letters, the Boston Public Library, Columbia University Library, Duke University Library, Goucher College Library, Harvard University Library, the Library of Congress, New York Public Library (Manuscript Division and the Berg Collection), Princeton University Library, Smith College Library, the University of Florida Library, the Library of the University of North Carolina at Chapel Hill, the University of Pennsylvania Library, the University of Virginia Library, the Valentine Museum (Richmond), the Virginia Historical Society, Wagner College Library, and Yale University Library. Miss Laura V. Monti, Chairman of Special Collections at the Research Library at the University of Florida, was of especial assistance to me during my research in the Rawlings Papers. Ellen Glasgow's literary executor, Mr. Frank V. Morley, clarified his role in the use of the Glasgow Papers and expressed his approval of this project. Mr. George V.

Moncure, trustee for the estate of Ellen Glasgow, and the Richmond Society for the Prevention of Cruelty to Animals kindly granted permission to quote from the Ellen Glasgow Papers.

The following citizens of Castine, Maine, gave of their time and memories and introduced a student from the South to the essence of Yankee hospitality: Dr. Harold S. Babcock, Miss Dorothy T. Blake, Mr. Francis W. Hatch, Mrs. Regis Strout, and Mrs. R. S. Wardwell. Likewise, the following citizens of Richmond, Virginia, offered their generous assistance: Miss Frances Brockenbrough, Mrs. James Branch Cabell, Mr. Glasgow Clark, Mrs. Douglas S. Freeman, Mr. H. L. Longerbeam, Mrs. Arthur Perkins, Mrs. James Asa Shield, Mrs. Garland S. Sydnor, Jr., Mrs. William R. Trigg, Jr., and others who wish to remain anonymous. Mrs. H. H. Rowe searched the records of Pet Memorial Park, Inc., for information about Ellen Glasgow's dogs. Mrs. Shield graciously discussed with me the life of her uncle, Colonel Henry W. Anderson, and granted permission to quote from his letters. Mrs. Cabell kindly granted permission to quote from the letters of James Branch Cabell and provided me with introductions to others who were of assistance. The Reverend Cranston Clayton of Chattanooga, Tennessee, read the manuscript and offered some useful suggestions.

My greatest debt of gratitude is to Professor Robert H. Woody of Duke University. From selection of the topic to completion of the final draft, his guidance, critical judgment, encouragement, and friendship have done much to transform what might have been a dull task into an exciting adventure.

# Contents

# *Illustrations*

xiii

*Ellen Glasgow*
*and the*
*Woman Within*

# 1

## Ghosts on Main Street

The old gray stucco house at One West Main Street in Richmond, Virginia, is said to be haunted. It is the house where Ellen Glasgow lived, wrote, and died. Believers in ghosts claim to have seen a vision of Miss Ellen in white, standing on the landing of the main staircase or in the garden doorway. The sound of a typewriter, perhaps made by magnolia pods tapping against a window, sometimes drifts down from the old study. One occupant climbed to the study on a sudden compulsion, heard the loud ticking of a clock in a clockless room, and "felt very close to Miss Ellen without knowing why."[1] Nonbelievers might feel close to Miss Ellen only through the reading of her novels; but if ever a house should be haunted with ghosts of the past and intimations of the future, hers should be. She steeped herself in the remarkable history of the Old Dominion, mystical experience became a part of her being, and as a writer she trained her spirit to flow backward through time and space in quest for man's origin and for his destiny.

One hundred and twenty miles from the sea, the River James splashed over falls at the foot of three hills destined to become Richmond. The red men who had built a modest village of twelve wigwams upon the hills gazed down at a river which they did not even know had been named the James by white men from across the sea. The men who landed at Jamestown in the late spring of

[1] Gloria Galloway, "Tap-Tap, Whoooo—Spooks Spin Tonight," Richmond *Times-Dispatch*, October 31, 1968, Sec. D, p. 1.

1607 pushed up the river in search for a passage to India. Deafened by the falls, and finding the river navigable no farther than the Indian village, they turned back to Jamestown. For half a century the activities of the white men at the falls were minimal and were checked by the red warriors. Then a prosperous merchant came from England to the falls, built a house named Belvedere, traded tools, medicine, pills, sugar, rum, molasses, white indentured servants, and black slaves for furs and tobacco to be shipped back to England.[2] His name was William Byrd, and his son, in the next century, laid out checkerboard streets over the hills and called the town Richmond after its likeness to the geographical situation of Richmond-on-the-Thames in England.[3]

Richmond-in-Virginia eventually became the home of men who cried for separation from England and who argued among themselves over the formation of a government for the new nation. In the course of the American Revolution, the capital of Virginia was moved from Williamsburg to Richmond, where after the war, James Madison, unimposing of voice and stature, persuaded his skeptical fellow Virginians to vote for the ratification of the Constitution of the United States. Thomas Jefferson drew the plans for the gleaming white Capitol with massive columns that stood on Richmond's highest hill, and John Marshall, the city recorder, supervised a lottery to raise the funds for its construction.[4]

In 1807, a dozen years after the cornerstone for the Capitol had been laid and when Thomas Jefferson was President of the United States and John Marshall was Chief Justice of the Supreme Court, the building became a shrine to a bitter disagreement between the two men who brought it into existence. The stage from the south brought Aaron Burr into town, formerly Jefferson's Vice President, but now a prisoner under heavy guard. At the belated instigation of Jefferson he was charged with treason and with preparing an expedition against a country at peace with the United States. Pres-

---

2 Paul Wilstach, *Tidewater Virginia* (Indianapolis: Bobbs-Merrill Co., 1929), 153.

3 W. Asbury Christian, *Richmond: Her Past and Present* (Richmond: L. H. Jenkins, 1912), 7.

4 *Ibid.*, 28.

ident Jefferson was called as a witness and refused to come. John Marshall presided at the trial in the Capitol, found insufficient evidence to prove the treason charge, admitted Burr to bail on the other charge, and by ironic coincidence dined with him on the eve of the trial.[5] Within five months Burr rode out of town a free man, fortuitously befriended by the Chief Justice, the ultimate winner of the ideological and personal conflict between Jefferson and Marshall. It was half a century before the nation again paid so much attention to Richmond.

In that half century Richmond saw layer upon layer of the debris of human hand and mind and heart spread over her hills. The day after Christmas, 1811, during a performance of "Raymond and Agnes, or The Bleeding Nun," the Richmond Theatre burned, causing the death of a number of prominent citizens. The Negroes in the gallery, having been provided with a separate entrance, exited safely.[6] In time, a memorial was erected, and the people of Richmond turned to other activities. They cobblestoned their streets, attended public hangings, welcomed Lafayette and Charles Dickens, and built their mansions. The west end became fashionable; and in 1841 David M. Branch, a wealthy tobacconist, built his Greek revival mansion at One West Main Street. He never lived in it, and in 1846 it was sold to a Davenport family. The growing city needed a cemetery, and a small group of men formed a stock company to establish a private burial ground on the banks of the James River. They fought and haggled for two years over the hillside that is called Hollywood, and in the late afternoon of June 25, 1849, a Baptist minister dedicated the cemetery that became the final resting place for American presidents, Confederate heroes, and especially Episcopalians.[7]

Deeper into the same summer, a handful of citizens braved the heat and the more awesome threat of boredom to attend a lecture on "The Poetic Principle" in the concert hall of the Exchange Ho-

---

[5] Albert J. Beveridge, *The Life of John Marshall* (Boston and New York: Houghton Mifflin Co., 1919), III, 343–97.
[6] Christian, *Richmond*, 78.
[7] *Ibid.*, 163.

tel. The lecturer was Edgar Allan Poe, and at the conclusion of the program he read "The Raven."[8] It was the poet's single performance in Richmond, and seven weeks later he was dead; the brief moment of art yielded to the more pressing matter of politics and the divisive issue of Negro slavery. In less than a dozen years the cannon fired over Fort Sumter, Virginia seceded from the Union, and her celebrating capital sparkled under the dancing fires of the greatest torchlight procession ever witnessed in Richmond.[9] Robert E. Lee made his dramatic decision to cast his fate with that of Virginia.

The fate of Virginia and of Richmond was spelled large when on May 29, 1861, a group of men headed by Jefferson Davis arrived from Montgomery and officially made Richmond the capital of the Confederacy. One of the Confederate cabinet members, a Jew from New Orleans named Judah P. Benjamin, took up his residence at 9 West Main Street, only a few doors from the Davenport mansion. He must have passed One West Main frequently as he alternated his time between his public duties at the Capitol and his private entertainment in his residence on Main Street where he operated a small gambling casino.[10] Richmond became a city of hospitals and prisons, able-bodied soldiers marching off to battle, and wounded or dead soldiers returning for inadequate medical attention or a hero's burial, roaming spies and speculators, anguished whites and bewildered blacks, gamblers and prostitutes. President Davis declared martial law, stubbornly tried to hold together the Confederacy, mourned the deaths of Stonewall Jackson and J. E. B. Stuart, and watched his people economically and politically and psychologically disintegrate before his eyes.

Down the hill from the Capitol, on the north bank of the James River, the operators of the Tredegar Iron Works fought as valiantly as the men on the hill to keep the Confederacy alive. Francis T. Glasgow, the superintendent of the blast furnaces that were scattered throughout western Virginia, wrote letter after letter recom-

---

[8] *Ibid.*, 165.
[9] *Ibid.*, 217.
[10] Robert Douthat Meade, *Judah P. Benjamin: Confederate Statesman* (New York: Oxford University Press, 1943), 191.

mending that the furnaces be closed for lack of grain to feed the workers, many of whom were Yankee prisoners, Confederate conscripts, and Negro convicts.[11] In December, 1864, his advice was heeded. The following April, Jefferson Davis and his cabinet began their flight across the Carolinas and Georgia. Behind them were smoking ruins that stretched from the north side of Main Street to the James River, but stopped short of the Tredegar Iron Works. The Confederacy was dead, and Richmond would continue to think of itself as its capital far into the next century.

Yankee cavalry rode down Main Street and hoisted the flag of the United States over the old Confederate Capitol. A Yankee major general took up residence in the White House of the Confederacy and restored order. Two hundred Union guns were fired over Capitol Square to celebrate Lee's surrender, and Union soldiers marched through the heart of Richmond by the thousands on their way home. Within two years the South passed into the era of reconstruction under military force, and Virginia became Military District Number One. The use of troops to bring about reconstruction in Virginia ended in 1870 and was shorter than the war. In the spring of that year a federal court had to decide who was the duly elected mayor of Richmond, a question of authority arising out of the confusion during the transition from Reconstruction to "home rule." The trial was in the Capitol. A gallery collapsed under the weight of the spectators; three hundred were killed, and heavy clouds of dust poured from the building.[12] A century later, an expression of unspeakable horror still darkens the countenance of many a Richmond gentlewoman as in a hushed tone she tells a passing tourist of the "Dis-AH-stah." The dust never cleared. A fog of history settled over Richmond, eventually permeated but not dissipated by an occasional towering structure of modernity, and worked its way permanently into the bloodstream of succeeding generations of Virginians.

---

[11] Charles B. Dew, *Ironmaker of the Confederacy: Joseph R. Anderson and the Tredegar Iron Works* (New Haven and London: Yale University Press, 1966), 168–69, 235, 252.
[12] Christian, *Richmond*, 317.

Before dawn on April 22, 1873, in an unpretentious house at First and Cary streets, a newborn girl uttered her first cry in an atmosphere that was growing heavy and stale under the proliferating melancholy memories of a happier age. Later she referred to her birth as an unhappy event, and she always felt stifled by the environment in which she lived.[13] She was born into a desperate era of social change and petty struggles for power. On the morning of her birth the horses that stood quietly in their stalls a few blocks away were dumb pawns in an act that symbolized the age. In recent months the city fathers had decreed that no locomotives would be allowed on Broad Street, a move calculated to lead to the removal of the tracks in order to grade and pave the street. The owners of the railroads obeyed the ordinance and used horses to pull their railroad cars. By April the railroad owners had surrendered, and horses that had once been used to prevent the change began the work of grading and paving. In the midst of progress the past seemed always to be hauntingly present, for in the next months the horses pulled along Broad Street wagonloads of Confederate dead who had fallen at Gettysburg and now were being removed to their final resting places in Hollywood Cemetery.[14] The baby girl was the eighth child of Francis T. Glasgow, the manager of the Tredegar Iron Works. She was named Ellen.

When a skinny-legged girl of fourteen, who believed passionately in ghosts, she moved with her family in 1887 into the Davenport mansion at One West Main Street. Frail of health, and already determined to be a writer, she entered what would be her home for the rest of her life. A large mirror ordered by James Madison and later purchased by her great-uncle hung in the front drawing room. There was marble tile on the walkway leading up to the steep steps and massive front door. It was a spacious house with four large rooms upstairs and four downstairs, a cavernous basement, a servants' wing, and a hallway with a broad staircase. The columned back porch faced a garden with a high brick wall around it. Time passed, and the house and garden became alive with the things that

---

13 Ellen Glasgow, *The Woman Within* (New York: Harcourt, Brace and Co., 1954), 5.
14 Christian, *Richmond*, 327, 331.

produce memories, the material of ghosts: the entanglements of love and hatred within a large family, the death cry of a loved one, the gentle voice of a lover, the laughter of important literary figures of the twentieth century, the barkings and whinings of pet dogs, the quiet and despair of loneliness, a backyard rose garden containing a tiny tombstone marked "Jeremy," and the persistent clicking of the typewriter. Finally, the house became an extension of the novelist's dual personality, and the boards between the two floors divided it into two worlds. Downstairs was the world of wit and gaiety, bright colors, and elaborate parties, the world where a public image was created and external history was recorded. Upstairs was a world of despair and self-pity, the place where novels were written for escape and companionship. It was the seething depository for the internal history of a solitary spirit. A housekeeper moved from one level to the other without sharing either, and only a small white dog was allowed to roam freely between the two worlds. Those worlds were the exclusive property of the trim, attractive, sixty-year-old woman with dark hair and eyes who in 1934 climbed the steep stairs from the main hall, entered the book-lined room on the northwest corner, carefully locked the door behind her, and sat down to write her autobiography. Ellen Glasgow was alone with her ghosts.

# 2

## *Let Glasgow Flourish*

"*L*ord, let Glasgow flourish," is the motto that three Glasgow brothers, Robert, Joseph, and Arthur, brought to America with them in 1765.[1] The dominant feature of their coat of arms was a green oak tree, a symbol of the family's faith in its ability to endure. Actually, they were not Glasgows at all; they were descendants of a family of Camerons from Glasgow, Scotland. During the Scottish wars in the seventeenth century, a branch of the Cameron family fled to northern Ireland in order to escape religious persecution. To distinguish them from another family of Camerons, they were designated as the *Glasgow* Camerons. In time they dropped the name Cameron and retained Glasgow as the family name.[2]

They arrived in America as Glasgows, driven by the twin demons of ambition and piety. Uncompromisingly devoted to Calvinism and courageously determined to preserve their family and faith in the new world, they carved out for themselves a wilderness plantation of four or five thousand acres on the banks of the James River in Rockbridge County in western Virginia. They named it Green Forest in order to perpetuate the Gaelic meaning of their family name; and after the American Revolution what was believed to be the first large brick house in western Virginia was raised on the plantation. Arthur Glasgow was only sixteen years old when he

[1] *The Glasgows and Their Name* (Printed pamphlet with no author or date given), in Ellen Glasgow Papers, University of Virginia Library.
[2] Olive Glasgow Titus to Ellen Glasgow, January 17, 1936, in Glasgow Papers.

came to America. The next two generations of his descendants were born in the brick plantation house. His son married into the Anderson family, and his grandson, Francis Thomas Glasgow, born in 1829, was also the nephew of General Joseph Reid Anderson, president of the Tredegar Iron Works in Richmond.

Francis Glasgow grew up at Green Forest, where his childhood training centered around instruction in the Presbyterian religion. As a lad of ten he was probably present at the funeral of his Grandfather Anderson and heard the minister console: "And if the Master was pleased to call his servant, and his servant was pleased to go, then why should we wish to retain him, since what is our loss is his eternal gain?"[3] Francis Glasgow was taught to believe firmly in the existence of heaven and hell and the inevitability of man's going to the one place or the other. His favorite biblical passages became those that threatened man with the possibility of eternal damnation, and he was convinced that every event in life, no matter how great or small, was the will of God. Thus indoctrinated, he left the plantation in his fifteenth year to attend Washington College in Lexington, Virginia. He took his degree in 1847 and then went to Richmond to read law. Dissatisfied and bored, he quit after two years and took a job with his uncle at the Tredegar Iron Works. A man of slight stature, in poor health, Francis Glasgow soon left his job and went back to the plantation of his father and the protection of the Scotch-Irish clan. On July 4, 1853, he married Anne Jane Gholson, his sweetheart from a neighboring county.

Anne Jane Gholson came from considerably different stock than did her husband. She was the daughter of Judge Yates Gholson and his first wife, Martha Anne Jane Taylor. Martha Taylor Gholson, who traced her ancestry back to Baron de Graffenried of Switzerland, the founder of the town of New Bern, North Carolina, died when her daughter Anne was an infant. Judge Gholson remarried and moved to Ohio where he became a judge on the Ohio Supreme Court, but he allowed his infant daughter to be adopted by her elderly great-uncle, Chancellor Creed Taylor of the Needham

3 Reverend Stephen F. Cooke, *Funeral Sermon on the Death of Colonel William Anderson* (Fincastle, Va., 1839), in Glasgow Papers.

Law School in Cumberland County, Virginia. Anne Gholson could find in her ancestry many of the leading names of the Virginia Tidewater aristocracy: Randolph, Yates, Woodson, Bland, Taylor, Gholson, and Creed.[4] According to the tradition of her class, she was a lifelong member of the Episcopal church. In the marriage of Anne Gholson and Francis Glasgow, the cavalier and puritan traditions of Virginia came into conflict and with significant effects upon the personalities of their children.

In 1854 Francis Glasgow resumed his work with the Tredegar Iron Works in Richmond, where the life of the young couple became intricately involved with the fortune of the business. In a score of years the fate of the family rose and fell with the tides of prewar anxiety, civil war, reconstruction, and financial panic that pulled upon the Tredegar. In those same years, Francis Glasgow recorded the births of ten children in the family Bible. His uncle, Joseph Reid Anderson, sold him one-sixth interest in the Iron Works and placed him in charge of managing business and promoting sales.[5] In less than three years General Anderson purchased the stock back from his nephew and placed him in a salaried position in which he was to remain for the rest of his life. It was a position that might have been more secure for a young man just beginning his family.

On January 31, 1855, Francis Glasgow recorded the birth of his first child, Emily Taylor. Annie Gholson was born July 9, 1857, and Joseph Reid on March 26, 1860. The Civil War came, and in 1861 General Anderson set up a foundry and machine shop near the Tredegar for ordnance work and placed Francis Glasgow in charge. As the war intensified, however, Francis Glasgow's knowledge of Rockbridge and Allegheny counties was too precious to be wasted, so by 1863 he was sent westward to assume the overall direction of seven Tredegar stacks in the mountainous region of Virginia.[6] His next child, Sally Cary, was born on January 4, 1863,

---

[4] *Woman Within*, 297–301. See also Thomas P. de Graffenried, *The De Graffenried Family Scrapbook* (Charlottesville: University Press of Virginia, 1958).

[5] Dew, *Ironmaker of the Confederacy*, 16.

[6] *Ibid.*, 108, 153–54.

at Fincastle, Virginia. As an infant she could have known nothing of the hardships her father was suffering. Three of the furnaces were destroyed by General David Hunter's Union soldiers, and much of Francis Glasgow's job consisted of trying to work rebellious labor under armed guard. Often he and his workers had to flee to the hills to hide from enemy troops. That job ended, however, for the Confederacy had fallen by the time his fifth child, Arthur Graham, was born at Buchanan on May 30, 1865.

Francis Glasgow was not out of work long, for General Anderson took steps to insure the operation of his business in spite of the misfortunes of war. He used his own men to guard the plant and protect it from being burned when Richmond was evacuated shortly before the surrender, and immediately after the war he applied to President Andrew Johnson for a pardon. The President had announced that such pardons would be available to former Confederates who declared their loyalty to the United States. The President granted the pardon to Anderson, there were no actual government confiscations, losses were light, and by the end of September, 1865, Anderson was back in business.[7] He brought his nephew back to Richmond to resume his post as business manager. There, five more children were born. Kate Anderson was recorded on January 14, 1868, and Francis Thomas on September 2, 1870.

Ellen was next, a sickly, premature baby who had to be carried about on a pillow. She was christened Ellen Anderson Glasgow, but often signed herself as Ellen Anderson Gholson Glasgow out of affection for her mother and respect for her mother's ancestors. The year of her birth was a year of financial depression and an economic setback for the Tredegar Iron Works from which it never completely recovered. In the 1870's and 1880's iron was giving way to steel, and the Tredegar Works, not having sufficient capital to make the transition, was doomed to exist as a small iron business unable to compete with the future industrial giants.[8] It meant relative poverty for the Glasgow family, which was still increasing.

Ellen was two when her father recorded the birth of a baby

7 *Ibid.,* 300.
8 *Ibid.,* 319.

brother, Samuel Creed, on October 14, 1875. Two weeks later the baby died of diptheria, a disease that also threatened the life of Ellen. Her sixteen-year-old brother, Joseph, died shortly thereafter; and the entire family, including the impressionable Ellen, was engulfed by grief and despair. A distraught mother no doubt clasped her surviving children to her breast in an unconscious effort to compensate for the loss of her sons. Later in life, her baby Ellen grew to love death.

The nearness of death had become an accustomed part of life in Richmond, a city devoted to the immortalization of heroes who had fallen in the war. While the Glasgows were burying their sons, the city was unveiling a statue of Thomas J. Jackson with the inscription, "Look! There is Jackson standing like a stone wall."[9] Richmond looked to heroes of the past for the inspiration to endure and prevail in the moment of defeat. The Glasgows, too, endured, and on January 31, 1877, the name of the final child, Rebe Gordon, was entered into the old family Bible. Ellen had a playmate, a shadow.

The three youngest children, Ellen, Rebe, and Frank, were put out to play in the bricked backyard protected by a black iron fence. Ellen was unwell and spent much of her time watching the other children's games and the lamplighter ignite the gas lanterns on Cary Street. One day, as a small child, she wandered into the street between a black dog and the boys who pursued him. Although rescued by her Negro mammy, she never forgot the incident, or the feelings of the hunted, or the terror of the dog and the shouts of the boys. Likewise, as a child, she saw an old Negro man taken away to the almshouse and began to suspect that life was full of cruelty and injustice. For comfort she clung to her Negro mammy, Lizzie Jones, who claimed to have cooked dinner for Robert E. Lee the night before the surrender.[10]

Lizzie Jones was devoted to the Glasgow children, and Ellen adored her. Often she took Ellen by the hand and walked to Capitol Square, to the toy store, or to a nearby park, and occasionally to

9 Christian, *Richmond*, 350.
10 *Woman Within*, 9, 18.

Hollywood Cemetery. She entertained her charge for hours with fairy tales and ghost stories. Between them they created an imaginary "Little Willie," who went with them everywhere. Mammy was the great love of Ellen's childhood. Ellen loved her mother, too, but apparently it was Mammy who gave her the personal attention and love that she craved.

Ellen's father conducted family devotions every morning and led her by the hand to the Presbyterian Sunday school. Later in life she moaned, "As a child I felt damned all day."[11] Her father offered her pennies and nickels not to ask too many childish questions, and when her feelings were hurt she begged a box of gelatine from the cook and hid under the bed to eat it.[12] Aunt Bec, her father's old-maid sister and a born raconteuse, told her the plots of Sir Walter Scott's *The Waverley Novels*, helped her identify the letters of the alphabet in *Old Mortality*, and ultimately taught her how to read and write.[13] Her brother Frank, whom Ellen idolized as a child, started to school, but Ellen was judged too sickly to go. Yet she had a normal child's curiosity and desire to learn. The conflict between her curiosity and her inability to attend school forced her to try to educate herself at an early age and made her more attentive to her natural surroundings. Inarticulate plants and animals became more real to her, and she was given the opportunity to develop those interests in her sixth or seventh year when her father bought a nearby farm for the family's summer home.

Jerdone Castle was an estate of some seven hundred acres in Louisa County, about thirty miles northwest of Richmond. The family spent all their summer days there, and Mr. Glasgow joined them for the weekends. It was a kind of paradise for Francis Glasgow's youngest children. Ellen was like an uncaged bird as she ran across the yard and fields, delighted to escape from the bricked-over

[11] Dr. Alexander Brown, Jr., to Marjorie Kinnan Rawlings, notes on a personal interview, in Rawlings Papers, University of Florida Library. Hereafter Marjorie Kinnan Rawlings is abbreviated as MKR, and this type of footnote without a date indicates that the information came from notes on personal interviews Mrs. Rawlings conducted in 1953 when she began to collect material for a biography of Ellen Glasgow. A date will indicate that the material is contained in a letter.

[12] Berta Wellford to MKR, in Rawlings Papers.

[13] *Woman Within*, 24.

yard with the iron fence around it. She and Rebe found a constant playmate and a lifelong bosom friend in little Carrie Coleman, whose father owned the adjoining farm. The children did not mind the abundance of ticks and the almost impassable road.[14] There were barns to explore and haystacks to slide down, trees to be named and "bell-like white flowers" to be picked.[15] The children had a bird dog, a pointer named Pat, who slept peacefully and undisturbed in the bed with Rebe even when his bulk was about to suffocate her.[16] Frank, who was about ten, found his little sisters to be acceptable playmates. The older girls were interested in having their friends visit for overnight parties in the large rooms upstairs. Occasionally they amused themselves by teasing the younger girls.

But the younger girls lived in their own world of anguish and joy, innocent of the implications of their childish games. Ellen's heart was broken when her beloved mammy left her to work for another family. But Mammy returned frequently and brought little Lizzie Patterson with her to join the girls at play. Lizzie was a delight. She lived at Reveille, a house that had the distinction of being haunted by at least two ghosts. One was the ghost of a young girl who had fallen down the front steps in her riding habit and broken her neck. The other was that of an old woman. One day a servant came to tell Mrs. Patterson that he was quitting. When asked why, he explained, "Miz Patterson, I laks ter hav' a room ter mah se'f." He could not be convinced. "But you *do* have a room to yourself," she said. "No m'am. There's an old woman that comes in and rocks in de rockin' chair every night."[17] So he quit, and the ghost of the old woman lives on. But even a friend who lived in a house with two ghosts was no satisfactory compensation for the loss of Mammy.

After the departure of Mammy, Ellen found herself suddenly alone and inclined to seek solitude in a barn, under a bed, behind

---

14 Arthur G. Glasgow to MKR, February 16, 1953, in Rawlings Papers.
15 Ellen Glasgow to Elizabeth Patterson, March 22, 1902, in Glasgow Papers.
16 Interview with Mr. Glasgow Clark, Richmond, Va., November 14, 1968.
17 Interview with Mrs. William R. Trigg, Jr., Richmond, January 10, 1969.

a tree or bush. Little Willie was no longer real to her. Often she emerged from her seclusion with a few lines of poetry and read them triumphantly to Carrie, Rebe, and Lizzie. Rebe was not impressed and complained, "If y'all are going to read po'try, I'm not going to play."[18] The poetry was put aside for some other pastime, such as the game in which either Ellen or Rebe would leave the room after pointing to a chair and saying, "That's *my* chair," daring the other to sit in it in her absence.[19] The consequence of sitting in the forbidden chair is unknown, but both girls developed a fierce sense of possessiveness which they eventually applied as freely to people as to chairs. Ellen, however, would not desert her "po'try," not even for the approval of her childhood playmates, or even after the devastating experience of overhearing her older sisters laugh at her childish lines.

Ellen accepted the difference between herself and her comrades-in-play at an early age. According to her own account, she was but seven when she wrote her first story, "Only a Daisy."[20] Barely one short page in length, the story was a milestone in the life of the author:

In a garden full of beautiful flowers there sprung up a little daisy. Everything was bright and cheerful around it, but the daisy was not content. "If I were only one of those roses," it said, "then I would be happy, but I am only a little daisy," and the daisy sighed and hung its head.

Days passed and the roses were carried away. There was to be a grand ball in the castle, for the young earl was going away. "If I could only be there but no one would think of taking me," said the daisy when the other flowers were carried away to grace the stands and vases on the night of the ball. "But I am only a little daisy," and it sighed again.

It was the evening before he should go away and the earl was walking in the garden with a young girl. "Let me give you a flower before you go," she said, "for it is the last time I will see you before you go," and she stooped to pluck a tall white lily that grew near, but the young man stopped her. "No," he said, "I will have this

18 Carrie Duke to MKR, in Rawlings Papers.
19 Rebe Glasgow Tutwiler to MKR, *ibid.*
20 *Woman Within,* 53.

little daisy. I will keep it and it will remind me of you." She
plucked the daisy and handed it to him. They stood together and
talked for a little while and then the girl turned and went into the
house. The young man stood still a moment, pressed the daisy to
his lips, then hurried away and was soon lost to sight in the darkness. And the little daisy was content at last to be "only a daisy."[21]

"Only a Daisy" is the summary of Ellen's own life at age seven.
Mammy was gone, Little Willie had vanished from her imagination, and Ellen had begun to create a private world of the mind in
which there were characters she could possess and force to be her
companions. Uncomfortable in the real world, she created a new
world more to her liking. Her earl in the story approved absolutely
of the daisy, whereas her real childhood friends had sent her away
with her "po'try." Ellen revealed a motivation for writing and a
self-image that stuck with her for the rest of her life. She thought
of herself as vastly different from her fellows; she thought of herself
as infinitely superior.

Her brief attempts to attend school did little to alter that image.
A public school system was flourishing in Richmond in the 1880's,
but it was customary for the children of the aristocracy to attend
schools that were privately run by teachers who gathered a few
students around them. Quite likely the school was held in an old
house, where the students were divided into only two groups,
labelled "Primary" and "Intermediate and Collegiate."[22] Ellen
reached the advanced age of twelve before she set forth into the
world of academia. Her doctor and her mother finally decided that
she was strong enough to attend Miss Lizzie Munford's school,
conducted in Miss Munford's home, but Ellen remained there for
less than a year. Her classmate Lucy Pegram walked to school with
her and sometimes went to her house after school to play.

Lucy also kept a diary, in which she described Ellen as a skinny
girl with a pale face who wore her hair in two long plaits. She and
Ellen ran down a back alley and entered the school by the back

21 The manuscript of the story is in the Glasgow Papers.
22 Richmond Female Seminary *Bulletin, 1879–80*, Library of the Valentine Museum,
Richmond.

door, because as Lucy explained: "I wish it was not a little disgrace to have a school, then we could go in the front door, but our school is very nice and Miss Lizzie is fat but not her waist, and she makes us pray first every day."[23] Ellen apparently endured the praying and the embarrassment according to the custom of the times, but she was frequently absent and may not have shared all of Lucy's experiences at school. One episode, however, that she undoubtedly discussed with her friends either at school or at home was a public hanging in 1885. Richmond was then a city with a population of more than sixty-five thousand, and public hangings were still practiced.[24] The prison was only two blocks from the Glasgow home. This particular hanging took place during recess, and Lucy duly recorded the event: "Somebody is going to get hung tomorrow because of murder, the postman told me. He did get hung at recess. All Miss Lizzie's servants came out in the yard and it was sorter dark, and they jumped and prayed and some of the children were afraid and cried but I jumped and prayed, too—it was fun."[25] Characters who had spent time in prison often appeared in Ellen's novels; and if she was not present at the school during the hanging, Lucy very likely shared her joy with her as they raided bread and preserves from Ellen's basement store room.

School girls in the 1880's found other and less morbid ways to entertain themselves. There were dancing classes where mothers and mammies looked proudly on and where boys misbehaved. Ellen was only an observer at such classes. Her frail health allowed her to skip after-school calisthenics and piano lessons that were taught by Miss Lizzie's sisters. She indulged in the practice of swapping lunches, perhaps attended the funeral of a cat, and thrilled to the visit of the organ grinder and his monkey, though she felt a little sorry for the monkey. She watched Negro convicts work in the backyard under armed guard, and she walked with her friends to Hollywood Cemetery. With her family she went to White Sulphur Springs, West Virginia, where if the climate was more amenable

23 Lucy P. Scrivenor, "Diary of a Richmond Girl" (typescript in Rawlings Papers).
24 Christian, *Richmond*, 393.
25 Scrivenor, "Diary."

than that of Richmond, the accommodations certainly were not. With Lucy she planned an ambitious literary endeavor: "Ellen and I are going to write a play about a robber. She wants to put a dog in but she is not going to let him bite anybody."[26] Most of all, Ellen looked forward to her summers at Jerdone Castle with her trees and her dog and the numerous places where she could hide and write.

But life, even at Jerdone Castle, was never the same for her after the loss of Mammy and the evaporation of Little Willie. When she was ten, her mother suffered a nervous breakdown that threw the whole family into an atmosphere of morbidity and terrified the young girl who held her so dear. Mrs. Glasgow clung tenaciously to her little girls and always humored their whims. When Miss Munford's school closed, she sent Ellen to a more famous private school, Mr. John H. Powell's Richmond Female Seminary at 3 East Grace Street. Mr. Powell advertised the school as "Complete in its Appointments and thorough in its Instruction from Kindergarten to Collegiate Department inclusive."[27] On the primary level, one could study geography, arithmetic, English grammar, and history; and on the intermediate and collegiate levels, one could study English, history, math, mental and moral philosophy, and the natural sciences. Ellen would have none of it. Her first day was a disaster. A greedy little girl ate her lunch, and because of her innocence of any knowledge of arithmetic or geography, Ellen was placed on a bench at the foot of the class. It made no difference that she was well-read. Her mother and father and Aunt Bec had read numerous English works to her, and she was already reading Charles Dickens. She did not like the strange children at the Richmond Female Seminary, and she did not think she should be on the bench at the foot of the class. She developed a severe nervous headache, jumped down off the bench, and fled home to the sheltering arms of her mother, who soothed her and assured her that she would never again have to go to school if she did not want to.[28] And she

26 *Ibid.*
27 Richmond Female Seminary *Bulletin, 1879–80,* Valentine Museum.
28 *Woman Within,* 41–50.

never again went. Later, one of the teachers at the Richmond Female Seminary was heard to observe, "I regret so that Ellen was never able to take an education."[29] As a new dropout, Ellen decided that she would rather be dead and even judged by her father's terrible God than have to return to school.[30]

School having ended, Ellen found other ways to pass her time. On one occasion when she saw a man mistreating a dog, she hurled herself out of a carriage and clung to the man's coat with one tiny hand while she beat him with the other.[31] When she was older, she and Lizzie Patterson darkened their faces and dressed up like gypsies, a pastime Ellen had enjoyed when much younger with her sisters and Mammy.[32] But Ellen and Lizzie developed the art far beyond those early ventures. They hung a little cart with red curtains, hitched a pony to it, drove along Franklin Street, and told fortunes for a fee. They stopped at the home where William Dean Howells happened to be visiting his brother. The writer saw the wagon coming, and said, "I want no gypsies on this place. Get out!" He grasped the pony's bridle, turned the wagon around, and ordered the children away.[33] At other stops the girls had better luck. They collected seven dollars for their day's work, but Ellen's father was not amused and sent them back with washed faces to return the money.[34] Years later Ellen Glasgow sat among the celebrities who gathered in New York City for William Dean Howells' eightieth birthday, and at yet a later date the little gypsy whom he had turned away from his brother's door accepted the Howells Medal for distinguished service in literature.

The religious zeal of Ellen's Presbyterian father, and his interest in the everlasting soul of his little girl, went beyond the disciplinary lesson in honesty that he gave her for the gypsy episode. His sister, Aunt Bec, carried Ellen daily to a Dwight L. Moody revival service

[29] Colonel C. C. Tutwiler, Jr., "Ellen Glasgow—The Writer as Reader," in *De Graffenried Family Scrapbook*, 217.
[30] *Woman Within*, 45.
[31] Berta Wellford to MKR, in Rawlings Papers.
[32] *Woman Within*, 34.
[33] Emma Gray Trigg, "Ellen Glasgow," *The Woman's Club Bulletin*, Richmond, IX (No. 2, 1946), no page given.
[34] Interview with Mrs. William R. Trigg, Jr., Richmond, January 10, 1969.

that opened in Richmond on January 4, 1885.[35] Every afternoon
they sat on the front bench under the watchful eye of the minister.
On the last afternoon of the meeting, Ellen heard the minister say,
"The little girl in blue on the front bench has been an example to
us all," and then announce that she would lead the gospel hymn.
With the help of Aunt Bec she started singing "Rescue the Perish-
ing," and dryly noted in her autobiography fifty years later: "That
was the end. The evangelist passed on to wider fields and to riper
harvests, while I relapsed, permanently, into 'original corruption,'
and was 'bound over to the wrath of God.'"[36]

Those who may believe in the doctrine of 'original corruption'
may find, it does seem, much in Ellen's youthful behavior and the
reaction of her relatives and other adults toward her to substantiate
their faith. In early adolescence Ellen fell desperately in love with
a Mr. Munford, a man more than twice her age. The day he married,
she became so furiously jealous that she threw herself on the floor
of the porch and kicked and screamed. Mr. Munford finally assuaged
her grief with the gift of a small gold ring, which she kept all her
life.[37] And she was but fourteen when her father decided to sell
Jerdone Castle. He gave her dog Pat to an unkind overseer. She
never forgave her father for that, and he increasingly became a
major villain in her life.

After selling Jerdone Castle, Mr. Glasgow bought the gray house
at One West Main Street. It was largely a family of girls who moved
into the new home. The oldest son, Arthur, was away at the Stevens
Institute of Technology at Hoboken, New Jersey. The soft-eyed and
delicate Frank was sent to the Virginia Military Institute because
his father thought it would "harden" him. Ellen's older sisters
were still unmarried and at home; the new house was largely theirs.
Ellen was unenthusiastic about it; her heart was broken over the loss
of the farm, and she had little affection for her older sisters. In her
new home on Main Street she retreated more and more to her

35 Christian, *Richmond*, 389.
36 *Woman Within*, 34–35.
37 Berta Wellford to MKR, in Rawlings Papers.

reading and her writing. Locked in a room or hidden under a bed, she applied her youthful hand and mind to the writing of short stories.

Dreams of adventure captured her childish imagination, and one of her earliest creations is an unpublished story called "The Prairie Flower."[38] Although innocent of the skills of spelling, grammar, and punctuation, the young author created a definite plot and employed a rather clever, if puerile, use of dialect. In the story, the sun is setting over a cowboy camp in West Texas. A rough-looking character, "brown Bill," checks to see if a younger cowhand, Bob, is asleep and then announces that he intends to marry a beautiful young girl with yellow hair, "Prairie Rose." Prairie Rose and her brother, "gintleman Jamie," are newcomers to the area and obviously are very different from their neighbors. Brown Bill decides that Gentleman Jamie has come to Texas "ter 'scape the perlice" and vows to find out what crime he has committed, hand him over to the authorities, collect a handsome reward, and make Prairie Rose his own. But Bob is not really asleep, and at the first opportunity he rides off to warn Rose and her brother. Coming to their cabin he peers through a "winder" and sees a little pine table spread with "a frugal repast of corn bread and meat." Rose "was not positively beautiful but she was beautiful when compared to the men at the camp and one old woman." The shape of her head and features are remarkably like those of Ellen's mother, and she is a Southern lady who insists that Bob must come in and eat before he reveals the bad news. Bob returns to the camp, leaving Rose and Jamie to discuss their plight. Sure enough, they are hiding from the "perlice." They have come West from some unnamed place, which it is safe for the reader to assume is Virginia, where Rose had a sweetheart named Harold Deacond. Her brother James had been told that Harold had betrayed Rose, so James supposedly had murdered Harold. Rose is an extraordinarily forgiving soul, for "child as she was she had never entertained one hard thought against her brother for robbing her of all her enjoy-

[38] The manuscript of the story is in the Glasgow Papers.

ment in the midst of her happiness." They decide to stay put and be on guard, and the reader must move to "Chapter II" to find out what happens.

What happens is that one day while James is out tending to his cattle, "brown Bill" comes up "very ruffly and used some very offensive language." When Brown Bill said something about Rose, James, "in the heat of his passion . . . had fallen upon him and felled him to the ground. [H]e had not killed him but had hurt him rather badly." So Brown Bill's cowboy buddies form a posse to capture Gentleman Jamie and string him from the nearest tree. At dawn the next morning, when they come to take James away, Rose is looking out of an upstairs window and notices that the men have no "pistoles." She rushes to a trunk and takes out two "pistoles"; and "just as the men had brought James under the rope and broke forth with a yell of triumph, a piercing shriek was heard among them and Rose sprang before her brother and leveled two pistoles at them with steady hands and flashing eyes said 'Come one step nearer and I will shoot!' " The men were dumbfounded. "Her hair which they had always seen tucked neatly under a little cap, fell uncontrolled nearly to her feet in shining masses glistening in the rising sun. Her face was as white as the loose dress she wore which clung around her giving her an unearthly appearance." The men thought she was a spirit returned from the dead. Before they "could collect their scattered wits . . . a party of horsemen galloped up headed by faithful Bob." Rose dropped her "pistoles" and fainted into the arms of—who else but Harold Deacond. The trouble between Harold and James had, of course, resulted from a misunderstanding and the two men now become bosom friends. Harold and Rose marry. Rose vows that she will always be as a sister to Bob, and James expresses his appreciation to Bob by promising to see that he is "well cared for and educated for the position of [his] sister's brother." The education must have paid off, for the young author assures the reader: "As he was still very young he was very easily broken of his old habits." Rose promises not to prosecute the men who had attempted the lynching, and everyone lives happily forever afterward.

Time passed, and Ellen acquired more skills of her trade. She learned to spell, and she was far more mature when she wrote "A Modern Joan of Arc."[39] She deserted the West, which she had never seen, for a setting nearer home. Although the story is undated and was never published, it was probably written in her mid or late teens. The villains are not cowboys; they are Yankees. The heroine of the story is a little girl named Sally who sits on the window-sill with "her little head quite aching from an unusual amount of thoughtfulness." She is thinking about how she would like to have her papa return from the dreary business of fighting the Yankees, and she is remembering a story her mama read to her about a maiden in France who dressed up like a soldier and went to war. An attack by the Yankees is eminent. Her mother is in the "quarters" trying to calm the slaves. Mammy is in the nursery singing to her baby brother. Sally decides that she will go off to fight the Yankees, climbs into a chair and takes down an old sword and a gray slouch hat that falls over her eyes. Dressed for battle, she sets out to confront the enemy. A little black girl warns her to turn back, for the Yankees will skin her alive. But Sally is not afraid, even if the Yankees threaten to burn her like the girl in the story. She is determined to bring her papa back; and she imagines that if she can not scare the Yankees away with the sword that she drags behind her, maybe she can win them over with politeness. The Yankees come, fail to be frightened by her sword, and bundle her up to return to her mother. She informs them that they are rude for not going away and diligently inquires if they intend to burn her. Safely home and reprimanded by her mother for running away, Sally then walks calmly over to the officer who had rescued her and thanks him politely for not burning her. So the story ends, not with the young heroine being consumed by flames, but with her assuming the gentle attitude expected of a young lady of Ellen Glasgow's class.

A disadvantage of precocity is the early end to the joys and in-nocence of childhood that it brings, and Ellen's childhood stories reveal her precocity with all of its disadvantages. The self-image

39 *Ibid.*

shown in "Only a Daisy" is present in an even more highly developed degree in the later stories. Both stories deal with a girl who is sensitive, delicate, bright, and maligned by circumstances. Nevertheless, she transcends her predicament with unique feats of heroism and innocently believes that happiness will be hers in spite of the odds. The heroines in both "The Prairie Flower" and "A Modern Joan of Arc" find their happiness only when they fall back into the manners and customs of a Virginia aristocrat. The stories are the product of Ellen's inner psychic tension, a touch of youthful romanticism, the traditional training of a young girl of the Tidewater aristocracy, and her omnivorous reading.

Stories of the American West were in the air in 1885 and were no doubt read or told to the Glasgow children. Ellen had already completed her reading of Sir Walter Scott and Charles Dickens and had begun Victor Hugo. She read Robert Louis Stevenson's *Dr. Jekyll and Mr. Hyde* and moved on to history and philosophy, whatever she could find in her father's library, including *The Westminster Confession of Faith*.[40] She virtually memorized John Stuart Mill and yearned for more philosophy. But books were scarce, and she had to read what she could find rather than what she wanted. A man from Charleston, South Carolina, named George Walter Mc-Cormack, who was courting her sister Cary, encouraged her appetite for books. Ellen was about sixteen when she first met Walter, and she was nineteen when he married Cary in 1892. Under his tutelage Ellen deserted her created worlds of cowboys and Yankees and plunged into treatises on evolution and political economy. Through her reading she was thrust prematurely into adulthood and confronted with the realities of life before she was fully prepared to cope with them. The exercise of a keen mind at an unusually early age perhaps made more troublesome Ellen's transition from childhood to maturity.

Through the eyes of maturity she saw the members of her family in a very different light. As children of ages ten and seven she and Rebe had lain in bed on weekend summer nights at Jerdone Castle

[40] *Woman Within*, 72–73. See also Tutwiler, "Writer as Reader," in *De Graffenried Family Scrapbook*, 216–21.

with the sheet pulled up over their heads, listening to their mother pace the floor and moan all hours of the night in an adjacent room.[41] Their father was there for the weekend after spending the week in Richmond. The little girls did not know why their mother walked the floor and moaned; they only knew that they were terrified. Before ten more years had passed Ellen believed that she knew. On weekdays when he was alone in Richmond her father allegedly had been having Negro women in to sleep with him.[42] True or not, Ellen and her mother accepted it as true, and Ellen later discussed it with her intimate friends. The emotional shock was too much for Ellen's mother, a woman who had enjoyed a sheltered childhood and then endured the agonies of giving birth to and rearing ten children in the South during the Civil War and Reconstruction.

The shattered nerves of her mother and a growing alienation from her father were realities with which Ellen had to live. Her mother went away to try to regain her health. While she was gone, Ellen's father disposed of Toy, a dog to whom his wife and two youngest daughters were devoted. The dog was old, and it may have been a humane act; but apparently Mr. Glasgow never tried to explain it to the girls, or at least they never tried to understand. Ellen blamed him, too, perhaps falsely, for the change in her brother Frank's personality when he returned home after four years at the Virginia Military Institute. Frank had developed a stony reserve and entered a state of depression from which he never recovered. He walked daily to a job his father secured for him at the Tredegar Iron Works, but he was only partly living. Ellen was never again close to him. She had to search beyond the haunting company of her mother and brother and the hated image of her father for her moments of diversion.

That diversion came, and her years between the ages of sixteen and twenty had their brief moments of excitement. At sixteen she visited in Charleston, South Carolina, and was invited to attend a St. Cecilia Ball. As a guest she was awarded the essence of old

41 *Woman Within*, 62.
42 This is a recurring comment in the notes in the Rawlings Papers on interviews with people who knew Ellen Glasgow well. It is also intimated, but by no means explicit, in *The Woman Within*, 62.

Charleston hospitality. A beautiful young girl, dressed in white organdy with a red rose in her elaborately curled hair, she was, as she later admitted, the belle of the ball. The following year she was presented to Richmond society, and she attended dances at the Virginia Military Institute and the University of Virginia. In the light of such a budding social life an older woman called her aside and told her about "the facts of life" as a precautionary measure. Although such education was customarily kept from Southern girls as long as possible, that information probably did not come as too much of a surprise to Ellen, whose greater concern was to ask her friend, Dr. George Frederick Holmes, to give her a private examination in political economy.[43] At that time women were not allowed in classrooms at the University of Virginia, but Ellen passed the same exam that Dr. Holmes gave to his students and no doubt harbored a smug feeling of superiority over the old lady who had been worried about her education. Although Ellen's relationships with boys in her teen years were most casual, she was not without her beaux, and for the moment it looked as if she would escape the effects of a troubled childhood and break into the traditional social life of her class.

That social life bored her, however; she was far more excited during the moments she spent writing in solitude than when she was dancing at one of the colleges. When she was eighteen, she completed a four-hundred-page manuscript of a novel entitled "Sharp Realities." Her mother knew she had been writing secretly and her sister Cary offered her some encouragement. Cary clipped the name of a New York critic out of a magazine and sent it to Ellen along with fifty dollars to help her get the novel published. Ellen persuaded her father to let her go to New York with a group of Richmond girls whose parents had decided that some exposure to music and art was a vital part of their education. She had experienced some minor difficulty with her hearing, and even though her Richmond doctors had assured her that it was nothing to worry about, she was to take advantage of the New York trip to consult a specialist.

[43] *Woman Within*, 78.

Once in New York, Ellen slipped away from the group and made an appointment with the publisher, an old man with a gray mustache and "red and juicy lips," who was more interested in her physical attractions than her literary talents.[44] The experience did not endear to her the male of the species, whom she already regarded with suspicion. Disgusted, she departed and resolved never to write again. The ear specialist told her that there was nothing that could be done for her hearing, so she might as well go back home and forget about it. Determined that her first trip to New York should not be completely spoiled, she accepted the invitation of an older man for dinner at a bohemian restaurant, the Black Cat. Her resolve never to write again vanished almost as soon as it was made, for as she sat in the restaurant she began to envision the setting and the people there in a new novel.

She tucked the vision away temporarily, and upon her return to Richmond burned the manuscript of "Sharp Realities." For a time she locked herself in her room with her books as an escape from the hostile circumstances of rejection, fear, and her father's terrible god, Jehovah.[45] She refused to attend divine services and thus further alienated herself from her father. In less than a year, 1891, she began work on a new novel, *The Descendant*. The manuscript was hardly a year old when her sister Cary married Walter McCormack; he continued to encourage Ellen to read and to write, and he gave her a subscription to the New York Mercantile Library. Cary was possibly the most brilliant of the Glasgow children, and her husband was a young man of considerable intelligence and a hypersensitive nature not unlike Ellen's. He liked to read, and often discussed books with Ellen. He loaned her a copy of Charles Darwin's *The Origin of Species* and urged her to continue her study of philosophy. Walter and Cary became the only living people to share her innermost life. They provided her with a brief interlude of security and hope.

That precious interlude ended as her mother's mental anguish increased. Mrs. Glasgow lived in morbid fear of bad news, and any

44 *Ibid.*, 97.
45 *Ibid.*, 51.

telegram or message, no matter what its contents, that came to the house had to be intercepted in order to alleviate her agony. In the fall of 1893, she made a final trip to White Sulphur Springs in an effort to cure her distraught nerves. Conditions at the springs were unsanitary, and she developed typhoid fever after she returned home. On October 27 she died. Her funeral, a high Episcopalian service, was conducted at One West Main Street, and her body was interred in the family plot in Hollywood Cemetery. Ellen cried for weeks. She destroyed part of *The Descendant*. An attack of influenza increased her suffering. The illness passed and she ceased to cry, but her hearing was never again normal. The effects of the influenza and the excessive crying had aggravated a hereditary malformation, and she began to slip helplessly into the world of the deaf.

In the spring of the following year, Cary and Walter came to Richmond. Cary planned to stay for a few days while Walter went to New York City allegedly to attend to business. Days passed and there was no news from him. When they heard, he was dead. He had taken a room in a boardinghouse and shot himself. He was twenty-six. Ellen said that his death was brought on by abject poverty as the result of frail health and the loss of family fortune during and after the Civil War and Reconstruction. His brother-in-law, Arthur, flatly called him a drunkard. It was whispered around Richmond that he was homosexual. His body was shipped back and buried in the Glasgow family plot in Hollywood Cemetery. Cary spent all of the insurance money for a tombstone. Every day for a year she walked to the cemetery and sat by his grave. For the rest of her life she lived at One West Main.[46]

For Ellen, it seemed as if life had ended before her twenty-first birthday. Small wonder that when she reviewed her life at sixty she believed that her first sensation had been terror at the sight of the setting sun: "Beyond the top windowpanes, in the midst of a red glow, I see a face without a body staring in at me, a vacant face, round, pallid, grotesque, malevolent. Terror—or was it merely

---

46 *Ibid.*, 99–100. Various notes on personal interviews in the Rawlings Papers, and other sources who wish to remain anonymous.

sensation?—stabbed me into consciousness. Terror of the sinking sun. Or terror of the formless, the unknown, the mystery, terror of life, of the world, of nothing or everything?"[47] The formless, the unknown, the mystery were embodied in memories of childhood, in shadowy stones on a hill in Hollywood. Her ears were closing and her world was growing silent. Her father shed no tears that she saw. Had he not said that everything that happened was the will of God, the will of his terrible Jehovah? So it was God's fault. She would hold *Him* personally responsible.

[47] *Ibid.*, 3–4.

# 3

## *A Rebel by Accident*

✦

"It was like living in a tomb," Ellen said of the gray mansion on Main Street that housed the half-warm bodies of the surviving Glasgows.[1] Clad from throat to ankle in black, and oblivious to the outside world, the Glasgow girls wandered through house and garden. Their father went daily to the Tredegar Iron Works and weekly to the Second Presbyterian Church, bowing silently to the will of Jehovah. Frank maintained the stony silence of the hopelessly depressed. The older brother, Arthur, had moved permanently to London in 1892 and escaped the morbid atmosphere. More than just grief tormented Ellen; she lived in terror of going deaf. She refused to bow quietly to the will of Jehovah or to retreat from life into a state of mental depression. There must be some other way to live, some untrodden path to truth that she was bound to find. She must reject the tradition of her father, she thought, and his terrible Jehovah who had brought her to this low estate. Never would she surrender! She would dream dreams and search for happiness with the only tools at her command. Cary had given her a subscription to the New York Mercantile Library. Meaning in life might be found, she desperately hoped, within the pages of the books that came to her from New York.

Cary read with her, too, at first. Cary thought that if she developed her mind she would be able to communicate better with her dead husband in another world. Ellen's concern was more immediate;

---

1 *Woman Within,* 101.

she yearned to live *now*. The books that came from New York were the works of German scientists and philosophers; Schopenhauer, Kant, Schelling, and Haeckel. Included were English novels and Edward Gibbon's *The Decline and Fall of the Roman Empire*, into which Ellen dipped recklessly despite a warning that the forbidden fifteenth chapter would undermine her faith. Faith had never been one of her strong points. She demanded answers to the question of why life was as it was, and for those answers she turned to works on political economy, environment, and evolution. *The Origin of Species* was her favorite companion, and she read it rebelliously to spite her father who offered to pay her to put the book away. Sentimental Southern novels, such as the works of Thomas Nelson Page, irritated her, because they seemed to evade life's hard realities, which could not be explained away with the simple excuse that the Civil War and Reconstruction were to blame for all the hardships of Virginians. At twenty-one she silently hoped that life would evolve upward, and she looked to the future, not to the past. *The Origin of Species* became her Bible, and in her own rebellious way Ellen had selected Darwin's book as the literature through which she would search for God.[2] When she returned to her manuscript of *The Descendant*, she formed it, almost reverently, into a commentary on her new-found Bible.

Her writing flowed from some uncontrollable psychic compulsion, and she needed but the smallest encouragement from the strange world of publishers. Two years after the death of her mother, a magazine accepted one of her stories, "A Woman of Tomorrow,"[3] which gave Ellen that spark of encouragement. Many years later she claimed that she wrote the story when she was fifteen, but she probably wrote it at least five years later than she remembered.[4] Neither "The Prairie Flower" nor "A Modern Joan of Arc" bespeaks of as much maturity, and "A Woman of Tomorrow" was not published until after her twenty-first birthday. The story of a young woman of Virginia who in order to become a successful law-

[2] *Ibid.*, 92, 93, 94.
[3] *Short Stories*, XXIX (May/August, 1895), 415–27.
[4] Virginius Dabney, "A Prophet of the New South," New York *Herald Tribune*, August 25, 1929, Sec. 12, p. 6.

yer sacrificed an opportunity to marry a young man who was bound to the traditions of the past, it no doubt reflects a conflict that must have been real in the mind of Ellen Glasgow at the time she wrote it. Marriage and the career of a novelist are not necessarily incompatible, but Ellen came to view them that way. For the woman in the story, who later regretted her decision, either marriage or the career alone could not be entirely fulfilling. It was her tragedy, and perhaps also Ellen's, that she could not have both. Ellen saw herself certainly as "a woman of tomorrow," successful in a man's world, but lonely and deprived in a woman's world. Weeping over the loss of the one did not prevent her from pressing toward the successful achievement of the other; Ellen completed *The Descendant* in 1895 and dedicated it to Walter McCormack, who more than all others probably sensed and sympathized with the turmoil within the young novelist.

*The Descendant* jolted the American literary world and the Glasgow household. The sentimental platitudes that one would expect from a sheltered aristocratic girl who had made only one brief trip away from the capital of the old Confederacy were simply not there; in their place was the unseen presence of Charles Darwin and John Calvin, whose philosophies were becoming strangely reconciled in the mind of the novelist. The story of Michael Akershem, the illegitimate son of poor whites in Virginia, who ran away to New York City and became editor of a socialist newspaper, the *Iconoclast*, the novel was intended to be a study of the effects of environment and heredity upon the personality and fate of the central character. Actually, the book is a bizarre mixture of Darwinism, Calvinism, unassimilated reading in philosophy, memories of Walter McCormack, and feminine romanticism. Akershem is introduced as a "variation from type," but the description of the landscape in the first paragraph of the novel seems to warn the reader that the ensuing events might well be the will of the terrible Jehovah: "In the remote West, from whose heart the wind had risen, the death-bed of the Sun showed bloody after the carnage, and nearer at hand naked branches of poplar and sycamore were sil-

houetted against the shattered horizon, like skeletons of human
arms that had withered in the wrath of God."[5]

As if fleeing from the wrath of God, Michael Akershem went to
New York where his plight was no less desperate than it had been
in Virginia, he contemplated suicide, and then accidentally he
discovered the *Iconoclast* and the work of his life. At twenty-six,
the exact age of Walter McCormack when he had taken his own
life, Michael Akershem became the editor of a controversial newspaper that was known all over the city, and he moved steadily toward his predetermined fate.

The rugged and brainy editor of the *Iconoclast* often took his
meals at a restaurant named the *Chat Noir*, the very restaurant
Ellen had visited during her first trip to the city. Painted black cats
decorated the walls, and a real one wandered around among the
customers begging for food. The conversation at the tables centered around Akershem's lectures on "Social Lies," and the editor
himself proclaimed that religion was useless, society must be destroyed, and that marriage was not a failure but a fake, essentially
the views of his young creator, who at eighteen, had considered herself a socialist and to prove it had joined the Richmond City Mission. Her actions were inconsequential, for inactive membership
in an organization apparently designed to dole out a minimum of
help to the poor fell far short of the reorganization of society for
which her character in the novel called. Yet in writing the novel
Ellen had found a channel for her activism in the words and deeds
of the characters in books.

As Akershem sat in the *Chat Noir* proclaiming his dislike for
women, one of the more emancipated members of the fairer sex
sat a few tables away calmly painting his portrait. She was Rachel
Gavin, a girl of Southern heritage who had escaped to New York
City in pursuit of the very unladylike ambition to become an artist. Like Ellen Glasgow, she wanted a career, not romance, and
she even felt the same aversion for physical contact with men that
Ellen had experienced when the publisher with "red and juicy

5 Ellen Glasgow, *The Descendant* (New York: Harper and Brothers, 1897), 3.

lips" had attempted to kiss her. "When one is in love," Rachel asked, "it doesn't nauseate one to be kissed, does it?" Rachel soon learned, however, that she could tolerate being kissed by Michael, and, contrary to their philosophies, they fell into that ancient fallacy of love. Though she had prided herself upon being a woman of reason, not sentiment, Rachel in love, the novelist notes, had not the sense to realize the inconsistencies in Michael's personality. Ironically, Michael "blushed because he himself had been born without the pale."[6] The emotional and intellectual imbalance that came with the hyperactivity of the glands, loosely described as "being in love," shattered Rachel's ability to paint, and her masterpiece was laid aside.

With Akershem, too, the work of the glands outweighed the work of the mind. His "Social Lies" began to sound empty, and he learned that "it is less easy to mould life than it is to wound one's hands in the attempt."[7] His urge to destroy society waned, and he became a murderer and a convict. While waiting for his prison term to expire, Rachel earned her bread as a commercial artist and secretly completed and displayed the masterpiece she had put aside when she first met Michael. When he was released after ten years in jail, Michael was suffering from tuberculosis, and he died in Rachel's arms.

The story of *The Descendant* is really Rachel's story, not Michael's. Rachel's triumph over her man and her success as an artist were the triumph and success Ellen hoped to achieve. But Ellen believed that she had the same enemy as Michael and Rachel: an unmitigable predetermined fate. Displaying the skill of ironic writing for which she eventually became famous, Ellen's description of the dying Akershem recalled the naked branches of poplar and sycamore that looked "like skeletons of human arms that had withered in the wrath of God." Charles Darwin quietly surrendered to John Calvin, and the novelist awaited, angry and impuissant, the certain coming of her own fate.

Two years later, the novel was published, and an "elderly kins-

6 *Ibid.*, 73, 83.
7 *Ibid.*, 122.

man" of Ellen's expressed shock that "a well-brought-up Southern girl should even know what a bastard is," much less write a book about one.[8] A young woman of gentle upbringing who had the termerity to write such a story in 1895 and fearlessly use the word "damn" could hardly be accused of shying away from the struggle for female emancipation that was popular in the 1890's. But writing a daring novel in the privacy of one's home is one thing, and trafficking in the real world of publishers is quite another. Nevertheless, Ellen bravely wrote to the Macmillan Company and received an encouraging response. She had a new friend, Louise Collier Willcox, whose brother, Price Collier, worked for the Macmillan Company. Mrs. Willcox urged her brother to allow Ellen to call upon him and to give her manuscript a fair consideration. In the meantime, Ellen was busy on her own. Three days after Christmas, 1895, she wrote a painstaking letter to the Macmillan Company, as lacking in humility as it was cautious in style, in which she informed the company that she would mail the manuscript during the first week in January. And at the time she mailed it she naïvely remarked that she would call in person about a week later to learn their decision, and she urgently requested that the manuscript be placed into the hands of one who could give it a quick and "adequate" reading.[9]

The publishers calmly ignored her plea for a definite answer within one week and took their time to discuss her manuscript among themselves. Ellen had mailed the manuscript to George P. Brett, the president of the company. In the meantime, Price Collier, in obedience to his sister's wishes, had lunched with her in New York. He had not read her manuscript at the time of the interview; he offered her no encouragement and suggested that she "stop writing, and go back to the South and have some babies."[10] His initial reaction seems to have been that he would have preferred not to be bothered with the whole business, but he re-

---

[8] Ellen Glasgow, *A Certain Measure* (New York: Harcourt, Brace and Co., 1943), 9.

[9] To Messrs. Macmillan & Company, December 28, 1895, January 8, 1896, Macmillan Authors, New York Public Library.

[10] *Woman Within*, 108.

luctantly wrote to Brett and asked to see the manuscript if some
final decision had not already been made upon it. Brett sent him
the manuscript with his opinion that the "new woman sort of
thing" had "rather been done to death lately" and the suggestion
that Miss Glasgow's promising talent might be developed with
some good advice and "not a little" additional training.[11]

Price Collier was also unimpressed with *The Descendant,* but
he was fearful that some rival publisher such as Harpers or Apple-
tons might make a hit out of it through the advertisement given it
by harsh critics. He found the theme of the new woman tiresome;
and he discovered that the manuscript itself was riddled with
"hobble-de-hoy vulgarity," silly attempts to appear socially sophisticated, superfluous descriptions of nature, bad grammar, and childish rhetoric. On the basis of his one-hour visit with the author, he
assured Brett that Miss Glasgow was completely without promise;
she was uneducated, did not know how to think, and lived in a
closed world. On February 7, several weeks later than the deadline
Ellen had requested, Brett wrote her a letter explaining that he
could not publish her book in its present form. He suggested that
a careful revision of her manuscript for reconsideration by his firm
would probably not be worth her while and tactfully concluded that
perhaps there were a dozen other publishers who would be more
interested in her type of work.[12] The Macmillan Company lived
to regret its decision, but at the moment there was no consolation
for Ellen.

Yet, she was determined not to give up. One who had adopted
literature as her defense against a host of personal demons was not
about to be allayed by one disenchanted publisher. She took the
manuscript to the University Publishing Company of Virginia,
which was run by a contemporary of her old friend, Dr. George
Frederick Holmes. He turned it over to a younger man in the firm,
a Mr. Patton, who liked the book and tried to find a publisher for it.
Patton sent it to the Century Company, which agreed to publish
it provided some changes were made in the first few chapters. Ellen

11 January 29, 30, 1896, Macmillan Authors.
12 *Ibid.,* February 2, 1896.

made the changes and returned it to Mr. Patton; and although she had already begun work on a second novel, she moved in a world of general exhaustion and nervous anxiety over the fate of her first book.[13] Cary begged her to take a trip to regain her strength. Arthur, who lived in London, offered to pay her expenses to come to England for the summer. Since she believed that there was nothing more she could do for *The Descendant* but wait, Ellen decided to accept the invitation. She sailed early in April, 1896.

Arthur arranged her passage with the daughter of his business partner and gave her the money to buy a new wardrobe. It had been three years since the death of her mother, but Ellen was still wearing the black garments of mourning. On board the ship she cried from homesickness. Her traveling companion, whom she had not met before, did not know that she was partially deaf. Even Arthur did not realize that his little sister was hard of hearing and thought that she was shunning him when she did not always answer his questions. He took her to dances and introduced her to his friends, most of whom she found boring.

But Ellen loved London. She bought a guide book and walked the streets alone. She sat by the drivers of the omnibuses and rode in hansom cabs through streets that seemed familiar to her from her reading. She wandered through museums and shopped for clothes, thinking that English women wore poor hair styles and dull clothes and were of little importance in English society, and considering herself to be quite superior in her new bright-colored garments; but she thrilled to catch a glimpse of the royal family on a balcony for a wedding parade, the ladies wearing high head dresses and long gowns.[14] The summer wore on, and she received a letter from a young man in Paris whom she had met on the ship. "May I dare to hope that you will let me write to you," he began. Ellen dismissed it as a "funny experience"[15] and continued her wanderings through book stores and dress shops, through the ancient British universities, and across the Scottish moors.

[13] *Woman Within,* 111–13.
[14] Ellen Glasgow to Cary Glasgow McCormack, April 28, 1896, in Glasgow Papers.
[15] Cited by Ellen Glasgow, *ibid.,* July 31, 1896.

Westminster Abbey was the place of her dreams. "The vaulted arches of the transepts, with the tinted light from the windows is as solemn as death—or life," she wrote to Cary. Charles Darwin was buried there; his grave attracted her like a magnet. To her mind Darwin had explained why she was bound by Fate; he had interpreted John Calvin. "To think what that stone, with the words 'Charles Robert Darwin, Died Nov. 12, 1887' covers," she later wrote. "Hundreds of irreverent feet cross it every day. One should just stand silent and think."[16] Some invisible power held her close to the grave, and she learned that writing poetry, too, was part of her fate. Unmoving, inspired by the words on the cold stone, momentarily receiving the colder spirits of Darwin and even Calvin, her only lovers, she wrote:

> England's greatness: this abides unchanging,
> Won by arms that sound no loud refrains:
> When all wars and warriors shall have perished
> Truth remains.[17]

The truth of Darwin and the truth of Calvin, the only eternal truth, Ellen slowly and fatefully was coming to believe, was no more than the ultimate lonely isolation of death.

In her own life Ellen marched toward that truth doggedly, prematurely, sometimes even unaware. Being deaf, she was both living and isolated from human companions whom she watched chatter with small talk at carefully arranged dinners. She had "rather take a plunge from London bridge," she said, than dine with one particular family of her brother's friends. The strain of trying to make a pleasant impression on Arthur's friends made her feel "bruised all over," and she thought a cricket match she attended with them was "more stupid" than baseball. She craved the isolation of the crowded thoroughfare, shunned the intimacy of private homes, and told Cary that the "chimpanzees in the zoo" were "the most in-

16 *Ibid.*, July 31, 1896.
17 Ellen Glasgow, *The Freeman and Other Poems* (New York: Doubleday, Page and Co., 1902), 52.

teresting people" she had met.[18] Perhaps they reminded her of Darwin and the Abbey that was as solemn as life.

In the solitude of her room she poured out her heart in letters to Cary. She went daily to the National Gallery and selected a few paintings to concentrate upon, and although she was surrounded by fine art, she was still engulfed by loneliness and exhaustion. More than four months had passed since she had left Richmond. "Life is very unsatisfactory," she wrote Cary, "but 'things are as they are and will be brought to their destined issue.'" Still she had heard nothing from Mr. Patton and *The Descendant*. All the time she begged Cary to find out what was happening to her book, she expected only another disappointment, the inevitable fulfillment of her predestiny. "Nothing makes life very bearable," she lamented. "One may travel from the North Sea to Jericho, and one cannot alter one jot or tittle one's nature or destiny." An abundance of the comforts of life meant nothing to her, because as she explained, "a dinner in ten courses is wearying to a lack of appetite."[19] For a change, perhaps in a vain effort to escape her destiny, she decided to go to Paris.

There, in September, she received a cablegram from Mr. Patton: Harpers had agreed to publish *The Descendant*. Harpers did not know who had written the book and planned to publish it without an author's name on the title page. One of their editors believed that it had been written by Harold Frederic, the popular author of the sensational religious book, *The Damnation of Theron Ware*. Ellen apparently had nothing to do with the decision to publish the book anonymously, and it was probably a decision Mr. Patton made alone in order to find a publisher. Perhaps he got the idea from Ellen's description of Rachel Gavin, the heroine in the novel who exhibited her painting anonymously. Ellen landed in New York before the end of September; nervously excited and terrified by her deafness, she called upon Harpers. The member of the firm whom she met, as he explained that her novel would appear in

[18] Ellen Glasgow to Cary McCormack, July 23, 31, 1896, in Glasgow Papers.
[19] *Ibid.*, September 9, 1896.

January, 1897, was amazed that the author of the novel he had accepted was a young Southern girl who had never before published.[20] To Ellen his words were a new birth; she was something she had never been before and something she would always be. She had come to life as a novelist.

January came, and with it *The Descendant* appeared in bookstores. No author's name was on the title page, and there was something of a mild sensation among reviewers who immediately began speculating about the authorship. Most thought it had been written by a man. Some thought it possessed power and force, but was too brutal and bloody, too dependent upon depressing philosophy. The book was unusual, for in 1896 only Harold Frederic's *The Damnation of Theron Ware* and Stephen Crane's *The Red Badge of Courage* achieved substantial sales in a market dominated by sentimentalists.[21] And in 1897 the reading public was still not ready for Ellen Glasgow's brand of realism. The best seller of the year was James Lane Allen's *The Choir Invisible*, a historical romance about a Kentucky pioneer, and the essence of the type of novel Ellen loathed.

Five months after *The Descendant* appeared, a reviewer for *The Critic* suggested that the author must have been a woman because of "certain delicacies of insight, such as no man could be expected to exhibit."[22] Two weeks later the same journal identified the author and published a striking picture of her.[23] Dressed in a frilly white gown and sitting in a massive carved wooden chair, Ellen had sparkling eyes and beautifully curled hair that compensated for a slightly unattractive nose. Except for the eyes, it could have been a picture of any Richmond debutante on the eve of her formal presentation to society. The eyes were not eyes that one wanted merely to look at; they were eyes that one wanted to look into. No less a person than Hamlin Garland recognized that the young novelist wrote from the bitterness of age, not the immaturity of youth, and

20 *Woman Within*, 123.

21 William W. Kelly, "Struggle for Recognition: A Study of the Literary Reputation of Ellen Glasgow" (Ph.D. dissertation, Duke University, 1957), 7.

22 "A Review of *The Descendant*," *Critic*, XXVII (May 22, 1897), 352.

23 C. T. Herrick, "The Author of *The Descendant*," *Critic*, XXVII (June 5, 1897), 383.

that she had the power and boldness that destined her to become a marked personality in literature.[24] *The Descendant* went into three editions, and Ellen believed that she had found her way.

Some slight rearrangements were made at One West Main Street. At the head of the stairs on the second floor, a tiny room that overlooked Main Street was set aside as Ellen's study. In that room she finished her second novel, *Phases of an Inferior Planet,* which she dedicated to Cary. She wrote a short story, "Between Two Shores," based upon her experiences on the ship during her trip to England; and what is more important, she studied the techniques of other writers. Wise enough to realize that her educational opportunities had been severely limited, Ellen set about the awesome task of educating herself to be a good novelist. The French realists, Balzac, Flaubert, and de Maupassant taught her that literature should be a photograph of life. She read Henry James and rejected him, but before 1900 she discovered Leo Tolstoy's *War and Peace,* the book she quickly decided was the greatest novel ever written. The reading of philosophy no longer stifled her style, but dissolved in her increasing ability to create plots and characters. Significant literary contacts, she learned, were as important as the academic development of her art. Paul Revere Reynolds became her agent, and she corresponded with Walter Hines Page, the associate editor of the *Atlantic Monthly* who had expressed an interest in helping Southern writers get published.

The books Ellen had loved most, with the exception of Tolstoy, had been written by or about Englishmen, and she was so convinced that Englishmen were more capable than Americans of appreciating her art that she became obsessed with the determination to secure an English publisher. Also, England was the home and burial place of Charles Darwin. Indifferently, she allowed her agent, Paul Revere Reynolds, to place her short story, "Between Two Shores," wherever he could; but she was adamant concerning the placing of her new novel with an English publisher. "So you see the book *must* be placed with an English publisher," she wrote him late in 1897. She was "perfectly willing to accept the lowest terms,"

[24] Hamlin Garland, *Roadside Meetings* (New York: Macmillan Co., 1930), 350.

she said, because the thought that she might not secure an English publisher was worrying her very much.[25] The novel must be published by "a wholly English house," not just an American company with a branch in London. Several months later, she urgently reminded Reynolds: "I don't know whether I explained to you that in the English transactions the question of financial return is the least to be considered."[26] Reynolds succeeded in placing the book with Heinemann in London, and Harpers agreed to bring out the American edition.

On the American side of the Atlantic, Ellen took her publishing problems to Walter Hines Page. She sent him a poem, "The Freeman," for publication in the *Atlantic Monthly*, and when she met him in the fall of 1897, she gave him a manuscript copy of *Phases of an Inferior Planet*, which he agreed to consider for possible serialization in his journal. But Ellen was obviously far more interested in his knowledge of publishing houses than in his ability as a literary critic. She was convinced that her book was very good, and she needed no reassurance from Page. She asked about the possibility of having Houghton and Mifflin bring out the second novel in its book form if it proved acceptable to the *Atlantic Monthly* and insisted that her only concern was to find a publisher who would "do justly and fairly" by her work.[27] In the same paragraph, however, she noted that she had "warned the Harpers" that she expected a "satisfactory royalty on the book rights," and there can be no doubt that she was particularly concerned about the financial success of her American editions.

Despite Ellen's queries about publishers and finances, Page conceived of his role as that of a critic. With tact and a considerable

25 November, 1897. The letters of Ellen Glasgow to Paul Revere Reynolds are published in James B. Colvert, "Agent and Author: Ellen Glasgow's Letters to Paul Revere Reynolds," in Fredson Bowers (ed.), *Studies in Bibliography: Papers of the Bibliographical Society of the University of Virginia* (Charlottesville: Bibliographical Society of the University of Virginia, 1961), XIV, 180, hereinafter cited as *Studies in Bib.*

26 January 27, 1898, *ibid.*, 182.

27 Ellen Glasgow to Walter Hines Page, October 28, 1897, November 22, 1898, in Blair Rouse (ed.), *Letters of Ellen Glasgow* (New York: Harcourt, Brace and Co., 1958), 24, 25, hereinafter cited as *Letters.*

amount of daring, he flatly told her that the subject of the book was badly chosen and that it should not have been written.[28] She naturally disagreed but maintained a speaking relationship with him anyway. A true diplomat, Page spoke of her great promise and advised her to drop attempts to write poems and short stories and to concentrate upon writing novels.[29] Ellen Glasgow was not one to take advice, unless it came from books, but at least on this occasion she accepted Page's comments graciously and vowed: "I will become a great novelist or none at all."[30] In that vow there was a determination to prove to Mr. Walter Hines Page that he was mistaken about the merits of *Phases of an Inferior Planet*.

Page was not mistaken, however. Ellen's long struggle to become a great novelist had just begun. *Phases of an Inferior Planet* was published by Harpers in 1898, and reviewers on both sides of the Atlantic agreed with Page's opinion.[31] Plot development and character analysis are blighted by the author's preoccupation with the theme that the earth is a planet "where mediocrity is exalted and genius brought low."[32] But the book does show some improvement in style over her earlier effort and is a noteworthy link in the development of the author's thought. Darwin, Mill, and even de Maupassant are discussed by the characters, and there is an emphatic attack upon organized religion and inane society. The tension Ellen felt as the progeny of an Episcopalian mother and a stern Presbyterian father and her memory of the death of her baby brother are used liberally in the story. Inevitably, the characters ultimately bow to fate, or the will of Providence, as the rebellious author gives the solution to the riddle of life in the strict Calvinistic terms with which she had been drilled at her Presbyterian Sunday school.

In the novel the child of a Catholic mother and a Presbyterian

[28] Walter Hines Page, *A Publisher's Confession* (Garden City, N. Y.: Doubleday, Page and Co., 1923), 47.

[29] Walter Hines Page to Ellen Glasgow, December 8, 1897. Cited in Burton J. Hendrick, *The Training of an American: The Earlier Life and Letters of Walter H. Page, 1855–1913* (Boston and New York: Houghton Mifflin Co., 1928), 336.

[30] To Walter Hines Page, November 22, 1898, in *Letters*, 25.

[31] Kelly, "Struggle for Recognition," 20–26.

[32] Ellen Glasgow, *Phases of an Inferior Planet* (New York: Harper and Brothers), 20.

father, born somewhere on a river in the South, the James no doubt, was listed twice in the family Bible: "Marie Musin, born April 24, 1868" and "Mary Ann Musin, born April 24, 1868."[33] The parents never reconciled their differences about religion: "Between the kisses of their lips each offered petitions to a patient Omnipotence for the salvation of the other's soul. As the kisses grew colder the prayers grew warmer."[34] One Sunday the girl went to the Presbyterian church and the next Sunday she went to the Catholic church. When she became of age she took the name of Mariana and departed for New York City and the unpromising career of an opera singer. She lived in a run-down apartment house that was inhabited mostly by artists and philosophers. Her neighbor, Anthony Algarcife, read Darwin and Mill and earned a meager living by lecturing at the Bodley College. Earlier in life, he had studied theology, but he gave it up when he decided that religion had been refuted by science.

Anthony and Mariana married, lived in excruciating poverty, and had a baby who "cried only once, and that was upon its entrance into the predestined conditions."[35] The baby died, and Mariana left to tour Europe with a singing group. But since she could not sing she secured her fortune by marrying a man whose uncle endowed her with a large sum of money. Algarcife went back to the priesthood and became the most famous priest in New York, renowned for his eloquent pulpit style, his almost fanatical dedication to his pastoral duties, and especially his brilliant answers to a series of anonymous anti-religious articles. What his parishoners did not know was that he wrote the anonymous articles, too, and they contained the true expressions of his beliefs. Mariana returned at the peak of his new career, and they decided to start over again, but she died before the scheme could be accomplished.

Because the characters live more on an intellectual than an emotional plane, the novel is complex but unreal, the work of one who had not blended thoroughly what she had learned from the

[33] *Ibid.*, 19.
[34] *Ibid.*, 19.
[35] *Ibid.*, 131.

reading of books with what she knew from the living of life. The ordeals of life which seemed hopeless to the novelist are displayed without subtlety and without striking the empathetic chord in the experience of the reader. She had not yet accomplished the coordination of human mind and human spirit in a well-conceived work of literature, but that skill would come surely as the awareness of her achievement as a novelist sparked some badly needed confidence in her worth as a person. By noting the solution to life's problems for the heroine of this novel, as opposed to the solution for Rachel Gavin in *The Descendant*, Ellen's weakness is illuminated. Rachel triumphed over her man, held his head in her arms as he lay dying, and presumably went on to greater achievement as an artist; but Mariana discovered that she had no talent and died prematurely. The possible relationship between the fates of Mariana and Rachel to Ellen's own equation of writing with living and her acceptance of death as a viable alternative to her unhappy life should not be ignored. If she could not write, as Mariana could not sing, Ellen did not want to live. Her entire second novel appears to have been written in an atmosphere of defeat that might have ended her career immediately had not fate saved her.

The time between writing a book and seeing it in print may be sufficient for an author's intellectual and emotional attitudes to change significantly, and Ellen's did. She took the bad reviews and negligible sales in stride, and rationalized the failure by pointing out that Harpers was in serious financial difficulty and had placed the book on the market virtually unadvertised. True enough, Harpers was in difficulty, but it is unlikely the book would have been saved by any amount of advertising. Ellen admitted that she wanted to be widely recognized, while at the same time in her own mind she was quite clear that for an author to be unknown and unpopular was a sign of greatness.[36] And besides, she was already engrossed in a new project, the magnitude of which she was convinced would make all her previous efforts seem trivial, the conception of which had dispelled grandly the old atmosphere of defeat.

[36] Ellen Glasgow to Walter Hines Page, May 12, 1900, in *Letters*, 32. See also *A Certain Measure*, 109.

The new project began in Roanoke, Virginia, in 1897. Little did the delegates who assembled there on August 11 for the state Democratic convention realize that they were being watched. Ellen was standing behind the curtain on the stage of the old opera house trying to get a little firsthand information about the democratic process in Virginia. A doorkeeper had smuggled her in, where she listened to speeches that lauded free silver, extolled a federal income tax, and praised economy in government.[37] She was viewing a small exercise in Southern progressivism, but what was being discussed did not concern her nearly as much as how men behaved at a convention. The perspiring delegates, pumping their palmetto-leaf fans and benumbed by heat, tobacco smoke, and oratory were, to her, representatives of the whole human race whose predetermined foibles and contradictory justifications for existence she intended to exploit.

By turning to Virginia for the background for her third novel, she escaped the agony of floundering for information that had swamped her when she tried to write about New York. Darwin still remained her friend, and she dropped names of philosophers occasionally, but for the most part she put aside her undigested reading of philosophy and entered a remarkably new phase in her writing career in which she blended with relative ease the life of the mind with the life of the human spirit. She thought about the advice Walter Hines Page had given her and fired off a letter to her literary agent, asking him to return a short story she had sent him for placement, because, she said, she was a novelist and would write no more short stories.[38] She wrote Page himself and explained that she was working on an ambitious work intended "not to amuse, or to sell, but to *live*, and if it does so I shall be content not to— after it is finished." Sure that her novel would be a masterpiece, she asked Page to advise her whether she should go abroad to develop her art. "It is well for a writer to be born in England if he can," she said, but she questioned the value of going to Europe to

37 William Larsen, *Montague of Virginia* (Baton Rouge: Louisiana State University Press, 1965), 60.
38 To Paul Revere Reynolds, January 28, 1898, in *Studies in Bib.*, 182.

pursue an "adopted talent." She did not really want any advice from Page, however, because she answered her own question in the same paragraph. Before even asking Page, she had resolved in her own mind to make the most of her environment. If she had any talent, she said, it would develop in America as well as anywhere; and she concluded incidentally that the setting of her new book was in Virginia.[39]

The scene of the new book was in Williamsburg from 1870 through 1897, a troublesome period of readjustment when the South was neither Southern nor American but merely defeated and struggling to make for itself again and in a new way a place of dignity in the nation it had helped to build and attempted to destroy. Williamsburg is disguised as "Kingsborough" in the novel, but the novelist paints a superb picture of the old town that "dozed through the present to dream of the past and found the future a nightmare."[40] The town she wrote about is the Williamsburg that was suspended in time between its eighteenth-century splendor as the capital of the Commonwealth of Virginia and its sterile twentieth-century resurrection as a washed and polished display of colonial America. To gather information Ellen and Cary went to Williamsburg in the spring of 1898. With pencil and pad, Ellen wandered through the dusty streets making notes on a man asleep in a hammock on a porch, a girl walking up the front steps of a house, the shrubs growing in a yard, a distinguished old college and a state mental hospital. She watched people of various kinds in action and committed those actions to her memory. Apparently, she talked to very few.

One afternoon as she and Cary sat on the porch of the Colonial Inn, they gazed at a tavern across the street and saw a shy young man sitting there alone. He was a Richmond lad, James Branch Cabell, and he was about to be graduated from the College of William and Mary. He was five or six years Ellen's junior; he was good-looking, shy, brilliant, and interested in things literary. In his veins flowed the bluest Virginia blood. According to Ellen's

[39] March 26, 1898, in *Letters*, 26, 27.
[40] Ellen Glasgow, *Voice of the People* (New York: Doubleday, Page and Co., 1900), 13.

account, that very spring the administration of the college had threatened to expel him on a homosexual charge, but his mother had brought an attorney up from Richmond and had had the case dismissed.[41] Ellen's eyes constantly drifted up from her book and rested upon the young man across the street, and her heart gave a little flutter. There was a young man with the potential of being to her exactly what Walter McCormack had been to her older sister Cary. Ellen and James met and talked casually, but their friendship was deferred for almost a score of years; and Ellen's romantic palpitations waned forever, a stroke of good luck which Cabell himself must have eventually come to regard with considerable relief.

Her research in Williamsburg complete, Ellen returned to Richmond and molded her observations into the novel. In the process a strange and wonderful thing happened. Her hatred of her family, her violent rebellion against religion, and her morbid obsession with intense personal problems were subdued into an easy and natural part of her being. They meshed into the means of her self-expression, no longer standing out as enemies against which she was hell-bound to write philosophical treatises. Even deafness, her greatest bugaboo, yielded to her command as she used it as both the cause and the excuse to closet herself alone with the growing novel. "Science had failed my body as ruinously as religion had failed my soul," she later lamented, in a painful moment of self-pity, but the tyrants that had driven her so furiously in producing her first works were now putty in her hands.[42] No longer the worshipper of either science or religion, she had achieved in a negative way, a balance between the two and thus put aside an obsession that had prevented her from creating characters who were real. The compulsion to run away from home to seek the settings of her stories had vanished; sitting calmly in her study in Richmond, she could write about Virginia and herself and her family, about the things she knew best. When she left Virginia she put her work aside; and when she returned, she brought home no foreign ideas.

*The Voice of the People* was not quite finished when Ellen, early

---

41 *Woman Within*, 131–33.
42 *Ibid.*, 138.

in 1899, went on an extensive tour with her sisters Rebe and Cary. Arthur paid for the trip, and the three sailed on February 4, 1899, for Egypt, where they spent the winter and spring.[43] They visited the pyramids and listened to a crier call the muezzin from a nearby minaret. They visited Greece, Turkey, Italy, and Switzerland. By May they were in Paris, Ellen anxiously worrying about being away from her work for so long and even wondering momentarily if writing was really worthwhile.[44] But she knew it was worthwhile, and she could not enjoy Paris as long as an unfinished novel lay in her study in Richmond.

Despite her private feelings, her name was still before the public. Her short story, "A Point in Morals," appeared in *Harper's Magazine* in 1899. The theme was dramatic: a doctor is faced with the decision whether to make available painlessly killing drugs to a condemned murderer who, rather than surrender to the law, is determined to kill himself in the only painful manner at his disposal. But Ellen lost the drama of the situation in a cold discussion of euthanasia, and the reader senses little of the real impact of the situation on the lives of the characters. It was her second short story and the last one which she would publish for almost two decades. This unhappy effort appeared while she was in Paris, far away from her new novel, and surely offered her no comfort about her future as a writer. The comfort she needed was the resumption of work on the novel she dreamed would be her masterpiece. But it must wait.

From Paris, the three sisters went to London for an extended visit with their brother. Ellen wandered through the village of Haworth in Yorkshire and breathed the atmosphere of the Brontës whom she admired immensely. In the desolation of the place she felt the loneliness of Emily Brontë's spirit and was reinspired to proceed with her own work.[45] She returned to America with a sense of urgency. By the end of the first week in September, she was back in Richmond, locked in her study, writing the final chapters of *The Voice of the People*.

[43] Ellen Glasgow to Paul Revere Reynolds, February 3, 1899, in *Studies in Bib.*, 188.
[44] Ellen Glasgow to Horace Traubel, May 25, 1899, in *Letters*, 27.
[45] *Woman Within*, 149–51.

With *The Voice of the People* Ellen Glasgow achieved her first triumph in the creation of a work of art in which she distilled her observations from twenty-five years of living in Virginia into the novel that is the first volume in her social history of the state. In her attempt at realism, she injected a certain measure of gentility in her rebellion against the evasive idealism of the extant conventions in Southern letters. She steered a clear course between sentimentalism and racism, a route that by accident carried her directly to the source of a literary mode that for the age was revolutionary. She had neither the time nor the desire to sing with Thomas Nelson Page the praises of a bygone era, and her aversion for cruelty caused her to abhor the brutalization of a race that became a fad with Thomas Dixon. Negroes, poor whites, and aristocrats speak in her novel in the dialects they actually used and live in the manner in which they actually lived in Virginia. Clear in her vision and plain in her language, Ellen recorded what she saw: Negroes who were individuals with the feelings of human beings, blatant corruption in a political process that flourished on hollow oratory about honesty, and affable aristocrats fading from life into an endless line of portraits that hung in dark and high-ceilinged hallways. And her women, black and white, move through the novel as they moved through life, gliding along a tightrope between their emotions and the reality of their lives, searching for lovers and husbands, accepting the joys and agonies of motherhood that dispersed the dreams of their youth.

Ellen corralled her reader behind the curtain of that opera house in Roanoke in 1897 and gave him a peek at a state Democratic convention in process. And he is not likely to forget the view of Negro mammies strolling white babies around Capitol Square, while inside the building a negligible sprinkling of Republicans and Populists and innumerable Democrats—ranging from colonels and generals who fought in the war to sunburned farmers who grew up in poverty after the war—gather under the shadow of Houdon's statue of George Washington to argue over the importance of railroads and the increasingly volatile issue of the suffrage for the black man. Nick Burr's stroll through Kingsborough on the day of his death must be traced to Ellen's reading of Tolstoy, and the reader hears the same sounds that Nick heard, sees the same things that Nick saw, even if he cannot quite experience the same feelings that the novelist attempted to breathe into her hero. Still more a Darwinian hero than a believable man, Nick is less real than the environment in which he lives; but for the most part the book is almost as good as Ellen conceived it to be. If it proved to be a success with the reading public, Ellen said, then she would "work on a series of Virginia novels as true as I believe this one to be."[46]

Confidence in the merit of her work led her to proceed boldly in her negotiations with publishers. She informed Walter Hines Page that she wished "the Messrs. Harper to continue to be [her] publishers,"[47] but Page was always one jump ahead of her, more than ready to lead her carefully toward the public recognition that she now deserved. He had recently become a partner in the new publishing house of Doubleday, Page and Company, and he asked to see the manuscript of *The Voice of the People*, hoping that he might be given the privilege to be its publisher. Harpers was in serious financial difficulty, operating on a subsidy from the banking firm of J. P. Morgan,[48] he explained. Ellen feared, and with good reason, that the firm of J. P. Morgan was acting as a receiver and could sell any of the books at any time. What she did not stop to consider was the possibility that the financial boost from J. P. Morgan might ease Harpers comfortably and soundly over into the next century, which is essentially what happened. Upon receiving Page's letter, she fired off an inquiry about Harpers to her literary agent. Also, she asked cautiously about Doubleday and Page as publishers and expressed skepticism about any new publishing firm.[49] The literary agent advised against making a change, but Ellen was wiser than her agent and yielded to Page.

46 To Walter Hines Page, December 2, 1899, in *Letters*, 29.
47 *Ibid.*
48 Hellmut Lehmann-Haupt, *The Book in America: A History of the Making and Selling of Books in the United States* (New York: R. R. Bowker Co., 1951), 26.
49 Ellen Glasgow to Paul Revere Reynolds, December 7, 10, 1899, in *Studies in Bib.*, 188.

Walter Hines Page learned quickly that Ellen Glasgow was not an easy customer. She was a woman devoid of knowledge of arithmetic and scarcely versant in matters of business, to whom even the simplest things had to be explained in great detail. Stubborn was she, too, because she informed him that she had changed her opinion "not a jot" about *Phases of an Inferior Planet* and that he must understand that clearly before she could consider letting him publish her new book. If that were clearly understood, then they might do business provided Page would read the manuscript immediately himself and say frankly what he thought of it and provided he would pay her a royalty large enough to repair her wounded feelings about the former novel.[50] To seal the partnership Page must say that he *believed* in the book. He did believe in it; and he not only read it immediately himself, he required every man in his firm who would in any way be connected with it, including the shipping clerk, to read it and to express his enthusiasm to Miss Glasgow when she came for a visit. The result was a partnership between publisher and author that led to a close personal friendship and the promotion of the business interests of both.

The reading public profited, too, from the new partnership. The best seller of 1900 was *To Have and to Hold*, a historical romance by Mary Johnston, who was also a native of Richmond and a friend of Ellen's. The novels she and Ellen published in 1900 had little resemblance to each other, but during the spring months *The Voice of the People* and *To Have and to Hold* seesawed for first place on the best-seller list in certain Southern cities and eventually leveled off to tie for fourth place in sales across the country for the month of August.[51] By the end of the year *The Voice of the People* was not in the top ten best sellers, but its total sales had been good and Ellen had every reason to be happy. Her novel was marred only by a certain insensitiveness of the hero. Nick Burr was not the sexual creature which the male of the species is inclined to be, and the novelist offered no explanation why he was not. To the contrary, she had tried diligently to create him as a real and wholly

---

50 Walter Hines Page, *A Publisher's Confession*, 47, 48.
51 Kelly, "Struggle for Recognition," 32–40.

virile male, but had failed. Ellen's knowledge of men as physical and emotional human beings was scarcely even academic, and the maturity of her art in this respect awaited the delayed sexual maturity of her own personal life.

# 4

## Romance in Life and in Fiction

Jn 1900 Ellen was happy for the first time in her mature life, but her happiness did not stem from the success of *The Voice of the People*. She was in love. At a tea in New York in the winter of 1899, she met the man whom she called "Gerald B—" in her autobiography. Little is known of him other than what she said in her autobiography, an account that is tantalizingly vague but revealingly entitled "Miracle—Or Illusion?"[1] How much of her imagination went into the writing of the chapter is impossible to say, but the existence of such a person has been confirmed by her sister who traveled with her and knew that Ellen was meeting someone.[2] Ellen said, probably by way of disguise, that he was a financier; but his identity remains elusive. He was a tall thin man who in physical appearance resembled her father. He was considerably older than she, married, and the father of two sons.

"I fell in love at first sight," Ellen said, when she recorded the story thirty-five years later.[3] Gerald spoke in clear, crisp tones that she could hear despite her deafness. He praised her first two books and told her that he thought she was beautiful. He called at her apartment in New York and presumably began a clandestine love affair with her. During the next seven years they met infrequently, usually when Ellen visited New York, perhaps at least once in

1 *Woman Within*, 153–68.
2 "Notes for a Biography of Ellen Glasgow," in Rawlings Papers.
3 *Woman Within*, 153.

Richmond, once on Prince Edward Island, and occasionally in Europe. He drove her in his carriage through the streets of New York, and when the horseless carriage was invented he took her along on his first drive in his sports car. They had a favorite Hungarian restaurant and a tune that years later to Ellen always elicited his memory.

Ellen believed that Gerald was the one great love of her life. She shopped for bright-colored clothes, wore the best Paris hats, and took on the outward semblance of happiness. At twenty-seven she had traveled and read widely, but her upbringing was proper, and she had never had even a serious dating relationship with a man. The extent of Ellen's physical relationship with Gerald remains an exercise for the reader's imagination, for Ellen cagily phrased her autobiography so as to leave the question open. It was certainly commensurate with Ellen's avowed philosophy to engage in sexual relations beyond those limits suggested by the society against which she rebelled, but it is interesting to note that the lovers in her novels written during the time she knew Gerald have no physical relations and their meetings sometimes appear ridiculously contrived. Ellen could have been deliberately avoiding the subject in print, and certainly the beginning of the twentieth century was still a time when the explicit discussion of sex in literature was not considered acceptable, even for a rebel. Nevertheless, Ellen said that she was in love with her "whole being," and undoubtedly at the time she wrote her autobiography she hoped that she would be remembered as a woman who had known sex.[4]

---

[4] *Ibid.*, 153–68.

In the Glasgow Papers at the University of Virginia Library, one letter is preserved which may or may not shed some light on Ellen Glasgow's relationship with Gerald:

Washington
[March 23, 1901]

*Elaine, My darling*—Again my heart is desolate and I have left you (after three years of weary waiting, *why* have these unhappy circumstances repeated themselves in my life. This is just a little wail I am sending I can't write. The train is so shaky. Those few fast fleeting hours, how they sped! but they are as pearls to me. Ah! my sweet you little know the preciousness and sweetness of yourself—and weren't you so cunning to let me see you—and I know I made your dear head ache—but I don't really believe I have seen you—it is a dream—was I actually there and could put out my hand and touch you. I could say so much but you will think I have lost my reason. I am long-

*The Battle-Ground*, the first novel that Ellen wrote during the time of her love affair with Gerald, was the work, Ellen said later, of "romantic youth";[5] but the romance in the story is in the literary style with which many writers of the time treated the Civil War, not the description of the relationships between the sexes. Nevertheless, the heroine, Betty Ambler, is very much in love with a young man who goes away to fight in the war. When he returns at the end of the war, Betty greets him by *shaking his hand*; and although they agree to begin life anew together, there is not a spark of genuine passion between them. Either ignorance or a conscious intention not to reveal that she had knowledge that a single young woman of her status was not supposed to have, might have prompted such a treatment of her hero and heroine, but the literary value of the book suffered badly on account of it. It is significant, however, that the female characters in *The Battle-Ground* are happier

---

ing to see you with all my heart—and I would have stayed until Monday—but really was afraid my elation and perfect delight at being with you might make you ill. How I hate to think of you having those suffering headaches it cuts me to the core of my heart to see you pale. You must get strong and well for *Nova Scotia*, for I am surely going with you. Such writing! My darling I must stop. Did you catch any *one* of those kisses sighs and looks I cast—as I passed you by this morning. And you promised to think of me when you were awake—but I—I was thinking *all* night of you—and still you taunt me with indifference. O! would that I had stayed over—but even then the parting had to come—Don't let *Cary* laugh at this letter—does she read them? I hate N. Y. I only love Richmond—it is now the most *perfect* stop, hallowed by my Elaine's presence. My darling good-bye a kiss, another, and yet another! And that makes my three. *I* am not content but I shall have to be—with my heart my thoughts and my tenderest greeting

Ever Elaine
Love
*Gray*

The date, the tone and content, and the possible use of pseudonyms all suggest that the letter could have been written by Gerald. It is the only letter of its kind to survive, and its survival might have been an accident. Late in the spring of 1901, Ellen made the trip to Prince Edward Island with her sisters Rebe and Cary; but if Gerald went along or met Ellen there, it remains a secret.

Professor Anne Scott, of Duke University, an authority on the history of Southern women, has suggested that the letter was written by a woman. It was not unusual, she says, for a nineteenth-century woman to write such a letter to a female friend, and the terms of endearment should by no means be interpreted as an indication of lesbianism. Ellen Glasgow did have a female friend named "Gray" who was married early in 1907; but no other information about her has been discovered, so there is insufficient evidence to conclude that she wrote the letter.

5 *A Certain Measure*, 5.

and more optimistic about their future than those in Ellen's earlier novels. Betty Ambler's fierce determination not to be defeated personally just because the South had been defeated is precisely the attitude that Ellen always adopted in the face of a difficult situation.

In *The Battle-Ground* Ellen compensated for the lack of credibility in the description of her lovers with an injection of realism based upon a more direct kind of historical research. As a social history of Virginia from 1850 through 1865, the novel was intended to show the impact of the Civil War on the lives of ordinary people. Ellen's mother had lived through the conflict and had told her many stories about it. She used that inherited knowledge and even dedicated the book to the memory of her mother. To be able to describe the lay of the land accurately she and Cary hired a carriage and rode up and down the Valley of Virginia touring the battlefields. A friend loaned her the complete files from 1860 through 1865 of three newspapers: The Richmond *Enquirer*, the Richmond *Examiner*, and The New York *Herald*.[6] Ellen read numerous diaries and letters, and *The Battle-Ground* emerged as her most carefully researched novel. The life on the plantation before the war is splendidly drawn with characters who are realistic because they are individuals;[7] and for realism the battle scenes rival, if not surpass, the work of Stephen Crane in *The Red Badge of Courage*. After *The Battle-Ground* appeared in March, 1902, it sold well and was reviewed favorably on both sides of the Atlantic.[8] Contemporary critics and readers were sufficiently enamored with the characters and impressive research to forgive the flaws that have become more obvious with the passing of time.

Six months later in the same year Ellen published a thin volume of her poems, *The Freeman and Other Poems*.[9] She was yielding to pressure from Walter Hines Page to keep her name before the public, but in many ways the volume of poetry was an anachronism.

[6] *Ibid.*, 21.

[7] Francis Pendleton Gaines, *The Southern Plantation: A Study in the Development and Accuracy of a Tradition* (New York: Columbia University Press, 1925), 174, 182, 184, 191.

[8] Kelly, "Struggle for Recognition," 42–52.

[9] New York: Doubleday, Page and Co., 1902.

Some of the poems had been written while she was in England in
1896 and 1899, and they represent an earlier phase of her life.
The poems are a grim reminder of the dark mood of Ellen's spirit
in the late 1890's; and to one who believed so strongly, if unwilling-
ly, in predestination, they were perhaps an ill omen about her
future. The tone of the volume as a whole is the yearning of a
lonely young woman for death. Life is hell, and there is no escape
from the wrath of God, perhaps not even in death:

> One, rising from a rotting tomb, beheld
>   The heavens unfold beneath Jehovah's breath
> 'Great God!' he cried, 'with Thine eternity,
>   Couldst Thou not leave me Death?'[10]

In verse Ellen spoke her mind to the terrible Jehovah and assured him that whatever he was for she was against. In "The Vision
of Hell" she mingled her hostility toward God, her hatred of cruelty, and her frustrated desire to achieve, in the poetic expression of
a philosophy of life that remained with her:

> O God, within the hollow of whose hand
>   A million worlds are tossed to win or lose,
> You choose the stronger for salvation, but
>   The damned I choose.
>
> I take my stand upon the weaker side,
>   I grasp the sinner's hand, I share his fate,
> The hell of those who failed, I choose, or those
>   Who win too late.
>
> .  .  .  .  .  .  .  .  .  .  .  .  .  .  .  .  .  .  .
> 'It is the damned you look upon,' God said:
>   'The earth is hell.'[11]

The hunter of Truth, she said in the poem entitled "The Hunter,"
must search the past for his own answer to the question of what is
Truth. That was precisely what she was doing in writing novels
about Virginia's past. The truth of the past agonies of Ellen's own
private soul was too grim for the reading public in 1902, and only

---

10 *The Freeman*, 21.
11 *Ibid.*, 45–46.

nine copies of the volume of poems were sold.[12] Her readers were not interested in Jehovah's great plan for her damnation; they wanted more well-conceived romances about Virginia.

As the author of two successful novels about Virginia, Ellen Glasgow's opinion was sought as that of an authority on the contributions made by the South to the American character. And she revealed that although she had rebelled against the extant conventions in Southern letters, she had rebelled not an iota against the aristocratic Virginian's attitude toward his nation and state. The life of the republic, Ellen said, rested upon the "simplicity of our social structure and our characteristic love of individual liberty." Preservation of the nation depended upon states' rights, and her fellow Virginians, George Washington, Thomas Jefferson, and Robert E. Lee, had created the principles upon which the republic must grow.[13] Ellen conceived her role in the increase of the South's contribution to the American character to be the creation of a series of novels depicting "Virginia as it is," and she was already at work on *The Deliverance*, a novel designed to take up the history of Virginia where *The Battle-Ground* left off.

Writing the new novel occupied only a part of Ellen's time, for in the summer and fall of 1902 she was engulfed in the kind of social whirl that was sometimes typical in the life of the aristocratic Virginian. To escape the heat in Richmond she went with her sisters for a vacation in the Adirondacks, and on their return they paid a September visit to Walter Hines Page at his country home in New Jersey.[14] Then they hurried back to Richmond where their brother Arthur was planning to be married on October 1 in a ceremony that would make any blue-blooded family proud.

Arthur had been in London for ten years and had already established an international reputation as an engineer. He was thirty-six years old when he returned to Richmond for his wedding in 1902. His bride was Margaret Branch, a woman of legendary beauty

[12] Ellen Glasgow to Howard Mumford Jones, July 8, 1935, in *Letters*, 187.

[13] Ellen Glasgow to Edwin A. Alderman, February 5, 1903, in Alderman Papers, University of Virginia Library.

[14] Ellen Glasgow to Walter Hines Page, June 20, 1902, September 25, 1902, in *Letters*, 38–39.

and charm, who claimed to be a direct descendant from those who came to Virginia in 1607, and who was a member of the wealthy banking family.[15] After the wedding the couple made their home permanently in London and were welcomed in the highest social circles. The ceremony itself was in St. Paul's Episcopal Church, a gala event that recalled the essence of the aristocratic Old South. The thoughts in Ellen's mind, however, undoubtedly were not all happy ones. Arthur had succeeded in winning the perfect mate, a match which brought honor and distinction to his family. At the moment, Ellen was in love with a married man whose wife would not give him a divorce, a situation that could only bring dishonor upon Ellen's family. Ellen's own chances to marry well, or even to marry at all, were not good; she was jealous of those who had succeeded where she seemed to be failing. She was proud to have Margaret Branch as her sister-in-law, but deep within her she ached when she saw what she might have been but was not.

A trip to New York City was always a welcomed change from Richmond, and after the wedding Ellen spent several weeks there. She asked Walter Hines Page to find her an apartment with three bedrooms, a kitchen, a dining room, and a bath. It must not be too high from the ground, a comfortable fireescape must be in sight, and it must not cost over $125 per month. Three bedrooms were necessary, she said, because she intended to bring her Negro mammy to do the cooking, and the mammy, who had never been out of Virginia, was set upon making the trip.[16] Ellen spent most of December in New York shopping for bright-colored clothes, visiting an ear specialist, talking to her publisher, and, no doubt, seeing Gerald.

The meeting with Gerald which she cherished most, however, was in the Swiss Alps in the summer of 1903. She sailed with Rebe and Cary early in July and by the end of the month was situated in "the most costly [hotel] in all Europe" at the foot of the Jungfrau.[17] Before leaving America she left the manuscript of *The Deliverance*

15 *De Graffenried Family Scrapbook*, 210.
16 Ellen Glasgow to Walter Hines Page, October 15, 27, 1902, in Page Papers, Harvard University Library.
17 Ellen Glasgow to Walter Hines Page, July 31, 1903, in *Letters*, 42.

in the hands of her publisher, and the trip was ostensibly a vacation to recover from the strain of writing the book. But the meeting with Gerald surely was no accident. When she recorded the event in her autobiography, she considered that meeting the most beautiful memory in her life:

A summer morning in the Alps. We were walking together over an emerald path. I remember the moss, the ferny greenness. I remember the Alpine blue of the sky. I remember, on my lips, the flushed air tasting like honey. The way was through a thick wood, in a park, and the path wound on and upward, higher and higher. We walked slowly, scarcely breathing in the brilliant light. On and upward, higher, and still higher. Then, suddenly, the trees parted, the woods thinned and disappeared. Earth and sky met and mingled. We stood, hand in hand, alone in the solitude, alone with the radiant whiteness of the Jungfrau. From the mountain we turned our eyes to each other. We were silent, because it seemed to us that all had been said. But the thought flashed through my mind, and was gone, "Never in all my life can I be happier than I am, now, here, at this moment!"[18]

Insofar as she admitted, Ellen never again was so happy. The summer and the year ended, and Gerald receded into the distance from which he emerged to see her only after long intervals. In January, 1904, *The Deliverance* was published, and the dedication read: "To Dr. H. Holbrook Curtis with appreciation of his skill and gratitude for his sympathy." Dr. Curtis was a famous aurist who was credited with miraculous cures and had accepted Ellen as a patient at his private clinic in New York. During some of her trips to New York, Ellen went every day to his clinic for treatment. According to one report, Dr. Curtis was the mysterious lover Gerald.[19] He was considerably older than she, married, and the father of one daughter. A member of medical societies in Europe and America, he must have traveled widely in Europe and could have easily met Ellen there. As a doctor his financial status was as comfortable as Gerald's must have been, and his similarity to Ellen's description of

[18] *Woman Within,* 164.
[19] In the notes that Marjorie Kinnan Rawlings made for a biography of Ellen Glasgow she said that Dr. Curtis was Gerald, but Mrs. Rawlings went into no detail and left no indication of the source of her information.

Gerald in the autobiography gives credence, but not proof, to the theory that he was Gerald. Dr. Curtis, however, lived fifteen years longer than Ellen said Gerald lived. If the year of Gerald's death in the autobiography is the year when he actually died and not simply the year that Ellen *said* he died because that was the year that their relationship ended, then Dr. Curtis and Gerald could not possibly be the same person. The nature of the story of *The Deliverance* and the fact that it was published at the moment when Ellen was most happy with Gerald make it logical for Ellen to have dedicated that novel to the man whom she called Gerald if she thought she could do it without giving away their secret relationship.

A young woman of almost thirty, Ellen was intensely and deeply in love with Gerald, and *The Deliverance* became a love story set in Virginia from 1878 through 1890. Ostensibly a novel about Reconstruction, *The Deliverance* is a magnificently conceived and beautifully written story about the love between Christopher Blake and Maria Fletcher, a dramatic relationship made possible only by the upsetting of Southern society during war and Reconstruction. Christopher Blake, frequently described as a perfect male animal, was a Virginia aristocrat who had been deprived of his rightful heritage. The pride and the legendary physical perfection of the aristocrat were all that remained; the war had denied him an education and had obliterated his family's wealth. Christopher was a common laborer in tobacco fields that had once belonged to his father. Maria, on the other hand, was the granddaughter of the former overseer of the Blake plantation. Though she was not of aristocratic lineage, she had acquired education and refinement, the very qualities that were supposed to be reserved for Christopher's social class. Traditionally, she was below Christopher's class, although in reality she was much higher. Ellen Glasgow created their love story with luminous irony as she deliberately attempted to prove, perhaps especially to herself, that traditional class consciousness should be inconsequential in love affairs. Ellen herself was engaged in a love affair that defied the social attitudes of her family, and the writing of the novel was an attempt to reconcile her love for Gerald with her training as an aristocratic Virginian. Circumstances brought about by the Civil War and Reconstruction make the love between Christopher Blake and Maria Fletcher seem to be an impossible situation, just as Gerald's marriage and Ellen's mindset made their own relationship seem impossible. The affection between Christopher and Maria appears more genuine than that of the lovers in *The Battle-Ground*. Again, an explicit discussion of sex is omitted, but in *The Deliverance* the institution of marriage is discussed at length by characters of both sexes who come from all stations of life as if it were an obsession with the novelist.

The old aristocratic lady viewed marriage as a duty which must be undertaken with a single eye to family connections, and she recalled how her father "had so high an opinion of marriage that if his fourth wife, and she was very sickly, were to die at once, he'd marry his fifth within the year." A plain farmer was convinced that the ceremony itself inevitably changed a mild-mannered girl into a shrew, and his female counterpart noted that after marriage wives seemed to be more concerned about their setting hens than their husbands' hearts. An aging Negro, Aunt Polly, was proud to have had nine *young* husbands and advised, "de mo' you git, de likelier 'tis you gwine git one dat's worth gittin' . . . ."[20] Even the title of the novel, *The Deliverance*, refers to the personal deliverance of a young woman of means who dared to marry the man she loved even though it meant a life of poverty. The subject of love and marriage was heavy on Ellen's mind when she wrote the book, and it was into the love stories that Ellen wrote her interpretation of the impact of Reconstruction on the South, an interpretation which perhaps quite by accident was extraordinarily realistic.

Ellen subtitled the novel "A Romance of the Virginia Tobacco Fields," and for the setting she rode through the tobacco fields of Louisa and Caroline counties and made detailed notes on the growing of tobacco in Virginia. Against that backdrop she created her Christopher Blake, a descendant of an aristocratic family whose estate has fallen into the possession of a corrupt overseer. Consumed

20 *The Deliverance*, 84, 137.

by hatred and revenge, Christopher deliberately ruined the life of the overseer's grandson, Will Fletcher, by driving him to drink and to murder. In a vain effort to absolve himself of his guilt, Christopher pretended that he committed Will's crime and went to prison in Will's place. Christopher was saved, however, not by his own actions, but by the love of the overseer's granddaughter, Maria Fletcher, who by the end of the story was the only heir to the Blake estate. Despite the obstacles, Maria and Christopher planned to marry, thus restoring the estate to the Blake family. They had defied the traditions of the past and looked to the future for their happiness, something which Ellen hoped that she would be able to do with Gerald.

The story is set at the end of Reconstruction, not during Reconstruction. Ellen Glasgow was not looking for the solution to the South's postwar problems, or her personal problems, in some past era such as Reconstruction or in the days preceding the war. For her, the solution lay in the future when revenge could be put aside and guilt could be absolved. The marriage of the planter's son and the overseer's daughter may be taken as symbolic of the resolution of the South's inner conflicts and as reflective of a kind of optimism that pervaded much of the South after the turn of the century, as well as reflective of the novelist's optimism, however temporary, about her own personal life. The era of Reconstruction represented a definite break in the continuing process of Southern history and was not a period to which Ellen Glasgow and later William Faulkner felt that they should turn in constructing their interpretations of Southern history in fiction. This ability to look to the future rather than sigh for the past was something new for a Southern novelist and perhaps more than anything else establishes Ellen Glasgow as the first realist in Southern letters. It was a fortunate side effect of her romance with Gerald.

In her literary treatment of the impact of Reconstruction, Ellen Glasgow shattered the precedents that had been set by Thomas Nelson Page and even George W. Cable. In *Red Rock*, published in 1898, Page, a Virginian and an aristocrat of even higher social standing than the Glasgow family, wrote his conscientious account of the era he saw as the "greatest humiliation in modern times."[21] *Red Rock* became the novelist's stereotyped description of Reconstruction, also accepted by many historians, as the rape of the South, in which a coalition of armed soldiers, illiterate blacks, unscrupulous whites from both North and South, and irresponsible politicians stripped native white Southerners of their property and their vote and turned the area into a kind of lawless wasteland. Some of the descriptive passages in *Red Rock* and *The Deliverance* are quite similar, but the novelists' interpretations are vastly different. In *John March, Southerner,* published four years earlier than Page's *Red Rock,* George W. Cable, of Virginian and New England ancestry, took quite a different approach to Reconstruction. Cable's claim to be a realist rests more soundly upon his earlier works in which he reproduced the infinitely varied dialects he heard in the streets of New Orleans, but by the end of his career in the 1890's, he had become an advocate of the rights of Negroes and thus sacrificed objectivity and even creativity to his devotion to a cause. In short stories, lectures, essays, and the novel, Cable argued for federal intervention in the 1890's as a last resort to insure the franchise of the black man and for a return to what he considered to be the more progressive period before 1877 when Reconstruction finally ended in the entire South. For Cable and for some historians, Reconstruction was an enlightened period when compared to the trends of the 1890's.[22] Yet his ambitious work failed as realism on the same grounds that Page's did, because both men were writing to please a particular audience and took their social responsibility too seriously. Edmund Wilson, the dean of American literary critics, denounced both *Red Rock* and *John March, Southerner* as devoid of literature, irritating, and boring.[23]

Ten years elapsed between the publication of *John March, Southerner* and Ellen Glasgow's *The Deliverance.* It was a crucial ten

---

[21] Thomas Nelson Page, *Red Rock: A Chronicle of Reconstruction* (Plantation Edition; New York: Charles Scribner's Sons, 1912), viii.

[22] Arlin Turner, *George W. Cable: A Biography* (Baton Rouge: Louisiana State University Press, 1966), 255–56, 261.

[23] Edmund Wilson, *Patriotic Gore: Studies in the Literature of the American Civil War* (New York: Oxford University Press, 1962), 583, 611.

years in the movement of Southern history. By 1904 Negro suffrage was no longer a burning issue; it had been virtually settled by a general rewriting of Southern state constitutions that barred black people from the polls, and Southern Progressivism was proceeding apace for whites only. Ellen Glasgow was writing at a time when the controversial issues that plagued Page and Cable were no longer viable, which may help account for the fact that in her symbolic romances she developed a far different and rather surprising solution to the problem of how the novelist should treat Reconstruction, a solution which perhaps could have occurred only to the mind of a woman. Thomas Nelson Page was of the opinion at the end of the nineteenth century that the hope for the future of the South lay in a return to the days "befo' de wah"; George W. Cable thought that the salvation of the South lay in the resurrection of the techniques of dealing with problems which were attempted during Reconstruction, especially the guarantee by force of the political rights of Negroes. But Ellen Glasgow, determined that her lovers should be reconciled and live happily ever afterwards, looked to the future for the solution of the South's problems. In a good humor when she wrote *The Deliverance,* she was learning to laugh at the follies of herself, her characters, and the history of her region, and with the combined use of satire and irony she created a highly successful literary technique and an increasingly realistic view of the South.

The trend which Ellen Glasgow began in *The Deliverance* was carried to its zenith by William Faulkner. Like Ellen Glasgow, Faulkner virtually ignored the Reconstruction years themselves in his chronicle of the imaginary Yoknapatawpha County, Mississippi. In "An Odor of Verbena," a story included in *The Unvanquished* and published in 1938, Faulkner wrote a remarkable parallel to *The Deliverance.* Faulkner's story takes place in Mississippi in 1874. Bayard Sartoris, twenty-four years old and a law student at the University of Mississippi, receives word that his father has been shot in the street by Ben Redmond. According to the Southern code, it is Bayard's obligation to kill his father's murderer in a fair fight. Bayard wonders if he will be able to face the situation as a man, rather than as only a Sartoris and a Southerner. Despite the pressures of the community to the contrary, Bayard had the courage to face his enemy unarmed and to seek a more permanent peace by ending the tradition that cried for revenge against one's enemies.

Bayard Sartoris has enough in common with Christopher Blake to suggest that William Faulkner and Ellen Glasgow had similar interpretations of the era of Reconstruction. Both novelists set their stories at the end of the actual Reconstruction years, skillfully employed the use of irony, and created characters who ultimately decided upon a complete break with the past and a single eye to the future in resolving their personal problems that were so intimately tied up with the history of the South. Christopher Blake's decision to serve Will Fletcher's prison sentence in an effort to absolve himself of his guilt and to marry the overseer's granddaughter is analogous to Bayard's decision to face his father's murderer unarmed in an attempt to break a vicious cycle of Southern honor. Whereas Thomas Nelson Page and George W. Cable looked back to the days before the war or to the political and social events during Reconstruction itself for their solutions to the South's problems, Ellen Glasgow and William Faulkner suggested that the hope for the South lay in the cultivation in a new era of the basic human passions of repentance, determination, and courage. Page's, and to an extent Cable's, characters reacted to their lots in life as Virginians and as Southerners, but the characters of Ellen Glasgow and William Faulkner reacted as universal men. Although the setting of Ellen Glasgow's novel and much of her characterization is closer to Page, the theme of her work is closer to Faulkner. *The Deliverance* is but one of a number of her novels that establish her as an important transitional figure from romanticism to realism in Southern letters. She was forced to take a hard look at the reality of her own life, especially her relationship with Gerald, and the result of that experience found expression in her novels.

The value of *The Deliverance* was instantly recognized, and the critics listed Ellen Glasgow's name among the American realists Hamlin Garland, Stephen Crane, Frank Norris, and Theodore

Dreiser. The subtitle, "A Romance of the Virginia Tobacco Fields," was good advertisement for the love story, and the readers of novels bought *The Deliverance* in such numbers that it became the second-best seller in the nation in 1904.[24] What contemporary readers and critics could not know, however, was the tenuous balance from which the woman had written the novel and the factors in her own personal life that had gone into it. Suspended for the moment in a love affair that was satisfactory, Ellen was on top of a world that was forever turning.

24 Kelly, "Struggle for Recognition," 60, 74.

# 5

## The Agony and the Sweat

*G*erald died in 1905, and the pen that the year before had produced the second-best seller in the nation fell from Ellen's fingers. In the summer of 1905 she and Cary were at an inn in Mürren, Switzerland. Gerald was in Europe at the same time and sent Ellen a note telling her of his serious illness. According to her own account, Ellen never saw him again. In August, while riding on a train in France, she read of his death in the Paris edition of the New York *Herald*.[1] It was the crowning blow to an agony that had begun perhaps two years earlier.

The strain of a clandestine love affair with a married man had begun to erode Ellen's happiness long before his death caused the mixed emotions of grief, guilt, and even relief. At Christmas of 1904 she should have been happy, enjoying the fame and fortune which the success of *The Deliverance* brought her, but she was not. She wrote bitterly to Walter Hines Page that the years had taken away everything but her work and that she could not forget her Gethsemane and her cross.[2] She was hard at work on a new novel, *The Wheel of Life*, a vague and rambling story of immorality and boredom among the socially elite in New York City. She said that she did not know whether her own life went into her book, but it was a book that "was wrung from life itself" and was

1 *Woman Within*, 164–68.
2 December 26, 1904, in *Letters*, 40–41. In *Letters* this letter is misdated "1902"; the original manuscript in the Walter Hines Page Papers is dated "1904."

not likely to be either understood or popular. But it was a book she had to write in order to live, she said.[3] To her neighbor and fellow novelist, Mary Johnston, she cried out that she hungered for God, even though she was so uncertain "of his being underneath us all." Lamenting her weakness in yielding to her impulses, but without specifying what those impulses were, she moaned that her suffering made her want to "rend the universe."[4] But she was powerless to find relief from her mental and physical anguish and fell deeper into a state of melancholia as the winter dragged into spring.

The winter of 1904 and 1905 was spent slaving over a new novel and making very little progress with it. In March, Cary had a major operation for the removal of a malignancy, and her precarious health cast another pall over the family. Ellen dared not look to the past or the future; she contemplated only the moment at hand and spent hours restlessly pacing up and down Main Street. She read the *Bhagavad-Gita*, the sacred literature of the Hindus, and Thomas à Kempis' *Imitation of Christ*. She thought of herself as a mystic who could envision worlds beyond the constricting one which she knew, and she believed that her mind was too large to be confined to the tiny planet of earth. Her physical health declined with her mental estate, causing her to decide to go with Rebe to Chase City in the southern part of Virginia for, as she said, "a fortnight of boredom and mineral water."[5] The trip did her no good, and she was scarcely home again before she was planning another vacation. In May she and Rebe went to Hurricane, New York, but Ellen was not cheered by American mountains that she said were crude and lacked atmosphere.[6] She yearned to return to the Swiss Alps where she had spent her happiest time with Gerald.

She planned to go to Germany in the summer to consult Dr.

3 To Walter Hines Page, December 26, 1904, in *Letters*, 41.

4 To Mary Johnston, February 3, 1905, *ibid.*, 46.

5 To Mary Johnston, Sunday [March, 1905], in Mary Johnston Papers, University of Virginia Library.

6 To Eleanor Robson Belmont, May 29, [1905,] in Eleanor Robson Belmont Papers, Columbia University Library.

Isadore Müller, a leading aurist.[7] She was still angry and depressed over her failing hearing, although she had just acquired a hearing aid that was of some help to her. It was a cumbersome device, consisting of a trumpet that she held to her ear and an instrument attached to her body that had to be cranked by hand. She presented a comical picture holding the trumpet with one hand and turning the crank with the other, which caused some members of her family laughingly to comment, "I can't broadcast Ellen! "[8] Ellen, however, did not think it was funny. She hoped that Dr. Müller could help her, but her visit to him must have been inconsequential for she never mentioned him again, and her hearing did not improve.

Chances are that she knew Gerald would be in Europe at the time she planned her visit to the aurist. By July, Cary had recovered sufficiently from her operation to make the trip abroad with Ellen and Rebe. By the first of August the three sisters were settled in a Swiss chalet with a view of the snow-covered Jungfrau. They were surrounded by German and English tourists, and Ellen danced happily with both nations.[9] Then came the fateful letter from Gerald and the dismal return to America. Ellen plunged again into the sacred literature of Hinduism and Buddhism and the writing of Nietzsche and Schopenhauer. She completed her novel in an ambivalent state of mental anguish and questing for peace and sent it to Walter Hines Page to be published. Page begged her not to take metaphysics seriously, but Ellen insisted that metaphysics was the science of the soul of man and the only thing on earth which a human being could take seriously.[10] Convinced that science had failed her body and orthodox religion had failed her soul, she turned to mysticism for comfort. And she believed that she saw the light.

Upon reflection, the death of Gerald became Ellen's opportunity for an excursion into a spiritual world that she had not known before. The summer of 1906 she spent once again at Hurricane, New

[7] Ellen Glasgow to Arthur G. Glasgow, March 27, 1905, in *Letters*, 47–49.
[8] Interview with Mr. Glasgow Clark, November 14, 1968.
[9] Cary Glasgow McCormack to Mrs. Walter Hines Page, August 4, 1905, in Page Papers.
[10] To Walter Hines Page, Christmas, 1905, in *Letters*, 49–50.

York, and this time found the countryside beautiful and refreshing. September found her in Montreal and Quebec. She displayed a kind of exuberance on the anniversary of the death of Gerald and acted as if the new spiritual experience triggered by his death had led her into an infinitely greater understanding of human existence. She wrote long letters to Mary Johnston in which she quoted from the *Upanishads* and said that for the first time in her life her soul was "clear and radiant out of a long darkness." She stood in the Adirondacks and gazed at the constellations and experienced "peace and exquisite pleasure from [her] friendship with the stars," a feeling of tranquillity that made her willing to lie down quietly and give up her life for "one of the thousand lives" she saw beyond.[11]

Mary Johnston claimed to be able to understand such an experience and encouraged Ellen in her quest for Truth in the mystical teachings of the religions of the East. A month later Ellen continued:

> For a year I was so dead that I couldn't feel even when I was hurt because of some curious emotional anaesthesia, and, like you, I had to fight—fight, a sleepless battle night and day, not for my reason but for my very soul. Then at the end of a year—at Mürren last summer I came out triumphant, and for three whole months it was as if I walked on light, not air. I was like one who had come out of a dark prison into the presence of God and saw and knew him, and cared for nothing in the way of pain that had gone before the vision. . . . The old sorrows, the old temptations, the old fights are like so many steps by which we go on and upward and always, I hope, to something bigger and higher than we knew before. . . . The exaltation may soften and pass into quiet, but the peace of the soul does not and cannot surrender to the old anguish again.[12]

Ellen explained that such moments of exhilaration were not permanent, but she failed to describe precisely those thousands of worlds she saw beyond. Before the month ended, she and Rebe started for home, descending into New York City and the real and less mystical world of dressmakers and book publishers.

In terms of her art, Ellen paid a dear price for the liberation of

11 August 15, 1906, *ibid.*, 52–54.
12 To Mary Johnston, September, 1906, in *Letters*, 55–57.

her soul. *The Wheel of Life* was published in January of 1906 and glided along on the popularity of the author's name, finishing the year as the tenth-best seller across the country,[13] but it was the greatest mistake of Ellen's writing career. The stage in the novel is crowded with no fewer than six major characters who live dull lives in the upper echelons of New York society. Men and women alike find it impossible to remain faithful to the partners to whom they are married or engaged and eventually give up on trying to find any real satisfaction in life. The book is basically the story of Laura Wilde, a poet who lives in New York City in semi-seclusion with her eccentric family, which has a Southern background. She has vowed never to marry, but is unable to resist her physical attraction to Arnold Kemper, a man known for his virility, love affairs, and talent for making a fortune on the stock exchange. His proposed wedding to Laura is cancelled at the last moment, because Kemper fell in love with one of his former wives. Laura seeks comfort from Roger Adams, a man whose wife led him to financial ruin by buying expensive clothes, taking dope, drinking, and running around with other men before she finally died of general dissipation. Since Roger and Laura have been similarly hurt, they form a platonic partnership and spend hours talking about life. Pages and pages are filled with tedious descriptions of ladies' fashions and soliloquies by women who are dying of boredom, because Ellen was again trying to write a volume of philosophy under the very thin disguise of a novel.

Many years later she commended a reviewer for discovering the "autobiographical basis" of *The Wheel of Life*, a book she said "was taken directly from experience."[14] The social world described in the novel is one which Ellen entered for brief periods of time when she was in New York City, and the novel is probably an accurate description of the world in which Gerald lived. Although too many of the facts are unknown to draw definite conclusions, it is almost certain that the key to the truth of her relationship with Gerald is to be found in this novel. The beautiful Laura

[13] Kelly, "Struggle for Recognition," 85.
[14] To Bessie Zaban Jones, April 18, 1938, in *Letters*, 238.

Wilde, a talented artist from the South who lives a very protected life in New York City, drifts through the novel probably as Ellen Glasgow's literary counterpart. Arnold Kemper, attracted to Laura and hoping to form an unlikely match with her, is probably the literary counterpart of Gerald. Both lover and his beloved are presented as real sexual people, attracted to each other, yet held apart by psychological eccentricities and conflicting inherited values. Laura seems to demand a complete separation of mind and body, at some points even believing that the activity of the flesh might dull her creative and philosophical mind. Emotions have to be rationalized before they can be accepted or enjoyed. This attitude of Laura's in the novel became typical of Ellen's attitude toward her own relationships with men. And Arnold Kemper is presented as a purely sexual creature, admired as such by Laura only from a distance. The novelist seems to be demanding that males of the species be perfectly proportioned and pleasing to the female eye, but that they be no more than intellectual companions for the female. Such an attitude is an exaggerated version of the way Southern aristocratic ladies were taught to view their men, which was precisely Ellen's heritage, though many Southern ladies must have enjoyed a psychological maturity that went beyond their traditional training. The story of Laura Wilde and Arnold Kemper raises intriguing possibilities concerning Ellen and Gerald, but no records have survived that make it possible to distinguish absolutely between the truth of life and the truth of literature.

*The Wheel of Life* was written under the shadow of the last painful years that Ellen knew Gerald and the months immediately after his death. Ellen was saying that life is like the turning of a wheel that takes man through the ages of impulse, illusion, disenchantment, and reconciliation. All of these ages were phases of the various stages in the author's relationship with Gerald. The age of disenchantment was obviously most real to her, but she did convey the ages of impulse and illusion convincingly. The age of reconciliation refers not to that time when man becomes reconciled to man, but to the time when man becomes reconciled to some cosmic force, Fate perhaps, that is far greater than he and that determines his destiny. The jilted Laura, who sometimes questions the existence of God, comes to believe that "the agony of joy was sharper than that of grief," which is the same attitude Ellen had adopted by the time she completed the novel. When Laura enters her age of reconciliation, she lapses into a kind of stoic existence in which nothing matters, for everything is beyond her control: ". . . that we're all drawn by wires like puppets, and the strongest wire pulls us in the direction in which we are meant to go? It's curious that I should never have known this before because it has become perfectly plain to me now—there is no soul, no aspiration, no motive for good or evil, for we're every one worked by wires while we are pretending to move ourselves."[15] Ellen combined an attitude she had learned as a child at the Second Presbyterian Church with her personal anguish and increasing skepticism to produce a half-baked philosophy and pessimistic view of life. Within a matter of months after the publication of *The Wheel of Life*, she believed that she had discovered the existence of a soul through her brief and superficial foray into mysticism, and she enjoyed a fleeting moment of exhiliration before the realities of life drew her attention again to the mundane ways of the flesh.

The peace of the soul, she soon learned, does and can surrender to the old anguish again. As if by magic, the anguish returned as soon as Ellen and her sisters arrived back home in Richmond. The house itself cast a foreboding shadow over Ellen's countenance. Her younger sister, Rebe, planned to be married on December 5, 1906, to Cabell Carrington Tutwiler of Philadelphia. The Reverend Frank Paradise, an Episcopalian minister from Massachusetts, whom Ellen and Rebe had met at Hurricane, New York, was invited to perform the ceremony. Ellen became more nervous as the date approached. Rebe had been her closest friend and traveling companion, and Ellen dreaded the thought of losing her. Ellen also looked askance at men in general and decidedly disapproved of Tutwiler. And she was jealous. Thirty-two years old, single, and already the veteran of one major love affair, marriage still did not seem likely in her foreseeable future. Now her younger sister was

15 Ellen Glasgow, *The Wheel of Life* (New York: Doubleday, Page and Co.), 454.

about to embark upon a potentially happy way of life which Ellen
thought that she herself would never know, and there was an air
of coolness in the family on the wedding day. Rebe went with her
husband to make her home in Philadelphia, and Ellen struggled
to check her resentment.

The Reverend Paradise remained as a guest of the family for ten
days after the ceremony and passed hours of his time talking with
Ellen about philosophy. Ellen found the clergyman handsome and
seduced him into an intellectual courtship, for which he was apparently easy prey. His interests were not entirely intellectual, and
when Ellen saw him off on the train, she had a new beau. Ellen bubbled that the Reverend Paradise had fitted in beautifully with her
family and friends, and that he always seemed to say the right thing.
To entertain him she gave a dinner and invited Governor Andrew
Jackson Montague, the very man whom nine years earlier she had
watched become the attorney general of Virginia as she stood silently behind the curtain of a Roanoke opera house. The dinner
was lavish: raw oysters, sweetbreads, pheasants, salad, ham, ice
cream, sherry, and champagne.[16] Everyone had a good time, and
the much-fêted Reverend Paradise returned to Massachusetts, increasingly the object of Ellen's compensation for the loss of Rebe.

As one of the reigning women of the household, Ellen's domestic
duties were usually less exciting than serving as hostess at a dinner
for the governor of Virginia. Her biggest headache was the management of servants who gave "fresh illustrations of imbecility
every day," allowed the house to remain embedded in dirt, and departed without notice, taking with them much of the silver and
linen. Some of her time was spent looking for new maids, since the
dispositions of the Glasgow girls and the alleged amorous attentions of Mr. Glasgow made One West Main something of a maid's
graveyard. At odd moments she wrote long letters to Rebe and
doted over her dog Joy. Small children who visited in the home remembered Ellen Glasgow as a tall figure in white, standing in the

[16] Copy of a letter from Ellen Glasgow to Rebe Glasgow Tutwiler, December 14,
1906, in Rawlings Papers.

darkened hall.[17] At family dinners, before passing the plate, sometimes she broke open all the baked sweet potatoes, searching for the one that suited her best.[18]

When Christmas came, Ellen filled stockings to be distributed among poor children, entertained Carrie Coleman's family for dinner, bought whiskey and plum pudding for the servants, and argued with her father. She paid for the whiskey and plum pudding herself and complained that her father was having an "economical fit," which necessitated their eating rabbits for a week and using the very poorest grade of butter. Arthur sent her and Cary each a check for twenty-five dollars. Ellen planned to give hers to the Society for the Prevention of Cruelty to Animals, but Mr. Glasgow immediately garnisheed part of Cary's for reasons known only to himself. And Ellen spent hers for a deluxe edition of Plato. After Christmas, Ellen donned a lace dress and pink coat and attended several local receptions, where she inspected ladies' gowns, admired their fashionable dogs, delighted in small gossip and petty insults, drank very little, and frequently suffered from boredom. The arrival of the New Year properly celebrated, she retreated to One West Main Street, where she hired a new battery of servants, personally oversaw the cleaning and refurbishing of their quarters, spent more and more time working on her new novel, and waited for Rebe to return for a visit.[19]

Rebe came home in February, expecting a warm and friendly welcome. She had received many letters from Ellen filled with the tenderest terms of endearment, admonishing her to wear her pretty clothes and be cheerful in Philadelphia, and telling her how much she was missed. Often Ellen concluded with "Love to Cabell." But Ellen just did not like Cabell, and the restraint which she mustered in her letters vanished when she saw her sister in person. Ellen, Rebe, and Cary became involved in an argument that left all three

[17] Interview with Mrs. James Branch Cabell, November 14, 1968.
[18] Interview with Mr. Glasgow Clark, November 14, 1968.
[19] Copy of a letter from Ellen Glasgow to Rebe Tutwiler, December 23, 1906, in Rawlings Papers.

angry. Cary reprimanded Ellen for her expressions of hostility against Rebe for getting married. Ellen accused Rebe of enjoying everybody else's company more than she enjoyed hers, but later apologized for her terrible temperament. It was a short-lived argument, for the sisters were writing tender letters to each other again by the end of May. Ellen condemned herself for her own "absorbing wretchedness" and even promised to try to feel at home with Cabell for Rebe's sake. Two days later, Ellen complained that men were so different from women that she did not know if she would ever be able to feel at home with Cabell—and she never did.[20] The close relationship among the sisters became confined to letters that conveyed a feeling of tenderness that was markedly absent when they were together.

Ellen filled her days with the writing of her novel, planning her summer, and preparing for a very enjoyable Memorial Day celebration. On May 30, Richmond was thronged with old soldiers, some of whom wandered aimlessly through the streets with satchell in hand and no idea where they would sleep. Ellen invited two of them in for coffee and chicken, and no doubt explained to them that she had recently joined the Colonial Dames and planned to go to Jamestown to celebrate their day. Even Mr. Glasgow had a tender spot for the veterans. After a parade on June 3, the Glasgow family invited a whole company of Texans in for dinner. The company was comprised of twenty-three men who had allegedly served under General Joseph Johnston. Tables were set up in the living room and dining room and friends were invited in to serve. Each man was given a mint julep, fried chicken, coffee, ice cream, and a cigar. Before leaving they stood in the hall and sang "God Be with You till We Meet Again." Ellen followed them out into the street and stood, tiny and silent, in front of the massive house as the aging soldiers presented arms to her before marching off in a parade.[21] Ellen attended the celebration of the Colonial Dames at Jamestown in a gay mood, but when she returned she found the gray house once again empty and depressing.

20 *Ibid.*, May 22, 24, 1907.
21 *Ibid.*, May 30, June 4, 1907.

For the second consecutive year, she was unable to go to Europe. Arthur had decided to send Cary abroad for her health, and the rest of the family had to be content to spend the summer at White Sulphur Springs, West Virginia. The White, as they called it, was a long-established resort for fashionable people to which Ellen was no stranger. She doubted that she would be able to find any relaxation on the American side of the Atlantic, but she consoled herself by having some new clothes made for the occasion and by renting two cottages so that she would not have to stay in the same one with her father. From the outside, the cottages were picturesque. Virginia creeper shaded rambling porches that were furnished with hammocks and small tea tables. Inside, Ellen said, they were shabby and dirty.[22] The entourage consisted of Ellen, her older sister Emily, Mr. Glasgow, Frank, and Louise Willcox. Rebe was to come down for a visit later in the summer, and a friend was to bring Joy, the dog, after the family got established. Ellen thought she would spend her time in an intellectual pursuit of the meaning of life and mull over her loss of Gerald through death and her loss of Rebe through marriage. So she bundled up her Plato and her Plotinus, her Schopenhauer and her Spinoza, her Kant and her Buddha, her Christ and her St. Francis, and struck out for the cooler climate of the springs.

Soon, however, she gave it all up in favor of golf. Golf, more than philosophy, she later admitted, helped her to endure life.[23] For ten years she played golf from Virginia to Maine to California and only gave it up when she became anxious that her deafness might cause her to get hit from behind by another golfer's ball.[24] When she grew tired of golf that summer at the White, she moved on to horseback riding. The latter sport occasionally necessitated a generous application of liniment to the badly bruised lady, but she was undaunted and wrote to Arthur in London, giving him precise instructions to have an English saddle made and shipped to her.[25]

[22] *Ibid.*, July 2, 1907.
[23] *Woman Within*, 177.
[24] Information obtained from a person who wishes to remain anonymous.
[25] August 14, 1907, in *Letters*, 57.

She despaired again, however, when the man in charge of the horses put her on one that was so old that it would not go faster than a walk unless the man got behind and kicked it.[26] Her habit was to call the beasts "mules," but nevertheless she arose before dawn to ride through sun and rain, doggedly determined to find health and sanity.

In the evenings she braced her spirit with a stiff drink of liquor and donned her finest white muslin to attend the balls.[27] Southern gentlemen had brought their daughters to display before potential suitors, and there was much swishing of fans, calling for mammies, giggling, and behind-the-scenes speculation about the size of dowries. The ladies of Ellen's age were married and had at least one baby whom they watched fondly as he played on the floor of the ballroom and aroused just a tiny spark of envy in the heart of one who was trying to convince herself that she was unfit for marriage. Ellen promised herself that if the good Lord permitted, she would spend her next summer in the British Isles.[28]

Perhaps the memory of those babies on the ballroom floor at the White prompted Ellen to keep the channels of her own heart open, because by the end of 1907 she was engaged to the Reverend Mr. Paradise. By her own admission that engagement was "frankly experimental"; and for the three years it lasted, Ellen enjoyed the most faithful attentions of a suitor, but she always assigned him a secondary place in her life. In November she finished *The Ancient Law* and sent it to Walter Hines Page. About three weeks later she and Lizzie Patterson went to New York City to discuss the new novel and to have a good time. They stayed in New York for most of December where they shopped, and Ellen went to see her ear specialist every day for some undefined treatment that did her no good. The year changed to 1908, and Ellen went back to Richmond to await the publication of her seventh novel.

*The Ancient Law* was published in the spring. Though the re-

---

26 Copy of a letter from Ellen Glasgow to Rebe Tutwiler, July 2, 1907, in Rawlings Papers.
27 Ellen Glasgow to Mary Johnston, July 20, 1907, in Johnston Papers.
28 *Ibid.*

views on both sides of the Atlantic were unfavorable and it had little popular success, the novel was a marked improvement over her previous effort and attracted the attention of several academicians who began to build Ellen Glasgow's reputation as a respectable literary artist. The novel is the story of an ex-convict who returns to his home in Virginia, and Ellen undoubtedly got the idea from an unidentified novel of a similar theme that she read three years earlier. Ellen was particularly touched by that novel, which she felt showed how intensive suffering was necessary in order to develop a finer insight into life, a deeper consciousness of the spirit. The self-giving of the released convict in the unidentified novel, Ellen said, made him more human and worthy of respect than the successful man of letters he had been before his imprisonment.[29] Ellen believed that her own trials had made her a better person; the penitentiary was only three blocks from One West Main Street, and her father was an active voice in behalf of prison reform, so her choice of a theme was not something foreign to her experience.

The development of the theme, however, was not commensurate with her talents. Daniel Ordway, the central character of *The Ancient Law*, lived more lives than is generally possible or than is aesthetically satisfying in a novel. He was an embezzler, convict, familial outcast, mill-town hero, rejected husband, unappreciated father, quasi-political activist, and ultimately a potential suicide. His baptism by fire was a bit too intense, and his refinement is never convincingly revealed by the novelist. Once again Ellen Glasgow was being more philosophical than she was creative. Her justification for writing the story seems to have been to celebrate some unexpected bond of human friendship, the "ancient law," that enables a fellow human being to overcome his tragedy and emerge as a stronger person. The novel concludes with praise for a friend whose helping hand saved a basically good person from misfortune. Ellen dedicated the novel to "My Good Friend Effendi," who undoubtedly must have offered her some comfort in

[29] Ellen Glasgow to Eleanor Robson Belmont, April 2, 1905, in Belmont Papers.

the difficult year when she was trying to recover from the loss of Gerald, perhaps unaware that he was doing so. "Effendi" stands for F. N. D., the initials of Frank N. Doubleday, Ellen's personal friend and a partner in the firm that published her novels.

By the time the novel was published, Ellen was extremely angry with the other partner in the firm, Walter Hines Page, who had been her best friend in the publishing business. Page had become the editor of *The World's Work*, and he had written or allowed to be published, an article that was critical of the opponents of vivisection, branding them as "sentimental" and "emotional."[30] Ellen's love of dogs and interest in the Society for the Prevention of Cruelty to Animals was already well established, and she took the article personally. She poured out a diluted measure of her wrath to Page, urging him to examine both sides of the argument in the future before he indulged in "animadversion with regard to its consequences, moral or otherwise."[31] Shortly thereafter, she visited Page in New York City and apparently parted from that meeting on a cordial note, but the idea was already growing in her mind that perhaps she should change publishers for her next novel. Her love for animals was much stronger than her appreciation for the publisher whose assistance had helped to make her a well-known author.

A change of publishers could wait, however, because a more pressing matter concerned her at the moment. She sat in her study on July 4 listening to the noisy demonstration of fireworks, almost daring to wish that the Bunker Hill monument was still in the quarry, and planning a trip to Europe in the late summer.[32] For reading matter she would take her Bible or Spinoza, whichever could be more conveniently fitted into her bags. The important thing to her was not what she read, but that for the first time since Gerald's death she would vacation again on that side of the Atlantic on which, she once lamented, she had not been born.

Ellen, Cary, and their friend Berta Wellford sailed for Venice

[30] "Life of a Monkey Against the Life of a Man," *World's Work*, XVI (July, 1908), 10417.
[31] June 26, 1908, in *Letters*, 58–60.
[32] Ellen Glasgow to Mary Johnston, July 4, 1908, in Johnston Papers.

on July 18. The ship was small and Ellen suffered from seasickness during the entire trip.[33] She spent two months wandering with her friends in Italy. She loved Assisi, which she said was a dream of colors and reminded her of St. Francis. There she met a Franciscan monk named P. G. Geroni who served as her interpreter and took her into his confidence when he realized that she had a deep feeling for St. Francis. An aristocrat who had known a great deal of suffering as a monk, he found that he and Ellen had some things in common and called occasionally at her hotel.[34] Geroni was captivated by Ellen's smile, and several years later wrote her letters trying to diminish her sadness.[35] The legend arose in Richmond that an Italian monk, likely to have been Geroni, eventually followed Ellen to America, stood on the steps of One West Main Street, clad in robe, rope belt, and sandals, and could get no one to answer the door.[36] Berta Wellford denied that the story of his visit to Richmond was true, but the friendship between Ellen and the friar was important enough for Ellen to comment upon it to her closest friends and for Geroni to take the pains to write a few letters to her in French, which he believed that she could read.

In Assisi that summer the charm of the town and the friendship of Geroni were marred by a hotel plagued by poor service, mosquitoes, and fleas.[37] Ellen felt that Berta and Cary enjoyed seeing everything together while she was left alone so much. She went to see an astrologer who told her that it was her inevitable fate to be always alone. It was a fate which she had selected for herself long before she met the astrologer. By the end of September she was back in New York. After a few days of visiting and shopping she returned to Richmond and the isolation of her study, where she completed her eighth novel, *The Romance of a Plain Man.*

To punish Walter Hines Page for his article about vivisection,

---

[33] Ellen Glasgow to Arthur G. Glasgow, July 23, 1908, in Glasgow Papers.
[34] Berta Wellford to MKR, in Rawlings Papers.
[35] P. G. Geroni to Ellen Glasgow, January 30, 1912, and May 2, 1912, in Glasgow Papers. The sadness mentioned in the latter letter may refer to the death of Cary.
[36] Interview with Mrs. William R. Trigg, Jr., January 10, 1969.
[37] Copy of a letter of Ellen Glasgow to Rebe Tutwiler, August 5, 1908, in Rawlings Papers.

she decided to change publishers. She acted on a whim, not a calculated reason, when late in 1908 she wrote the company that had rejected her first novel twelve years earlier and offered them a second chance to become her publisher. George P. Brett was still president of the Macmillan Company, and he naturally was interested in the work of a novelist with an established reputation. Ellen assured him that her new novel had greater elements of popularity than anything she had written and that she was willing for him to give it his consideration if he would promise to do his best by it.[38] By Christmas they had agreed to do business, and Ellen promised to deliver the novel in January.

When Brett read the manuscript, he immediately regretted that he had signed the contract before seeing the novel. He wrote a three-page letter to Ellen Glasgow expressing his deep disappointment and suggesting that she completely rewrite the last half of the book.[39] She was indignant and fired off a telegram explaining that she was physically unable to rewrite the novel and asking to be released from her contract. Brett would release her from the contract only on the condition that if the book were published by another firm, it should not be changed from its present form and material.[40] Within two days Ellen decided that her health had improved and she would be strong enough to rewrite the book and let Brett publish it. When she returned the completed manuscript in March, Brett sent her a check in accordance with their agreement and did not take the trouble to reread the manuscript.

The book came out in May. Its theme paralleled that of *The Voice of the People*, but the development of plot and characters was far inferior to the earlier novel. Set in Richmond from 1875 through 1908, *The Romance of a Plain Man* is the story of Ben Starr, the boy who grew up in poverty but who was eventually offered the presidency of the Great South Midland and Atlantic Railroad. As a boy, Ben was fascinated by little Sally Mickleborough, a girl with red shoes and a Church Hill address who had

38 Ellen Glasgow to George P. Brett, December 12, 1908, Macmillan Authors.
39 *Ibid.*, January 26, 1909.
40 George P. Brett to Ellen Glasgow, January 28, 1909, *ibid.*

once called him common. He decided that the way to avoid being common was to become rich. Driven by his ambition and helped by General Bolingbroke, he became wealthy and finally married Sally, whose family wholly disapproved because of his ancestry. Pursuit of wealth resulted in neglect of Sally, who really was not particularly concerned with money. A financial panic plunged Ben into bankruptcy and forced Sally to take in laundry during her husband's illness. Eventually Ben got a second chance, remade much of his fortune, and attained his goal in life when he was offered the presidency of the Great South Midland and Atlantic Railroad. The same day the offer came he realized that his wife needed him to travel with her for her health, so he decided to decline the position out of devotion to his wife. His real ambition in life had been to become worthy of a woman from a higher social class, and to the mind of the novelist, their match was undoubtedly doomed to hardship and perhaps failure.

The story had a mildly successful popular appeal and enjoyed modest sales during the summer of 1909.[41] By the end of the year the Macmillan Company had sold 23,317 copies, paid the author $6,995.10 in royalties, and realized a profit of only $216.39.[42] Before January of the next year, Ellen bought the plates from the Macmillan Company and turned them over to her former publishers, Doubleday, Page and Company. She explained that her reasons were both financial and sentimental, but she had really never forgiven Brett for his frank expression of disappointment with the novel, a blow that was more devastating to her ego than Page's editorial about vivisection.

Ellen had rushed her rewriting of *The Romance of a Plain Man* in order to plan a trip to England in the spring. She had grown accustomed to paying little attention to her brother Frank and no doubt did not realize the gravity of his illness before she sailed. Frank suffered from insomnia and often went horseback riding on Sunday for relaxation, but his father believed that riding on Sunday was a sin and forced him to give it up. Every day the two

[41] Kelly, "Struggle for Recognition," 99.
[42] Ellen Glasgow File, Macmillan Authors.

of them walked to their jobs at the Tredegar Iron Works. Frank was thirty-nine years old in 1909, single, and believed never to have had any romantic relationship with a woman. Ellen had scarcely landed in London before she received word that he was dead. In the early hours of the morning of April 7, he pencilled a codicil to his brief will in which he directed that one thousand dollars in cash be paid from his bank account to each of his dear sisters.[43] He ate breakfast as usual with his father and then walked with him to the Tredegar Iron Works. In his office, during the day, for reasons that have never been explained, he shot himself. Ellen did not come home for the funeral. She continued her vacation in England with her close friend Lizzie Patterson, but Frank's death cast a pall over her trip. Nevertheless, she avoided formal mourning and continued to wear bright clothes. She met May Sinclair, the British novelist and suffragette, and marched with her through the streets of London in behalf of woman's suffrage. She tried to keep busy and to enjoy her trip.

At the end of the month May Sinclair invited Ellen to a tea. Ellen wore a brown satin suit and a brown hat with a plume in it. Twenty women and two men sat in chairs in a circle in the center of the room. All were drinking tea and eating bread and butter in funereal silence. May Sinclair greeted Ellen and Lizzie in a whisper and placed them in chairs with their backs only two inches from a hot stove. There they sat, not saying a word, the perspiration pouring off their foreheads, gazing at a Negro girl who sat alone in the middle of the room and at a man who nervously and silently clinched and unclinched his fists. Finally, the nervous gentleman passed around a plate of plum cake, which seemed to insult everyone, and Ellen tried to look as insulted as the rest. May Sinclair darted around serving tea and "looking like a frightened mouse and not opening her lips during the entire occasion." A writer, Kate Douglas Wiggin, came in with her publisher and sat down next to Ellen. Ellen found the writer conceited, but she thought the publisher was quite attractive. The publisher even smiled

[43] Last Will and Testament of Francis T. Glasgow, Jr., Office of the Clerk of the Chancery Court, Richmond City Hall, Richmond, Va.

when Ellen leaned over and told him that if she had seen him sooner she would not have run away from him! It was the only smile of the evening, for as Ellen noted, "a smile is an uncommon sight in merrie England. They take their pleasures sadly, yet I suppose they take them just the same." Being partially deaf made her nervous about meeting new people, and she was shocked when an old lady in the street later told her that the party had been given in her honor. To Ellen it had been a painful occasion at which she was so embarrassed that she was "positively as awkward [as] the English." Lizzie Patterson dreamed about funerals all night, and Ellen tried to cheer herself up by eating bread puddings and visiting old cemeteries. And in private she laughed heartily at the experience.[44]

Except for the tea, the vacation was not one of Ellen Glasgow's more memorable trips to England, and by the middle of July she was back home. She walked into the house on Main Street and into the gloom that hung there because of the death of Frank, the illness of Cary, and the presence of an aging father who was becoming "more irascible and dictatorial."[45] She wanted to escape that atmosphere at all costs, so she planned a trip to Colorado immediately. She invited her friend Julia Sully to go with her, and they set out on a train sometime in August.

As the train glided across the plains, Ellen pulled out her letters from Frank Paradise and read them to Julia. One letter contained a photograph of the gentleman, which Ellen admired excessively as she raved to Julia about how handsome her fiancé was. In the same letter was a poem which she read and destroyed indignantly. She told Julia that even if the Reverend Paradise was extraordinarily handsome, she could not marry a man who wrote poetry so badly.[46] The experimental engagement was broken the following year, and Ellen consigned to the flames all of her fiancé's love letters and poems.[47] Frank Paradise eventually married, deserted

[44] Ellen Glasgow to Cary McCormack, April 28, 1909, in Glasgow Papers.
[45] *Woman Within*, 183.
[46] Interview with Mrs. William R. Trigg, Jr., January 10, 1969.
[47] *Woman Within*, 179.

the ministry, and went to London to live with his family. Fifteen years passed and Ellen's friend Louise Collier Willcox glimpsed him on a train. When his wife could not hear, he told Mrs. Willcox to tell Ellen that he still loved her and that "it is the same love."[48] Ellen responded by sending him a letter and a copy of her current novel. He praised her work, sent her a photograph of his wife and children, and told her that he cherished his memories.[49] Many years later, when Ellen wrote of him in her autobiography, her memories of him were fonder than her feeling for him had ever been at the time of their engagement.[50] On that August day in 1909 when she tossed his poem out of the window, she tossed him out of her mind and braced herself for what she hoped would be a healing vacation in Colorado Springs.

The hampers of flowers that Denver people brought to her at the train depot did little to cheer her, and she wrote home to Lizzie Patterson: "Oh, well, I'm still very sad, my Elizabeth—What is the use—and to what end is it all?" Her melancholy moods frightened Julia Sully, and surely Ellen's letters home were not calculated to bring much joy to her friends. Even with her Acousticon she could not hear general conversation, and she tired of circulating among "wives with delicate husbands and husbands with delicate wives." "Life is over for me, my Lizzie," she wrote, "and the shade of the old woman at Verrey's looms larger every day. *That* is my end."[51]

The people at the resort, however, refused to allow Ellen Glasgow to drown herself in her own thoughts. A "cowboy in a sombrero" served her breakfast every morning, and her fellow vacationers insisted upon paying their respects to a popular novelist. The driver of the stage coach showed her a full-page newspaper story about her visit, which ended with the contention: "Now that Miss Glasgow has come, the Rocky Mountains have their Boswell." The people at the resort affectionately began to refer to her as "the

---

48 Louise Collier Willcox to Ellen Glasgow, August 17, 1924, in Glasgow Papers.
49 Frank I. Paradise to Ellen Glasgow, August 2, 1925 and October 17, 1925, *ibid.*
50 *Woman Within*, 178–80.
51 August 13, September 2, 1909, in Glasgow Papers. The old woman at Verrey's must refer to some experience Ellen and Lizzie had while traveling in England the previous spring.

Boswell of the Rockies," and a hermit who had moved west to escape a blighted romance poured out his life's story to the always sympathetic Ellen.[52] She was something of a hermit herself, and at the end of September she returned to Richmond to bury herself in a new novel and in a new cause.

The novel was *The Miller of Old Church* and the cause was woman's suffrage. In *The Romance of a Plain Man* her most splendidly drawn portrait was of an aristocratic old lady who defied the conventions of her family in order to read a daily newspaper and who died of exhaustion after participating in a march for women's rights. In the fall of 1909 Ellen and Cary entertained at a tea in Richmond in honor of Miss Laura Clay, a suffragette from Kentucky, which was attended by a few "bold spirits" who glanced about warily as they ascended the steps to make sure that they were not being watched by any strayed male.[53] Later in the season, the mother of Ellen's best friend, Carrie Coleman, invited the ladies to her home and there the Virginia League for Woman Suffrage was born. Mrs. Lila Meade Valentine became its president, and Ellen Glasgow was made third vice president. It was not a good way to win friends in Richmond. Rumors about them "arose from the 'better' Richmond parlors as though from a miasmic jungle. Finally, certain gentlemen of the ex-Confederate capital, alarmed at [their] growing appeal, formed an Anti-Suffrage League" to crush the ladies' organization.[54] Virginia later refused once and for all to ratify the Nineteenth Amendment which allowed women to vote, but for the time being the ladies were undaunted. Ellen joined the march down Main Street to Capitol Square, and garbed in a formal evening dress, she made at least one public speech in Richmond and one in Norfolk in behalf of woman's suffrage. There were limits to her participation, however, for in a note to Mary Johnston she promised that she would take part in a march only if it did not rain and if the march would not be too long.[55]

[52] Ellen Glasgow to Cary McCormack, September 3, 1909, *ibid.*
[53] *Woman Within*, 185.
[54] Marshall W. Fishwick, *Virginia: A New Look at the Old Dominion* (New York: Harper and Brothers, 1959), 255.
[55] Undated note in Johnston Papers.

Suffrage for women, Ellen Glasgow believed, "is an inevitable fact in the social development of the race, and sentiment is as powerless to stay its coming as it is to stem the advancing tide of evolution."[56] Yet she developed a sense of humor about the movement and in an interview with a reporter from the New York *Times* in 1913 declared that it did not make any difference if women proved to be unfit to vote because men were unfit too.[57] Her involvement in the movement, however, was only casual. Her first concern was for her novel, and in 1910 she was interrupted by the deaths of both Tiny and Littlest, her pet dogs. In fact, her most serious contribution to the suffrage movement was a poem published two years later:

### The Call

Woman called to woman at the daybreak!
    When the bosom of the deep was stirred,
In the gold of dawn and in the silence,
    Woman called to woman and was heard!

Steadfast as the dawning of the polestar,
    Secret as the fading of the breath.
At the gate of Birth we stood together,
    Still together at the gate of Death.

Queen or slave or bond or free, we battled,
    Bartered not our faith for love or gold;
Man we served, but in the hour of anguish
    Woman called to woman as of old.

Hidden at the heart of earth we waited,
    Watchful, patient, silent, secret, true;
All the terrors of the chains that bound us
    Man has seen, but only woman knew!

Woman knew! Yes, still and woman knoweth!—
    Thick the shadows of our prison lay—
Yet that knowledge in our hearts we treasure
    Till the dawning of the perfect day.

56 Note, dated 1910, in Glasgow Papers.
57 March 23, 1913, Sec. 6, p. 11.

Onward now as in the long, dim ages,
  Onward to the light where Freedom lies;
Woman calls to woman to awaken!
Woman calls to woman to arise![58]

Ellen left most of the marching and speech-making to others, while she secluded herself in her study and completed *The Miller of Old Church*.

For the setting of the novel, she selected the Southside section of Virginia; she had inspected carefully the rural estate which she named Jordan's Journey and listened to the native speech that "was still tinctured with the racy flavour of old England."[59] She wove her observations into a complex plot involving the rivalry between two families, the Gays and the Revercombs. The Gays owned Jordan's Journey and were the descendants of the old aristocratic landowners. The Revercombs included the miller and small farmers. At the beginning of the twentieth century, the Revercombs were more industrious than the decadent Gays. The only living members of the Gay family were Jonathan Gay, his mother, and his Aunt Kesiah. Jonathan's uncle, for whom he was named, had, some twenty-one years earlier, sired a female child by his overseer's daughter, Janet Merryweather. Abner Revercomb had been engaged to Janet and sought revenge by murdering old Jonathan Gay. The murder had never been solved, but the whole community lived in the knowledge of the truth and tacitly approved of the crime.

When the novelist picks up the story, the illegitimate daughter, Molly, is about to reach her twenty-first birthday, at which time she will receive a substantial yearly income from her father's estate provided she agrees to live with the Gay family. Abel Revercomb, the miller, was in love with Molly and wanted to marry her; but when she learned of her inheritance she decided to live at Jordan's Journey with the Gays. Consequently, the miller married the insipid and flat-chested Judy Hatch, who was really in love with a young minister. Jonathan Gay secretly married Abel's sister, Blos-

[58] *Collier's Magazine*, XLIX (July 27, 1912), 21.
[59] *A Certain Measure*, 127–28.

som Revercomb, but he refused to announce the marriage because he was afraid that the knowledge of his marrying across class lines would cause his mother to have a heart attack. And besides, he admired Molly Merryweather, whom he did not want to know that he was already married. The miller's wife died when she slipped on a log while running across a creek to see if the preacher had been injured in a buggy accident. Blossom Revercomb leaked the news that she was married to Jonathan Gay, and her infuriated uncle, Abner Revercomb, murdered the young Jonathan just as he had murdered his uncle more than twenty years earlier. Molly Merryweather then prepared to marry the miller, with whom she had been in love all along; and the novelist succeeded in suggesting that the only character who had any possibility for happiness was the one with the blood of both classes flowing in her veins. Typically for Ellen Glasgow, the leading male character, though he was stronger, had to work diligently to become worthy of the leading female character who had, even if by sheer accident, some aristocratic blood in her ancestry.

The plot line dealing with the mixing of classes through matrimony is supplemented with a secondary thread about the mixing of Presbyterians and Episcopalians in the rural community. Numerous minor characters are constantly discussing the merits of one denomination against the other, primed by the arrival in their midst of a young minister who was determined to educate the Presbyterian community in the ways of high church Episcopalian doctrine. Ellen was the offspring of a Presbyterian father and an Episcopalian mother and had listened to arguments on both sides at home. At the time she was writing *The Miller of Old Church* she was engaged to an Episcopalian minister, the Reverend Frank Paradise. The subject of religion was often the object of her sharpened wit, and she no doubt enjoyed herself immensely while discussing it through the characters of her rural Virginians. Sarah Revercomb, the mother of the miller, possessed the "inflexible logic of Calvinism" and treaded "softly in the way of pleasure lest God should hear." To her mind, it was not the will of God for human beings to be happy, and she was not about to try to counter Divine Purpose.[60]

But the miller, Sarah's son, had gone over "neck and crop to the Episcopals," in the words of Solomon Hatch, who noted that the miller recited the creed a bit too loud, because "when a man once takes up with a heresy, he shouts a heap louder than them that was born an' baptised in it."[61] Solomon's own daughter defied the ancient ways of her family, too, not because she was intelligent enough to think about doctrine, but because she fell in love with the Episcopalian minister. The entire community rallied to the minister's side upon the occasion of funerals and weddings, even though many were critical of his theology of baptism and his insistence upon the excessive repetition of the creed. Old Adam Doolittle summed it up after the wedding of Abel and Judy, when he said: "Ah, that young parson may have his faults, an' be unsound on the doctrine of baptism, but he can lay on matrimony with as pious an air as if he was conductin' a funeral."[62] And he could do it without even looking in the book.

Such characterization reveals a revival of Ellen's talent, development of her sense of humor, and promise for future production that was lacking in her previous three novels. Hard work and slow recovery from mental depression were beginning to pay off in better writing. The book enjoyed a modest popularity, and Northern reviewers especially liked it.[63] For the moment it looked as if the dark phase of life into which she had been plunged since the death of Gerald was about to end. The novel was published in May, and its dedication read: "To my sister Cary Glasgow McCormack in loving acknowledgment of help and sympathy through many years." Those were the last words that Cary read.[64]

Cary died in August, 1911. She alone among Ellen's close relatives

---

[60] Ellen Glasgow, *The Miller of Old Church* (New York: Doubleday, Page and Co., 1911), 290.
[61] *Ibid.*, 10.
[62] *Ibid.*, 340.
[63] Kelly, "Struggle for Recognition," 122, 126.
[64] *Woman Within*, 191.

had encouraged her to be a novelist, and to turn her deafness to
her own advantage. In 1910 Cary had been stricken with terminal
cancer, and for most of a year she lay in a downstairs bedroom
dressed in gowns and bed-jackets Ellen bought for her and attended
by a trained nurse, Miss Anne Virginia Bennett. Much of the time
Cary was unconscious, and during the last months of her life the
family simply waited. The end came on August 19, 1911, and the
members of the Glasgow family in Hollywood Cemetery numbered
more than those left at home.

Mr. Glasgow was eighty-one, recently retired from his job at the
Tredegar Iron Works, and inclined to live in the past, except on at
least one occasion when he made an offer of marriage to Cary's
nurse.[65] His son's suicide two years earlier had left him stunned,
but he passed through Cary's death without visible emotion. Ellen
reacted typically; she grew bitter and angry. Religion was not a
joke now; she loathed the God of John Calvin and of her father,
the God whose will had brought this new tragedy to pass. Grief
did not cripple her as it had done when she lost her mother; she
was angrily determined to escape from all the tragedy and illness
of her life. She fled to New York City and took an apartment overlooking Central Park, thinking that she had left One West Main
Street forever.

For more than thirty years, the gray house on Main Street had
been the home of Ellen's body and soul. Even when she tried to escape, the house and its memories, perhaps even its security, seemed
to hold a strange psychic power over her, and she spent only a few
months of each year in New York. While she was waiting for Cary
to die, her thoughts went back to her mother, and from there to
the whole institution of the Virginia lady, until out of her death
watch was born the idea for a tragic novel enshrining the Virginia
lady. Petersburg was the scene of the story, though Ellen called it
Dinwiddie in the novel. With a small black notebook and a pencil,
she roamed the streets of Petersburg, making descriptive notes about
people and houses she saw.[66] She wrote sketches of her characters,

---

65 "Notes for A Biography of Ellen Glasgow," in Rawlings Papers.
66 This notebook is preserved in the Glasgow Papers.

sentences, phrases, words, and chapter titles. Then she put her notes aside and went back to New York City for about six months.

On the last day of December, 1911, Ellen looked out over Central Park and took up her pen to send New Year's greetings to her friends, but she looked forward to the new year with terror. To Daniel Maurice Murphy, handsome brother-in-law of Edwin Markham, lecturer, book reviewer, and faith healer whose formula for happiness had allegedly restored physical and mental health to many, she wrote wistfully that there was no need for her to wish him a Happy New Year since he was already so happy, but she wished that the peace he possessed so abundantly might pass on to others. "Remember that you promised to be my friend," she cried, "and I need your friendship."[67] Ellen was not at her apartment when Murphy called, and she apparently abandoned forever her fleeting interest in faith healing; but for a woman so completely hostile toward religion, it was the ultimate cry of desperation.

What Ellen lacked in faith, she tried to make up in human companionship. In New York she sought the friendship of the novelist James Lane Allen, by now a lonely old man who had outlived his popularity. Although she disliked his novels and he had once written her an insolent letter making fun of her anti-vivisection crusade, they enjoyed a warm, if often bizarre and even pathetic, friendship for about four years. Allen's personality was even more temperamental than Ellen's, and it was perhaps inevitable that a rupture would come; but for the time being they needed each other. Ellen found him "fine and noble and very faithful at heart," but possessing a "perverse streak of sensitiveness, or egoism." She might have added that his personality was very much like her own. Their friendship blew hot and cold because each easily offended the other.[68] Allen declined her first dinner invitation by writing what he later called a "frivolous note" that was uncomplimentary of women in general.[69] Ellen simply ignored it, but when he later apologized and begged her to be his friend, she instantly forgave him and engaged

[67] December 31, 1911, in Anna Katharine Markham Papers, Wagner College Library, Staten Island, N. Y.
[68] To Grant C. Knight, June 29, 30, 1929, in *Letters*, 92, 93, 94.
[69] October 27, 1911 and November 4, 1911, in Glasgow Papers.

him in a playful exchange of what he called "dreadful quotes." In a few weeks, when she was in bed with a cold, Allen went over to her apartment to care for her, began to refer to himself as her doctor, and teased her about being a "perverse" woman.[70] The friendship was cultivated with an exchange of flowers, light conversation, and a birthday cake, but it never served any greater purpose for Ellen than to alleviate the loneliness of the moment.

She was homesick for Richmond, but she wrote to her friend Lizzie Patterson that she dreaded going back to the old place.[71] Yet, she always went back, as if she could not help herself. By the end of 1912 she had returned frequently enough to complete her novel in her study at One West Main Street. She called the novel *Virginia*, and she dedicated it "To the Radiant Spirit who was my sister Cary Glasgow McCormack." Doubleday, Page and Company published it in May, 1913, and the critics hailed it as her best work. But the public would not buy it. Of all of her novels since her first two, it was her least popular.[72] Among feminists, Willa Cather and Edith Wharton were giving her almost insurmountable competition. In an era of feminine activism, readers were not interested in the tragedy of a Southern lady trying to live by an obsolete code.

Virginia Pendleton in the novel was such a lady. The daughter of an Episcopalian minister, she grew up in Dinwiddie, Virginia, in the 1880's and was reared according to the theory that the less a young girl knew about life the better prepared she was to deal with it. She was beautiful, sheltered, and devoted to her children and husband, but she was unable to cope with her husband's career as a modern playwright or his attraction for women who were more intellectually alive than she was. Her marriage was a failure, her children outgrew her, and her life became meaningless long before she was an old woman. A tragic, pathetic figure, Virginia is a symbol for the universal conflict between the ideal of what a Southern lady was supposed to be and the reality of a woman's life in

[70] November 26, 1911, *ibid.*
[71] April 12, 1912, July 3, 1912, October 12, 1912, *ibid.*
[72] Kelly, "Struggle for Recognition," 135, 141, 143.

the early twentieth century. Years later, Ellen Glasgow explained her meaning: "And so, in this minor tragedy of a woman's life, we see the effects of the years wearing away and obliterating a single dream of identity, an individual illusion of happiness, which is encircled by the wider curve and sweep of time, as time wears away and obliterates yet one other discarded mould of perfection. For fantastic as her image appears nowadays, the pattern of the lady had embodied for centuries the thwarted human longing for the beautiful and the good."[73] Her comment upon the book is as tragic as the title character, because it is more a comment about Ellen Glasgow than it is about Virginia Pendleton. Ellen herself was one day an old fashioned Southern girl and the next day a modern intellectual in total rebellion against the traditions of her past. In all of her life she was not able to shed either role, nor was she able to reconcile them. She was both the "mould of perfection" and the one who cast it away.

The novel was misunderstood at the time it was published. A lady in Richmond approached Ellen and said: "Do you really think, my child, that a young girl could be inspired to do her duty by reading *Virginia*? I do not deny that there is truth in your book; but I feel that it is a mistake for Southern writers to stop writing about the War."[74] To be popular was to be a poor novelist, Ellen believed, and her literary reputation since 1904 had proved her to be correct. Her poorer works had sold the most copies. She had a sufficient income from her earlier works, and now she had the satisfaction of having written once again what she and a substantial number of critics considered to be a good novel. The character of Virginia is one of her stronger characters, because she is consistent and the literary counterpart of much of the novelist's own life. The well-bred Southern lady was always very much a part of Ellen Glasgow, and always very much in conflict with the intellectually alive modern woman. The part of Ellen Glasgow that was Virginia Pendleton, the novelist understood much better than the part of

[73] *A Certain Measure*, 96.
[74] *Ibid.*, 84.

her that was a rebellious, lively woman seeking to cast off the traditions that brought Virginia to ruin.[75] Perhaps that is why the latter role fascinated Ellen Glasgow more; perhaps that is why she tried to pretend that Virginia was based upon what she knew of her relatives, not upon what she experienced in her own life.

In the spring of 1914, Ellen Glasgow, now the modern woman, sailed for England, anticipating the realization of her dream of a lifetime: meeting her favorite living English authors. Her traveling companion was Louise Collier Willcox, a writer and book reviewer who had been educated by private tutors in England, France, and Germany, and eventually had settled with her husband in Norfolk, Virginia. She had helped Ellen get her first novel published, and she was the perfect companion for the trip. Ellen's old friend, Walter Hines Page, was ambassador to London, and he was among the first to entertain them after their arrival. His dinner was uneventful and boring because Ellen was too excited about the next few weeks when she would meet Thomas Hardy, John Galsworthy, Arnold Bennett, Joseph Conrad, and Henry James.

Thomas Hardy had been one of her mentors, and she thrilled to hear the small, immaculate man talk of his work. Hardy was equally impressed to find someone who had read all of his works. The friendship was sealed when Hardy discovered that Ellen loved dogs and introduced her to his wire-haired terrier, Wessex. From Hardy's Max Gate, Ellen went to the home of Joseph Conrad in Kent. Conrad, she said, had "a lovable personality, capricious and fascinating." She had her photograph made with him in his yard, and she felt that they were natural friends. Within a few days she dined with John and Ada Galsworthy, both of whom represented to her the essence of the British aristocratic tradition. The next afternoon was spent with Arnold Bennett. Ellen found that the author of *The Old Wives' Tale* had a scintillating wit and stuttered when he talked. She discovered also that he condescended toward all things

75 Louis D. Rubin, Jr., "Ellen Glasgow and James Branch Cabell," in Louis D. Rubin, Jr., and Robert D. Jacobs (eds.), *South: Modern Literature in Its Cultural Setting* (Garden City, N.Y.: Doubleday and Co., 1961), 122.

American, including American literature, but often she agreed with him.

At a reception given by the Ranee of Sarawak she met Henry James, whom she found "imposing, urbane, and delightful; but it was a dubious pleasure to have him begin one of his hesitating, polysyllabic, and endlessly discursive soliloquies." Ellen saw James only in crowds and was often pushed along "before he had found the exact right beginning, middle, and end of the involved sentences he was laboring to utter." She saw James only in the houses of her wealthiest acquaintances, suspected that he had no feeling for the lowly, cringed at the thought of his "moral problems," and thought him "foppish in manner"as compared with Hardy or Conrad.[76] Yet she accorded him his due as an artist. Ellen never admitted it, but surely a pang of envy crept into her heart as she saw an American who had lived and made his literary reputation in England, an ambition which she herself had once considered early in her career.

In the home of her brother and at the American embassy she heard frequent talk of a possible uprising in Ulster, but no mention of the war clouds over Europe. Early in July she sailed home on the German *Imperator*, which included among its passengers Theodore Roosevelt who was returning from a trip to Africa. Walter Hines Page arranged for her to dine with Roosevelt on board, and although she had labelled him as "a roving barbarian of the West who goes to Africa to kill animals," she was captivated by his charm. When talking, he was careful to turn slightly in her direction and pitch his voice so that she could hear. And he had read her books. So she concluded that all he needed to make him a great human being was simply not to have been born a Roosevelt. Before the month was out, the *Imperator* docked at New York, and Roosevelt and the English writers faded into the memory of a single pleasant and all-too-brief interlude in Ellen's life. Within weeks, the First World War broke out in Europe, and England was never again the same for her.

[76] *Woman Within*, 197, 201, 202, 204–205, 206–207.

Ellen's health had improved, and her outlook on life was decidedly more optimistic after her return from England. In her apartment overlooking Central Park she began to work on a new novel, *Life and Gabriella: The Story of a Woman's Courage*. It had been a long time since she could write about a woman's courage. She wrote half the novel between the late summer of 1914 and the late summer of 1915. While working on the novel, she revived her interest in poetry. Symbolic of her new lease on life, she called herself "John J. Newbegin, Esq." and sent a copy of her poem, "Albert of Belgium," to prominent poets for their comments. George Sterling, Edward Robeson Taylor, and Edwin Markham all liked the poem and apparently failed to see through the pseudonym.[77] The poem was couched in violent imagery, but dealt with the duty, honor, and courage of an individual monarch. It was a poetic expression of the same courage Ellen was treating in *Life and Gabriella*. The pseudonym was no more than a passing fancy, apparently never making its way into print or holding Ellen's interest longer than for the single poem. But the favorable response from respectable poets contributed to her light mood as she planned a trip to California with Carrie Coleman, her friend from childhood.

Ellen was happy as the train made its way westward. There was little of the gloom and despair that had darkened her earlier trip to Colorado. Carrie Coleman was chatty and gay. In San Francisco where Ellen was invited to serve as hostess at the Virginia Building, reporters and photographers crowded around her, but she dodged them with an almost neurotic aversion. One lucky reporter evaded her every effort to avoid the public, ingratiated himself to her, and took her and Carrie on an eleven-hour tour of the area.[78] Ellen wrote to her other childhood friend, Lizzie Patterson Crutchfield, that she adored California, wanted to visit it again and perhaps even live there. On August 14, she and Carrie started back to Virginia,

[77] George Sterling to John J. Newbegin, June 1, 1915, Edwin Markham to John J. Newbegin, June 2, 1915, Edward Robeson Taylor to John J. Newbegin, June 1, 1915, all in Glasgow Papers.

[78] Copy of a letter from Ellen Glasgow to Rebe Tutwiler, July 27, 1915, in Rawlings Papers.

as Ellen said, "leaving our hearts behind."[79] Carrie later told the reason: "Both of us fell in love, Ellen with a colonel in the army."[80] To Ellen, her colonel apparently never was very important, because as soon as the vacation was ended, she returned to her apartment in New York, the completion of her novel, and to another lover.

In the remaining months of 1915 she completed *Life and Gabriella*. The only one of her novels not written in Richmond, it is the story of Virginians in New York City. The heroine, Gabriella Carr, grew up in Richmond in the same era as Virginia Pendleton in *Virginia*, but refused to become a slave to the code for a Southern lady. Gabriella worked in a dry goods store in Richmond, properly run by a former general of the Confederate Army, but she eventually left for New York and marriage to a man whose primary interests were money and other women. After several years during which two children were born, the marriage ended in divorce, but through her own courage and talent as a designer of women's clothes, Gabriella made a highly successful venture into business. At the age of thirty-nine she fell in love with Ben O'Hara, a dashing Irishman who lived in the apartment below her. Gabriella at thirty-nine was only a few years younger than Ellen at the time she was writing the novel.

Ellen described Ben O'Hara as "a vivid impression of height, breadth, bigness, of roughened dark red hair," "a big, strong, simple creature," "a fine animal" with "the look of exuberant vitality which accompanies perfect physical condition," and "big and efficient."[81] Years later Ellen said he was based on a character she had actually known in New York: "Of them all, the improbable figure of Ben O'Hara is the only one that conformed to an original model. But for an accidental acquaintance with his counterpart, it is unlikely that Gabriella's break with the past would ever have assumed the shape it wore at the end."[82] The original model was

79 To Lizzie Patterson Crutchfield, August 12, 13, 1915, in Glasgow Papers.
80 Carrie Duke to MKR, in Rawlings Papers.
81 Ellen Glasgow, *Life and Gabriella* (Garden City, N.Y.: Doubleday, Page and Co., 1911), 367, 369, 388, 444.
82 *A Certain Measure*, 101.

an Irishman named Mulhern who owned the apartment house where Ellen was living in New York City. Ellen's friends described him as "terribly virile" and "big and attractive."[83] He called many times at Ellen's apartment, and Carrie, who stayed with Ellen at the apartment much of the time, dismissed the relationship lightly as "only a physical attraction," and "an infatuation, only an infatuation."[84] Berta Wellford believed that it was reasonable that Ellen would have had an all-out love affair with Mulhern,[85] and certainly Ellen enjoyed a freedom in New York City that she would not have dared to attempt in Richmond. She made Mulhern and her attraction to him real in her novel.

When *Life and Gabriella* was published in 1916, the critics did not approve, but the readers enjoyed the story of Gabriella and her Irishman and placed the novel fifth on the best-seller list for the year.[86] Any breath of optimism or courage that Ellen had known while writing the book was long gone by the time the novel appeared in print. Even her memories of a pleasant interlude in California, and perhaps even Mulhern himself, had become a part of the forgotten past. Someone supposedly asked her: "Why don't you write an optimistic novel about the West?" She replied drily: "If there is anything I know less about than the West, it is optimism."[87]

Late in 1915, her oldest sister, Emily, died in Richmond, and Ellen went home. She had little or no feeling for Emily whom she later falsely accused of maliciously burning papers that she had stored in a closet. Actually, papers which Ellen had designated not to be destroyed were not destroyed, and Ellen had indicated herself that she intended to throw out the things in the closet.[88] After the death of Emily, only Ellen, her father, and the nurse, Anne Virginia Bennett, remained at One West Main Street. Ellen grieved far less for her sister than she did at the prospects of having to live again in a constricting environment. Carrie Coleman came over for

83 Anne Virginia Bennett to MKR, in Rawlings Papers.
84 *Ibid.*
85 Berta Wellford to MKR, *ibid.*
86 Kelly, "Struggle for Recognition," 157.
87 Cited, *ibid.*, 162.
88 Anne Virginia Bennett to MKR, in Rawlings Papers.

Christmas dinner, as had become her custom, and tried to cheer her up. Lizzie Crutchfield sent her some memento of their happy childhood days together and invited her to a New Year's party. Ellen replied: "I am coming early to the party: I shall stay late, and I shall try very hard to look festive."[89]

She planned to return to New York City early in January, but if she made the trip it was cut short. In the middle of the month, her father slipped on the ice on the steps at One West Main Street. He died on January 29, 1916. His funeral was conducted from the Second Presbyterian Church, with the Elders serving as pallbearers. Among the letters of sympathy was a note from a man in Memphis recalling how Mr. Glasgow had given him a start in life and on one occasion had given him a decent suit of clothes so that he might attend church.[90] It was a typical act of generosity by a man whose good intentions had often inspired nothing but resentment from Ellen. As a famous citizen of Richmond, Francis Glasgow's death was marked with considerable public notice. His daughter later wrote only one sentence about his passing: "At eighty-six, he had died, like a Roman, superbly, without fear, without reluctance, but without haste, as if he were starting off on an expected journey."[91]

The gray house on Main Street had gaslights, crumbling paper, and oppressive memories. The place itself, not the death of her father, depressed Ellen. She wandered there alone, except for Anne Virginia Bennett who agreed to remain as her companion and secretary. Arthur promised that he would repaint the house and put in white tiled bathrooms and electric lights.[92] The tiny room at the head of the stairs that had been her study became a bathroom, and the large second-floor room on the northwest corner became her study. For months Ellen wandered in a daze, not caring what happened. In the spring she planted every inch of the yard in flowers, but she felt that she could not remain in Richmond.[93] In

---

[89] December 27, 1915, in Glasgow Papers.
[90] Sam Everett to Ellen Glasgow, January 30, 1916, *ibid.*
[91] *Woman Within*, 215.
[92] Ellen Glasgow to Arthur Glasgow [Summer, 1916], in *Letters*, 63–64.
[93] Copy of a letter of Ellen Glasgow to Rebe Tutwiler, November 4, 1916, in Rawlings Papers.

a dozen years she had labored to produce six novels, only two of
which were really creditable.[94] For the moment, she cared about
neither her life nor her work. Courage and optimism did not come
easily to her, but despite her sharp cynicism, she struggled valiantly
to develop both qualities. The leadership she promised to give
Southern letters was slipping from her, because the agony of her
personal life for the last decade and the sweat of her creative labor
had not combined as they might have done to produce the kind of
literature that others would accept as excellent and attempt to
imitate. Yet a seed of genius was visible in her work, dormant perhaps, but always potentially capable of coming to life. At forty-
two Ellen Glasgow had accumulated quite a reservoir of the agony
and sweat of the human spirit, the real materials out of which great
novels are created. If she could control her talent and endure disillusionment, that reservoir could become the source from which a
talented novelist might create her best works; or it might be a sea
upon which a lonely woman drifted to the edge of the universe.

[94] Ellen Glasgow, *Virginia* (New York: Doubleday, Page and Co., 1913), and *The
Miller of Old Church*.

# 6

## The Edge of the Universe

$\mathcal{J}$f a house is haunted, fresh paint, new bathrooms, and a well-planted garden will not dispel the ghosts. Ellen believed that One West Main Street was haunted, not literally, but by the memories of her mother and father, and Walter, Frank, Cary, and Emily. "The house belonged to the dead. I was living with ghosts," she wrote. "They are ghosts, too, of all I had known and loved in my life."[1]

All that she had known and loved in life was gone; a vast emptiness surrounded and terrified her. For solace she looked to someone who was not a ghost and not even a member of the family. Anne Virginia Bennett had been associated with the Glasgows for more than five years as a nurse for the ill or dying, but Ellen had been away much of that time and had formed no close relationship with her. Anne Virginia had no interest in literature and regarded Ellen's writing as only a way to earn a living. She was not the person Ellen wanted to fill the void in her life, but she became a prop who helped Ellen to continue to exist. Ellen was willing to lean heavily upon her, but she needed something more. Reading philosophy, writing books, and even playing golf were not enough. At forty-two she craved love and companionship even more than she had as a young woman. Her youthful vow to avoid marriage had become a heavy burden, but she was intelligent enough to know that that vow and the mysterious psychological reasons for which she had made it were sure indications of a personality that was incompatible with

1 *Woman Within*, 222.

marriage. She was not optimistic when she accepted a friend's invitation to a luncheon in order to meet a prominent Richmond attorney who also happened to be an eligible bachelor. At least her brother Arthur would be present, and the reputation of Henry W. Anderson was sufficient to arouse her curiosity.

The luncheon was on Easter Sunday, 1916, and the meeting was like a resurrection for Ellen. Anderson was a few years older than she, robust, literate, well-dressed, and refined in his manners. Ellen felt an immediate physical attraction to him.[2] She welcomed his call a few days later and eventually staked her happiness on his increasing attentions. Anderson was a brilliant lawyer accepted in the best social circles in Richmond, Paris, and London. He had played golf with President Taft, and a portrait of the President hung in the library of his home on Franklin Street. Energy, ambition, and intelligence accounted for his remarkable success in his profession.

The son of a distinguished country doctor, he was born in Dinwiddie County, Virginia, on December 20, 1870, in the last days of Reconstruction.[3] His ancestry was impeccable, but the war and Reconstruction had reduced the family to modest circumstances. In 1840 his father had been graduated from the fine medical school at the University of Pennsylvania; and his mother, an Episcopalian from Prince George County, Virginia, was related to the Harrisons. His father provided private tutors for his education as a youth, but there was no money for college. Henry worked on a railroad in Crewe, Virginia, and eventually became secretary to the president of Washington and Lee University, which enabled him to work his way through the law school and take his degree in 1898. In 1901 he became a partner in the Richmond law firm of Munford and Anderson. As a young man he established a friendship with Lady Hadfield of England, the sister of an attorney general of the United States and formerly Miss Frances Wickersham.

2 *Ibid.*, 225.
3 Unless otherwise noted, this sketch of Anderson is reconstructed from his biography in *Who's Who in America* and a description of him by his niece, Mrs. James Asa Shield of Richmond.

Lady Hadfield became credited with having an enormous effect upon Henry Anderson. Her name was given to one of his nieces, and it was reported that it was through Lady Hadfield's influence that Anderson developed the formality and elegance of an English gentleman.[4] She sent him a British housekeeper and thus began his practice of employing British rather than Negro servants.[5] Richmond regarded him with a mixture of respect and resentment, not only because of his British household, but also because he was a member of the Republican party. Yet his dinner parties were well attended and his company was sought. It was typical of Henry Anderson that he should strive for his manners and household to be more aristocratic than those of Richmond's entrenched aristocracy, many of whom resented his challenge to their closed society. Ellen, who by ironic coincidence had been entertained by Lady Hadfield during her visit in London in 1909, condescendingly looked upon Anderson as one who was not her social equal, although in terms of ancestry, education, and refinement of manners, he was her superior.

Social equal or not, Ellen could not disregard her strong attraction to him. His hair was sandy brown, his skin was tanned, and his eyes were close-set in his head. He was plagued by extreme near-sightedness and wore frameless glasses, which accented his appearance as an English gentleman. An Anglophile herself, Ellen admired his British manners and household. Witty and commanding in conversation, he talked much as she did. He was convinced that human beings were happiest in medieval times when they were building the great castles, the ruins of which Ellen had spent days of her time in Europe admiring. The church had no attraction for him; the Bible he regarded as only history. He was both modest and pompous, at times downright shy. He shunned nothing that might lead to his self-improvement; his ambition was to become a justice on the Supreme Court of the United States. Ellen observed that he had "learned to enter a room, very slowly, as the leading actor walks

4 Maude Williams to MKR, in Rawlings Papers.
5 Anne Virginia Bennett to MKR, *ibid.*

on the stage awaiting applause."[6] When he walked into the luncheon
on that Easter Day, Ellen silently applauded, not only because she
liked what he was, but because she dreamed of what he might become to her: an escape from the ghosts of her past.

The past receded as Henry Anderson called more and more frequently at One West Main Street and often dined on Ellen's back
porch. Each was alone and needed the other. They talked about
philosophy, politics, and art and discovered that they had some
things in common. Ellen became Henry's "Dear Vardah," a name
assigned to her by an astrologer and picked up by Anderson as a
term of endearment. He missed her in the summer when she went
to New York and Maine for a vacation. He wrote her of his loneliness; and he told her of his desire to help people, not to gain political fame.[7] Ellen approved of his goals, she answered his letters,
and she favored him with a poem entitled "Song." It was a poem
she had written and published four years earlier and merely sent
to her new suitor:

> Long, long ago upon another star
> I heard your voice and looked into your eyes;
> The worlds are many and the way is long,
> Perchance I may have missed you in the skies
> But still the memory beckons from afar,
> And still I search the face of the earth
> For one I loved upon another star.
>
> My feet have followed the eternal quest,
> The way that leads through water and through fire;
> Somewhere before my soul had come to birth
> Mine eyes have seen the face of my desire.
> Always I weary of the things that are,
> Always my heart is hungry for its dream
> Dreamed long ago upon another star.[8]

[6] *Woman Within*, 224.

[7] Henry W. Anderson to Ellen Glasgow, June 19, 1916. All letters of Henry Ander-
son to Ellen Glasgow are in the Ellen Glasgow Papers in the University of Virginia
Library. They are quoted here by permission of Colonel Anderson's niece, Mrs.
James Asa Shield. The letters of Ellen Glasgow to Henry Anderson have not survived.

[8] *Harper's Monthly Magazine*, CXXV (June, 1912), 103.

Poetry was not Anderson's forte, but he stayed up all night writing his response:

### An Answer

#### I

As in the shadow of the dark'ning night,
I turned from the ways of the passing throng
Your hand came forth as a flash of light,
Blowing a message—'twas just a "Song."

#### II

It speaks of the days of the long ago,
The aching dreams of another world.
Of the mystic stars our souls did know,
Ere they went out through gate of pearl

#### III

To yield themselves to the Greater Will,
To bear new life to forms of clay,
To play their part, though dreaming still,
In God's great scheme of destiny.

#### IV

Perchance 'twas there our souls were One
Back at the dawn of Earth's Young Day
When fate stepped in, and this was done—
Our souls were parted and launched away,

#### V

To roam the world, as the Hindu Dreams,
Haunted by jugs of the beautiful past,
To seek its Mate by Hills and Streams,
And when united find Heaven at last.

#### VI

Then why do we look or sigh again
For sweet dream dews of the earlier Star,
To quench the thirst of the weary strain,
Or cool the fever of the "things that are"?

## VII

The search is over, for this we know
That Love is God, and "God is Love,"
That through its power e'en here below,
We compass the realms that were above.

## VIII

And yielding our all, our souls may claim,
The perfect joy, the endless youth,
And find in Love's consuming flame,
That the Hindu's dream is really truth.[9]

Ellen liked his "Answer" and his willingness to follow where she led. Like the Reverend Frank Paradise before him, he was becoming an intellectual companion, willing to discuss Ellen's interest in philosophy and mysticism, which she had not abandoned.

Neither had she abandoned her wandering ways. In Maine she was staying in the cottage of Dr. Pearce Bailey, a founder of the Neurological Institute of New York, and a man reported to be very much in love with her. Anderson and others of Ellen's friends believed that Bailey had asked her to marry him, but she had refused.[10] Anderson was plainly jealous and wrote Vardah that he hoped she would not like Dr. Bailey's place or its owner too much.[11] Ellen returned home, alone, late in August. Her time with Anderson was brief, however, for with him business always came before pleasure; and early in September he sailed for England on the R.M.S. *Adriatic*. On board the ship he had plenty of time to write letters, and he continued his courtship by mail.

A unique pattern formed early in their romance, and it was the same pattern that had characterized the relationship between Abel Revercomb and Molly Merryweather in *The Miller of Old Church*. If any feeling of inferiority had urged Anderson along his compulsive drive toward success, Ellen preyed upon that feeling. It was probably not unusual for a man of Anderson's class and generation

9 August 4, 1916.
10 Anne Virginia Bennett, Carrie Duke, and Henry Anderson to MKR, in Rawlings Papers. Dr. Joseph Collins, a colleague of Dr. Bailey's, indicates in a letter to Ellen Glasgow, dated April 8, 1945, that "P. B." had once loved her. In Glasgow Papers.
11 August 16, 1916.

to tell his lady that he did not deserve her love, but Ellen undoubtedly did not hesitate to tell her suitor that she was far superior to him and thus prompt numerous letters in which he told her of his unworthiness and his desire to achieve the high plane on which she lived. Yet Anderson's passion was for politics more than it was for romance. His romantic duties fulfilled in the opening paragraphs, Anderson often lapsed into a heated expression of his political views, especially his strong belief that Woodrow Wilson was unfit to be President of the United States and was "an infliction upon the country by an angry God."[12] On board the *Adriatic* he wrote:

> *Vardah*, my dear, I have just read again your letter to the Steamer, and I shall read it each day, to cheer yet humble me. It cheers because it breathes the fine spirit of *you*; it humbles me because it brings to me so strongly a sense of entire unworthiness. There is nothing for me to do but to keep trying, even if I keep failing to rise to the spiritual heights which are your home. If I should fail always know that I have tried and I shall try, and your spirit and influence may make it possible. . . .[13]

He went on to urge her to continue to write, for he needed the comfort of her letters; they were all he had at a time when he found President Wilson's speeches "impossible" and believed that the President was "the most dangerous demagogue and opportunist of our time."

Once on the foreign shore, Anderson's letters came less frequently, reflected very little homesickness for Vardah, and indicated that he was having a good time in England. He stayed through the fall and into the winter. Ellen did something she had never done before: she planned a winter trip to London, allegedly to visit her brother.[14] Her trip did not materialize, and at Christmas both she and Anderson were in Richmond. They exchanged the greetings of the season and expressed their anxieties about the role of America in the First World War. The darkening war clouds and the

[12] August 31, 1916.
[13] September 8, 1916.
[14] Ellen Glasgow to Arthur Graham Glasgow, December 14, 1916, in Glasgow Papers.

lengthy separation while she was in Maine and he was in Europe to Ellen's mind made their future uncertain, but Anderson reassured her: "What the future holds I cannot say, but it will always hold you, like Beatrice to Dante leading me from the depths of material things to the heights of idealism which we may well call Paradise."[15]

Paradise was something that had been almost edged out of Ellen's philosophy. She felt that she and Anderson were growing apart and that the ghosts of the past were again rushing in to fill the void in her life. For the first time in almost twenty years, she broke her promise to Walter Hines Page that she would not write any more short stories. In December, 1916, she published "The Shadowy Third," a ghost story about a haunted house in New York City. Ellen combined the experience of living in her "haunted" house in Richmond with a nurse as a companion and her fresh memories of her life in New York to write one of the most intriguing and successful of her literary creations.

"The Shadowy Third" tells the story of Miss Randolph, a nurse who grew up in Virginia and moved to New York City to practice her profession. A very famous and handsome surgeon, Dr. Maradick, invited her to move into his home and care for his invalid wife. It was rumored that the doctor had married Mrs. Maradick originally for her money and that the marriage had never been happy. They had had one child who had been dead for several years. Mrs. Maradick suffered from hallucinations; she believed that she saw her child playing with toys around the house. Her husband thought she was insane and threatened to put her in an asylum. The nurse, Miss Randolph, was astonished to discover that she also could see the child, and she protested vehemently when Dr. Maradick finally did put his wife in the asylum. Mrs. Maradick died there, and Miss Randolph stayed on in the house as the doctor's secretary. Then she saw the child again, skipping rope in the garden. Late that night an emergency call came for the doctor. She called him from the foot of the stairs. He had just returned from a date with the woman he intended to marry, the woman with whom he had supposedly been

15 December 27, 1916.

in love before he married Mrs. Maradick. The doctor came down the stairs whistling and with a light step. He tripped, pitched forward, and lay dead at the foot of the stairs. In the bend in the staircase was a child's jump rope. Miss Randolph, burdened with Ellen's philosophy, was convinced that "something had killed him at the very moment when he most wanted to live."[16]

The ghost story was a new experiment for Ellen. "The Shadowy Third" is somewhat autobiographical, but it was written to earn money. In 1916, after the death of her father, Ellen had the responsibility to keep up a large house. Though she inherited a small trust fund from her father, and was given a larger one by her brother, she still felt insecure since she had no management ability. She turned that aspect of the household over entirely to Anne Virginia Bennett who once had taken some business courses. Ellen and Anne Virginia were sitting before the fire one night when Anne Virginia said: "Ellen, we need money. Why don't you write a story?"[17] Ellen agreed and wrote "The Shadowy Third." She sent the story to her agent, with the warning note that she did not care to take less than a thousand dollars, and that she would like, if possible, to get more.[18] *Scribner's Magazine* bought the story, and other publications eventually asked to reproduce it.

Spurred on by its success, Ellen wrote "Dare's Gift" the ghostly tale of an ancient estate on the James River, where "the psychic force of its memories" drove sensitive women to insanity even when they did not know the details of its past. The estate, Dare's Gift, had once been the home of the beautiful Lucy Dare, a belle of Virginia who was in love with a Yankee soldier during the Civil War. The soldier left the battle front to visit Lucy at Dare's Gift. She learned that he had information that would lead to the fall of Richmond, and she placed her love for Virginia above her love for the soldier by betraying him to the Confederate Army. He was shot while leaping from a balcony, and Lucy Dare never recovered from the trauma of the experience. The story was published in two parts

[16] Richard K. Meeker (ed.), *The Collected Stories of Ellen Glasgow*, (Baton Rouge: Louisiana State University Press, 1963), 72.
[17] Anne Virginia Bennett to MKR, in Rawlings Papers.
[18] To Paul Revere Reynolds, November 26, 1916, in *Studies in Bib.*, 195.

in *Harper's Magazine* in February and March, 1917, and it represents Ellen's tendency to integrate her ghosts and her lovers, which is perhaps a revealing insight into her own attitude toward her relationship with men. In her next story, however, she deserted her ghosts and wrote a tale that was blatantly autobiographical.

Scarcely had she decided that she was growing distant from Anderson than she slipped back into the loneliness she had known before she met him. In February, 1917, she published "Thinking Makes It So," the story of Margaret French, a forty-three-year-old poet who was without love and forced to write stories in order to support her family. One day Margaret received a letter that said: "My Poet, I have read your poems, and I love you because of them." Her admirer, John Brown, envisioned his poet as a bright young woman, dressed in a rose-colored dress. Margaret replied: "Dear Lover of my Poems, if I had known that my verse was for you, I think I should have made only songs of joy, never of sadness." She went out and bought herself a rose-colored dress. Other letters were exchanged; then came a letter saying her admirer wanted to meet her. She was terrified, fearing for him to discover that she was a dowdy, middle-aged woman. She refused to allow him to come, but he came anyway, unexpected and unannounced, lean, middle-aged, and plain. When Margaret entered the room in her rose-colored gown, he said: "My beautiful, I should have known you among a hundred women, for you are just as I dreamed of you."[19]

Ellen took her title from *Hamlet* and her theme from her own life. In 1916, she was writing stories to earn a living and trying to imagine herself into happiness and romance. When she met Henry Anderson, she no doubt believed that her dreams were beginning to be fulfilled as they were for Margaret French in her story. Anderson had quickly recognized Ellen as a sensitive, emotional person who must be handled cautiously. He feigned an interest in her work, and no doubt much of his talk of his unworthiness of her was no more than a suitor's attempt to please the subject of his admiration. For her part, Ellen tried to develop an interest in politics, a

[19] Meeker (ed.), *Collected Stories*, 76, 79, 89. Originally published in *Good Housekeeping*, February, 1917.

topic that bored her. Anderson assured her that they were not growing apart,[20] and they decided to write a political novel together.

The result was *The Builders*, a novel not published until 1919, but begun early in 1917. Set in Richmond in 1916, it is the story of Caroline Meade, a trained nurse who is hired by David and Angelica Blackburn to care for their daughter. They live in a splendid house, Briarlay, on Monument Avenue. David Blackburn is falsely accused of beating his daughter and of infidelity to his wife. Actually, the beautiful Angelica is the one who is unconcerned about her child and cares little for her husband. Caroline gets involved in an emotional entanglement with Blackburn, is asked to leave by Angelica, and eventually goes to France as a Red Cross nurse. David Blackburn is highly suspect in Richmond because he is first a Republican and then an Independent. Above all, he is an idealist whose political views are precisely those of Henry Anderson.

Anderson helped Ellen collect her materials and proofed many of her early chapters. Ellen read his speeches and incorporated them into her book. He sent her a documentary list of facts concerning 1916, several letters about Southern conditions, and copies of his speeches. He accepted the project as his own, always tactfully commending Ellen for her work: "I have read the chapter several times. It is very good, indeed. I have some suggestions, and think *we* can make it a strong chapter."[21] Sometimes his letters were filled with information for the novel:

> The only part which I questioned at all was . . . where you speak of the emotional vulgarity of the time being due to a more adventurous spirit. I somehow doubt this, though it may be true. If so in the past the spirit of adventure took a different form and a more abstract one. The present time is restless, and discontented, with that vulgarity which comes with the levelling influences of Democracy—expressing what it calls freedom in bad manners, rather uncertain of itself it is the more assertive. This is always the consequence of the breaking up of old orders and bring[ing] in New, but it is essential to the broader development of mankind.[22]

[20] *Ca.* January 1, 1917.
[21] April 29, 1917. Italics mine.
[22] Undated.

Together they worked through the spring and summer of 1917. Though it was a period not without its difficulties, it was the happiest time in their courtship. Occasionally they argued, and Ellen apparently wrote depressing and highly critical notes to Anderson. Her depression made him unhappy: "I am so miserable today I am wishing I had never been born," he wrote. Sometimes he tried to comfort her: "My dearest, I idealize you always, and look up to you in all things for beauty and purity, and inspiration!" Usually he accepted all of the blame for her unhappiness: "Mine is a cold and lonely path, Vardah, and those who cross it seem only to feel the chill—God grant me that I may not bring its chill to you, but only warmth and beauty."[23] Whatever the contents, every day for months a servant would carry a message from Franklin Street to Main Street and wait for a reply. Once there was only a folded sheet of stationary labelled "To Vardah" that contained a pressed flower. Often the note said no more than "Good Morning, my dear—A bright and happy day to you! H."; or "I did enjoy our hour last night—Henry." There were words of encouragement, apologies for having hurt her feelings, Easter and birthday greetings, and numerous notes saying that he would be down for dinner.

Dinner for two was served on the back porch of One West Main Street in perhaps the most romantic setting imaginable. The servants' wing and carriage house blocked the view of the backyard garden from Fouschee Street, and high brick walls on the other sides granted privacy. The yard was thickly planted in flowers, especially roses of many varieties, including microphylla roses that were never quite perfect. Lining the banister around the porch and the steps leading down to the garden were potted ferns and flowering plants. Sturdy doric columns rose for two stories from the porch to add a kind of authentic grandeur to the scene. There Ellen and Henry dined alone and talked about their novel, their lives, and the subject that was on the lips of most Americans that year: World War I. There they faced the possibility that Anderson's increasing devotion to the work of the Red Cross might necessitate his leaving the country. Ellen dreaded that possibility. She was in love.

23 Undated notes.

On July 18 she received an urgent letter from him: "I *want to see you*. I decided finally to go to Roumania. Everyone seemed to think it my duty to go, a chance to render service for which I have been asking—but I shall go with a heavy heart."[24] On the following night Ellen made a note for posterity: "Thursday the nineteenth of July 1917. I became engaged to Henry this evening."[25] For months that brief note to herself was the most tangible proof she had of her engagement, because the following day the bridegroom-to-be left on a venture that changed the course of their lives.

Henry Anderson was awarded the title of colonel, placed in charge of the Red Cross Commission to the Balkans, and given the responsibility to keep Rumania in the war on the side of the Allies. Included in the Commission were some of Richmond's most prominent citizens and Ellen's brother, Arthur.[26] As the train made its way westward from New York to Chicago to Vancouver, Ellen received almost daily telegrams, postcards, and notes from Anderson. He described the trip, lauded the competence of the members of the Commission, said he was getting used to being called "Colonel," and was obviously enjoying himself. He found it tedious, however, to have to salute through the English, French, and American anthems and warned that after the Commission reached Russia it might be difficult to get out letters.[27] At Vancouver the party boarded the R.M.S. *Empress of Russia* for a ten-day voyage to Japan. Soon they were on a train crossing Russia. On the sixteenth of September they arrived in Rumania.

Letters suddenly became less frequent, the result of the problems of censorship and the enthusiasm with which Anderson plunged into his work. Ten days after his arrival in Rumania, Anderson wrote Ellen a letter that she never forgot: "The Queen has also attended a number of private entertainments in our honor, granted us one private audience and has asked me to come tonight for a

---

[24] July 18, 1917.
[25] Written on a half sheet of stationary with no other markings on it, this note is preserved in the Glasgow Papers.
[26] The Commission had thirty-eight members, including twelve doctors and eleven nurses.
[27] August 10, 11, 12, 13, 1917.

private talk over work."[28] Richmond soon became alive with gossip about Anderson and the Queen. Anderson was accused, no doubt falsely, of allotting an unfair proportion of Red Cross funds to Rumania, and the whole world knew that Queen Marie of Rumania was a woman accustomed to choosing her own lovers.

At the time of World War I, Queen Marie was not yet forty years old, had been the wife of Ferdinand I since she was sixteen, and was the mother of six children. The granddaughter of Queen Victoria, Marie was born and lived in England until the time of her marriage. From a shy bride of sixteen, she had risen to a position of authority in the government of Rumania unprecedented for a woman. Her beauty was legendary, and much of her success as a monarch must be traced to the way she daringly flaunted her beauty and exercised her womanly wiles. "Probably not since Helen of Troy or Cleopatra," noted her biographer, "has there been a more desired woman than Marie of Rumania."[29] Often Marie entertained her guests in her private chambers, which were decorated entirely in gold. She placed her summer palace at the disposal of Colonel Anderson. He became infatuated with her. She gave him expensive gifts, including a miniature of herself in a silver case and a jewel-studded cigarette case that had been especially made for her in Paris. She worked side by side with him in the care of her people who suffered bitterly from the ravages of war. She liked Anderson personally, and she was grateful for the work of the Red Cross.

In October the Red Cross Commission to the Balkans sailed for home, but Colonel Anderson was not with it. He explained to Ellen that he could not come home yet because he must remain to serve in Rumania.[30] His letters contained little of his previous comments about his unworthiness of her, but he sometimes mentioned his homesickness and his concern for her and her book.[31] He complained that her letters did not reach him on account of the censors, and Ellen sat at home suffering miserably because she felt that

28 September 26, 1917.
29 Mabel Potter Daggett, *Marie of Roumania: The Intimate Story of the Radiant Queen* (New York: George H. Doran Co., 1926), 134.
30 November 26, 1917.
31 *E.g.*, January 25, 1918.

he did not write often enough.[32] In March, 1918, the Germans overran Rumania; the Queen stood in stony majesty, greeted her conquerors and bade farewell to her friends. Henry Anderson gripped Marie's hand with emotion and then fell to his knees and kissed the hem of her dress.[33] By June he was back in New York.

Ellen had changed considerably by the time Anderson returned home. The winter and spring had been difficult for her. Anne Virginia Bennett had joined the Red Cross in March and gone to France as a nurse. Ellen was alone except when Carrie Coleman came over to spend the night. The horrors of war and the anxiety over not hearing from Anderson preyed on Ellen's mind. "Night after night," she wrote, "I saw, in imagination, the gangrened flesh on barbed wires, the dead, stiffened in horror, the eyeless skulls and the bared skeletons, the crosses and poppies, the edge of the universe."[34] Afraid of being alone again, she believed the rumors and gossip about Anderson and the Queen. When he appeared to her in his uniform, glittering with the decorations of seven countries,[35] looking hale and vigorous, and talking of the Queen and the Princess Ileana and his plans to return soon to Rumania, Ellen believed that she had lost him forever.[36]

Anderson endured bravely, perhaps proudly, the gossip that reached his ears; he tried to console Ellen, but she refused to be consoled. She marched determinedly toward the edge of the universe, a place known only to the distorted and mystical mind that believes it can escape the present and see simultaneously into the past and the future. Anderson came to dinner on July 3, 1918. He and Ellen argued, and he left early. Ellen was in despair; she could find no comfort in religion, philosophy, or human relationships. "Ghosts were my only companions," she wrote. "I was shut in, alone, with the past."[37] She went to her room, closed the blinds, and dressed for bed. She took sleeping pills in an excessive quantity,

[32] Carrie Duke to MKR, in Rawlings Papers.
[33] Daggett, *Marie of Roumania*, 239.
[34] *Woman Within*, 233.
[35] Serbia, Rumania, Greece, Russia, Montenegro, Czechoslovakia, and Italy.
[36] *Woman Within*, 235.
[37] *Ibid.*, 237.

wishing for death. Death did not come. She believed that she saw passing before her the figures of all those whom she had loved,[38] and the unassorted imaginations of a troubled mind caused her to wish for death more than for life.

The agony of her depression she thrust upon Anderson. "I am doing my best," he wrote her. "Yet I am always under the shadow of your terrible threat. This is not criticism."[39] He tried again to explain why he had remained in Rumania and to assure her of his continuing affection and his anguish over her depression. Their future became uncertain, but the engagement was not broken and Anderson's return to Rumania was not postponed. Rumania had been liberated by the Allies, and early in November, Anderson was on his way back. He had scarcely had time to reach Europe before Ellen received a letter from his mother expressing her great satisfaction that Henry was planning to marry her and her deep faith that God was a "very present help in time of trouble."[40] The trouble to which she referred was the separation because of the war, not the real problems which Ellen and Anderson were facing.

By the time Anderson arrived in Europe, the war was over. He and Ellen corresponded more frequently, but their letters were increasingly impersonal. The Queen went to the Peace Conference and brought back significant territorial gains for Rumania. No doubt Anderson approved of the increase in the territory of Rumania, but he was disillusioned with the conference. "My own private impression of the Peace Conference," he wrote, "is that a lot of professors and theorists have succeeded in making a mess of Europe."[41] Yet Anderson's personal popularity in the Balkans soared; he admitted that he was offered and rejected the crown of Albania.[42] His mission had ended, and it was time for him to go home to Richmond.

In Richmond, life for Ellen Glasgow proceeded at a dreary pace. Anne Virginia Bennett had returned from the war, and no longer

[38] *Ibid.*, 239.
[39] Undated.
[40] Laura E. Anderson to Ellen Glasgow, November 19, 1918, Glasgow Papers.
[41] July 3, 1919, *ibid.*
[42] Henry W. Anderson to MKR, in Rawlings Papers.

did Ellen have to live alone, but her best friend, Carrie Coleman, had just announced that she would marry Frank Duke. The subject of marriage, especially if it meant the loss of one of her female companions, was especially bitter to Ellen. Yet she invited her friend to be married in the drawing room at One West Main, and no doubt tried to hide her gloomy feelings during the ceremony. Had Ellen but known it, the marriage of Carrie would not change their close friendship. Frank Duke lived less than five years after the wedding, there were no children, and Carrie did not move away. After the ceremony, Ellen returned to her novel. It was something to occupy her mind, and Henry Anderson had urged her to complete it, hoping it would improve her mental outlook.

*The Builders* was published in the fall of 1919.[43] It was the first of her novels with which Ellen Glasgow had considerable assistance, and it was the only one which she ever allowed to be serialized in a magazine.[44] The plot was weak, and the novel was ignored by both book reviewers and buyers. Yet it is replete with Anderson's political thought, a fact that becomes of more interest since Anderson moved into positions of greater leadership in the Republican party in the 1920's. The leading character, David Blackburn, is critical of President Woodrow Wilson in 1916 and is gossipped about by the ladies of Richmond because he joined the Republican party, the party which in Virginia was still considered to be the party of Negroes. Blackburn eventually deserts the Republicans and becomes an Independent. Anderson never went quite that far, but he did lead a group determined to give the Republican party a new status in Virginia. In the novel, Blackburn explains to a friend from New York City that the South is solid politically because of its reaction to the trauma of Reconstruction. He considers Reconstruction a wrong worse than death; but since Virginia had limited the suffrage in 1902 and made the votes of Negroes negligible, he feels that the Solid South is harmful to Southerners and regards "the liberation of the South from this political tyranny as the imperative duty

---

[43] Ellen Glasgow, *The Builders* (Garden City, New York: Doubleday, Page and Co., 1919).

[44] *Woman's Home Companion*, October, November, December, 1919.

of every loyal Southerner."[45] That is precisely what Anderson said a few years later in his campaign speeches.

Almost as if by magic, when Anderson was out of the country and unable to assist with the novel, the characterization of Blackburn was dropped and Ellen concentrated upon the development of his fickle wife. The character of Blackburn was tapered off with comments by his friends, that his country seemed to be more important to him than any living creature, an attitude that Ellen adopted toward Anderson long before she finished the novel. The book was stillborn; Ellen's heart was not in it by the time it reached the press. Her lack of concern for it, as well as the financial consideration, no doubt accounts for her unprecedented decision to allow it to appear in serial in a woman's magazine.

When Anderson returned from Europe in the fall of 1919, Ellen gave him an inscribed copy of *The Builders* which tactitly acknowledged his assistance. But her warmth toward him had decreased, and it was becoming obvious that there would be no wedding. The decision not to marry was never clearly made, and the engagement was abandoned rather than canceled. After his final return from Europe, Ellen asked Anderson if he still regarded himself as engaged to her. His response surely did not erase the doubt from her mind:

> You ask if I regard myself as engaged to you. Of course I do, and there has not been a word or suggestion to the contrary. Even when in your last letter you said I could do as I pleased it did not affect my view of that in the least. We entered into the engagement in good faith by mutual agreement, and any change in status should be by mutual agreement. The only difference between us seems to be that you seem to regard it as irrevocable while I feel that if circumstances arise which would render unwise the carrying out of that agreement, we should change or end it—but by mutual consent in a dignified and proper way. And if either of us feel that those conditions have arisen it is a duty however painful to say so frankly. This is all I have ever claimed or done, and all I am seeking to do now. In my view of it I cannot do less.

45 *The Builders*, 119.

I am distressed, my Dear, to have given you pain or distress. It has been the most painful experience of my whole life—I am sorry that the doom which seems to hang over my life has involved yours.[46]

The relationship deteriorated further, and Anderson suggested that they postpone the marriage until April and both take "treatment" in order to get in shape for it.[47] No date was ever set and no public announcement was ever made. Ellen's increasing criticism of Anderson was becoming unbearable for him. She wrote him numerous bitter letters in which she accused him of all sorts of social improprieties, even using their friendship to material advantage. With good reason, Anderson was highly insulted; and he took upon himself the impossible task of trying to maintain his patience, defend himself, and not offend Ellen at the same time:

I am wondering if it ever occurred to you that your judgment might be wrong. You judge me so freely and with such apparent sureness that your conclusions are right that it makes me strong in my belief that no human being is or can be capable of judging another. Your judgment seeks not only to cover the present but to sweep back over the past and to wipe out my character, my sincerity, everything, in one sweeping decree—a decree as tragic as it is sweeping, and as wrong as it is tragic. I have made no decision, but must, of course, accept yours. You wrote me a letter, which from anyone else would have been unbearable, even offensive. From you it just hurt—hurt me as I have never been hurt. . . . It is true that I have endeavored to throw around our association a normal atmosphere to overcome if possible the insistently morbid view you have maintained for two years past. . . . I have tried to get you to go on a trip out of the shadow and loneliness of that house, all to no avail. God alone knows how I *have* tried and I am willing to leave it to him.

If when you turned away it was meant to be forever, I cannot change it. It is your house and your life is your own. You must decide for yourself. . . . I shall go forward the best I can. . . . Your pity I do not desire. I have so lived that I can face man and God with courage for I have been honest and sincere. I deny the rights or power of man—even you to judge me. By God's judgment I abide.

[46] Undated letter written in pencil while Anderson was ill in bed.
[47] Undated, but almost certainly written around January 1, 1920.

I have so often expressed the fear that the course you insisted upon sailing would lead to wreckage, yet I could not believe it! Since you have "turned away forever" I accept it, and go forth to face life as best I can shadowed by one great failure! Yet I know in my conscience I have done my best—a poor best perhaps but *my* best—my honest best!

Henry

If you should want me at any time I am ready to come to you or serve you.

H.[48]

The argument dragged on through the summer until Ellen finally decided to go to Maine for a few weeks. Anderson made the mistake of sending her a note saying he was glad she had decided to go away and hoped that she would regain her health.[49] Ellen was incensed and told him so, because she thought he meant he was glad to be rid of her. So Anderson attempted one more time to explain his meaning:

> You seem to read into my letters things I never think of but I really think this is due to the rather morbid state of mind which you have developed in recent months. I simply undertook to emphasize the importance of each individual living his or her own life in its daily activities and *not* living it by another's standards, or what might be thought to be another's view point. This seems to me an elementary principle both of philosophy and of happiness. But my dear, why not throw all this abstract discussion aside and enjoy your trip, and regain your strength and poise? It isn't a question of whether I wanted you to go on your account or mine but of restored health and strength which you can get from the trip. . . . I just laugh off these constantly recurring misunderstandings due perhaps to my stupidity. . . .[50]

Henry Anderson liked to avoid disagreeable situations. He attempted to solve the conflict by bringing his "sense of humor out of storage" and urging Ellen to do likewise. The situation *was* becoming laughable, and Anderson finally and wisely rescued them both by openly laughing. In a playful vein, Anderson replied to

[48] Tuesday, no date.
[49] August, 1920.
[50] August 26, 1920.

one of Ellen's letters: "Dear, *Dear*, DEAR! what a blast! If I am as bad as your last note says why bother with me at all? Anyhow, the withered and stricken remains of me will come down tonight and be converted into a metaphorical grease spot on the rug."[51]

The therapy of laughter ultimately provided the cure. Ellen picked up her work again. In October, 1920, she published "The Past,"[52] the story of a Mrs. Vanderbridge who saw the ghost of her husband's first wife come and sit at the table with them every time her husband was thinking about his former spouse; but ultimately the living second Mrs. Vanderbridge triumphed over the dead first Mrs. Vanderbridge. As in "The Shadowy Third," a nurse also can see the ghost and serves as the narrator. Ellen went to such lengths to explain the mystery of the ghost that the story loses its impact, but it is intriguing as a possible reflection of the triangular affair involving Ellen, Queen Marie, and Henry Anderson. Ellen had about convinced herself that she was the victor in the affair and accepted the whole episode as an exciting venture of the mind and an intensive lesson in human experience that might be useful in the development of her art.

She began another novel, and on December 4, 1920, she felt well enough to go down to the College of William and Mary to be initiated as an honorary member of Phi Beta Kappa.[53] But her contact with Anderson remained close. When his mother died in January, he poured out his heart to her in a long personal letter expressing his tenderest feelings for his mother and a kind of profound religious faith that Ellen probably did not appreciate. When in the summer of 1921 the Republican party named Henry Anderson as its candidate for governor of Virginia, Ellen took a lively interest in the campaign.

Ellen's interest in politics was at first philosophic. In her earlier novels she had already lauded the type of character who dared to break with the tradition of the past and on his own personal initiative achieve a considerable measure of success. Henry Anderson's

---

51 Undated.
52 *Good Housekeeping,* October, 1920.
53 Mrs. William A. Kraus to MKR, February 16, 1950, in Rawlings Papers.

rise to political prominence and financial success was precisely the story she had told several times before she ever met him. As one who dared to be different, Anderson was to politics in Virginia what Ellen Glasgow considered herself to be to literature in the South. The courage to dare to be different from the ways of the past while at the same time drawing vital nourishment from it was the subject of a speech she delivered to a woman's club in Richmond in March, 1921.

Under the title "The Dynamic Past" the speech was published in *The Reviewer*, a local fledgling literary journal organized by the friends of James Branch Cabell. "To me Virginia's past is like a hall hung with rare and wonderful tapestries," she said, ". . . but it is not a place in which we should live and brood until we become like that ancient people whose 'strength was to sit still.' " No matter how splendid the past, it should provide the seeds for the future. "It is tomorrow, not yesterday, that needs us most." Washington, Jefferson, and Lee were all men who dared to break with tradition and look forward, not backward. Art, culture, and politics are all linked together, she argued, and all must move forward together, drawing their strength from that which was good in the past without becoming a slave to some bygone era. "Here in Virginia we need liberation not from the past, but from the old moorings which have held the past and ourselves anchored in stagnant waters."[54] The principles of Washington, Jefferson, and Lee, she concluded, call Virginians to go forth from the haven of the past with wisdom and courage.

The speech could almost have been written by Henry Anderson. He and Ellen Glasgow were in the habit of proofing each other's work, and it is very likely that he commented on "The Dynamic Past" privately before it was ever delivered or published. Although the speech contains a few barbs against the worship of material success, a weakness of which Ellen was prone to accuse Anderson, it is as much an expression of Anderson's attitude toward the past and the future as it is Ellen's, and its theme is reiterated time and again in his campaign speeches.

[54] *The Reviewer*, I (March 15, 1921), 73–80.

When Henry Anderson accepted the nomination for governor at the Republican state convention in Norfolk on July 14, 1921, he stepped forth with the same courage for which Ellen had called in her speech. Ellen immediately offered to take part in the campaign, an offer that Anderson accepted provided she would not let it interfere with her book.[55] Anderson was not especially ambitious to become governor of Virginia, and he looked upon his candidacy as the fulfillment of his duty to the state he loved. He made a valiant effort to keep his politics on a high level, untainted by the racism which had become such a characteristic part of elections in Virginia. He campaigned for roads, schools, the destruction of a corrupt political machine, and escape from the doldrums of the Civil War that still lingered over the Old Dominion. He asked for the repeal of the poll tax that had been instituted in 1902 primarily as a means of disfranchising Negroes. Ironically, the race issue suddenly became the major one in the campaign. The Democratic candidate, Lee Trinkle, charged that Anderson's attempt to repeal the poll tax would restore suffrage for black people and set Virginia back half a century. Anderson retaliated by saying that the Republican party in Virginia was "a party of white citizens." He was right. For the first time in its history the Republican party in Virginia was a party of white citizens. Since Negroes had been disfranchised, they were considered of little value politically. In fact, they were considered of such little value that when Anderson was told at the convention that they would bolt the ticket he reportedly remarked, "Fine."[56] Negroes did bolt and named John Mitchell, Jr., black editor of the Richmond *Planet*, as their candidate for governor.[57] In the popular jargon Anderson became known as the "lily-white" candidate, and Mitchell was the "lily-black" candidate. As a Democrat in the yet Solid South, Trinkle's victory was almost assured.

With the battle lines thus drawn, Ellen Glasgow edged into the

[55] Henry Anderson to Ellen Glasgow, no date.

[56] Andrew Buni, *The Negro in Virginia Politics, 1902–1965* (Charlottesville: University Press of Virginia, 1967), 81–83.

[57] For a study of the career of John Mitchell, Jr., see Ann B. Field, "Negro Protest in the New South: John Mitchell, Jr., 1863–1902" (M.A. thesis, Duke University, 1968).

fray in spirit if not in action. The ideas she had put forth in "The Dynamic Past" she elaborated upon in an untitled political speech which she probably never delivered.[58] She addressed her fellow Virginians as one who spoke only out of loyalty to Virginia, not to any political creed. Her ancestors had all been Democrats and she had been bound to the Democratic party, she said. She joked: "As a little child I believed that the 'publicans and sinners of the Bible meant Virginia Republicans, and my Father used to say that one of the first sensible questions I ever asked him was 'Are there only angels and Democrats in heaven?'" And then she planned to tell them that in the coming election the Republican platform was far more constructive than anything the Democrats had to offer. She lamented the fact that Virginia had not had a statesman for twenty years and was in the hands of a monarchical political machine. The Republican party had the right principles and the ablest men, she said. Then she leaped into the race question, almost with the exact words of Anderson himself:

> That a small and ineffectual minority such as the negro race in Virginia—without education, without experience in government, without property, and without influence of any sort, should constitute a serious menace to the established rule of the white people —is a proposition that could be advanced only by the Democratic Party in Virginia or to Alice in Wonderland. If the Democratic machine would devote a little of the energy it expends on the manufacture of political mud to the removal of the genuine substance, both our mental and our material avenue might be made more dignified as well as more comfortable.

Following the party line, she said that the roads and schools that Virginia needed so desperately were likely to be given only by the Republicans. The Democratic platform she found irrelevant; she expected that party "to rise at any moment and give three cheers for mothers!" She explained that Robert E. Lee had broken with the tradition of the past in his search for truth and that Virginians in 1921 must follow his example. And she concluded that the Repub-

[58] The manuscript of the speech is in the Glasgow Papers in the University of Virginia Library. I have found no press releases or other indication that the speech was ever delivered.

Francis Thomas Glasgow, a stern Scotch-Irish Presbyterian, had fundamentalist beliefs that his daughter Ellen found intolerable. She believed her father to be harsh and cruel, and they never understood each other.

Anne Jane Gholson Glasgow was a Tidewater aristocrat. Although Ellen's middle name was Anderson, from her father's family, she often signed herself Ellen Anderson Gholson Glasgow.

In 1875, when Ellen Glasgow was two years old, two of her brothers died. Her mother's grief and despair deeply affected the sensitive child.

Ellen wrote her first story when she was seven. "Only a Daisy," a one-page summary of her life, revealed a self-image that remained with her for the rest of her life.

At eighteen Ellen had completed a four-hundred-page manuscript of a novel entitled "Sharp Realities." She was also growing deaf.

This picture of Ellen Glasgow, made in 1897, was used to advertise
her first novel, *The Descendant*.

Ellen Glasgow was hardly the typical, demure southern girl of the 1890's that she appears to be here. Already she was devoted to Darwinian science and had published her first novel.

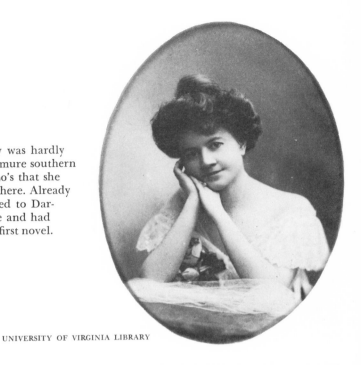

The Glasgow family traditionally spent their summers at White Sulphur Springs, West Virginia. Here Ellen is shown during the 1890's.

Sometime after 1905 this picture was made of Ellen (hand on newel post) with her sister Rebe, her brother Frank, who committed suicide in 1909, and her father.

At thirty-three Ellen Glasgow became engaged to the Reverend Frank Paradise, an Episcopalian minister from Massachusetts. The "experimental" engagement lasted for three years before she broke it.

Ellen Glasgow was the guest of several British authors during her visits to England. She is shown with Joseph Conrad in his garden in 1914.

Anne Virginia Bennett was Ellen Glasgow's companion for thirty years. Jeremy and Billy, the dogs pictured with her, held unusual places in Miss Glasgow's affections.

Colonel Henry W. Anderson in his World War I uniform, with decorations, about the time of his engagement to Ellen Glasgow.

At fourteen Ellen Glasgow moved into One West Main Street, Richmond, and the old house remained her home for the rest of her life.

Miss Glasgow's upstairs study at One West Main. It was in this room that at age sixty she secretly began her autobiography, *The Woman Within*, which was published posthumously.

Colonel Henry W. Anderson, of Richmond, courted Miss Ellen on this porch overlooking the back garden at One West Main. She received other visitors here, including many notables in the literary world.

In 1938, when Miss Glasgow was elected to the American Academy of Arts
and Letters, she asserted that "all such honors are entirely empty
and not worth a straw," but that same year she accepted honorary
degrees from the University of Richmond and Duke University.

lican platform was designed from a human rather than a political perspective, a phrase that either she or Anderson had placed in the mouth of her character David Blackburn in *The Builders*.

Ellen was not much of a campaigner, and neither was Anderson. She dreaded making speeches and public appearances and could not be persuaded to do so even out of love for Virginia. Anderson excelled at oratory, but he did not really want to be governor.[59] Campaigning bored him, and he made no effort to adapt his style of life to political expediency. His English chauffeur drove him in his foreign car into a town where he was to speak. Meticulously dressed in the costume of a British gentleman, Anderson made his speech, stood quietly for his chauffeur to open the door for him to get back into the car, and then moved on. His style was a far cry from the back slapping and carnival atmosphere that Virginians had grown accustomed to at election time. Even Democrats admitted privately that Anderson's speeches were impressive and that his goals for Virginia were realistic.[60] His defeat was probably due more than anything else to the handicap of the Republican label.[61] After the election Anderson returned to his duties as an attorney and counselor for a national Republican administration; and Ellen turned to the completion of her novel, a task she had never completely laid aside for the campaign. By the end of the year the novel was finished, and Ellen, with her brother's money, went to New York City to take an expensive serum treatment for her ears. The treatment had supposedly wrought some miraculous cures but was of no avail in her case.[62]

The novel, *One Man in His Time*, published in May, 1922, contributed as little to her literary reputation as the serum treatment did to the cure of her deafness. Though Anderson supplied none of the actual work on it, the novel vaguely reflected Ellen's affair with him and his campaign for governor. For the first time in her

[59] Henry W. Anderson to MKR, in Rawlings Papers.
[60] Douglas S. Freeman to MKR, *ibid.*
[61] The final count was Trinkle, 139,416, Anderson, 65,933, and Mitchell, 5,046, in Buni, *Negro in Virginia Politics*, 87.
[62] Ellen Glasgow to Arthur Glasgow, December 27, 1921, and January 5, 1922, in Glasgow Papers.

career she felt behooved to place a note in the front: "No character in this book was drawn from any actual person past or present." But characters were drawn, however poorly, from actual persons. The novel is supposedly the story of Gideon Vetch, a political mystery who triumphed over both parties to become governor of Virginia and yet retained an aloofness from the people who voted for him and to whom he was devoted. The appearance of a jaded old woman in Capitol Square adds an element of mystery. Vetch's daughter eventually learns that the old woman is her mother and that Vetch is not her father and has never been married. The old woman was a circus performer who years before in California was spotted by Vetch with her child in her arms as she was being dragged off to prison for knifing a man. Vetch took the child and reared her as his daughter. As governor, Vetch was murdered while trying to prevent a strike, but the reader is not likely to care. The character of Vetch is poorly developed and seems unreal. Other characters occupy more of the novelist's attention, but even they are not successfully drawn. Without doubt, it was Ellen's most feeble attempt to create a novel and was obviously written under great nervous strain. The reviews were harsh, and the sales were poor.[63] One of the few good reviews was written by a local young newspaper man and historian, Douglas S. Freeman, whose motive must have been more to assuage the feelings of the hometown novelist than to write an honest critique of her book.[64]

Though the book failed as a creditable novel, some of the conversations of minor characters reveal Ellen's mental state at the time she wrote it. An aging woman who has been disappointed in love moans that "there ought to be something more permanent than love for one to live by." She is told by a friend that there is courage and is advised to buy a "hat that can look the world in the face."[65] Ellen was struggling valiantly to recover from the strain of the previous years. She had once told her sister: "Rebe, if you get de-

---

63 Kelly, "Struggle for Recognition," 183.

64 In a letter to Douglas S. Freeman, dated May 24, 1922, Ellen Glasgow thanks him for his good review of her book. Freeman Papers, Library of Congress.

65 Ellen Glasgow, *One Man in His Time* (Doubleday, Page and Co., 1919), 296, 297, 315.

pressed, buy a red hat."[66] The cure of Ellen's depression required more than a red hat, however, and one of her characters revealingly comments that "if the penalty of depression was psychoanalysis, it was worth while to pretend to be gay."[67] Ellen had come to know about psychoanalysis through her friendship with doctors in New York City who were associated with the Neurological Institute and through her own need for therapy.

In the summer of 1922, Henry Anderson helped her select a new therapist,[68] and she periodically resorted to psychiatric care for the rest of her life. Anderson did all that he could to help her to recover. At Christmas he sent her a jade necklace from Tiffany's and playfully told her to look as much like an oriental barbarian as she liked.[69] But Ellen faced the new year with uncertainty, unsure what role her one man in his time might play next and no doubt painfully aware that in the year the literary world greeted T. S. Eliot's *The Wasteland* and James Joyce's *Ulysses,* her own literary output and reputation had reached its lowest point.

The new year brought little change in the relationship with Anderson, and Ellen spent much of her time writing short stories. Her earlier success with ghost stories prompted her to write another one in January and February.[70] The ghost in "Whispering Leaves" is a Negro mammy, dead for several years, but who comes back to take care of a little white boy who believes that he can see and talk to her. The story takes the same style as the earlier ghost stories. A female visitor from outside the home can also see the ghost, whereas none of the other members of the family can. The story is too long, and as one critic lamented, contains "enough horticultural detail to fill a gardening magazine."[71] But Ellen kept working and in the remainder of the year wrote three other stories.

"The Difference," published in June in *Harper's Magazine,* deals

---

[66] Rebe Tutwiler to MKR, in Rawlings Papers.

[67] *One Man in His Time,* 70.

[68] Henry Anderson to Ellen Glasgow, July 3, 1922, in Glasgow Papers.

[69] Christmas, 1922.

[70] "Whispering Leaves" was originally published in *Harper's Magazine* in January and February, 1923.

[71] Meeker (ed.), *Collected Stories,* 164.

with what was rapidly becoming her favorite theme: the moral superiority of woman over man. Margaret Fleming received a letter from her husband's mistress. It turned out that the mistress was an artist who took on many lovers as a part of her philosophy of self-development; Mr. Fleming could not understand why his wife should be upset because, as he explained, the little affair was no more to him than "recreation." Ellen pursued the battle of the sexes further in "The Artless Age," published in the *Saturday Evening Post* in August, and easily the most frivolous of her stories. A Virginia lady was trying to find a proper mate for her handsome son, only to have him run off and marry a rude girl who had deliberately made herself obnoxious in order to catch his attention. And the proper girl ran off with a man old enough to be her father.

The final story of the year was "Jordan's End," the most popular of the Glasgow stories and perhaps the best constructed. Jordan's End is the name of a decaying house in Virginia and is symbolic of the end of the Jordan family whose male members all die insane because of generations of intermarriage. The last Jordan is mercifully murdered by his wife who had promised him that she would do it when he, too, was ultimately afflicted with the insanity. With the completion of "Jordan's End," Ellen collected seven of her stories into a volume entitled *The Shadowy Third and Other Stories*, published in October, 1923.[72]

Her interest in short stories was waning as she began to mull over an idea for a new novel. She published only one more story, "Romance and Sally Byrd," in December, 1924.[73] Sally Byrd had the misfortune at nineteen to fall in love with a married man who failed to tell her about his wife. Her lover had no intention of getting a divorce, and she was only one of many he had treated so. Sally Byrd thought that romance was over for her, but then she discovered a handsome man who lived on her street and took new hope. Like Sally Byrd, Ellen was beginning to look around for

---

72 Ellen Glasgow, *The Shadowy Third and Other Stories* (Garden City, New York: Doubleday, Page and Co., 1923). Included in the volume are "The Shadowy Third," "Dare's Gift," "The Past," "Whispering Leaves," "A Point in Morals," "The Difference," and "Jordan's End."

73 *Woman's Home Companion*, December, 1924.

male companions other than Henry Anderson and believed that she had found them.[74] She was coming to the end of the most difficult phase of her life, which began with her fear of living alone in a house that to her mind was haunted by memories and which ended with a traumatic love affair that permanently colored her outlook on life and gave the final shape to her philosophy. It is no coincidence that the stories she wrote during the time deal with real and imagined human relationships.

Ellen left the unpublished manuscript of a story, "The Professional Instinct," that was undoubtedly written during the time she knew Anderson.[75] It is the story of Dr. Estbridge, an analytical psychologist whose dream is to be appointed to the chair of physiology at some unnamed university. He is bored with his wife and interested in a beautiful philosophy professor of thirty-eight whose ambition is to become president of a college in St. Louis, Missouri. The woman is offered the presidency of the school, but the chair in physiology goes to Estbridge's rival. The woman agrees to give up her profession to run away with him to Shanghai. Minutes before the train is to leave, the doctor receives word that the man who had originally been offered the chair has been killed in an accident and the position can be his. So he is willing to desert the woman who had given up all for him in order to stay and achieve his ambition. Ellen was probably wise never to publish the story, for it adds little to her work. Yet there were times when she felt that Anderson's devotion to his country and to Virginia were far more important to him than his devotion to her.

By 1924, however, the strain of the relationship with Anderson had eased. They had settled into a platonic friendship that lasted for the rest of Ellen's life. On special occasions Anderson sent her

[74] By 1923 Ellen Glasgow had become acquainted with the doctors at the Neurological Institute in New York City, several of whom became her suitors. She had also become friends with the British author Hugh Walpole, who had visited her several times in Richmond and whom she was prepared to pursue relentlessly.

[75] In the Glasgow Papers a letter from Dr. Pearce Bailey to Ellen Glasgow, dated March 8, 1916, indicates that he was helping her collect information for the story then. "The Professional Instinct" is published in Meeker (ed.), *Collected Stories*; and in *Western Humanities Review* XVI, No. 4 (Autumn, 1962), 301–17, with an introduction by William W. Kelly.

gifts—flowers, clothing, books, jade earrings to match her necklace, and the reproduction of a gold cup from a museum in Athens to be used as a holder for her hand phone. She gave him silver bowls which he was fond of collecting. Every Tuesday when Anderson was in town they dined together on her back porch. But the engagement of politics to art was ended forever; their careers took different and predictable courses. In the Republican 1920's Henry Anderson held a number of important advisory posts with the United States government, and President Herbert Hoover even wanted to appoint him to the Supreme Court of the United States. The prize was snatched from his fingers, however, by Bascom Slemp, a Republican congressman from Virginia and old political enemy of Anderson's who refused to concur and thus blocked the appointment in its earliest stages.[76] In the Democratic thirties and forties, Anderson was reduced to making speeches critical of the administration, but as the receiver for the Seaboard Air Line Railroad Company and later as chairman of its board of directors, he was scarcely idle, and his financial success was assured. Ellen was left to work out her own salvation in the only way that she knew: she wrote *Barren Ground.*

76 Interview with Mrs. James Asa Shield, January 9, 1969, Richmond.

# 7

# Barren Ground

When she began *Barren Ground,* Ellen believed that she had
"found a code of living that was sufficient for life or for death."[1]
That code is a philosophy of life so without feeling, so without
emotion, that its adherent might as well be dead. It is the code
of an agonized mind determined to avoid human relationships and
their demands of giving and receiving. She adopted it as a simple
means of survival in the aftermath of the rupture of her painful
relationship with Henry Anderson, but its roots stretch back into
her childhood. In a vain effort to rationalize her fate, Ellen said
that if falling in love had been bliss, then falling out of love was
"blissful tranquillity."[2] Actually it was hell and she knew it. She
lost herself in work and created a character, Dorinda Oakley, who
became a mechanized human being totally drained of humanity,
the person whom Ellen imagined herself to be.

Dorinda Oakley could have been created only by an embittered
and cynical woman. More than any other character in her novels,
Dorinda Oakley is Ellen Glasgow. Ellen herself said that *Barren
Ground* was "a rich harvest" gleaned from the whole of her life[3]
and that she and Dorinda were "connected, or so it seemed, by a
living nerve."[4] It is the most autobiographical novel she wrote and
perhaps for that reason remained her favorite book throughout

1 *Woman Within,* 271.
2 *Ibid,* 244.
3 *Ibid.,* 270.
4 *A Certain Measure,* 163.

her life.[5] She put her whole heart, she said, into a book in which she *believed*.[6] Ellen had decided to withdraw from her fellow human beings whom she accused of having caused her pain, but she did not intend to leave them in peace. As surely as her attempt to commit suicide was to punish Anderson for his infatuation with the Queen of Rumania, her writing of *Barren Ground* was an essay to prove once and for all her superiority to Anderson in particular, men in general, unfriendly critics, and even her fellow craftsmen whose popularity exceeded hers. The philosophy of Dorinda Oakley is the philosophy that Ellen Glasgow at fifty-two adopted as her own standard and elaborated upon later. A bleak philosophy arrived at late in life, the plateau of stoic endurance ultimately provided her with a footing from which she could laugh at the foibles of *homo sapiens*, especially the male of the species. Before she laughed, however, she took her readers step by step with Dorinda Oakley to that barren plateau where no sane person would wish to go or dare to stay.

The time of Dorinda's life coincides with that of the novelist. Dorinda is a young woman of twenty in the 1890's when the reader first meets her, and a cynical woman in her fifties in 1924 when the novel ends. The child of a Presbyterian family in rural Virginia, Dorinda was drilled in the theology of Calvinism. Like Ellen, she believed that her mother's ancestry was superior to her father's and that the mating of her mother and father was a mistake that caused her to inherit the tragic "conflict of types."[7] Dorinda's mother was the granddaughter of a Presbyterian missionary who settled in the Valley of Virginia and through "ingenious Presbyterian logic" somehow managed to reconcile his religion with his willingness to buy and sell Negro slaves.[8] From him Mrs. Oakley had inherited an unshakeable belief that "If you ain't got religion to

[5] Ellen Glasgow to Bessie Zaban Jones, March 6, 1941, in Bessie Zaban Jones Papers, Smith College Library; March 29, 1931, in *Letters*, 107; to Signe Toksvig, October 8, 1944, in *Letters*, 354.
[6] Ellen Glasgow to Hugh Walpole, August 23, 1923, in *Letters*, 69.
[7] *Woman Within*, 14; *A Certain Measure*, 158.
[8] *Barren Ground*, 7.

lean back on, you'd just as well give up trying to live in the country."[9] In her younger years Mrs. Oakley had a preference for Presbyterian missionaries, and was engaged to one who died shortly
before the wedding. As a second choice she married Joshua Oakley
purely because the shape of his head reminded her of an apostle.
After her marriage she suffered through temporary periods of insanity, much as Ellen's own mother had done; and all of her life
Mrs. Oakley dreamed of palms waving over sandy beaches and
naked black babies being thrown to crocodiles. Only her Presbyterian faith allowed her to endure as the wife of a poor farmer in
Virginia.

Joshua Oakley, Dorinda's father, has little parallel to Ellen's
father. Oakley belonged to the class in Virginia known as "good
people," the class that had no gallery of "important" ancestors
and which existed by hard work and little show of progress. Joshua
Oakley was "land poor"; he owned more acres of land than he could
work and allowed much of it to grow up in broomsedge, obstinately
refusing to rotate crops or try anything new on his farm. Because
of his type of mentality—"a cornfield at Pedlar's Mill was as permanent as a graveyard"[10]—he and his neighbors were engulfed in
the poverty of the soil. His sons were no account, and Dorinda
clerked in a country store to help support the family.

The country store was owned by Nathan Pedlar, an industrious
man with a wife and large family, who was sometimes willing to
experiment with new ideas. His wife was ill and obviously about to
die. Yet she maintained a "feverish optimism" and always planned to
get out of bed the next day, but she never did. She droned on about
milking the cows, paying the taxes, and ordering piece goods for
sale in the store. In play, her younger children conducted a mock
funeral around a hole in the rug which they designated as an open
grave. Dorinda watched the scene in desperation and wondered
if the trivial things after all were the only things that mattered
in life.

9 *Ibid.*, 101.
10 *Ibid.*, 18–19.

But Dorinda's mind was elsewhere. She yearned to get away. The whistle of the train haunted her. Like her creator, as a child she had read the yellowed theology books of her great grandfather and *The Waverley Novels* that were in the family library. She had decided that in spite of her mother's faith, religion was not enough for her. She remembered her childhood as a time of loneliness and fear and the house in which she grew up as a foreboding place that seemed to wait for disaster. She felt a kinship with the land that was grown over with broomsedge, because "she was caught like a mouse in the trap of life."[11] Dorinda Oakley felt exactly as Ellen had felt in 1893 when she stood by her mother's grave and realized that she was going deaf and that there was nothing she could do about it. As Ellen had done, Dorinda looked for her escape in companionship with a member of the opposite sex.

Escape came in the person of Jason Greylock, but the novelist hints that one who had lived so uncomfortably with the doctrine of predestination as she and Dorinda had done might have guessed that she would be unlucky in love. Jason Greylock was a young doctor who had come back from New York to live with his father, also a doctor, who was gradually drinking himself to death. Jason hated Pedlar's Mill as much as Dorinda did. He believed that there was failure in the very air and that if one stayed there long enough, he would cease to care about anything. He was convinced that people would fight to stay in a rut but not to get out of it.[12] In a vain effort to avoid the rut, Dorinda and Jason planned to marry in the fall just as Ellen and Henry Anderson had planned to marry before the First World War. Mrs. Oakley warned Dorinda that marriage for most women was "just the struggle to get away from things as they are"; and Dorinda herself suspected that love and happiness were interchangeable terms only to a woman, for Jason apparently had some deep anxiety about their engagement.[13] Even as, in a passage in the novel so inconspicuous that the reader might easily miss it, Dorinda allowed Jason to make love to her, she was tor-

11 *Ibid.*, 56.
12 *Ibid.*, 111–12.
13 *Ibid.*, 103, 108.

mented by the "sense of impermanence" and fear that she might "drop back again into the dull grey of existence."[14]

And drop back she did, for Jason soon went to New York allegedly on a brief business trip. He and Dorinda were supposed to be married when he returned, but he did not write and Dorinda suffered just as Ellen had suffered when Henry Anderson did not write to her from Rumania. In his absence Dorinda went to an old Negro woman for advice and encouragement. The old woman told her what she no doubt suspected: "Befo' de week's up you is gwinter be mah'ed, . . . en dar ain't a livin' soul but Aunt Mehitable gwinter know dat de chile wuz on de way sooner—" But Dorinda suspected also that she would never marry Jason. In an encounter with Jason's drunken father she learned that Jason had gone to New York to marry Geneva Ellgood to whom he had been engaged before he met Dorinda and whose brothers had spirited him away at gun point. Thus, Dorinda was involved in a triangular affair much as Ellen had been with Anderson and the Queen. Jason returned with his wife, and Dorinda attempted to murder him. She decided that life was over for her, she was finished with romance, and that there must be "something in life besides love."[15]

In her search for something besides love, Dorinda went to New York, wandered the streets alone, hungry and pregnant, and noticed that the sea of rooftops looked like fields of broomsedge. She felt no sense of sin; everything "was embraced in the elastic doctrine of predestination." In an accident she lost her unborn baby as inconspicuously as she had gotten it, and the whole episode becomes so minor that the reader is likely to forget it. In the hospital she met a doctor who offered her sympathy and a job. He introduced her to a bachelor friend, another doctor with whom she vacationed in Maine much as Ellen had vacationed in Maine with Dr. Pearce Bailey. When the possibility of marriage arose, Dorinda explained that the thought of physical lovemaking made her "sick all over," and that she had "finished with all that."[16]

14 *Ibid.*, 114.
15 *Ibid.*, 138, 192.
16 *Ibid.*, 198, 246.

Whether that particular psychological maladjustment is one from which Ellen herself suffered is a matter of sheer speculation, but it is worth noting that Dorinda is not the first of her characters who suffered from it. Molly Merryweather in *The Miller of Old Church*, published in 1911 and five years before Ellen even met Anderson, bitterly explained that she hated lovemaking and that when she saw "that look in a man's face and [felt] the touch of his hands upon [her she wanted] to strike out and kill."[17] Ellen's relationships with the opposite sex had been stormy to say the least, and the increasing incidence of known or alleged homosexuals among her male companions might lead one to suspect that Ellen was more comfortable with men who were not likely to make physical demands upon her. Even Anderson's statement to her that he tried to throw a blanket of normalcy over their morbid association may have meaning that penetrates into their physical relationship.[18] Certainly Ellen's disregard as a child for her father and disdain as a woman for men in general is an established fact. Molly Merryweather was saved by finally getting the one man whom she really loved. But the novelist, who believed that she had lost the one man—Gerald—whom she herself could ever love, was not so optimistic about the fate of Dorinda Oakley. Dorinda left New York and the only decent man who might have made an appropriate husband for her when her mother wrote that her father was dying. Predestination, the novelist asserts, had taken the decision out of Dorinda's hands.[19]

Back on the farm in Virginia and lonely, Dorinda decided that "farming, like love, might prove presently to be no laughing matter." But there was nothing left for her in life but work, so she plunged into the life of the farm with such a passion that it became her only existence. She bought dairy cows and rotated crops until she conquered the broomsedge and was easily the most modern and successful farmer in the area. Dorinda lost herself in the work of running her farm just as completely as Ellen lost herself in the writing of *Barren Ground*. Dorinda's father and mother died, but

17 *Miller of Old Church*, 69.
18 Henry Anderson to Ellen Glasgow, Tuesday, n.d., in Glasgow Papers.
19 *Barren Ground*, 248.

she was beyond grief; she believed that dying was the happiest part of her mother's life. A Negro woman became Dorinda's closest companion, just as Ellen's closest companion was her secretary and nurse: "The affection between the two women had outgrown the slender tie of mistress and maid, and had become as strong and elastic as the bond that holds relatives together."[20] Jason lived nearby, but he had become an alcoholic and his wife eventually went insane and killed herself. Occasionally Dorinda remembered him as he had been; but her real triumph came when his farm was sold for taxes and she bought it in. Ellen Glasgow was determined to prove that "For once, in Southern fiction, the betrayed woman would become the victor instead of the victim."[21] It was a strange victory, however, for Dorinda had become as barren as the soil had been at the beginning of the novel.

Ellen often ignored good stopping places in her novels, and she dragged her heroine through 150 more pages and two more triumphs over the inferior male. Dorinda married the widower Nathan Pedlar because he was "almost emasculate in his unselfishness" and willing to live with her in a platonic relationship. The union contributed to the development of the farm, but it did little for Dorinda's character. Nathan was never treated as any more than a superior hired hand, and after about ten years of marriage he died a hero while rescuing others in a train accident. His widow was not grief-stricken; at his funeral her most serious thought was that she was glad that the burial was an "Episcopal service which circumscribed the rhetoric of clergymen." But the town remembered him as a hero and erected a monument in his honor. Dorinda was convinced that men were inadequate as husbands and lovers, and only as "heroes, dedicated to the service of an ideal, were worthy, she felt, of the injudicious sentiments women lavished upon them."[22] After all, Henry Anderson had come home from World War I as a hero and had enjoyed the admiration of all except his fiancée.

[20] *Ibid.*, 276, 333, 340.
[21] *A Certain Measure*, 160.
[22] *Barren Ground*, 362, 432, 440, 456.

Having safely disposed of Nathan, the novelist turned her attention back to the already doomed Jason Greylock. An alcoholic living in poverty, he ultimately landed in the local poorhouse. In fact, it was the sight of a woman leaning against the whitewashed wall of an almshouse that gave Ellen the idea to write *Barren Ground*.[23] Dorinda went to the almshouse and volunteered to take Jason to her home and care for him, not because she had any feeling of compassion for him, but as her final vengeance against the man who had done her wrong. When he died in her home, a servant noted: "You'd 'low jes' ter look at 'im dat hit wuz a moughty pleasant surprise ter find out dat he wuz sholy daid."[24] The servant meant that Jason himself seemed pleased at his own passing, but the reader cannot help suspecting that the one who was really pleased was Dorinda Oakley.

Dorinda mourned not for Jason or "the love that she had had and lost, but [for] the love that she had never had." The end of expectancy, she understood, was the worst that could happen to her. In a weak attempt to end on a note of optimism, Ellen allowed Dorinda to tell herself that she would be strengthened and refreshed by "the spirit of the land" and find "the serenity of mind which is above the conflict of frustrated desires." Dorinda's stepson teased her that she might marry again, but Dorinda's final comment, and the final comment of Ellen, is that she is "thankful to have finished with all that."[25]

When Ellen completed *Barren Ground* in 1925, she thought she was glad to be "finished with all that." And she sent Henry Anderson a copy of the completed work just to make sure that he understood that she was glad to be finished. He understood without her telling him and wrote her a polite note congratulating her on a fine piece of work, but mildly protested that Dorinda's reaction to Jason upon her return to Virginia was a little unnatural and melodramatic.[26] The entire story is really unnatural and melodramatic, and

23 *A Certain Measure*, 159.
24 *Barren Ground*, 500.
25 *Ibid.*, 504, 509, 511.
26 Henry Anderson to Ellen Glasgow, Sunday Night, n.d., in Glasgow Papers.

the only themes that the reader is likely to remember at the end of more than five hundred pages is a vengeful heroine who prides herself on her ability to live without love as a form of superhuman courage and the transformation of the land from barren ground into productive soil. A whole catalogue of human evils, including murder, suicide, illegitimacy, poverty, ignorance, natural and accidental death, a hostile environment, and all sorts of inherited weaknesses are paraded before the reader, but he scarcely realizes that they are happening. They are but minor episodes in a life rendered tragic because they are so minor. Ellen intended for them to be minor. "Behind the little destinies of men and women," she wrote, "I felt always that unconquerable vastness in which nothing is everything."[27]

Yet the book is a near brilliant literary accomplishment, and the objectionable monolithic quality of Dorinda is lost in the sheer artistry of the telling of her story. The imagery, the use of colors, the descriptive power of the novelist, even the length of the book itself, convey that "unconquerable vastness" in which Dorinda Oakley, and perhaps even Ellen Glasgow, are so terribly insignificant. What endures is not the pathetic, frustrated woman, Ellen-in-Dorinda, who prided herself on her acumen, but was never bright enough to accept the truth that the mind can never be entirely separated from the body; what endures is the unconquerable broomsedge that overspreads the same land that is farmed by generation after generation of human beings, who have and must pass away once their brief time on earth is spent.

The reading public would not buy a view of life that was so somber, so painfully real, and the novel was not a best seller.[28] But the critics took notice, and it was reviewed by such leading literary men as Carl Van Doren, Stuart Sherman, James Branch Cabell, and H. L. Mencken. Mencken, recent discoverer that in terms of culture the South was the "Sahara of the Bozart" with a single oasis supplied by the work of James Branch Cabell, was not uncritical of *Barren Ground*. He felt that Miss Glasgow had no intimate

[27] *A Certain Measure*, 158–59.
[28] Kelly, "Struggle for Recognition," 225.

knowledge of her "flea-bitten yokels" who were her main characters and that she had created a novel "somehow weak in its legs."
Nevertheless, he did concede that *Barren Ground* contained excellent work, bold imagination, and careful planning.[29]

Carl Van Doren referred to Ellen Glasgow as "the one important
realist" of the new dominion of Virginia,[30] and the reviewer for the
*New York Times Book Review* proclaimed: "Southern romance is
dead. Ellen Glasgow has murdered it."[31] He accused her of overkill,
however, and lamented that the author obviously intended to come
to the same conclusion no matter what events transpired in the
meantime. Both he and Carl Van Doren compared *Barren Ground*
to Edith Wharton's *Ethan Frome*, much to the credit of Mrs. Wharton. Louise Collier Willcox, Ellen's friend for a quarter of a century, praised the book highly in a shallow review in which she
found it comparable to Thomas Hardy's *The Return of the Native*.[32]
And she told Ellen that she intended to send a copy of it to "poor,
old Mr. Paradise," Ellen's former fiancé who no doubt also was
interested to learn that Ellen had "finished with all that."[33]

In England, where reviewers discovered that the barren ground
of Virginia was comparable to the British countryside and where
the readers of novels were willing to take their literature with a
more melancholy flavor than in America, *Barren Ground* found a
quite favorable reception.[34] It remained, however, for a gentleman
of letters in Richmond and a literary critic on Ellen's own side of
the Atlantic to write the reviews that boosted her literary reputation and sealed her fate for the future.

James Branch Cabell wrote his first review of a Glasgow novel,
and he proclaimed, gentlemanly and more or less honestly, that

29 Mencken, "New Fiction," *American Mercury*, V (July, 1925), 382–83.

30 Van Doren, *"Barren Ground,"* *New Republic*, XLII (April 29, 1925), 271.

31 H. I. Brock, "Southern Romance is Dead," *New York Times Book Review* (April
12, 1925), 2.

32 Willcox, "Four Distinguished Novels," *Virginia Quarterly Review*, I (July, 1925),
261–264.

33 Louise Collier Willcox to Ellen Glasgow, April 12, 1925, in Glasgow Papers.

34 Kelly, "Struggle for Recognition," 223. The Glasgow Scrapbook in the Glasgow
Papers contains many of these English reviews.

*Barren Ground* was the "best of many excellent books by Ellen Glasgow." Taken collectively, he said, her books were a "portrayal of all social and economic Virginia since the War Between the States."[35] The phrase stuck, and in the minds of critics and historians Ellen thereafter was labeled a "social historian." She came to believe that the plan to create a complete social history of Virginia had been hers from the beginning, but until Cabell first used the phrase and suggested that in retrospect a complete social history was what she had created, the phrase never appears in her writing. To the grave and beyond, they feuded politely over who suggested the theme first, but the creation of the label undoubtedly belongs to Cabell. Nevertheless, the fact that the Glasgow novels do comprise a complete social history of Virginia since the Civil War is not accidental, and Ellen's correspondence with her publisher at the time she was writing *The Voice of the People* in 1899 suggests that she had the idea, if not the well-laid plan and label, for her "social history" long before Cabell began to explain her to the public.[36] In spite of the controversy, Ellen appreciated Cabell's review, eventually reciprocated with favorable comments on Cabell's work, and occasionally even turned to him for advice. Cabell's review of *Barren Ground* marks the real beginning of his friendship with Ellen Glasgow, for it was her habit to consider anyone who recognized the merit of her work to be worthy of her friendship. Years after her death, Cabell wryly remarked: "She liked good reviews, you know."[37]

Indeed she did like good reviews, and Stuart P. Sherman, literary editor for The New York *Herald Tribune*, wrote one that warmed her heart and which is perhaps the most important of her entire career. Sherman was a man of some stature as a literary critic, and he proclaimed once and for all that Ellen Glasgow was a "significant leader of contemporary realism." Before reviewing *Barren Ground*, he read her earlier novels and then suggested that she had preceded

---

[35] Cabell, "The Last Cry of Romance," *Nation*, CXX (May 6, 1925), 521.
[36] To Walter Hines Page, December 2, 1899, in *Letters*, 28–29.
[37] James Branch Cabell to MKR, in Rawlings Papers.

Theodore Dreiser and Edith Wharton in her use of realism. "The fighting edge of romance," he wrote, "is always reality."[38] Ellen Glasgow wrote "romance with blood in it," he said, playing upon her most famous utterance of the year and of her life: "What the South needs is blood and irony."[39] Blood, she later explained, was needed to give new life to Southern literature that was satisfied "to copy instead of create," and irony she believed to be "the safest antidote to sentimental decay."[40] Sherman thought she had given not only the South, but the entire nation what it needed in the way of literature. Looking back to *The Voice of the People* which was published in 1900, he noted: "Realism crossed the Potomac twenty-five years ago, going north!"[41] He suggested a need for a collected edition of the works of Ellen Glasgow, but he humbly petitioned that in such an edition *Barren Ground* be pared down by at least 20 percent "out of a tender regard for the brevity of a man's life and the artistic satisfaction of going through some passages of it swiftly—indicating rather than exhausting their interest."[42] But in general his praise was unsparing and delineated for her a place of importance in American letters with more foresight than perhaps even he was aware.

A dozen years before Margaret Mitchell published *Gone with the Wind*, Dorinda Oakley stands like a sexless Scarlet O'Hara against a setting less dramatic than the Civil War and Reconstruction and without the accompaniment of a Rhett Butler. The selfish personality, the feeling of being wounded by circumstances, the bitter determination to rise above tragedy, and the ultimate turn to the land as a source of strength are shared by both characters. Ellen Glasgow played to the hilt the agrarian image as a symbol of human nature five years before the Southern literary mythmakers took their stand in Nashville and made that image the genre for a whole

38 Sherman's essay, "The Fighting Edge of Romance," is reprinted in Stuart P. Sherman and others, *Ellen Glasgow: Critical Essays* (Garden City, N.Y.: Doubleday, Doran and Co., 1929), 1.
39 Cited in Vernon Loggins, *I Hear America . . . : Literature in the United States Since 1900* (New York: Thomas Y. Crowell Co., 1937), 192.
40 *A Certain Measure*, 28.
41 Sherman and others, *Ellen Glasgow*, 2.
42 *Ibid.*, 2.

era in Southern letters.[43] And the pervading, almost living, power of the land to control the lives of the people who live upon it became a furrow plowed time and again by William Faulkner and writers of lesser stature as they tried to create out of the materials of the human heart some artistic prop to help man to endure and to prevail. Ellen's contemporary critics could not envision the role she would play in the continuing evolution of literature. Neither could they guess her real motivation for writing *Barren Ground*, but Stuart P. Sherman came closest to it when he said that she was "a feminist with a vengeance."[44]

A furious desire for revenge had driven Ellen to write *Barren Ground*: revenge against Henry Anderson for leaving her for the Queen of Rumania and against the whole male sex for not supplying at least one from their number to be her appropriate suitor, revenge against her poor health, heredity, and environment, revenge against the merciless years she had struggled and failed to create a great novel, and revenge against the grim doctrine of predestination that often brought her to hopeless despair. In creating a character who suffered through tragedies comparable to the novelist's own real or imagined misfortunes and causing that character ultimately to triumph over those tragedies, Ellen attained the revenge that she sought and enjoyed her own personal triumph. While writing the story of Dorinda Oakley, Ellen cast off psychological burdens that had become unbearable; and the favorable critical acceptance of the novel proved to herself, perhaps to her public, and to such of her intimates as Henry Anderson that she was as capable of sublimating personal and professional handicaps as Dorinda was of transforming the barren soil into fertile pasturage.

Once Ellen had had her revenge, tasted of triumph, and adopted a philosophy to live by, she was able to laugh as she never had done before. A sense of humor had long been a part of her personality, but now she cultivated it as a public image and as an artistic technique. She laughed at the things that had tormented her; she laughed at life and religion and love. A woman with a sense of

---

[43] Twelve Southerners, *I'll Take My Stand* (New York: Harper and Brothers, 1930).
[44] Sherman and others, *Ellen Glasgow*, 9.

humor, she asserted, could find "an intellectual life more permanently satisfying than emotional experiences." In a public interview after *Barren Ground* had been published, she admitted that
the attitudes of Dorinda in the novel were her own. She explained
that marriage was a practical matter and that some women "remained unmarried because they were too romantic to compromise."
It was as good an excuse as any for her spinsterhood and one which
even she no doubt came to believe. Her own misfortunes in love
she never admitted or discussed publicly in her lifetime; and when
asked if her heart had ever been broken, she exclaimed whimsically:
"Ah, I know nothing of broken hearts! I have never seen one."[45]

But she did know. It was a broken heart that finally led her into
the barren and emotionless regions of human existence from which
she created her favorite novel. The creation of *Barren Ground* with
its philosophy of self-containment, by which Ellen believed that it
was possible for a woman to live, afforded her only temporary satisfaction. Until her dying day she insisted that the female who was
best adjusted to life was the one who had finished with love, the one
who like Dorinda Oakley had become indifferent to the male and
had settled down comfortably to endure the remainder of her life.
But it was a difficult role even for the accomplished novelist to play.
To give not a whit of oneself to another and to receive not a whit
of the self of another is inhuman; it is a philosophy which Ellen
Glasgow named with exquisite choice: Barren Ground.

[45] Marguerite Moores Marshall, 'Loveless Woman May Live Gallantly," New York
*Evening World*, n.d., Glasgow Scrapbook, in Glasgow Papers. This clipping is included among the reviews of *Barren Ground*.

# 8

## *Of Dogs and Men*

In spite of herself, Ellen Glasgow remained within the realm of human fellowship. In her writing and in her life, she set about to justify the ways of Dorinda Oakley to the realities of human existence. With satire and irony, with pathos and levity, she manipulated the men in her novels and in her life with the expertise of a professional artist who also happened to be a woman who knew all too well the bitterness of a broken heart. Men are morally inferior to women, she decided, and deserve nothing from women but amusement and contempt. Yet men cannot escape their attraction and need for the superior female. "Man and woman both sprang from monkeys," she said in an uncorrected note for some later novel, "but I think woman has sprung the fartherest."[1] At the same time, though Ellen would not admit it, the females, too, even Ellen herself, enjoyed immensely the attentions inferior men paid to them. Inevitably flattered, Ellen must have smiled triumphantly when she received two anonymous and undated valentine telegrams: "If you were seven and I were nine, I'd say 'Please be my Valentine' "; and "Give me just a little sign that you will be my Valentine."[2]

Yet it is the nature of human beings to love, and if Ellen would not, or could not, love a man, or perhaps a woman, she could love a dog. The affection she had for living creatures, Ellen transferred

[1] Glasgow Notebook, in Rawlings Papers.
[2] Glasgow Papers.

quite naturally to dogs. It is not unusual for a child to love pets. It is not necessarily shocking that a little girl should become blazingly angry, as little Ellen did, when her father gave her favorite dog to an overseer whom Ellen regarded as a cruel master. But when that little girl had become a woman who shows such utter devotion to dogs as to dismay men who want to court her, and reveals herself as the principal reason for the Society for the Prevention of Cruelty to Animals becoming one of the most conspicuous and powerful organizations in Richmond, this particular trait stands out as a primary revelation of an eccentric personality.

This dog-love played a part in ending the close relationship between Ellen Glasgow and Henry Anderson. On Christmas Eve, 1921, he presented her with a prize Sealyham puppy. She named the dog Jeremy after the title character in a novel by her friend Hugh Walpole.[3] She was already cooling in affection for Anderson; her love-at-first-sight with Jeremy may have marked the end of the process. Anderson, for his part, probably wished to gain his freedom from Ellen and shrewdly expected that Jeremy, in her possession, would make his effort easier. If so, he was right.

Ellen's attachment to Jeremy was stronger than her feeling for any human being. A white pedigreed Sealyham with black spots, Jeremy brightened One West Main Street, welcomed guests at the door, and brought a considerable amount of pleasure to his mistress. The details of Jeremy's daily care rested with Anne Virginia Bennett who loved dogs as much as Ellen did and often became jealous of affection that Jeremy showed to Ellen.[4] Through the eyes of those who loved him, Jeremy became famous as a dog with an extraordinary personality. He ushered party guests into the parlor and overnight guests up to their rooms, and occasionally when he welcomed a guest whom Ellen disliked he crawled apologetically into her presence after the guest had departed. At Christmas time he was awarded presents from various members of the family, usually toy animals that squeaked. On one occasion he delighted his mis-

[3] Ellen Glasgow to Hugh Walpole, April 29, 1922, in Walpole Papers, New York Public Library, Berg Collection; Carl Van Vechten to Oliver L. Steele, September, 1960, in Van Vechten Papers, Yale University Library.
[4] Anne Virginia Bennett to MKR, in Rawlings Papers.

tress by chewing up a Sunday school book. Jeremy chose his own companion from the dog world when about a year after his arrival at One West Main he met in the street a French poodle named Billy. Jeremy began to sit in the window and wait for Billy to pass, to bark at him, and then to run down the steps to invite him into the house. Soon Ellen managed to buy Billy from his owners, and the two dogs became inseparable. They were taken for daily rides in the car, and household and vacations were often adjusted to their comfort.[5]

Unlike men, dogs were creatures Ellen could possess and control, and dismiss when she did not feel like being bothered with them. The dogs provided her an emotional prop at a time when her disillusionment with men had brought her to the verge of suicide. Her affection for dogs perhaps reveals that her anti-maleness involved sexual aversion. Perhaps her love for pets involved a feminine need to take care of some living creature. It sprang also from human egotism, the desire to dominate, to have her own way. And it made her a favored candidate for the presidency of the Richmond Society for the Prevention of Cruelty to Animals.

The Richmond SPCA had been chartered in 1892, and Ellen had become a member the following year when she paid her one-dollar fee.[6] For thirty-two years the Richmond chapter remained dormant; it became a vital force in Richmond's society only when Ellen Glasgow accepted its presidency in 1924. She was listed as the first vice president of the Society from 1911 to 1924, but she was rarely present at the annual meetings, and her work consisted of no more than contributing her name to the letterhead.[7]

A radical change occurred when Ellen grasped the helm in 1924. For twenty years under her leadership the Society prospered and exerted actual power in Richmond. The Society bought an old grocery store at 203 South Jefferson Street and turned it into an

[5] The story of Jeremy is told in *Woman Within*, 246–48; "A Celebrity of the South," *National Humane Review* (October, 1929), 13; and "Ellen Glasgow's Pet Sealyham Terrier Had Canine Personality," Richmond *Times-Dispatch*, September 8, 1929, p. 14.

[6] Interview with Mrs. Arthur Perkins, Richmond, November 15, 1968; SPCA Scrapbook, Ellen Glasgow Memorial Shelter, Richmond.

[7] "Minutes of the Richmond SPCA," scattered dates, Ellen Glasgow Memorial Shelter, Richmond.

animal shelter. The cost was six thousand dollars, half of which Ellen paid out of her own pocket.[8] She had letterheads printed with the motto "Help is Better than Sympathy" and immediately set to work. She turned the SPCA into a social organization with a non-rotating board of directors manned by the elite of Richmond. The annual meeting of the board was often held at One West Main Street and ranked as one of the gala social events of the year.[9] In a mimeographed letter to the members written in January, 1926, Ellen urged them to attend the annual meeting at her home, promising that it would be most interesting, because of the progress made in the development of the shelter, a dog pound, and "horse exchanges."[10] The members came, enjoyed the party, discussed the plight of the homeless animals of Richmond, and contributed their money, some because they were genuinely concerned with the work, and others because they were afraid to refuse Miss Ellen. In time the board came to include Henry Anderson, the editors of Richmond's leading newspapers, and most of Ellen's close friends.

For Ellen, however, the work of the Society was far more than a social event. She kept the commissioner of Virginia highways stirred up over the inhumane treatment of mules used in construction work, and she waged such a vigorous battle against vivisection that she all but defeated research work in Richmond medical circles.[11] She even wrote the American ambassador, Alexander Weddell, a native of Richmond, and protested the torture of horses in Argentina, a protest that must have seemed absurd to the natives of that country where horses were so plentiful that even beggars rode them.[12] She used her friendship with Douglas Southall Freeman, editor of the Richmond *News Leader*, in an attempt to enlist that paper as an active ally. Freeman, a member of the board of directors of the SPCA, gave his support when the cause seemed worthy and

8 Interview with Mrs. Arthur Perkins.

9 Interview with Mrs. Garland S. Sydnor, Jr., Richmond, November 14, 1968.

10 John Stewart Bryan Papers, Virginia Historical Society, Richmond.

11 H. G. Shirley to Ellen Glasgow, April 26, 1929, Firm of Munford, Hunton, Williams and Anderson to Ellen Glasgow, January 26, 1926, Dr. J. Shelton Horsley to Ellen Glasgow, May 19, 1927, all in Glasgow Papers. Dr. William Porter to MKR, Rawlings Papers.

12 Alexander Weddell to Ellen Glasgow, July 18, 1936, in Glasgow Papers.

managed to find some tactful excuse when it did not.[13] He always maintained a cordial relationship with the president of the Society and perhaps contributed to her extraordinary success.

When not working for the Society and the welfare of dogs in the flesh, Ellen indulged her interest in animals by collecting manufactured dogs. It became her chief hobby, and her collection of china, porcelain, and pottery dogs grew to seventy-eight pieces by the time of her death and came to occupy a place of importance in Richmond's Valentine Museum. She catalogued them herself, giving a brief description of the various items and something about the conditions under which they were acquired. They include Staffordshire, Rockingham, Crown Derby, lustre, Whieldon, Chelsea, Leeds, Worcester, Bow Derby, and ironstone ware. There are more than thirty pairs of Staffordshire spaniels, the most popular dogs of Victorian England and a breed that has become rare both in china and in life. They were sometimes called "comforters," and chains around their necks indicate that they belonged to the plain folk of England. Ellen owned a pair that she said stood for a hundred years on the same mantelpiece in a house in Goochland County, Virginia, and which an expert in New York told her were the best that he had ever seen.[14]

There are other pairs and singles that came from England or Italy that were gifts from her friends or purchases made during her visits to those countries. A pair of Rockingham poodles, the traditional pets of the British aristocracy, was given to her by Lady Eve in London in 1927 and was reported to be 110 years old at that time. In England, Carrie Duke bought her a spaniel said to be the smallest Chelsea dog ever made, and Ellen bought for herself a pair of bronze lustre ware hounds which the dealers in England said was the only pair they had ever seen. A pair of Whieldon ware poodles she listed as "my pets" and noted that they came from William Wordsworth's Grassmere and belonged to the eighteenth century. Her most valuable piece was a Crown Derby pointer, dated 1780,

[13] Ellen Glasgow to Douglas Freeman, November 19, 1924, Douglas Freeman to Ellen Glasgow, December 10, 1924, and January 22, 1935, all in Freeman Papers.
[14] Ellen Glasgow's listing of her collection is preserved in the Glasgow Papers.

and sent to her as a gift from her British publisher in 1928.[15] James
Branch Cabell, who shared her interest in ceramic dogs on a somewhat smaller scale, gave her a Chinese Scribe's water dog, dated
1680. The menagerie occupied a glass cabinet in Ellen's study and
overflowed to mantelpieces, desks, tables, and other display areas
around the house.[16]

The Glasgow collection of china dogs is extraordinarily fine, and
as a hobby it was an interesting and innocent enough pastime for
Ellen. It was offensive to no one and remains a valuable contribution to the knowledge and history of that particular form of art.
Ellen's interest in the real creatures, however, is another story. Her
friends and acquaintances often found her excessive attachment to
dogs repulsive and attributed it to various causes, not always complimentary. A distant relative said her love of dogs was a compensation for her deafness; she could talk to a dog and need no answer.[17]
Irita Van Doren, Ellen's friend and literary executor, thought that
Ellen's love of animals was a fetish and that many of her remarks
about dogs were nauseating.[18]

Some of the stories told about Ellen Glasgow and dogs seem to
provide ample evidence that her acquaintances had good reason to
be offended by her attitude toward dogs. During a vacation in
Spain when it appeared that a hired driver was going to take her to
see a bull fight, Ellen poked him in the back with her umbrella
until she made him understand that she did not want to see a bull-
fight.[19] Perhaps it was during the same trip that Ellen heard about
a bus that ran off of a cliff in Spain in order to keep from hitting a
dog. Upon hearing the story Ellen's first comment was, "What happened to the dog?"[20] At least one Richmond doctor thought that
Ellen's love of dogs was a manifestation of an unhealthy personality,
as when being shown an old magazine cartoon depicting a woman

15 C. S. Evans to Ellen Glasgow, December 21, 1928, *ibid.*
16 Jane Davenport Reid, "The Ellen Glasgow Collection of Ceramic Dogs," *Commonwealth*, XVI (February, 1949), 13, 30, 31.
17 "Notes for a Biography of Ellen Glasgow," in Rawlings Papers.
18 Irita Van Doren to MKR, *ibid.*
19 Roberta Wellford to MKR, *ibid.*
20 Interview with Mr. Glasgow Clark, Richmond, November 14, 1968.

kneeling beside the gravestone of "Fido" with the caption "Puppies or Humanity?" Ellen became visibly shaken. The same doctor, irate because of the threat Ellen had posed to medical research, believed that her excessive affection for animals, as if they were people, represented an aberrant emotional outlet resulting from lack of sexual fulfillment.[21] The evidence is clear that from the time she became president of the SPCA she displayed a greater emotional attachment to dogs than to men, but to attribute her love for animals to sexual frustration is probably too facile an explanation. She continued to pursue the male of her own species with glee, probably unaware of some latent hope that she would land her man yet, or at least break some hearts in the process.

One man who had the misfortune to become acquainted with Ellen at the time she was beginning to separate from Anderson was Hugh Walpole, British writer, lecturer, and confirmed bachelor. In 1920 he came to America to give a series of lectures, and Ellen invited him to visit her in Richmond.[22] Walpole came in April, perhaps more interested in visiting James Branch Cabell than Ellen Glasgow, but he stayed at One West Main Street and was entertained in a lavish style. He was even treated to a private concert on Ellen's back porch by the Negro Sabbath Glee Club. When he departed he and Ellen were on a first-name basis, and Ellen was far more infatuated with him than he was with her. An exchange of warm letters followed in which Ellen praised his books and he thanked her for her hospitality. Flattery agreed with Walpole, and he wrote Ellen that he thought of Richmond as his American home.[23] She was thrilled and began to express her eagerness to visit Walpole in his own home in England and to assure him that "at any hour of any day your American home awaits you."[24] Her letters grew longer and increased in warmth with repeated emphasis on her desire to visit him in England. She even pleaded with him to help her recover from absorption in her personal life and find her place again

[21] Dr. William Porter to MKR, in Rawlings Papers.
[22] Ellen Glasgow to Hugh Walpole, February 2, 1920, in Walpole Papers.
[23] July 23, 1920, in Glasgow Papers.
[24] August 10, 1920, in Walpole Papers.

in the literary world. And after she named her dog for his character Jeremy, she added that the dog was at her side, "barking his love to you."[25]

Walpole did not reciprocate her enthusiasm. He made the mistake of saying that *One Man in His Time* was not as good as Ellen's earlier work, and he apparently incurred a mild portion of her wrath.[26] The minor rift was repaired, and he visited again in Richmond in 1922 and 1926.[27] Hugh Walpole never had a high opinion of Ellen Glasgow as a writer. He accused her of "a fierce clutching of her literary reputation," and the chances are that he strongly disapproved of female writers in general.[28] But his and Ellen's friendship lasted for a decade with brief interruptions when she would become agitated over something he had said, exactly as she had responded to some of Anderson's innocent remarks. In 1927 she visited him briefly in England;[29] but three years later when she wrote him that she expected to be in England and wished to call upon him, he did not answer her letter. At first she was hurt, then offended, and finally bitter, and their friendship came to an end.[30] Such a conclusion was perhaps inevitable, for Ellen was hypersensitive to criticism and had a tendency to grasp her friends possessively, while Walpole easily, and no doubt correctly, might have construed her excessive attentions toward him as a threat to his cherished bachelorhood.

The bitter ending of their friendship may have confirmed in Ellen's mind that the Barren Ground philosophy she had formulated in 1925 was sound. Or it may have shown only that this particular woman was simply unable to sustain a happy relationship with any man. Nevertheless, surprisingly, Ellen had friends who never saw this tragic weakness, this abnormality, in her makeup, did not be-

25 March 29, 1921 and August 30, 1921, April 29, 1922, *Ibid.*

26 Hugh Walpole to Ellen Glasgow, July 24, 1922, August 16, 1922, November 2, 1922, in Glasgow Papers.

27 Rupert Hart-Davis, *Hugh Walpole: A Biography* (New York: Macmillan Co., 1952), 228, 274, 281.

28 *Ibid.*, 281.

29 Ellen Glasgow to Hugh Walpole, July 6, 1927, in Walpole Papers; Hugh Walpole to Ellen Glasgow, July 9, 1927, in Glasgow Papers.

30 Carl Van Vechten to Oliver L. Steele, September, 1960, in Van Vechten Papers.

lieve it was there, and were shocked that such a gay and wholesome person as Ellen Glasgow could author such a book as *Barren Ground*, the book she regarded as the watershed in her personal and literary life.

The writer Carl Van Vechten was one such friend.[31] The Ellen Glasgow he knew was the woman vacationing on Cape Cod in the summer of 1925. Accompanied by Anne Virginia, Jeremy, Billy, and her niece, Ellen seemed happy enough. The weather was hot and mosquitoes were plentiful, and she played golf with paper napkins wrapped around her legs and arms to protect them from the insects. Her game was never very good, but she laughed and enjoyed herself, revealing nothing of the woman who had written *Barren Ground*. She was the happy, carefree person whom Carl Van Vechten knew. But Henry Anderson, and to a far lesser degree, Hugh Walpole, knew that the Ellen who had written *Barren Ground* was just as real, if not more so, as the Ellen who laughed and played golf on the shores of Cape Cod.

A man who saw both sides and was able to live with both sides of Ellen Glasgow was Joseph Collins, one of the founders of the Neurological Institute of New York. He was a friend of Dr. Pearce Bailey, the doctor who had been fond of Ellen earlier but who died before the publication of *Barren Ground*. Dr. Collins, a bachelor, was interested primarily in abnormal psychology. He had a taste for things literary and perhaps a more-than-scientific interest in the psychology of writers. He wrote a number of books, none of which added much to the medical or literary professions, but which were couched in terms that appealed to the prurient interests of the populace. Two of them mention Ellen in a manner perhaps deliberately calculated to please her but sadly lacking in any serious information about her.[32] In other books he included an analysis of the female personality, psychological sketches of certain writers, discussions of various sexual aberrations and advocacy of the liber-

---

[31] Carl Van Vechten to Ellen Glasgow, April 18, 1925, in Glasgow Papers.
[32] Collins, *The Doctor Looks at Love and Life* (Garden City, N.Y.: Garden City Publishing Co., 1926), 205, contains a few words of praise for *The Romantic Comedians*; and *Taking the Literary Pulse* (New York: George H. Doran Co., 1924), 68–72, praises her for telling the truth about life in a good writing style.

ation of sex from the bonds of church and tradition.[33] He was undoubtedly devoted to his profession and the promotion of knowledge within it, and it was no more than an accident that his attitudes toward medicine and literature caused him to have a great deal in common with Ellen Glasgow.

Some writers went to Dr. Collins for medical treatment, and this may have been the way Ellen first met him. Their relationship became more social than medical, however, and he visited her in Richmond and she visited him in his apartment in New York. True or not, he liked to think of himself as one of her lovers and once bragged that he and Ellen had had a "very close relationship indeed."[34] Although they saw each other infrequently they became lifelong friends, a feat that may be attributed to Collins' talents as a psychologist since he was the only man with whom Ellen maintained a sustained and satisfying relationship.

Some of Ellen's friends, however, found Joseph Collins objectionable. One woman thought he was a sinister-looking man who was involved in an illicit relationship with another lady of her and Ellen's acquaintance.[35] According to one report, it was well known that he was homosexual. Sometimes he was accompanied by young boys in public and allegedly had a French boy living with him to whom he was especially devoted and about whom Ellen expressed concern. At a cocktail party in the late 1930's, shortly after the publication of John Steinbeck's *Of Mice and Men*, Collins frankly explained that Lennie, a character in the novel, received sexual gratification every time he squeezed anything, especially a rat. That interpretation, which was not uncommon, was of particular interest to Ellen, who was not exactly unfamiliar with the problem of bestiality. At any rate, she found it amusing and laughingly called Collins a dirty-minded old man who was fond of French boys.[36] Such

[33] Collins, *The Doctor Looks at Marriage and Medicine* (Garden City, N.Y.: Doubleday, Doran and Co., 1928); *The Doctor Looks at Literature* (New York: George H. Doran Co., 1923), *The Doctor Looks at Life and Death* (New York: Farrar and Rinehart, 1931).

[34] Source withheld.

[35] Source withheld.

[36] A description of this party by an eyewitness is preserved in the Rawlings Papers.

conversation, even in public, was apparently not offensive to either and perhaps even characteristic of their friendship. But it was not characteristic of most of Ellen's social relationships, and generally her allusions to sex in conversation and in her books were tactfully and satirically restrained to the kind of light banter that takes place among the characters in one of her most popular novels, *The Romantic Comedians*.

In a matter of only a few months in the summer of 1926, Ellen wrote *The Romantic Comedians*, a novel as light and entertaining as *Barren Ground* had been dark and depressing. It was a novel, as she said later, written as an experiment for her own private diversion.[37] The experiment was extraordinarily successful, and her private diversion became the delight of thousands of readers. Ironically, in spite of the marked contrast between *Barren Ground* and *The Romantic Comedians*, the latter novel was written from precisely the same motivations that inspired the tale of Dorinda Oakley's grim pilgrimage through life. In *Barren Ground* Ellen poured out her own most private emotions that had tormented her during the crisis years of her relationship with Henry Anderson. In *The Romantic Comedians*, in which she was really making fun of Anderson in particular and the whole area of male psychology, she disguised those same emotions by laughing heartily at what she insisted was the tragic fate of her hero who was unable to control his passions.[38] In *Barren Ground* she celebrated the bizarre courage and victory of the female; in *The Romantic Comedians* she satirized what she considered to be the tragic weakness of the male.

Set in Richmond in 1923, *The Romantic Comedians* is the story of Judge Gamaliel Bland Honeywell, an aging lawyer of sixty-five who has just buried his faithful wife of thirty-six years and now wishes to take a girl of twenty-three as his bride. The girl, Annabel Upchurch, yields to the urgings of her mother, whose motivations are entirely financial, and accepts the Judge's proposal. Amanda Lightfoot, the belle to whom the Judge had been engaged as a youth, no longer attracts him because she is old, but she has re-

[37] *A Certain Measure,* 211.
[38] *Ibid.,* 223.

mained "faithful" to him all of her life. The Judge's twin sister, Mrs. Edmonia Bredalbane, has run safely through four marriages and constantly reminds the Judge of his age. She reminded him also that "in the case of twins, there is usually a strong and a weak one, and, fortunately for me, I was the strong one of us two."[39] She tries to encourage the Judge to forget Annabel and marry Amanda, but the Judge cannot be dissuaded and the marriage takes place.

The honeymoon was somewhat exhausting for Honeywell, and in a matter of months Annabel ran away with a man her own age. Annabel's mother frantically hoped that her daughter's new lover was not a lover "in the discreditable European sense of the word; merely her lover in the superior, though more tragic, American fashion."[40] It is a most revealing distinction to be drawn by Ellen Glasgow, who in her day perhaps made love on both continents, but who undoubtedly thought of her own recent love affairs as the superior and tragic American variety. The different attitudes toward love affairs in America and Europe are further explained by Mrs. Bredalbane, who ought to know: "As provincial as you are in America, it is hopeless to try to make you understand that behaviour as much as beauty is a question of geography, and that my respectability increases with every mile of the distance I travel from Queenborough [Richmond]. In France, my reputation is above reproach; by the time I reach Vienna, I have become a bit of a prude; and contrasted with the Balkan temperament, I am little more than a tombstone to female virtue."[41] That Balkan temperament had cost Ellen one fiancé, and it is no coincidence that various characters in the novel see the World War as marking a major change in the social code. But poor Judge Honeywell, only a male and a lawyer like Henry Anderson, is not bright enough to share the observations of his twin sister. He only knows that he has lost Annabel and feels much older than his sixty-six years. Inevitably, he notes that there is no comfort in philosophy or religion. He checks into a hospital supposedly to die. But his vital functions perk

39 *The Romantic Comedians*, 226.
40 *Ibid.*, 270–71.
41 *Ibid.*, 310.

up when he notices a nurse even younger than Annabel and thinks: "There is the woman I ought to have married!"[42]

*The Romantic Comedians* owes almost as much to Henry Anderson as *Barren Ground* did, for Ellen accused Anderson of chasing after a group of younger people in a vain effort to remain young.[43] It is no coincidence that Judge Honeywell is a lawyer without morals, that the World War has had an extraordinary social impact even upon Richmond, and that the female character in the book who is happiest is one with the "tranquil immunity of a mind that had finished with love."[44]

As with *Barren Ground* the critics raved. The public, which had shunned *Barren Ground*, bought *The Romantic Comedians*, and within a few months of its publication in September, 1926, more than 100,000 copies had been sold.[45] The Book-of-the-Month Club used it for its November selection, and at a 15 percent royalty Ellen began to pocket one of her largest earnings from a novel. Publicly, Joseph Collins announced that "Miss Glasgow knows the pathology of love as well as the psychology."[46] He said that Judge Honeywell was a good example of consistent behavior and that the love of an old man burns as fiercely and more devastatingly than that of youth.[47] Privately, he suggested to Ellen that she should have allowed her judge to do more lovemaking.[48]

For the taste of Richmond, however, the Judge did quite enough. The book caused a mild sensation in Ellen's hometown, as one critic summed up: "How indelicate to probe beneath a Virginian gentleman's delightful exterior!"[49] Ellen no doubt enjoyed the agitation in Richmond, for, from her earliest novel, she had been a rebel against the customs of her native city and state. When she turned to

---

[42] *Ibid.,* 345.
[43] *Woman Within,* 244.
[44] *The Romantic Comedians,* 305.
[45] Kelly, "Struggle for Recognition," 239.
[46] Collins, "Ellen Glasgow's New Novel A Tragedy of Old Age," *New York Times Book Review* (September 12, 1926), 5.
[47] *The Doctor Looks at Love and Life,* 205.
[48] To Ellen Glasgow, n.d., in Glasgow Papers.
[49] Eudora Ramsay Richardson, "Richmond and Its Writers," *Bookman,* LXVIII (December, 1928), 451.

the satirical treatment of one of Virginia's most idolized institutions, the gentleman, she consummated this rebellion with an unprecedented *coup de grâce* and accidentally hit upon the literary style that was her forte.

She planned to repeat the performance on a more elaborate scale, but for the moment she was tired. Even though *The Romantic Comedians* had "bubbled out in one year"[50] and might appear to the casual reader to have been a relaxing exercise coming so soon after *Barren Ground*, Ellen was exhausted from the sheer labor of the task and still not entirely free from the emotional trauma that had inspired both it and *Barren Ground*. The good reviews and large sales no doubt helped her feelings, but they were not enough. She planned another trip to England, both as a means of relaxation and as a kind of triumphant entry during which she would renew her friendship with British writers and present herself as at least one American writer worthy of their acceptance.

Ostensibly, the purpose of the trip was to take various European cures for her troublesome nerves. At least that is what she told her brother Arthur, who usually responded to such a letter with a check to cover the expenses of the cure. Although a doctor could not find anything wrong with her, she complained that anytime she tried to make a decision she felt completely exhausted, and she hoped that the doctor would suggest a summer in England.[51] She was hinting for her brother's financial assistance and seeking her doctor's sanction for a trip she intended to make anyway. The decision was made, and in June, 1927, she sailed with Carrie Duke on the S.S. *Olympic*. Henry Anderson wired flowers to her on the ship and wished her a bon voyage.[52]

The farther the S.S. *Olympic* moved from America the better Ellen began to feel. In England she did take the waters, perhaps as much because it was a fashionable thing to do as because it was supposed to have some medicinal value, and her trip became a pleasant social event rather than merely another chapter in her medical his-

50 Ellen Glasgow to William H. F. Lamont, February 19, 1928, in *Letters*, 90.
51 To Arthur Glasgow, April 11, May 5, 1927, in Glasgow Papers.
52 To Ellen Glasgow, June 18, 1927, *ibid.*

tory. She arrived in London and spent some time with her brother at Moncorvo House. And she mailed picture postcards to "Mr. Billy Bennett" and "Mr. Jeremy Glasgow" at One West Main Street, Richmond, Virginia. She sent Billy a picture of a landscape where she thought he would like to run and said that she hoped that he and "precious Jeremy" had had their drive today.[53] On other cards, she sent Billy a picture of a Skye Terrier, which she thought he might like to have for a playmate; and she sent Jeremy a picture of a Sealyham so that he could see the stock from which he had sprung.[54] And finally she sent "Mr. William Bennett" a postcard picture of the first Girls' Sunday School in Gloucester with the note on the back: "A Sunday School for darling Billy to chew."[55] Ellen not only wrote cards to Jeremy and Billy, she also had clothes and collars especially made for them in London.

From London she went to Harrogate where she soaked herself in sulfur baths; and from Harrogate she embarked, with the aid of Arthur's car and chauffeur, on a motor trip over most of England. She was interested primarily in dogs, ruined cathedrals, almshouses, and writers. In August she met the Duchess of Hamilton, a lady who had nine dogs as her daily companions, which had been given to her by a policeman who had rescued them from a sack as they were being taken to a medical college. The Sealyham she discovered to be the most fashionable breed in England and she yearned for one to take home with her, but she finally decided that Jeremy and Billy did not need a companion. She was thrilled to discover that there was a branch of the humane society in almost every village in England and that her heart was not wrung constantly by the sight of work animals along the road.[56] Compared to Virginia she thought that England was a paradise for dumb creatures.[57] By accident she stumbled upon the Animal Rescue League in a poor section of London and discovered a small house owned by three women where

[53] To Mr. Billy Bennett, July 3, 1927, *ibid.*
[54] To Billy Bennett, July 10, 1927; to Jeremy Glasgow, July 10, 1927, *ibid.*
[55] August 31, 1927, *ibid.*
[56] Ellen Glasgow to Anne Virginia Bennett, August 7, 1927, in *Letters*, 86.
[57] Ellen Glasgow to Rebe Tutwiler, August 11, 1927, Ellen Glasgow to Anne Virginia Bennett, August 19, 1927, in Glasgow Papers.

fifty-one thousand animals had been put to death during the last year. The mere thought made her rather sick, but she said she was glad to see what people and animals have to endure.[58] Since the deceased animals were beyond her reach, she lavished her sympathy upon the poor women who had to live in such an environment.

The poor, as long as they were at a safe distance and not likely to interfere with her life, had always been a special object of her sympathy. That sympathy, coupled with her appreciation of the British literature that had celebrated the poor, caused her to find the almshouses of England particularly fascinating. In every village where it was possible she visited the almshouse. At the almshouse in Dorchester, to which Thomas Hardy referred her, she discovered one old woman and six old men, "and the old woman complained of the old men to us exactly as if she had been married to all of them!"[59] At Glastonbury, the almshouse was composed of seven tiny cottages where seven old women lived. Each had a tiny flower garden by the door, and one was filled with roses. Ellen stopped at the one with the roses and met a Mrs. Curtis who lived there with her crippled daughter and raised roses while trying to exist on the pittance allotted to them. Ellen gave her some money and then talked with her about roses. When Mrs. Curtis discovered that yellow roses were Ellen's favorite, she promised to raise one from a slip and name it "Ellen Glasgow." The movement of time, however, obliterated the woman and her roses, and Ellen's botanical namesake never came to be.[60]

For the moment she was more interested in buildings that were enhanced by the movement of time, the abbeys and cathedrals that had been celebrated frequently in English literature. In fact, she spent a major part of her vacation visiting them, an interesting pastime for a woman who had so little use for that faith for which they supposedly stood. She visited Waltham, Bath, Tintern, and Fountains abbeys, plus a number of more obscure places; and she was particularly impressed by the beauty she found in ruins. Time and

58 To Anne Virginia Bennett, August 14, 1927, Glasgow Papers.
59 To Rebe Tutwiler, August 24, 1927, *ibid.*
60 Copy of a letter from Ellen Glasgow to Rebe Tutwiler, August 31, 1927, in Rawlings Papers. See also *Woman Within*, 254–56.

again she wrote: "England has certainly reason to be grateful to Henry VIII who destroyed abbeys and created ruins!"[61] The English cathedrals she thought to be the most beautiful ever built by man, and she could not decide whether York or Canterbury was her favorite.[62] The home of Gray's "Elegy Written in a Country Churchyard" thrilled her. A trip through Burnham Beeches with its beech trees as large as California redwoods, she said, was so beautiful that it hurt and reinforced her belief that trees have spirits.[63] She shopped for antiques and clothes, but nothing meant as much to her or stuck so soundly in her memory as the beauty of the ruined abbeys and cathedrals.

Not even her visits with British writers excited her as much in the long run as the abbeys. She postponed a trip to Westminster Cathedral in order to have lunch with Frank Swinnerton, but she later went back to see the cathedral.[64] She wrote Carl Van Vechten that she had had "a beautiful time with Hugh [Walpole] in London," but she failed to mention that visit in her autobiography which was written some years after the end of her friendship with Walpole.[65] Her efforts to see Virginia Woolf, whose works she admired immensely, were all in vain. Her visit with May Sinclair was depressing, because May Sinclair had been crippled by a stroke or paralysis and had become overweight.[66] Joseph Conrad had died in 1924, and his widow greeted her cordially but was no substitute for the famous novelist.[67] Mr. and Mrs. Harold Nicolson spent a full day with her and introduced her to the essence of English hospitality, although virtually the only thing Ellen had in common with them was the same publisher in London.[68]

Perhaps it was Thomas Hardy whom she looked forward to see-

[61] To Anne Virginia Bennett, July 27, 1927, in Glasgow Papers; copy of a letter to Rebe Tutwiler, July 30, 1927, in Rawlings Papers.

[62] To Anne Virginia Bennett, July 27, 1927, to Rebe Tutwiler, August 11, 1927, in Glasgow Papers.

[63] To Rebe Tutwiler, July 30, August 11, 1927, *ibid.*

[64] Frank Swinnerton to Ellen Glasgow, August 13, 1927, *ibid.*

[65] July 27, 1927, in Van Vechten Papers.

[66] May Sinclair to Ellen Glasgow, August 9, 1927, Ellen Glasgow to Anne Virginia Bennett, August 14, 1927, in Glasgow Papers.

[67] Ellen Glasgow to Anne Virginia Bennett, August 25, 1927, in *Letters*, 87–89.

[68] *Woman Within*, 257.

ing most. Although he had become old and ill, he greeted her as cordially as he had done thirteen years earlier and acted as if he were genuinely glad she had come. But his beloved wire-haired terrier Wessex had died of old age only a few months before Ellen's visit and had been buried in the Hardys' garden.[69] Hardy showed Ellen the grave, and the two of them stood there and mourned. Yet she called Thomas Hardy "the youngest old man that ever lived," and believed that her visit with him was among the highlights of her summer.[70]

Ellen's visits with the celebrities, however, was in no way comparable to the excitement of her trip of 1914 or to what she had expected when she left home in June. Thirteen years and the World War had wrought many changes, and she must have felt a little like a relic of the past. The image of herself she took home and preserved was the lonely woman wandering through almshouses and ruined abbeys and the Burnham Beeches, not the famous writer who had rubbed shoulders with others of her breed in another country.

In the moorland country she felt "absolutely alone with the earth as God made it" and in tune with the landscape that most perfectly expressed her feeling toward life.[71] On a late August afternoon she had her chauffeur drive her and Carrie Duke out to Dartmoor. Ellen deserted the car and wandered for hours over the heath, until she came to a low hill called "Gibbet Tor" where people used to be hanged. She added some small white stones to a little pile, as was the custom of visitors to that lonely spot. The bracing air rustled her skirt and chilled her hands and face as she watched the sun set over the moors. The color of the heather changed from purple to brown to russet black and finally to a kind of brown and violet darkness. Ellen stood there on the summit of the world, alone and forsaken, savoring the bittersweet taste of melancholia, the roundness of the earth curving away from her.[72]

---

69 *Ibid.*, 199.

70 To Helen MacAfee, January 31, 1928, in *Letters*, 89.

71 *Woman Within*, 257.

72 Copy of a letter from Ellen Glasgow to Rebe Tutwiler, August 26, 1927, in Rawlings Papers.

That feeling lasted but a night. In less than two weeks her ship docked at New York. Henry Anderson wired gardenias to her on board, and he was waiting on the shore to welcome her home.[73] In Richmond she dropped back into her prosaic existence. She tried to resign from the board of trustees of the Richmond Public Library, a position she had held for only two years, but the mayor refused to accept her resignation for at least four months, and by then she had weathered the crisis that caused her to attempt to resign.[74] That crisis was a controversy over whether the Richmond Public Library should buy Sinclair Lewis' *Elmer Gantry*. Some felt the novel advocated vice and hypocrisy and was unfit for the Richmond library, but Ellen was quick to express her unequivocal opposition to such censorship.[75] She explained that those who did not like the book did not have to borrow it and added that although Mr. Lewis was an important novelist, he was no master of his art and his "four hundred and thirty-two unalluring pages" read "more like a moral tract than a novel." Perhaps she recalled the days when she craved books so desperately and found them unavailable in Richmond. At any rate, she was a staunch friend of the public library and on at least one occasion attended a convention of librarians with James Branch Cabell and insisted upon staying after the session until she had shaken hands with every librarian present.[76]

James Branch Cabell, though he had the disadvantage in Ellen's mind of being a male, was beginning to occupy a role of increasing importance in her career. They had never been close until he wrote a favorable review of *Barren Ground*, and then their friendship blossomed overnight. Yet it was more professional than personal and was largely a case of two weary travelers of different temperaments stranded together in a tiny oasis in the "Sahara of the Bozart." In 1927 Cabell published a new book, *Something About Eve:*

[73] Ellen Glasgow to Anne Virginia Bennett, September 14, 1927, in Glasgow Papers.
[74] J. Fulian Bright to Ellen Glasgow, May 21, 1928, *ibid*.
[75] "Ellen Glasgow on Censorship and Sinclair Lewis," *American Library Association Bulletin*, LVI (July, 1962), 618. Two letters from Ellen Glasgow to the librarian, March 14, 1927, and August 23, 1928.
[76] Miss Throckmorton to MKR, in Rawlings Papers. See also Thomas P. Ayer to Ellen Glasgow, April 3, 1926, in Glasgow Papers.

*A Comedy of Fig-Leaves*, dedicated "To Ellen Glasgow—very naturally—this book which commemorates the intelligence of women." In his preface to that volume in a collected edition of his works, Cabell explained that his purpose was to exonerate the role of woman in the beguilement of man.[77] The theme of the story is man's attempt to find fulfillment in a region called Antan, which is the home of all poets.[78] The hero who travels that "woman-haunted way" never quite makes it, but his lingerings are because of his own human weaknesses, not the fault of the women.

Ellen appreciated the dedication, but she was convinced that the book told more about Adam than Eve and accused Cabell of saying that only the man aspired toward unattainable perfection while the woman desired only more of man.[79] Cabell liked to joke with Ellen over their differing interpretations of the roles of the sexes and once remarked, "Ellen, it seems to me that your ladies do not always behave like gentlemen." To which Ellen replied, "But James, I am sure that your gentlemen are very often ladies." Each had a splendid sense of humor, but perhaps Ellen got the upper hand when she noted dryly that "The funniest word James ever wrote was the word 'Episcopalian' in *Who's Who*."[80]

The joking ended, however, when their respective publishers began to bring out collected editions of their works at about the same time. By 1930 Doubleday had produced the first four volumes of the *Old Dominion Edition* of the works of Ellen Glasgow, and the McBride Company had started to bring out the *Storisende Edition* of the works of James Branch Cabell. Ellen and Cabell agreed that each would review the collected edition of the other. Cabell's review appeared in April, 1930, and reiterated his belief that Ellen's books composed a complete social history of Virginia. He added

[77] New York: Robert M. McBride & Co., *Storisende Edition*, 1929, xiii.
[78] Desmond Tarrant, *James Branch Cabell: The Dream and the Reality* (Norman: University of Oklahoma Press, 1967), 183.
[79] *A Certain Measure*, 233–34.
[80] Julian R. Meade, *I Live in Virginia* (New York: Longmans, Green and Co., 1935), 193, 194. See also Virginius Dabney, "Prophet of the New South," New York *Herald Tribune*, August 25, 1929, Sec. 12, p. 18.

that her theme was "The Tragedy of Everywoman, as it was lately enacted in the Southern States of America," a theme which he found "dreadful" and "embarrassing." In comparing her work to his own, he could only conclude "that never while life lasts can the two sexes quite understand each other," but he ended by contending that hers was art of a superb quality.[81]

Ellen returned the favor. In less than two months she announced that Cabell's multi-volumed Biography of Manuel "sins in being superior." She slyly chided him for creating male characters who were no more than apes reft of their tails and embarrassed because they had not yet adjusted their fig leaves, and for his males' "indestructible capacity to be shocked by the loss of prudery in woman." But she concluded that he alone among American writers had dared "to look into the encompassing void and to laugh because it is bottomless."[82]

The mutual criticism with Cabell was a fortunate event in the development of Ellen as a writer and as a critic, because it became a facet of her broader evaluation of the novel in the South. Two years before she and Cabell wrote their reviews of each other's works, Ellen had produced an essay entitled "The Novel in the South," which exhibits a penetrating knowledge of her subject and her region, and hints that she had a great capacity for leadership in the field of Southern letters. Although Cabell probably had little to do with the ideas expressed in it, the stimulation of his increasing friendship in the late 1920's probably encouraged Ellen's interest in criticism. Cabell himself had always been more interested in literary criticism as a form of art than Ellen had, and eventually he played a significant role in the actual writing of Ellen's major critical work.[83] But Cabell had the good sense to remain aloof from Ellen's personal problems and was the one male of her intimate acquaintance during the decade of the 1920's whose influence upon her writ-

[81] James Branch Cabell, "Two Sides of the Shielded," *New York Herald Tribune Books* (April 20, 1930), 1, 6.

[82] Ellen Glasgow, "The Biography of Manuel," *Saturday Review of Literature*, VI (June 7, 1930), 1108–109.

[83] *A Certain Measure.*

ing was more professional than personal. Ellen's essay on the novel in the South reinforced Cabell's contention that she was a social historian.

"The Novel in the South" takes a strictly historical format and is as much a comment on the history of the South as it is a criticism of Southern letters.[84] In the aftermath of Reconstruction, Ellen contended, historians and novelists were not allowed to interrogate. Instead, they found a retreat in Old Virginia for almost every mortal dwelling except the imagination of man. The Old South, she said, generated "complacency, self-satisfaction, a blind contentment with things as they are and a deaf aversion from things as they might be," which stifled both "the truth of literature and the truth of life" and settled "like a cloud of honey bees over the creative faculties of the race." Bringing her pet peeves and her undying wit to play, she said that the Southern gentleman's certainty that he had been created in the image of his Maker gave him dignity and "confirmed his faith in the wisdom of his Creator." And, of course, the gentleman's favorite institution was the Protestant Episcopal Church, which was "charitable toward almost every weakness except the dangerous practice of thinking."[85]

The Civil War and Reconstruction afflicted the mind of the South with "a bitter nostalgia" and resulted in "a mournful literature of commemoration." Such literature she found "false to human behavior" and therefore doomed to extinction. The South had been content to borrow rather than to create, and no literary magic could be worked until the Southern novelist "forgot that he had been born, by the grace of God, a Southern gentleman."[86] Southern novelists who after the turn of the century began to forget the old days and to concentrate upon human imperfections rather than so-called inherited perfections, awakened an interest in ideas and held the future of Southern letters in their hands. Like so many of the younger Southern writers, Ellen had come to view the industrial development of the South as a threat to destroy the very

[84] Ellen Glasgow, "The Novel in the South," *Harper's Magazine*, CLVIII (December, 1928), 93–100.
[85] *Ibid.*, 95.
[86] *Ibid.*, 96.

conditions that nourished the lives of Southern artists and therefore a powerful stimulation of an impressive mass of literature of revolt.

The term "New South" had already become the popular label for the post-Reconstruction South caught in the throes of industrial development and social readjustment. Ellen characterized the era as accurately as any professional historian could have done and pointed out its significance for the future of Southern letters:

> Adaptable by nature, and eager, except in moments of passion, to conciliate rather than to offend, the modern South is in immediate peril less of revolution than of losing its individual soul in the national babel. After sixty years of mournful seclusion, the South is at last beginning to look about and to coquet with alien ideas. With an almost disdainful air, the Southern mind is turning from commemoration to achievement. Noise, numbers, size, quantity, all are exerting their lively or sinister influence. Sentiment no longer suffices. To be Southern, even to be solid, is not enough; for the ambition of the new South is not to be self-sufficing, but to be more Western than the West and more American than the whole of America. Uniformity, once despised and rejected, has become the established ideal. Satisfied for so long to leave the miscellaneous product "Americanism" to the rest of the country, the South is at last reaching out for its neglected inheritance.[87]

The advance in the South of "what the world has agreed to call education," Ellen feared, was bringing with it a corresponding decrease in the art of living, and forcing the "aesthetic emotions of the South into revolt" in a drive to perpetuate both freedom of thought, beauty, pleasure, and picturesque living. Such a drive would produce the novelists of the future, and if their novels were to be great Southern novels they must have "the elemental properties which make great novels wherever they are written in any part of the world: power, passion, pity, ecstasy and anguish, hope and despair."[88] And she believed that Southern novelists in the new era were capable of doing just that.

Ellen's prediction that it was entirely possible that the best writing in the United States would be done in the South caused her to

[87] *Ibid.*, 98.
[88] *Ibid.*, 98–99, 100.

be hailed by a young Richmond newspaper man, Virginius Dabney, as a prophet of the New South. Dabney was remarkably perceptive, and from his reading of her novels and personal interviews, he extracted her opinions on topics other than literary ones. She told him that the modern South faced three dangers: the exploitation of Southern labor by Northern capital, "mad industrialism" which would destroy the freedom and charm of living, and the surrender of intellectual integrity to the Fundamentalist point of view. Speaking of Fundamentalism, she said, "We should never bargain with the forces of ignorance," her eyes flashing angrily.[89]

And she had as little use for Prohibition as she did for Fundamentalism. Before the Prohibition amendment went into effect, she stocked her cellar thoroughly, and she unashamedly served spirits in her home throughout the dry era. She looked upon Prohibition as a sham and pretense and noted that, "In the South we are substituting murder for a mint julep and calling it progress."[90] The whole idea of Prohibition was devoid of humanity and mercy, she thought; and when a policeman remarked to her that her home was situated near the heart of the bootlegging district, she delightedly responded that she was glad to know that the bootlegging district had a heart.

She objected also to the "movies" and by 1929 had attended only three—*The Birth of a Nation*, *Oliver Twist*, and *The Man in the Iron Mask*. She enjoyed *The Birth of a Nation*, but the other two she found to be horrible distortions of the books upon which they were based.[91] Despite her penetrating insights into the era in which she lived, this prophet of the New South was far more at home in her antebellum house on Main Street and surrounded by the accoutrements of the Old South than with the supposedly stimulating conditions of the new age that would bring about a mass of literature of revolt, of which she considered herself to be the chief exponent. Her criticism of the New South perhaps concealed her preference for the Old.

89 Dabney, "A Prophet of the New South," pp. 6, 7, 18.
90 *Ibid.*, 7.
91 *Ibid.*, 18.

The roles of essayist and prophet, however, were strictly extra-curricular for Ellen Glasgow. In the late 1920's she was a novelist primarily interested in the comedy of manners, particularly the manners governing the relationship between the sexes in Richmond, Virginia. In 1929 she published *They Stooped to Folly*: *A Comedy of Morals*. The dedication read: "To James Branch Cabell . . . in acknowledgment of Something About Eve . . . this book that commemorates the chivalry of men." Chivalry was a myth, Ellen contended, epitomized by Virginius Littlepage, a fifty-six-year-old lawyer who is the leading male character in the story. According to his chaste and naïve wife, Virginius is mercifully unendowed with a "lower nature"; but in reality, beneath his impeccable exterior, his mind wanders into forbidden pastures, and his roving eye comes to rest cautiously upon the enticing charms of a mischievous divorcée. And yet he is less anxious to seduce the woman than he is to be careful not to provoke a family quarrel that might interfere with his regular rendezvous with his bootlegger. This characterization of Virginius Littlepage, Ellen no doubt believed, sufficiently proved that the myth of the chivalry of men was built upon a foundation of shifting sand.

Concomitant to the myth of the chivalry of men is the myth of the "ruined" woman. Virginius Littlepage is surrounded by three generations of Virginia ladies who stooped to folly by loving too hastily and whose degree of ruination is contingent upon the generation to which each belonged. They are Virginius' old-maid sister Agatha; the middle-aged grass widow Mrs. Dalrymple; and a young girl named Milly Burden. Agatha was ruined simply because as a young woman she had been engaged to a man who jilted her, and according to the custom of her generation she was no longer fit to belong to another. Mrs. Dalrymple, of good birth but easy virtue, had been involved in a scandal that resulted in her loss of both husband and lover, and for penance she plunged into Red Cross work in Europe during World War I. In the country of Berengaria, she became involved in heroic deeds and posed for her picture in the peasant dress of the country while presenting an American check to the Queen. That picture was published in the Sunday supplements of American newspapers, and her reputation was mightily improved. Ellen lifted this description entirely out of the life of Queen Marie of Rumania and included it in the novel as another attack upon Henry Anderson. Mrs. Dalrymple's tactics paid good dividends, and after the war she was able to hold her head erect as she walked through the streets of Richmond. Milly Burden was a child of the twentieth century, the most thoroughly ruined of the three, and the least repentant of all. She gave herself to an unstable youth, Martin Welding, who departed shortly after their liaison for the war in Europe. She never told him of her illegitimate baby, and she never admitted any qualms of regret or conscience for having loved him.

Other ladies, too, are presented as victims of the system. Louisa Goddard remained single all of her life because she had loved Virginius in silence from her youth and was the best friend of his wife. Virginius' daughter, Mary Victoria, went to the Balkans to work with the Red Cross and became infected with the moral laxity that Ellen had come to associate with that region. Mary Victoria returned home married to Martin Welding and believing that she could reform him. She could not, and he eventually left her as he had left Milly.

The completed novel was not a well-organized plot with all the traditional parts of a good story, but a series of humorous tableaux held together loosely by their relationship to Virginius Littlepage. But when it appeared in print in the fall of 1929, it was greeted with applause and compared to *The Romantic Comedians*. Most reviewers in America and in England approved, though some felt that Ellen did not develop her characters sufficiently.[92] Although the Literary Guild chose it as one of its selections, *They Stooped to Folly* suffered in comparison with *The Romantic Comedians* and did not achieve the same high level in sales as the earlier novel. Nevertheless, H. L. Mencken gave it some good advertisement when he called it "the Southern attitude toward fornication."[93] No

92 Kelly, "Struggle for Recognition," 256–57.
93 H. L. Mencken, "Two Southern Novels," *American Mercury*, XVIII (October, 1929), 251.

doubt Mencken's personal pleasure would have been increased, and perhaps his review would have been enriched, if he could have known that while the novel was in the planning stages, Ellen had announced in her annual report to the SPCA, perhaps with a mischievous grin, that "a small cat house was built by contributions of money and material given for that purpose by several of our members."[94]

Another mild sensation rippled through certain social circles in Richmond whose members were dismayed that Miss Ellen had once again exposed wild oats growing in sacred Virginia soil. Douglas S. Freeman, editor of the Richmond *News Leader*, took what was for him a characteristically cautious approach to the problem. He pointed out those areas in Richmond that Miss Ellen had used as the setting for her story and reserved his adulation for the author instead of her novel.[95] He thus produced a review that was pleasing to Ellen and inoffensive to her critics.

Ellen enjoyed creating a mild sensation in Richmond, which she took as a sure indication that she had succeeded in saturating her novel in blood and irony. Gossip she did not mind, as long as the reviews that got into print were slanted in her favor. And besides, more entertaining than anything she wrote in *They Stooped to Folly*, and during the very months that she was completing the novel, was a little charade of her own she was acting out in New York with a doctor named Ward A. Holden.

Dr. Holden was a bachelor and a friend and contemporary of Joseph Collins. In the spring of 1929 he became infatuated with Ellen, who was flattered by his fascination and teased him relentlessly. During one of her trips to New York she snuggled into his arms and rested her head on his shoulder while they watched someone try to force milk and whiskey down the throat of an ill dog in a vain effort to save its life.[96] The blood pounded through the doctor's veins, but Ellen was more interested in the dog. And she told

[94] "To the Richmond SPCA," a printed page torn from an unidentified book, in Rawlings Papers.

[95] The manuscript of Freeman's review of *They Stooped to Folly* is preserved in the Freeman Papers.

[96] Ward A. Holden to Ellen Glasgow, May 22, 1929, in Glasgow Papers.

Holden her Barren Ground philosophy; she told him that she was thankful to be "finished with all that." By way of explanation to Holden, perhaps, she added a comment that at some time she jotted down for posterity: "I have had as much love and more romance than most women, and I have not had to stroke some man the right way to win my bread or the wrong way to win my freedom."[97] But Holden was persistent and wrote her a letter, tender and intimate, that recalled their evening:

> You were fascinating that lucky Friday evening, Ellen dear! Your expressive mobile face, your wonderful waved black hair, your exquisite white shoulders and arms and tiny hands, your trim aristocratic legs, your black gown with the metal ornament applied to the left of the skirt and the varicolored soft batisk scarf that trailed behind you—all made up a picture not to be forgotten. And it was indeed lovely to hold you in my arms, and indeed delicious to kiss your sweet lips—sophisticated certainly, but not primitive![98]

Ellen was not impressed and apparently wrote back that her hair was not black and reminded him again of her Barren Ground philosophy. Holden was undaunted, and replied: "Perhaps it might have been delightful to be considered a Perfect Lover for a woman who still had illusions about love, but it would be infinitely more delightful to have a little share in the affections of one who now believes herself to be beyond such illusions." Apparently Ellen responded with a question about his life and interests; for he took her question lightly and replied in fun that he had been interested in painting and the opera, but the glory of his life had been "affectionate friendships with fine women," which, when they degenerated into love affairs, led to the usual antagonisms. He reminded her that when women ceased to be amorous, they became argumentative; and he suggested that she must have had some hard knocks "to lose so early the illusions that most women cherish to the end." He complained that her letters were too impersonal and

---

[97] "Miscellaneous Pungencies," a small collection of undated sayings in Ellen Glasgow's handwriting, *ibid*.
[98] April 29, 1929, *ibid*.

insisted that he longed to hold her in his arms no matter what thoughts filled her mind.[99]

But Ellen wandered off into a discussion of the various connotations of the words "love" and "affection" and led him toward a more philosophical than biological relationship.[100] Once he asserted that only the lovely vistas she saw would be theirs, the exact response that Ellen had elicited many times from Henry Anderson.[101] He wrote playful letters throughout the summer and apparently saw her when she stopped in New York in August. He flattered, chided, and begged. Finally, he realized it was no use and gave up.[102] The dialogue with Holden was no more than a pleasant diversion for Ellen; and it is just as well that he capitulated to her irrevocable commitment to her Barren Ground philosophy when he did, because at the end of the summer Ellen was plunged into what was for her among the greatest tragedies of her life.

On September 5, 1929, Jeremy died.

Ellen was in Maine resting from the completion of her novel and trying to escape from the strain of Jeremy's long illness when she was suddenly called home. She rushed back to Richmond in order to be with Jeremy in his last hours.[103] She found him in the final stages of pneumonia, but she believed that he recognized her before his death. Jeremy had been ill for almost a year. In December, 1928, he had had a gall bladder operation but had partially recovered. In July, 1929, his condition worsened and it became necessary for him to have a second operation. The operation was performed not by a veterinarian, but by a famous surgeon in Richmond. Specialists from New York and Philadelphia were consulted by telephone, and everything known to medicine was tried in an effort to save his life.[104] When it seemed as if he would recover, Ellen

99 May 22, 1929, June 5, June 23, *ibid.*
100 Ward A. Holden to Ellen Glasgow, July 13, 1929, *ibid.*
101 June 23, 1929, *ibid.*
102 Only two letters available after August, 1929—one dated 1932 and one dated 1936—both bespeak of an impersonal relationship. *Ibid.*
103 "A Celebrity of the South," *National Humane Review* (October, 1929), 13.
104 "Ellen Glasgow's Pet Sealyham Terrier Had Canine Personality," Richmond *Times-Dispatch*, September 8, 1929, p. 14.

went to Maine on her doctor's recommendation to try to prevent a nervous breakdown.

Her nerves were not helped much when she received the doctor's bill some weeks after Jeremy's death. She was incensed, not because of the amount, but because it read: "Services for dog." She thought it should have read: "Services for Mr. Jeremy Glasgow."[105] Jeremy's loss was as serious to her and Anne Virginia as if he had been a near relative, and the arrangements for his funeral were made the same as if he had been a person. A local undertaker embalmed his body and placed it in a baby's casket. Interment was in Ellen's backyard garden, and the grave was marked with a marble stone.

From Virginia, New York, and England, sympathy notes poured in at One West Main Street, and the Sunday edition of the Richmond *Times-Dispatch* ran an extended obituary.[106] From England, Hugh Walpole and the writer Radclyffe Hall sent their sympathy.[107] Radclyffe Hall assured Ellen that animals have an afterlife and that Jeremy was still very near her. Carl Van Vechten told her that he understood her anguish and knew that she would never get over it.[108] Joseph Collins expressed deepest sympathy and said that "intense love has terrible exactment.[109] James Branch Cabell, Mary Johnston, and Henry Anderson all said that they understood the deepness of her bereavement.[110] John Stewart Bryan, president of the College of William and Mary and chairman of the board of trustees of the Richmond Public Library, had written her at the time of Jeremy's first illness that he had once lost a horse by sudden death and could understand the concern she felt over her faithful dog.[111] Such notes were of little consolation to Ellen, who was gripped with a sense of "the futility of all things."[112] After Jeremy's

105 Interview with Mr. Glasgow Clark.
106 September 8, 1929, p. 14.
107 Hugh Walpole to Ellen Glasgow, September 20, 1929, Radclyffe Hall to Ellen Glasgow, September 29, 1929, in Glasgow Papers.
108 To Ellen Glasgow, September 10, 1929, *ibid.*
109 To Ellen Glasgow, September 11, 1929, *ibid.*
110 September 9, September 28, and no date, 1929, respectively, *ibid.*
111 January 9, 1929, *ibid.*
112 Ellen Glasgow to James Branch Cabell, no date, but reference to death of Jeremy places it in fall of 1929, in Cabell Papers, University of Virginia Library.

burial she went back to Maine, but she often awoke during the night with stabbing pains in her heart and felt so perfectly miserable that she could foresee nothing remaining in life to make it worth living.[113]

For most of a year she drifted in a state of dazed grief, and then she fled to England, back to Harrogate, to rest and to recover. Before sailing in June, 1930, she told her sister that she would rather be dead than going,[114] and from on board the S.S. *Homeric* she wrote Anne Virginia that she awakened from her sleep "either in tears or in a panic" and that she looked forward with relief to the time when she would be in Hollywood Cemetery with Jeremy.[115] Carrie Duke was with her in England and they had a pleasant visit with Radclyffe Hall, but it rained constantly, and Ellen was so weak that she had to spend part of her time in a nursing home at Harrogate.[116] The summer passed, and she visited Paris and Scotland, which in retrospect she decided that she had enjoyed but which she never admitted in her letters to Anne Virginia. "I cannot say that I have had one hour of genuine pleasure—or even one moment," she wrote. "The best, I think, was when I came unexpectedly upon that field of flaming poppies. Though I am much better, I am still too easily exhausted and too drained of emotional strength to enjoy anything. And I think always of Jeremy and the pity and terror of life."[117]

The summer ended and with it her last glimpse of England. She returned to Richmond only slightly refreshed and unhappily aware that the Barren Ground philosophy of Dorinda Oakley, which she had imagined sufficient for life or death, was sadly inadequate to cope with the pity and terror of life.

[113] Ellen Glasgow to Anne Virginia Bennett, October 16, 1929, in Glasgow Papers.
[114] Copy of a letter to Rebe Tutwiler, June 12, 1930, in Rawlings Papers.
[115] June 16, 1930, in Glasgow Papers.
[116] *Woman Within*, 258.
[117] To Anne Virginia Bennett, August 24, 1930, in Glasgow Papers. See also *Woman Within*, 261–63.

# 9

## Madame Paradise
## Afloat in the New South

*A*nne Virginia and Billy welcomed Ellen home from England, and to the same dreary house on Main Street. The novelist was fifty-seven years old, somewhat embittered by her past defeats, but still determined to make the most of what life remained for her. She knew that she would never recover from the death of Jeremy, and feared that her inner life would never be calm and peaceful; still she had her art and a public image to create. Personal and professional maturity brought increased control over a troubled psyche, which she wove intricately into the plots of her novels, but buried forever from the eyes of her contemporaries in a highly secretive autobiography.

A regional novelist who correctly considered her novels to have universal significance, in the 1930's she floated upon the ever rising tide of the New South by giving to the world her best novels, which are set in Virginia but transcend in theme their sectional connections. The New South is the post-Reconstruction South in which industry and business sparred with agriculture to usher in a new political, economic, and social order. To Ellen Glasgow it was an era of noisy industrialism, foul odors, strange men in high political places, bad taste in literature, and a maze of broken class lines. It was a place "where pirates had deserted the seas and embarked afresh as captains of industry."[1] The industrial process, she felt,

1 Ellen Glasgow, *The Sheltered Life* (Garden City, N.Y.: Doubleday, Doran and Co., 1932), 146.

182

offered little hospitality to letters, and she was disheartened "to be obliged to live and work in an age that seems to have lost not only all standards but even all respect for what we used to think of as artistic integrity."[2] Yet it was the era in which she lived and she was always an unwilling participant and a detached observer with the alert mind and ready pen needed to chronicle the period.

By temperament and heritage she was so anchored in the gracious-living tradition of the Old South that visitors at One West Main Street inevitably felt that time had been turned back a century or more. At the coming-out ball in Richmond for her niece, Ellen appeared as Madame Paradise of Williamsburg, friend of Samuel Johnson. Her dress of brocaded silk with flowers on a cream-colored background and real lace in front was designed by a local artist, Margaret Dashiell. A Negro girl was hired to follow her as her slave and hold her hat and prayer book.[3] A more appropriate costume could not have been chosen, for as Madame Paradise, Ellen savored for one brief evening the kind of living that she loved; and as the friend of Samuel Johnson she imagined herself to be in the eminent role of leadership in literature that she desired.

Out of costume, but in character, Ellen Glasgow attempted briefly to play the role of Samuel Johnson to a younger generation of Southern writers whose works were already making her novels seem antiquated. She was encouraged by three outstanding professors of English who appreciated her work and sought her friendship. In June, 1930, the University of North Carolina awarded her the honorary degree of Doctor of Letters, and she found in Chapel Hill a small group of literary people who enjoyed her work, and the experience caused her to remember that weekend as one of the truly happy occasions of her life.

---

2 To Allen Tate, January 30, 1933, in *Letters*, 127.

3 Margaret Dashiell to MKR, in Rawlings Papers. The precise date of this ball has been impossible to determine, but it probably took place in the late 1920's. The niece, Arthur Glasgow's daughter, married in 1935, but there is some indication that her marriage must have been a number of years after her coming out ball. Marjorie Glasgow Congreve to Ellen Glasgow, August 5, 1934, in Glasgow Papers; Arthur Glasgow to Ellen Glasgow, October 31, 1934, and July 5, 1935, in Rawlings Papers.

There she met Howard Mumford and Bessie Zaban Jones.[4] Jones
was a professor of English whose career eventually carried him to
the University of Michigan and to Harvard University, and his
approval of the work of Ellen Glasgow and willingness to write
laudatory articles about her naturally made him one of her favorite
scholars. He and his wife maintained a cordial relationship with
her for the rest of her life, including occasional visits in each other's
homes, but their friendship was not on a deep personal level and
was confined for the most part to an exchange of letters. Yet those
letters were often concerned with casual as well as literary matters,
and less than a year after their meeting Ellen playfully wrote to
Howard: "The spring is here. Doesn't it tempt you?"[5] With Bessie
she discussed such things as her health, their vacations, the life in
Cambridge, and the art of letter writing.[6] The Joneses were Ellen's
closest friends among major literary scholars, but she was acquainted
with Edwin Mims, a professor at Vanderbilt University who praised
her work and eventually expressed an interest in writing her biography;[7] and the triumvirate of professors was completed by James
Southall Wilson, Poe Professor at the University of Virginia.

Ellen suggested to James Southall Wilson that there was a need
for a Southern Writers Conference and met with him during the
spring of 1931 to discuss the possibility of making such a conference
a reality.[8] Wilson took the initiative to get the University of Virginia to host the gathering, while Ellen, James Branch Cabell, Du-
Bose Heyward, Stark Young, Thomas Wolfe, and Paul Green
composed an informal committee to plan the event. Ellen approached the project with gusto and in a rare good humor even
expressed a wish to meet some of the students who were "more interested in literature than football."[9]

---

[4] Ellen Glasgow to Bessie Zaban Jones, January 16, 1933, in Bessie Zaban Jones
Papers; September 27, 1938, in *Letters*, 243–45.
[5] April 15, 1931, in Howard Mumford Jones Papers, Harvard University Library.
[6] In Bessie Zaban Jones Papers.
[7] To Ellen Glasgow, August 4, 1941, in Glasgow Papers.
[8] James Southall Wilson to Ellen Glasgow, January 10, February 19, and March 17,
1931, *ibid.*
[9] James Southall Wilson to Ellen Glasgow, October 19, 1931, James Southall Wilson
Papers, University of Virginia Library.

On October 23 and 24, 1931, the writers gathered on the Lawn
of "Mr. Jefferson's University" where a lazy serpentine wall and
rows of gleaming white columns, surrounded by the splendor of
the autumn's colors, made the alma mater of Edgar Allan Poe and
Woodrow Wilson seem to rest serene and timeless. There was no
schedule and no program; participants spoke only if they wished.
It was a weekend of quiet conversation and sightseeing, an opportunity for some to make new friends and for others to indulge in
heavy drinking. Among the thirty writers who attended were Ellen
Glasgow, William Faulkner, Sherwood Anderson, James Branch
Cabell, Emily Clark, Donald Davidson, Allen Tate, Paul Green,
and DuBose Heyward. Two eminent Southern historians, W. E.
Dodd and U. B. Phillips, were there.[10] Dodd assured those writers
who were unhappy about increasing industrialism in the South
that they could relax because the Depression had killed the machine
age. James Branch Cabell refused to speak publicly, explaining that
the reason he wrote was because he did not know how to speak;
but he did suggest privately that writers practiced their craft because it was fun, and why worry about Truth since no one knew
what that was anyway.[11] DuBose Heyward felt that the militant
spirit against organization at the conference was an appropriate
symbol of the area the writers represented and was "a milestone
along the highway of culture in the South,"[12] but Paul Green
spoke about the loneliness of the creative life and stirred up a
ripple of controversy when he approved of the machine age that
had been so soundly damned the year before by some of the writers who were present.[13] Struthers Burt avoided the controversy and

[10] The other guests included: Katherine Anthony, John Peale Bishop, James Boyd,
Herschel Brickell, Katherine and Struthers Burt, Mary and Stanley Chapman, Isa
Glenn, Caroline Gordon, Archibald Henderson, Mary Johnston, Josephine Pinckney,
Alice Hegan Rice, Cale Young Rice, Amélie Rives (Princess Troubetskoy), Mrs.
Laurence Stallings, and Irita Van Doren.
   Those writers who were invited but did not attend were Burton Rascoe, Herbert
Ravenel Sass, Laurence Stallings, Julia Peterkin, Thomas Wolfe, and Stark Young.
[11] Emily Clark, "A Weekend at Mr. Jefferson's University," *New York Herald Tribune
Books* (November 8, 1931), 1–2.
[12] DuBose Heyward, "South's Authors Compare Notes at U. Va.," clipping from an
unidentified newspaper, in Glasgow Papers.
[13] Josephine Pinckney, "Southern Writers Conference," *Saturday Review of Lit-*

even the whole topic of writing and concentrated on his lunch.[14]

The person of greatest interest was the small man in his mid-thirties whose novels were already making those of his colleagues appear decidedly second and third rate. William Faulkner rarely left Mississippi, was bashful in public, and usually spoke only three words: "I dare say."[15] In a relaxed mood he rode several of the writers through the hills in a convertible and sang "Carry Me Back to Ole Virginny." His drinking habits were as famous as his novels, and some of the participants who deliberately plied him with liquor were duly rewarded with a more intimate knowledge of Faulkner the drinker than of Faulkner the novelist.[16] The conference was mostly a pleasant vacation, a weekend house party, during which "several writers who had hated one another's books learned to like one another's personalities so well that they resolved henceforth to tolerate their books."[17] The writers agreed it was a great pity they had to go to New York to get their books published, but no one had any concrete suggestions for a change. A similar gathering was planned for the following year in Charleston, South Carolina, but it was poorly attended and the idea was thereafter dropped. The conference at the University of Virginia remained as the unique and single meeting of a kind of open air Southern Academy of Arts and Letters where, in spite of the Eighteenth Amendment, the mint juleps were too much in abundance, and the individualistic personalities of the participants were so accented that it became clear that writers are created more by accident than by design and are not likely to perpetuate their own kind.

As individualistic as anyone there, Ellen Glasgow hovered over the gathering like a *grand dame*, prepared to condescend out of a sense of duty to impart wisdom to the fledglings who were possibly quite unaware that she had reached any higher plain of

*erature* (May 7, 1931). Both Allen Tate and Donald Davidson had contributed articles to *I'll Take My Stand*, a book that defended the agrarian tradition of the South especially as a vital literary symbol.

14 *Ibid.*

15 Clark, "Weekend at Mr. Jefferson's University," 2.

16 Stark Young to Ellen Glasgow, November 10, 1931, in Glasgow Papers.

17 Clark, "Weekend at Mr. Jefferson's University," 2.

achievement than they had. She bubbled with the charm of an aristocratic lady of the Old South and at least in Allen Tate found a youngster who thought that as a person she was greater even than her art. He thought her admirable character was possible to her generation but not to his, and he affectionately dubbed her "Miss Ellen" in the gracious Southern tradition of a gentleman who genuinely admires and respects an older lady.[18] She was as sincerely attracted to him, and cultivated his friendship as a worthy intellectual companion and a potential reviewer of her books.[19]

At the commencement of the conference Allen Tate's "Miss Ellen" was the star of the show. She alone had a prepared speech, which she delivered at the beginning of the program. In it she attempted to set forth the distinction among the truth of life, the truth of history, and the truth of fiction. At least one observer pronounced it "brilliant and witty."[20] Actually, she had approached her task with malice aforethought and the firm intention to give a piece of her mind to her junior colleagues, especially Mr. William Faulkner, who were writing so freely about violence and decadence that she considered them to be in bad taste. She had entitled a rough draft of her speech "Are We Maggots?" In the draft she accused America of being a masochist among nations and warned that a lack of pity and understanding on the part of novelists threatened to negate any progress man had made through evolution.[21] Fortunately, she discarded the title, subdued her ire, and prepared another speech of considerably more value.[22]

She was personable, witty, entertaining, and almost profound. She explained that she had chosen as the main character of her first novel the illegitimate son of illiterate poor whites because she had always been on the side of the underdog. But now that times had changed and the underdog was on top, especially in the

18 Stark Young to Ellen Glasgow, January 11, 1932. Young quotes from a letter he received from Allen Tate. In Glasgow Papers.
19 Ellen Glasgow to Stark Young, January 12 and March 6, 1932, in *Letters*, 112, 114.
20 Donald Davidson, "A Meeting of Southern Writers," *Bookman*, LXXIV (February, 1932), 495.
21 The draft of this speech is in the Glasgow Papers.
22 The draft of this speech, entitled "Notes for a speech before Southern Writers Conference at U. Va.," is in the Glasgow Papers.

novels of most of her hearers, she had decided to champion the well bred, whom she believed to be the outcasts of the machine age. After that initial mild rebuke to the Southern Academy, she ended her introduction by joking about herself: "When I was asked, as the only woman on this committee, to bid you welcome to Virginia, I modestly replied that women come before men only in shipwreck." With that she made the audience her own and proceeded to comment upon the diversity among Southern writers as a fair indication that the South at last had become a part of the world and made life itself the chief concern of its literature: "We are, I think, less interested in any social order past or present than we are in that unknown quantity which we once called the soul and now call the psychology of mankind. Into this world of psychology we may look as into a wilderness that is forever conquered and yet forever virgin. Here and there, we see our own small trail which leads on to that vanishing point where all trails disappear."[23]

From psychology she moved to Truth and suggested that there are many kinds of Truth which are the legitimate concerns of the writer:

> There is, for example, what we have agreed to call the truth of life. Then there is that vastly different truth, the truth of art, which includes history and fiction. This, of course, is merely a way of saying that modern psychology or the Theory of Relativity or both together have demolished our conception of truth as an established principle superior to and apart from the thinking subject. We no longer think of truth as a fixed pattern outside of ourselves at which we may nibble for crumbs as mice at a loaf. All of you who write fiction must have had the shock of finding that when we break off a fragment of the truth of life and place it, without shading or shaping, into the truth of fiction, it sheds a meretricious glare of unreality. And many of us have tried at least once to be so supremely honest that we have taken a single character or incident or even a phrase directly from life—only to be told that this single character or incident or phrase is the one false stroke in an otherwise truthful portrait of experience.[24]

23 *Ibid.*
24 *Ibid.*

Unfortunately, she did not elaborate sufficiently upon her distinctions among the different kinds of Truth, but the fact that she drew the distinctions must have been of considerable interest to both the novelists and the historians present. But most of the participants had come for a vacation, not a discussion of philosophy, so either because Ellen did not find enough congenial company or because she actually did develop a severe headache, she went back home at the end of the first day and ended her dreams of becoming mistress of a Southern Academy.[25]

Ellen's brief forays into the social and organizational world of writers were always excursions she made in her leisure time and tasks to which she was never willing to devote a full measure of her energy. She liked to pour all of her mental and physical strength into her novels, and at the time the Writers Conference was being planned and taking place she was at work on her masterpiece. *The Sheltered Life* was published in September, 1932, eleven months after the conference. The advent of its publication commanded the entire front pages of the book sections of both the New York *Times* and the New York *Herald Tribune*, partly because Ellen had become friends with the book editors of both papers but especially because the novel was worthy of such attention. She had taken the background of her own girlhood and placed it in conflict with the philosophy of life that she accepted in her adulthood.[26] The same events in the novel are viewed by the young and by the old, neither of whom has any safe refuge from the crumbling shelters of religion, convention, and social prejudice, unless it be in death.

Ellen set *The Sheltered Life* in Richmond between 1910 and 1917, deliberately choosing the time of America's entry into the First World War as the climax of the story, for in her own life the First World War marked the dissolution of her own shelters. Jenny Blair Archbald, nine-and-one-half years old when the story opens, is obediently reading *Little Women* for a penny a page, but bored and anxious to "live." She is wildly attracted to George Birdsong, a

25 James Southall Wilson to Ellen Glasgow, November 16, 1931, in Glasgow Papers.
26 *A Certain Measure*, 201, 204.

man almost four times her age, just as Ellen at the age of twelve pitched a formidable temper tantrum when her Mr. Munford married a woman his own age. Jenny Blair lives with her mother, grandfather, and two old-maid aunts in a formerly aristocratic section of Richmond that is becoming run down and polluted by the odor from a nearby chemical factory. Her grandfather, General Archbald, is an old man given to meditating upon his youth and opportunities that were lost because he surrendered to the social code of his peers. Jenny Blair's mother is the inevitable female character in a Glasgow novel who discovers that love in its physical expressions is overrated and is thankful to be "finished with all that." Aunt Isabella has been jilted by her fiancé and bangs out her frustrations on a piano. Eventually she marries a man who does not have the proper social pedigree but who provides her with a happy home. Aunt Etta was born so ugly that no man will look at her and suffers from sexual frustrations so severe that she has become demented. John Welch is a young doctor who, with the innocence and determination of youth, thinks that he can reform the world. Eva Birdsong is a woman of legendary beauty who sacrificed her plans for a career in order to marry George Birdsong and leads a useless and miserable life as the community's symbol of perfect beauty. Though married to the prettiest woman in town, George Birdsong is incapable of fidelity, often consorting with other women, including the stoic, black wash-woman. With superb literary technique, Ellen Glasgow deftly weaves the story of their interrelated lives, subtly and sensitively revealing the power and the inadequacies of the wisdom of the past.

Time passes and Jenny Blair becomes eighteen. She begins to taunt George, unaware of the tragedy she invites, until he finally kisses her and a passionate attraction develops between them. When Eva is in the hospital for an operation, Jenny Blair meets George in a garden described exactly as the garden in back of One West Main Street, and a dramatic climax occurs one afternoon shortly after Eva has returned home. George had just returned from a hunting trip with a large supply of ducks. He tied them together in pairs with bright colored ribbons and laid them around in his den to be distributed among his friends. Jenny Blair waited for him in the garden, but Eva saw him go out to meet her and called him back. And Jenny Blair knew that Eva was going to kill him before she heard the shot and saw him lying with blood on his lips among the ducks with blood-specked beaks and bright ribbons around their necks.

The novel received a critical and popular acclaim that Ellen had never known before. Henry Seidel Canby of the *Saturday Review of Literature*, Isabel Paterson of the New York *Herald Tribune*, J. Donald Adams of the New York *Times*, Stark Young of the *New Republic*, Allen Tate, and Mary Johnston all had glowing words of praise.[27] Ellen's publishers were ecstatic and informed her that this was the first time a novel of theirs had ever made the front page of the book review section of the New York *Times* and that a second edition was being printed even before the first was placed on the general market.[28] The public liked the book, too, and *The Sheltered Life* climbed to fifth place for the year on the best-seller list.

Ellen was elected to membership in the National Institute of Arts and Letters, and it was commonly assumed that she would win the Pulitzer Prize. But when the award was announced in May, 1933, it went to *The Store* by T. S. Stribling. Ellen's friends and critics were dismayed, and Lewis Gannett, book critic for the New York *Herald Tribune*, publicly denounced the Pulitzer Prize Committee for its decision.[29] Miss Ellen pretended to be unperturbed and wrote to Gannett: "Nothing really matters but to preserve, at whatever cost, one's own sense of artistic integrity."[30] Actually, she was indignant and wrote to Allen Tate, who had notified her that he was "positively furious" about it:

> I never thanked you for what you said of the Pulitzer Prize Committee, but I appreciated your indignation. So many different persons seemed to feel that indignation over choice. . . . Such ex-

27 Kelly, "Struggle for Recognition," 265, 279, 284; Allen Tate to Ellen Glasgow, September 9, 1932, in Allen Tate Papers, Princeton University Library.
28 Page Cooper to Ellen Glasgow, August 16 and August 23, 1932, in Glasgow Papers.
29 Undated newspaper clipping, *ibid.*
30 May 25, 1933, in *Letters*, 135.

pressions give me pleasure—but I have lived too long in a world that "encouraged mediocrity" and in a country that consistently preferred the amateur to the artist. After more than thirty years of this one becomes accustomed, if not reconciled, to the national apotheosis of the average. But I still resent the kind of books the North considers representative of the South.[31]

The writer Isa Glenn summed up the feelings of a number of people when she wrote to Ellen, "I am very indignant, honey. I hold, and I'm sure all of us hold, that *The Sheltered Life* should have got it. Well—damn it!"[32] But the damage could not be undone, and the result was that a small group of critics connected with the most prestigious journals for reviewing new novels rallied to her support and for almost a decade devoted their magazines to the rectification of the error.[33] But the shelter of superior literary recognition proved to be as elusive for Ellen Glasgow as the shelters of religion, convention, and social prejudice had been for the characters in her novel, and when the Pulitzer Prize was finally awarded to her in 1942 she had ceased to care about it.

The Great Depression was well underway in 1932, and Ellen was more concerned about financial security than she was about literary fame.[34] Even so, she fared better during the Depression than did most Americans. Help came to her through the generous gifts of her brother, Arthur Graham Glasgow, "whose affection is a shelter without walls" Ellen said in her dedication of *The Sheltered Life*. Arthur Glasgow was the only surviving male member of the family, and in the tradition of his Scottish ancestors had assumed the role of head of the clan. He saw Ellen infrequently and did not especially enjoy reading her novels, but he was proud of

31 July 4, 1933, *ibid.*, 139–40. See also Allen Tate to Ellen Glasgow, May 24, 1933, in Glasgow Papers.

32 May 7, 1933. Other letters include Daniel Longwell (an editor for Doubleday, Doran and Co., and a friend of Ellen Glasgow, but in a precarious position because his firm had also published *The Store*), May 19, 1933; Jean Kenyon Mackenzie, May 8, 1933, Henry S. Canby, May 8, 1933, James Branch Cabell, May 5, 1933, and J. Donald Adams, May 8, 1933, all in Glasgow Papers.

33 Henry Seidel Canby of the *Saturday Review of Literature* and Stark Young of the *New Republic* were the leaders of this movement, but J. Donald Adams of the New York *Times* and Irita Van Doren of the New York *Herald Tribune* gave their support.

34 Ellen Glasgow to Daniel Longwell, June 22 and August 12, 1932, in *Letters*, 117, 121.

her fame and was glad to contribute to her support. He gave generously through two trust funds, a number of outright gifts, and occasionally by remodeling the house which actually belonged to him. As a founder of Humphreys and Glasgow, Ltd., a London-based gas company, Arthur had become quite wealthy.

Under Arthur's management and direction, one trust fund was created in 1908 so that Ellen and her brothers and sisters would receive a yearly income. Since the death of her father in 1916, Ellen had received one-half of the total income from that fund. In 1926 Arthur established a second trust fund for her alone with an initial investment of $165,000.[35] The income from these two funds, along with her royalties, provided her with a comfortable livelihood. A statement of her income dated June, 1931, indicates that she received $8,156.53 from the two trust funds and $3,427.70 from her personal dividends and royalties for a total of $11,584.23. It has been impossible to determine whether this figure is for six months or a year, but even if it covers the longer period, it represents an excellent income for that year. In the first six months of 1932 her income from all three sources dropped to $3,425.40, a figure still considerably higher than what many Americans earned for the entire year.[36]

But Ellen was not willing to adjust her scale of living. She spent money lavishly for clothes, trips, doctors, and dinner parties. Early in December, 1931, she wrote Arthur that she had had to borrow four thousand dollars the previous summer in order to take her vacation and that her stocks had gone down. In the same letter she told him of a young man who had committed suicide, and warned that she could understand the tragedy because to her the mystery was "not why a few are unable to bear life, but why the whole world doesn't end its existence."[37] Arthur responded with a check for six thousand dollars as her Christmas present.[38] On other occasions

[35] Arthur Glasgow to MKR, February 3, 1953, in Rawlings Papers.
[36] Rawlings Papers. No source given.
[37] December 16, 1931, in Glasgow Papers.
[38] Ellen Glasgow to Arthur Glasgow, January 7, 1932, *ibid.* Ellen Glasgow to Arthur Glasgow, April 5, 1932, thanks him for another gift of money without specifying the amount, in Rawlings Papers.

Arthur bought her new cars, usually a limousine with a glass to separate her compartment from that of the chauffeur, and paid for her medical expenses. He alone made it possible for her to have the leisure and comfort she needed to write her novels.

On a personal level, however, there was little love between Ellen and Arthur. A tall man with a stern expression, Arthur tended to inspire fear even in the members of his family. He was occasionally willing to laugh at himself and could be personable with anyone who dared to joke with him.[39] Apparently Ellen never bothered to try to break down the barrier between them. She lived in terror of his visits, for Arthur liked to lord it over people and complained bitterly about the service when he visited Ellen. Often he would not stay at One West Main Street, but chose instead the home of Colonel Henry Anderson where British servants provided service more to his liking.[40] Eight years Ellen's senior, he had been away at college when she was an adolescent and had moved permanently to London by the time she was twenty. As a boy of eleven he took a canal boat to Lexington and stopped at two places uninvited, where he told the servants who met him at the landing: "Tell Miss Sally Mc-Corkel, Arthur Glasgow has come for the day," and "Go up and tell Colonel Paxton, Arthur Glasgow is here." He rebelled against his father's insistence that he go to the Presbyterian rather than the Episcopalian Sunday school and could not be coerced by whippings. Eventually he offered to compromise with his father and either go to church or take walks with him. Mr. Glasgow hesitated, then chose the latter.[41] From childhood, Arthur was accustomed to having his own way. He believed that Ellen had no use for him except for what he did for her, and it would appear that his generosity with her was payment for the fame she brought to the family name rather than the devotion of a brother to his sister.

Though Ellen spoke kindly of Arthur she avoided him, and they rarely corresponded about anything other than financial matters. In the 1930's, of ten siblings, only Ellen, Arthur, and Rebe were

39 Interview with Mrs. James Branch Cabell, November 14, 1968.
40 Interview with Mrs. James Asa Shield, January 9, 1969.
41 Arthur Glasgow to MKR, in Rawlings Papers.

still living. Each had a strong will and refused to make conces-
sions to the other. Ellen and Rebe went for several years without
speaking to each other, and Arthur and Rebe got into unseemly
arguments over whether Ellen cared for them. Ellen talked as if
she had never loved any of her siblings except the "dearest brother"
who had committed suicide and the "beloved sister" who had died
of cancer, though it is certain that she loved their memories more
than she had ever loved them.[42] Arthur, Ellen, and Rebe sometimes expressed a superficial devotion to each other, but beneath
the surface each had a sufficient measure of their father's iron will
to carry them through life in their relations with each other with
the miasmic malice of a nest of copperheads under the sweet Virginia flowers, or the microphylla roses that were never quite perfect.

Woven far more intricately, and sometimes with no less malice,
into the shelter of Ellen's family life than her brother and sister,
was Anne Virginia Bennett, the woman hired to be a companion
and secretary but who became much closer to Ellen than any blood
member of her family. Anne Virginia grew up on a tobacco farm in
Virginia and received her nurse's training before she joined the
Glasgow family in 1911. During the First World War she served
with the Red Cross in France, was widely rumored to have been in
love with and jilted by a prominent Richmond physician, and
returned home not only dejected, but actually ill with a case of
tuberculosis. After a time in a sanitarium she came back to Main
Street to stay. She stood over Ellen sometimes like a guardian angel,
sometimes like a prison guard, refusing to allow her to be disturbed when she was writing and often refusing to allow her to
be disturbed when she was not writing. A tall, buxom woman with
the figure of Britannia, she was sometimes given to black moods
that got on Ellen's nerves and discouraged others from coming to
the home.[43] When not in a dark humor, Anne Virginia could be
very kind and pleasant; and Ellen became almost helplessly de-

---

[42] The excessive affection Ellen Glasgow expresses in *The Woman Within* is in conflict with contemporary accounts.
[43] Interviews with Mr. Glasgow Clark, November 14, 1968, and Miss Frances Brockenbrough, January 9, 1969, Richmond.

pendent upon her. Some of their friends believed that Anne Virginia had coerced Ellen into keeping her by reminding her and Arthur that she could have been their stepmother had she chosen.[44]

Anne Virginia and Ellen had little in common, but by a sheer accident of fate they were brought together at a time when each needed the other. They formed a bizarre relationship in which Anne Virginia became intensely jealous of anyone who tried to wait on Ellen, and Ellen treated Anne Virginia as her personal possession. When they visited in New York, Ellen would not allow Anne Virginia to call on her sister in Brooklyn, except over the telephone, because she did not want to be left alone.[45] They shared a love of dogs and a dislike of men. Ellen liked to think of men as intellectual and social inferiors and unsatisfactory lovers, but she enjoyed teasing them and often sought their company. Anne Virginia hated men almost violently. She appreciated Arthur's generosity, but had no use for him as a person and suggested that he had no sympathy with Ellen's deafness.[46] At the time Ellen and Henry Anderson were engaged, Anne Virginia reportedly told Anderson to his face that she hoped Ellen would marry him so that she could divorce him in less than twenty-four hours. And she found repulsive the habit of James Branch Cabell of greeting Ellen with a kiss on the cheek.[47] Ellen sometimes tried to avoid Anne Virginia but was never deliberately unkind and certainly had a genuine affection for her.

Anne Virginia never complained of bad treatment and was fiercely devoted to Ellen all of her life. She became intricately involved in Ellen's daily routine, did all of the bookkeeping, tended to all of the household details, typed Ellen's manuscripts, and took her side against members of the family when they argued. She slept upstairs in a room that adjoined Ellen's, but Ellen usually locked

---

44 Irita Van Doren and others to MKR, in Rawlings Papers.
45 Interview with Miss Brockenbrough.
46 To MKR, May 7, 1953, in Rawlings Papers.
47 References to Miss Bennett's hatred of men occur frequently in letters and interviews, including the following: Anne Virginia and Carrie Duke to MKR, in Rawlings Papers; Ellen Glasgow to Hugh Walpole, May 19, 1920, in Walpole Papers.

her door from the inside. Anne Virginia would arise at 6:30 A.M., go downstairs, and see that a servant built the fires and prepared breakfast to be served to Ellen in bed. She and Ellen breakfasted together in Ellen's bedroom and often planned the meals for the day. Ellen locked herself in her study from 9 A.M until 2 P.M., while Anne Virginia walked the dogs, typed, supervised the servants, or arranged flowers when they were available. In the afternoons they went for automobile rides together or invited two other ladies, usually Carrie Duke and Berta Wellford, in to play bridge.[48] Sometimes they did not play bridge at all, but simply listened to Ellen tell funny stories about the SPCA or talk about the characters in her novels.[49] Theirs were anything but intellectual gatherings, and literature as such was usually not a topic of conversation. Berta Wellford was a woman of intelligence who appreciated literature, but Carrie Duke probably never got all the way through one of Ellen's novels. She would hold a book at arm's length and work her lower jaw up and down as she struggled over the words, but she always knew the characters and plots because Ellen told her. Trivial gossip oozed out like grease as Ellen dominated the conversation, and her faithful Anne Virginia kept a wary eye and sixth sense tuned to the needs of her mistress, doggedly determined that hers would indeed be a sheltered life.

Even a sheltered life with a modicum of luxury during the Great Depression could be dreary, especially for one easily depressed by the sight of suffering and constantly plagued by ill health. The kidnapping of the Lindbergh baby angered her so much that she declared modern American society "to be at the mercy of criminals."[50] She was not unaware of the suffering the Depression was causing, and she had a genuine feeling of pity, her favorite emotion, for those whose predicaments seemed hopeless. Physically, she suffered as helplessly as many of her nighbors suffered financially. She visited a Doctor Wolf in New York, apparently a specialist in

[48] Anne Virginia Bennett to MKR, in Rawlings Papers.
[49] Interview with Miss Frances Brockenbrough. Miss Brockenbrough, a friend of Carrie Duke's, was occasionally a partner at the bridge games.
[50] To Arthur Glasgow, March 5, 1932, in Glasgow Papers.

nervous disorders, who Stark Young told her might be able to cure her, but he could not.[51] Her nervous condition was complicated by a painful sinus infection that prompted her to go to the Johns Hopkins Hospital in Baltimore for six weeks in the summer of 1933. Her sister Rebe went with her, and the two of them spent all of June and part of July in a small unairconditioned room in a hotel, where Ellen received daily visits from doctors and endured a great deal of pain.[52] Her physician was a famous ear and throat specialist, but the treatment was so painful and the results so negligible that Ellen told Arthur she had "endured infinitely more than life is worth."[53] Arthur responded to her lament by offering to pay for an "after cure" at Blowing Rock, North Carolina, where at least the climate would be cooler, but Ellen declined because she felt that she was getting too far behind with her work and that the financial situation was too bad.[54]

Life was "a continuous adjustment of character to calamity," she said, for although she believed that the condition for which she had been treated had improved, she returned home from Baltimore with a bad cough and a dampened spirit.[55] Her Johns Hopkins specialist suggested that she return in the fall for a minor operation that might help the cough, but upon the advice of her friend, Dr. Joseph Collins, who disagreed with the Baltimore specialist's diagnosis, she went in the fall to a Dr. Faulkner at the Manhattan Eye and Ear Hospital, where she gained no help but merely another opinion on the cause of her trouble.[56] Although it was difficult to

51 Stark Young to Ellen Glasgow, September 14, 1932, March 29, and May 2, 1933, ibid.
52 Ellen Glasgow to James Southall Wilson, June 8, 1933, in Wilson Papers; to Virginia Tunstall, June 14, 1933, in Virginia Tunstall Papers, University of Virginia Library; to William Lyon Phelps, June 18, 1933, in William Lyon Phelps Papers, Yale University Library.
53 June 17, 1933, in Glasgow Papers.
54 Arthur Glasgow to Ellen Glasgow, June 30, 1933, in Rawlings Papers; Ellen Glasgow to Allen Tate, July 4, 1933, in Letters, 140.
55 To Arthur Glasgow, July 21, 1933, in Glasgow Papers.
56 Dr. James Bordley, Jr., to Ellen Glasgow, September 14, 1933, Dr. Joseph Collins to Ellen Glasgow, September 26, 1933, in Glasgow Papers; Ellen Glasgow to Allen Tate, July 4 and 5, 1933, to Stark Young, October 30, 1933, to J. Donald Adams, November 2, 1933, in Letters, 140, 141, 147, 148; Ellen Glasgow to Sara Haardt Mencken, October 30, 1933, in Sara Haardt Mencken Papers, Goucher College Library.

be witty when in pain, for many years Ellen had cultivated a sense of humor to help her cope with the infelicities of life, and it was ultimately that sense of humor that provided her some relief from her physical suffering. After winter attacks of influenza that had laid both her and Anne Virginia low, she wrote to James Branch Cabell: "Well, it seemed to me that we needed only this to complete our despondency—I had almost written 'ruin,' but I remembered in time that, though fallen in spirit, we are still perfect ladies!"[57] Except for casual references to her illnesses in her letters, Ellen was too much of a lady and often too busy with other activities to be a chronic complainer. Her complaints occasionally got into print, but more often they fell only on the ears of Anne Virginia and Arthur.

Miss Ellen the Sufferer was virtually unknown to her public, but Miss Ellen the Hostess on Main Street was often the talk of certain literary factions of the social world in both Richmond and New York City. Guests were lavishly entertained at One West Main Street. Well remembered was the June party for Hugh Walpole in 1920 when the Negro Sabbath Glee Club stood on the backporch and sang their spirituals.[58] It was a strict imitation of a custom of the Old South and one which Ellen often employed at her parties.[59] Aunt Roberta, a distinguished looking Negro lady dressed in a lace cape, who was the grandchild of the mammy of Ellen's mother, was often present to greet the guests and to take their wraps.[60] The guests included such literary figures of Ellen's day as Hamlin Garland, Stark Young, Caroline Gordon and Allen Tate, James Lane Allen, James Branch Cabell, Burton Rascoe, Sara Haardt and H. L. Mencken, Marjorie Kinnan Rawlings, Gertrude Stein, Henry Seidel Canby, Carl Van Vechten, Douglas Southall Freeman, a host of representatives of publishing companies, and even a good sprin-

[57] Sunday, [1931], in Cabell Papers.
[58] Carl Van Vechten, "Introduction," in Padriac Colum and Margaret Freeman Cabell (eds.), *Between Friends: Letters of James Branch Cabell and Others* (New York: Harcourt, Brace and World, 1962), xiii. See also Emily Clark, "Ellen Glasgow," in Sherman, and others (eds.), *Ellen Glasgow: Critical Essays*, 48.
[59] Margaret Just Butcher, *The Negro in American Culture* (New York: Alfred A. Knopf, 1956), 48–49.
[60] Ellen Glasgow to Carl Van Vechten, April 3, 1941, in *Letters*, 284.

kling of English professors. She knew few of these people well, and
even fewer of them knew her well. She counted Stark Young and
Carl Van Vechten among her closest friends, but there were long
periods of time when she did not see them. Even James Branch
Cabell, who lived in the same town, did not spend much time with
her, and Ellen probably felt much closer to his wife, who was un-
interested in literature, than she did to him. The literary celebrities
whom she entertained when they passed through Richmond or
invited to cocktails when she was staying in a hotel in New York
did not form the coterie of her intimate friends. Yet Ellen sought
their company almost neurotically, virtually begged them to come
to visit her, and once they came entertained them as extravagantly
as she could.

At the same time, as James Branch Cabell said, she was "frankly
and frigidly exclusive as to which inhabitants of Richmond she
would allow to enter her impressive mansion as social equals"[61] and
on at least two occasions cancelled invitations to literary ladies
whose morals she discovered left much to be desired. Referring to
one of these ladies, she commented, "I'd rather have kleptomania
than nymphomania."[62] The lady in question was no doubt Elinor
Wylie, whom she refused to invite to a dinner party but later included at an afternoon tea, believing, perhaps, that wickedness was
diluted in a large afternoon crowd.[63] And by claiming to be ill
she cancelled an invitation to Rebecca West when she heard that
the British writer was having some difficulty with her son by H. G.
Wells. Such cancellations were rare, however, and the guests who
came to see Miss Ellen and to see her house were never disappointed. Their hostess always had herself and her house ready for
them.

As Ellen grew older, she became plump, but never excessively
fat, and she tried diligently to maintain her youth. She wrote to
the aging Princess Troubetskoy, her friend and fellow novelist of
Virginia, for detailed information about the best beauty prepara-

61 James Branch Cabell, *As I Remember It* (New York: McBride Co., 1955), 231.
62 Emily Clark, *Innocence Abroad* (New York: Alfred A. Knopf, 1931), 67.
63 Source withheld.

tions, and assiduously followed the Princess' advice.[64] A weekly trip
to the beauty parlor kept her hair tinted a dark auburn color,
and she must have spent hours on her toilette. The ritual began
with the application of Dr. Woodbury's facial soap and Helena
Rubenstein's pasteurized cleansing cream. During the initial stages
of the preparation of her skin, Ellen kept her *Rouge en crème*, a
mixture of geranium and raspberry, tucked between her thighs
because the Princess had told her never, *never* to use artificial
heat to bring it to the proper consistency.[65] The job was finished
with Lady Esther's face powder and Dorothy Grey's dark red
*D'Espague* lipstick.[66] Then Miss Ellen turned to her wardrobe,
which consisted of the best and most expensive gowns from Paris
and New York. She loved clothes more than she loved books and
spared nothing to make sure that she always had the latest styles and
brightest colors. On one occasion she was a sensation in a low-cut
red lace dress, and on another when she wore a deep blue dress
with glittering stones around the low neck and a sunburst in her
hair.[67] In the evenings she often carried a large purple fan made
of ostrich feathers.[68] Her ankles were slender and her feet were
tiny, traditional marks of aristocratic beauty, and she chose shoes
to match her wardrobe from as many as forty-eight pairs that she
sometimes had in her possession at one time.[69] Preceded by a bouncing white dog, Miss Ellen descended into her spacious hall, swished
her ostrich plumes and rippled and purred as she circulated through
parlor and drawing rooms with her guests.

The house was furnished and decorated appropriately for such
a hostess. There was a dark marble fireplace in every room, and if
the weather was cool, a soft coal blaze crackled in each grate. The
walls of the hallway and parlor and drawing rooms were painted
ivory and gray, the furnishings included Sheraton and Hepple-

[64] September 28, 1937, in *Letters*, 226.
[65] Amélie Rives Troubetskoy to Ellen Glasgow, October 6, 1937, in Glasgow Papers.
[66] *Ibid.*, September 9, 1931, September 10, 1937, December 26, 1937.
[67] Leonie Villard to Ellen Glasgow, September 9, 1932, *ibid*; Mrs. William R. Trigg,
Jr. to MKR, in Rawlings Papers.
[68] Burton Rascoe, "Ellen Glasgow Deplores Real Estates and Dry Spies," clipping
from an unidentified newspaper, in Rawlings Papers.
[69] Frances Williams to MKR, in Rawlings Papers.

white, and the floors were covered with Oriental rugs.[70] A Chinese
Chippendale desk and Victorian rosewood chairs were in the back
drawing room. Blue damask curtains were in both drawing rooms,
and red linen and silk from Italy hung at the windows in the dining
room. When dinner was served, a fine linen table cloth was spread
over the mahogany table that was formally set. Scattered through
the receiving rooms were hand-painted fire screens, a dark blue
velvet Chesterfield sofa, a William and Mary highboy, and a small
Queen Anne chest.[71] Sometimes guests were allowed a glimpse of
her upstairs study, a room dominated by bookshelves, paintings
of dogs, and the large collection of porcelain canines. There was
a Hepplewhite couch, the customary dark marble fireplace, and in
the corner a beautiful and massive colonial desk that had been used
by Ellen's ancestor, Creed Taylor. Too high from the floor to be
accessible when sitting in an ordinary chair, it had a special chair
with it that must have caused Ellen's feet to dangle more than a foot
from the floor when she sat in it. A typewriter on a small table was
near the desk. A Buddha was on the desk, a Botticelli print over the
mantlepiece, and "The Burial of Latané," the picture of a Confederate woman reading the burial service for one of General J. E. B.
Stuart's fallen officers when a federal officer refused to allow a
clergyman to perform the rite, completed the room.

The events that transpired sometimes were not commensurate
with the surroundings. Ellen tried to be a gracious hostess, but her
deafness was a painful handicap. Her voice had a slight crackle and
her articulation was so precise that it irritated.[72] She used a hearing
aid that resembled a portable telephone, which she carried in her
hand and from which a cord was attached to her person. For her to
hear her guests they had to speak into the receiver at rather close
quarters.[73] Those whom she did not like, it is reported, were entertained in the parlor on the southeast corner of the old house. There
Ellen often made a witty or profound remark and then pointed her

[70] Rascoe, "Ellen Glasgow Deplores."
[71] Anne Virginia Bennett to MKR, in Rawlings Papers.
[72] Henry S. Canby, "Ellen Glasgow: A Personal Memory," *Saturday Review of Literature*, XXVIII (December 22, 1945), 13.
[73] Cabell, *As I Remember It*, 225.

ear trumpet in the direction of the guest for an instant reply. The guest usually became flustered and embarrassingly incapable of a quick answer. Those whom she liked she entertained across the hall, and critics who had given her good reviews saw nothing but the full force of her charm. She had a barbed tongue, however, for those who had given her bad reviews. At a party in the home of James Branch Cabell, she marched up to a critic who had written favorably of *The Romantic Comedians* at the expense of her earlier work and said fiercely: "Young man, I am not a woman to develop at my age. If I have not already achieved I never will!"[74] The chances are that Miss Ellen intended to be as witty as she was malicious, for she could be quick to forgive and rarely dwelled upon a bad review; her social relationships no doubt would have been more cordial had she not been handicapped by partial deafness. To save herself the embarrassment of having to hear others, she often dominated conversations and spoke her mind so positively that she appeared to be harsher than she ever intended to be.

Her most famous party was given for Gertrude Stein in February, 1935. Gertrude Stein was a friend of Carl Van Vechten's, and it was through him that Ellen happened to invite her and her companion, Alice B. Toklas, to Richmond. Ellen was not enthusiastic at first, because as she said, she liked to avoid "Modern Fads and People who Lecture."[75] But she was willing to entertain Miss Stein as a favor to Van Vechten. Ellen did not happen to have a book of Stein's on hand and was not an admirer of her art, and she asked Carl Van Vechten to send her a Stein volume in advance so she could get it autographed at the party.[76] The book was sent, duly inscribed during the visit, and Ellen and Gert got along well together.[77] But the party itself became the talk of the town, for the word got out that Ellen Glasgow was entertaining Gertrude Stein,

[74] Hunter Stagg to MKR, November 28, 1953, in Rawlings Papers.
[75] To Carl Van Vechten, January 30, 1935, in *Letters*, 173.
[76] Ellen Glasgow to Carl Van Vechten, January 27, 1935, in Van Vechten Papers; Carl Van Vechten to Ellen Glasgow, February 6, 1935, in Glasgow Papers.
[77] Ellen Glasgow to Gertrude Stein, n.d. and April 30, 1935, in Gertrude Stein Papers, Yale University Library; Ellen Glasgow to Alfred Harcourt, February 7, 1935, in *Letters*, 174.

and a guest at the Jefferson Hotel, located across the street, who happened to admire Miss Stein decided to crash the party. Miss Ellen's parties simply were not crashed, and she was momentarily at a loss for what to do. But the uninvited guest was quite capable of taking care of herself. She circulated briefly among the guests, then walked up to Miss Ellen, kissed her on the cheek, and said, "No one had a more delightful time than I."[78] Ellen claimed that she lacked the courage to be rude to anyone in her own house "even when rudeness was the better part of morality,"[79] but she enjoyed the embellishment the story received through the local gossip mills and did nothing to alter it. Perhaps she really felt that the event was not unworthy of the guest of honor, for she wrote in her private notebook: "Gertrude Stein—a wise overgrown child., as obvious as an infant. Likes obvious things. Barnum discovered that people are always willing to pay for the pleasure of being fooled. 'Alice, Alice, Gert is eating chocolate!' "[80] Anne Virginia Bennett enjoyed their visit immensely,[81] and the whole episode was but another notch in the reputation of Miss Ellen, who had become so famous that a local cab driver liked to point out her house as the residence of the lady who "writes real hot novels."[82]

No one wanted to miss a Glasgow party, and those who were invited to stay overnight were treated to a rare luxury. The huge guest room, decorated in pink, was upstairs on the same side as Ellen's study. It had an open fireplace, two modern four-poster beds, an adjoining sun room, and bath. In the morning a small Negro boy, one of the cook's children, slipped into the room and started the fire. Then a maid came in and drew the bath. After the guest had been allowed sufficient time to bathe, the maid returned with a breakfast tray. The tray was covered with hand-made Italian lace and there was always a little vase contining a flower. After break-

---

78 Mrs. William R. Trigg, Jr., to John Cook Wyllie, February 23, 1959. in Wyllie Papers, University of Virginia Library.
79 To James Branch Cabell, July 22, 1935, in Cabell Papers.
80 "Record Book," in Glasgow Papers.
81 Carl Van Vechten to Ellen Glasgow, February 6, 1935, *ibid.*
82 George H. Tucker, "When Ellen Glasgow 'Arrived,' " Norfolk *Virginian-Pilot*, undated clipping in Library of the Valentine Museum, Richmond.

fast, hostess and guest chatted in the study, rode around town, or occasionally took an all-day trip to Williamsburg. At lunch time Anne Virginia brought in canapés, and she was followed by a maid who carried a silver tray on which there were eighteenth-century goblets filled with mint juleps or old fashioneds. Lunch was prepared by the cook, James Anderson, a Negro who served Ellen faithfully in that capacity for forty years. A major crisis was precipitated when he was sick and unable to work, but fortunately he was usually on the job.[83] His kitchen was in the basement of the servants' wing, and he always cooked on a coal range, using no shortening other than real butter. Smithfield ham, chicken, and beaten biscuits were usually on the menu. A formal dinner consisted almost certainly of diamond back terrapin. There were vegetables, fruits, salads, and elaborate desserts. The best wines were served, and though Ellen ate very little herself, she encouraged her guests to eat heartily.[84] A weekend visit at One West Main Street was an experience long to be remembered.

Those who sought out Miss Ellen for an interview or advice, however, did not always receive such cordial treatment. One such was Julian Meade, a youthful Virginian who aspired to become a writer. Miss Ellen granted him an interview, but told him in advance at what hour he must leave. She was cordial, but not inclined to encourage the young man. They remained amiable until Meade published his book, *I Live in Virginia*, and Miss Ellen was infuriated over what had to say about her. There was a good measure of truth in his portrait, but he had placed too much emphasis on her bitter attitude toward youth and cynicism toward life in general.[85] The result was a caustic exchange of letters in which Mr. Meade was no gentleman and Miss Glasgow was no lady.[86] Miss Ellen tried to use her influence to stop the book from being reviewed and suggested that it should be called trivial gossip that was not worth publishing. She said that her hospitality to "discour-

[83] Ellen Glasgow to Bessie Zaban Jones, May 9, 1937, in *Letters*, 219.
[84] Irita Van Doren to MKR, in Rawlings Papers.
[85] Julian R. Meade, *I Live in Virginia* (New York: Longmans, Green and Co., 1935), 186, 188, 190.
[86] Julian Meade to Ellen Glasgow, June 17, 1936, in Glasgow Papers.

aged and unhappy youth" had been exploited and that the young writer was as clear a case of "arrested mental development" as she had ever encountered.[87] Her literary friends rallied to her support, and Mr. Meade became *persona non grata* among the very people who might have promoted his career.[88] Julian Meade was a frustrated young man who dared to say what he thought about conditions and writers in his native state and thus wrote a commentary of some lasting value. On the other hand, Miss Ellen engaged in some trivial gossip of her own about Mr. Meade and a certain amount of calculated malice turned what should have been a petty episode into a major event. In dealing with those whom she liked, she was witty and charming, but Julian Meade was not one of her favorites.

There were certain topics, rather than persons, which were likely to arouse her ire. Always temperate toward Jehovah, the subject of religion, especially in its Presbyterian and Episcopalian manifestations in the state of Virginia, was sure to bring on a verbal tirade. Although she held fast to many of the ethical teachings of Christianity, she denounced it thoroughly as a philosophy and could find no good in the Christian Church. On one occasion, Dr. Robert Norwood, rector of St. Bartholomew's Church in New York, visited in Richmond to conduct Lenten services at St. Paul's Episcopal Church. Alex Weddell, United States ambassador to Argentina and a native of Richmond, invited Ellen, the Reverend Norwood, and his Richmond hostess, Mrs. William R. Trigg, Jr., to cocktails. There were only five persons at the gathering. Ellen, dressed in a bright varicolored costume, sat on a couch, and the minister sat in a chair facing her. Early in the conversation the subject of religion was raised, and the minister spoke positively about the reality of divine love and the certainty of immortality. Ellen's eyes sparkled and she struck back with a joyous denial of those very things. The sparks, and even the fur, flew as Ellen lost her temper, became bitter and rude, and acted as if she were thoroughly enjoying the

87 To Stark Young, n.d., in *Letters*, 196–97.
88 Emily Clark to Ellen Glasgow, July 14, 1936, Stark Young to Ellen Glasgow, April 15, 1937, Julian Meade to Stark Young, March 24, 1937, Margaret Mitchell to Stark Young, n.d., all in Glasgow Papers.

encounter. Mr. Norwood could not surrender without negating his calling; he was calm and persistent. The battle ended in a draw, and some days later Ellen said simply that the clergyman was "a dreadful man." And the Reverend Norwood remarked that Miss Ellen was one of the most unhappy people he had ever met and one of the most charming.[89]

Miss Ellen's charm was reserved primarily for those who told her they liked her books; and her social consciousness, when it extended beyond her devotion to certain quadrapeds, consisted of fleeting generosities bestowed upon suffering individuals always in a situation that demanded of her no deep personal or Christian involvement. A soldier who wrote her a letter to tell her how much he had enjoyed *Barren Ground* was rewarded with an invitation to One West Main where Miss Ellen toasted his health in sherry before the fireplace in her parlor and then invited him into her dining room to a meal of roast turkey and dressing, green beans, baked hominy, escalloped eggplant, pickled pears, cranberry gelatin, caramel ice cream and cake. After dinner they drank coffee together in the parlor where Miss Ellen told him funny stories, chatted about writers who had visited her, and gently made fun of Virginians for always talking about the Civil War.[90]

The same hospitality that she had lavished upon the famous she graciously accorded to the soldier who was one of her fans, and he learned nothing of the woman who could be rude when irritated by a personality or a philosophy. He saw the other and better known side of Ellen Glasgow, the woman who did such things as attempt to get a local newspaper to use its influence to help a teenager who was sentenced to be executed,[91] took a small boy who had no money down to Miller and Rhoads Department Store and bought him a complete outfit,[92] personally bought the food for a horse whose owner could not afford it, gave money to her servants and former

[89] Mrs. William R. Trigg, Jr., to MKR, April 16, 1953, in Rawlings Papers.
[90] "From a Soldier's Letter," Ohio State [University] *Lantern*, undated clipping in the Glasgow Papers. The soldier was Kendall Falke, class of 1942, Ohio State University.
[91] Ellen Glasgow to Douglas S. Freeman, June 8, 1928, in Freeman Papers. The results of this effort are unknown.
[92] Margaret Dashiell to MKR, in Rawlings Papers.

servants during the Depression even though she refused to contribute to a poetry magazine on the excuse that money was too
tight.[93] Every Christmas she carried food and gifts to the African
Old Folks Home, and she almost single-handedly made certain that
the humane society was not dropped from the community fund
during the hard times.[94] Those who were afflicted with her own
malady of deafness were the special recipients of her sympathy,
which took the form of advice about hearing aids and some expression of understanding the problems they faced. Often her ges-
tures were futile, though warm and human, such as the time she
met a Mr. Gunston who was also deaf. They ended up holding
hands, looking at each other, and both saying: "Do you hear me?
Do you hear me?"[95]

The lack of communication between Ellen and Mr. Gunston
was in some ways typical of her relationships with those who had no
hearing problems, for the complexities of her personality were un-
fathomable to her contemporaries. To posterity, however, she
granted a boon in the form of an intensely personal memoir that
probed into her own psyche with candor and is indeed what she
liked to call "a journal of the inner life."[96] Ellen believed firmly
that everything possible to be known about a great novelist should
be known, and to insure that the whole truth of her own life be
told and told properly, she elected to tell it herself. "It seems to
me" she once wrote, "that the only excuse for writing the life of
a person is that truth shall be served."[97] In 1934, under the working
title of "The Autobiography of an Exile" she began *The Woman
Within*.[98] In preparation for the task she read James Joyce's *Portrait of the Artist as a Young Man*[99] and apparently set out to prove

93 Ellen Glasgow to Virginia Tunstall, June 14, 1933, in Tunstall Papers; Robert
Boswell to Ellen Glasgow, January 22, 1931, in Glasgow Papers.
94 John Selby, "Work and Friends Make Life Interesting for Miss Glasgow," Richmond *Times-Dispatch*, March 20, 1938.
95 Margaret Dashiell to MKR, in Rawlings Papers.
96 To Gene Saxton, March 15, 1936, in Saxton Papers, University of Virginia Library.
97 To Grant C. Knight, June 29, 1929, in *Letters*, 93.
98 A few pages of her earliest draft are preserved in the Glasgow Papers. The book
was published posthumously by Harcourt, Brace and Co., in 1954.
99 Irita Van Doren to MKR, in Rawlings Papers.

that her own suffering had been greater than that of any other artist. A comment in a letter to Bessie Zaban Jones at the time she was beginning the autobiography is revealing: "This brings me to your question:—'Have you liked your life?' And I answer, not one day, not one hour, not one moment—or perhaps, *only one* hour and one day. When I read of D. H. Lawrence and all the other strutting, sad-eyed martyrs of literature, I tell myself that they do not know the first thing about suffering. So long as one is able to pose one has still much to learn about suffering."[100] She did not tell her friend what her one moment of happiness had been, but it was obviously that day in the Alps with Gerald, the memory of which, according to the autobiography, she cherished to the end of her life. She saturated her suffering in self-pity and even warned that it was difficult for her to tell "where memory ends and imagination begins,"[101] but the document she produced is extraordinarily frank and accurate for an autobiography.

Ellen could afford to be frank, for she did not intend for the journal of her inner life to be published during her lifetime or the lifetime of Henry Anderson, who occupied two full chapters of her story. Since Lizzie Patterson Crutchfield often visited to discuss their childhood experiences, it is not surprising that one-third of the book is devoted to her childhood and youth. She had a tendency to telescope events back into childhood that happened later in her life, did not confess to quite all of the formal education she had, and was often melodramatic; but she was never deliberately dishonest, and she produced the kind of complete account of her early years that could have been written by no one but herself. The autobiography reads like a woman talking to her psychiatrist and attempting to psychoanalyze herself. Ellen was undergoing periodic psychiatric treatment at the very time she was writing the autobiography, and the influence of the therapy is obvious. She saw herself as a split personality who owed her maladjustments in life to a tragic conflict of types inherited from an Episcopalian mother and a Presbyterian father. Her attempts to resolve that conflict

---

[100] February 7, 1934, in *Letters*, 151.
[101] *Woman Within*, 281; to J. Donald Adams, April 28, 1936, in *Letters*, 211.

generated her literary creativity and led her into some of the most difficult and unhappy human relationships.

Her bitterest chapters are those that deal with Henry Anderson, one of which has the uncomplimentary title of "Fata Morgana." She gave no characterization of the whole man and wrote about him only from her narrow and intensely personal perspective. She insisted that his letters to her be preserved and she disguised his name so thinly that his identity was immediately obvious to anyone who had known him. With Gerald she was far more cautious, and his identity remains elusive. And her more fleeting liaisons she did not mention at all. Despite the rampant self-pity, her moments of happiness with Gerald and during her visits in England are sufficiently chronicled that the reader cannot help suspecting that she did not suffer quite so much as she pretended and must have found her extraordinary success in her own lifetime to be at least some consolation for the agonies of her inner conflicts. Her memoir presents her as the "woman who is shrieking but cannot be heard,"[102] but it also shows her to be the typical and perhaps the only "Great Lady of Richmond" of her day.[103]

She continued to work on the manuscript periodically throughout the late 1930's and early 1940's. As the chapters piled up she sealed them in brown envelopes and placed them in her silver chest and later transferred them to a black brief case which she locked and labelled "Private and Personal." The brief case was then deposited in her bank with the instructions that it should never be entrusted to the mails. In 1935 she made a contract with Harcourt, Brace and Company to publish the manuscript posthumously at the discretion of her literary executors.[104] Eventually she selected Frank V. Morley of Harcourt, Brace and Company and Irita Van Doren as her literary executors and charged them with the sacred responsibility to carry out her instructions with regard to her autobiography. Ellen created the manuscript with

---

102 Alfred Kazin, "The Lost Rebel," *New Yorker*, XXX (October 31, 1954), 130.
103 John Cook Wyllie, "Ellen Glasgow Left a Revealing Work," Richmond *News Leader*, November 1, 1954, clipping in the Glasgow Papers.
104 *Woman Within*, viii, ix.

more care than anything she ever wrote, because to her it was the most living of her works and her greatest gift to posterity. No one read the manuscript during her lifetime, and it was almost ten years after her death that it was published.

Readers in 1935 could not have known it, but they really did not have to wait twenty years to learn what was in Ellen Glasgow's autobiography. In 1935 she published *Vein of Iron*, a novel she had begun in 1932 and worked on consistently while the idea for the autobiography was forming in her mind. The events that happened to the fictional characters in *Vein of Iron* are the very episodes in the life of the real person in *The Woman Within*, and if large sections of the two books were printed in parallel columns their extraordinary similarities would be immediately obvious. In August, 1933, Ellen went back to her ancestral home in Rockbridge County, Virginia,[105] where the James River cuts through the Blue Ridge Mountains, and quietly transformed the memories of the first Glasgows in America and their local mountain folk descendants into the characters of *Vein of Iron*. The story takes place between the years 1901 and 1933 and traces the development of Ada Fincastle from a young girl in Ironside, Virginia, to a mature woman in Queenborough during the Depression. The fictitious town of Ironside is the Glasgow-Buena Vista area of Virginia, and Queenborough is Richmond.

And Ada Fincastle is so very much like Ellen Glasgow. Ada's father is a Presbyterian minister turned philosopher and consequently defrocked, and her mother is from the Tidewater region of Virginia. The union of the purest strains of the Tidewater with the sturdy Scotch-Irish of the Valley, Ellen was convinced, had caused her own inheritance of the tragic conflict of types; and she set out with enthusiasm to explore the consequences of that union in her story of Ada Fincastle, a girl whose development she considered to be almost directly opposite to that of Virginia Pendleton Treadwell in *Virginia*.[106] Ada's grandmother and her neighbors are all staunch

---

[105] Ellen Glasgow to Allen Tate, September 30, 1933, in *Letters*, 145; "Notes on Rockbridge," looseleaf notebook, in Glasgow Papers.
[106] Ellen Glasgow to Allen Tate, June 4, 1933, in *Letters*, 137; *A Certain Measure*, 168.

Presbyterians who exist by the doctrine of predestination, but no one of them really cares that their children chase and taunt Toby Waters, the village idiot boy, in the very shadow of the church. No one, that is, except Ada, who has pity for the boy and sometimes imagines herself to be in his place.

Ada falls in love with Ralph McBride, a neighbor lad who is poor but mentally gifted and begins to work his way through Washington and Lee University as part-time secretary to the president, much as Henry Anderson had done in real life. But Janet Rowan, a beautiful and temperamental girl, tricks Ralph into marrying her. Ralph goes off to fight in World War I, and Janet eventually runs away with another man. Typically, for Ellen Glasgow, World War I marks the watershed in the lives of most of the characters. Ralph returns home for a visit, makes love to Ada on Thunder Mountain in a scene which is the only genuine love scene in the entire Glasgow corpus and which is very similar to Ellen's description in the autobiography of her own rendezvous with Gerald in the Alps many years earlier. Ralph returned to the war, and Ada did not tell him that she was pregnant until after the baby was born.[107] The shock of Ada's illegitimate pregnancy killed her grandmother and made Ada an outcast in the town. The children who had once chased the idiot boy now chased Ada, and the idiot boy's mother rescued her by tossing on the children slops that she had collected for the pigs. The description of Ada's emotions is similar to Ellen's description in the autobiography of her own childhood terror when she wandered out into the street between a black dog and a band of children who were chasing it. Ada had inherited in her character a vein of iron from her Scotch-Irish ancestors that enabled her to endure. Ralph returned, married Ada, and moved to Queenborough along with the entire Fincastle family. The Depression came and the family suffered severely. John Fincastle made his way back to Ironside so that he could die in the land of his ancestors. Ralph and

[107] It is interesting to note that Ellen Glasgow's two most autobiographical heroines, Dorinda Oakley in *Barren Ground* and Ada Fincastle in *Vein of Iron*, both have love affairs analogous to Ellen Glasgow's own experience and both became pregnant.

Ada went back for his funeral and decided to stay there in the old manse and try to make a new beginning. The manse itself represents the continuity from one generation to the next and is as much alive as any flesh and blood creature, just as One West Main was to Ellen much more than some inert building of wood and stone.

Ellen worked on *Vein of Iron* with more enthusiasm than she had on any other novel and was convinced at the time it was completed that it was her best work.[108] She believed that she had shown how religion, philosophy, love, and simple human relationships were not the things that had enabled man and traditions to endure, but that survival depended upon that kind of stoic fortitude which she called a vein of iron.[109] The distillation of her own struggles through life, the novel was an intensely personal creation with her, and she was determined that it should get the best possible treatment from her publisher. For the second time, she changed publishers.

Largely through the influence of Irita Van Doren and the lucrative offer made to her by Alfred Harcourt, she left Doubleday in favor of Harcourt, Brace and Company.[110] Walter Hines Page was dead, and by the mid-1930's her friend old Frank Doubleday had moved to the background.[111] Doubleday, Doran and Company had published the novel in 1932 that won the Pulitzer Prize, the very same year they published *The Sheltered Life*, and the bitter memory of that event no doubt influenced Ellen to look for another publisher. Daniel Longwell, an editor for Doubleday, Doran and Company, made a desperate effort to retain her business by offering to allow her to write her own contract, but she could not be deterred.[112] Since 1929, Alfred Harcourt had been trying to become Ellen's

[108] To Bessie Zaban Jones, December 29, 1933, in Bessie Zaban Jones Papers; to Irita Van Doren, August 2, 1934, to Bessie Zaban Jones, January 8, 1935, to Irita Van Doren, June 18, 1935, to Bessie Zaban Jones, August 10, 1935, all in *Letters*, 160, 171, 185–86, 193. With the passage of time she went back to *Barren Ground* as her favorite.

[109] To Stark Young, n.d., in *Letters*, 190.

[110] Irita Van Doren to Ellen Glasgow, June 15 and 28, July 14 and 30, 1934, all in Glasgow Papers.

[111] Kelly, "Struggle for Recognition," 286.

[112] Ellen Glasgow to Irita Van Doren, August 12, 1934, in *Letters*, 161–62.

publisher, and in 1934 he succeeded.[113] His terms were generous: an advance of twenty thousand dollars on the basis of 15 percent royalty to twenty-five thousand copies, 20 percent royalty after twenty-five thousand copies sold, and a guarantee of fifteen thousand dollars spent on advertising.[114] The terms were extraordinarily good and no doubt a powerful factor influencing Ellen's decision, but she still insisted that her publisher show the proper enthusiasm for her work and believe in the novel.[115] The book was an instant success and neither publisher nor author had any reason to regret the new partnership.

For the second time in her life, one of Ellen Glasgow's novels commanded the entire front pages of the book review sections of the New York *Times* and the New York *Herald Tribune*, critics as a rule praised the novel, and the public bought it. The Book-of-the-Month Club selected it, more than 100,000 copies were printed, and it became the second-best seller of 1935.[116] It was the first of her novels to be made into a motion picture, an agreement which Ellen made purely for financial reasons.[117] Fresh rumblings that Ellen Glasgow deserved the Pulitzer Prize once again came to naught, but the critical and popular success of *Vein of Iron* so soon after the similar reception of *The Sheltered Life* definitely placed her on a new plateau of achievement and recognition. Ellen, of course, was most aware of her achievement. Even the role of Madame Paradise, friend of Samuel Johnson, could not contain her. She had created art that was timeless and had done well to put down

---

[113] Alfred Harcourt to Ellen Glasgow, November 1 and 4, 1929, June 15, August 2, and 10, 1934, in Glasgow Papers.

[114] Ellen Glasgow to Irita Van Doren, August 2, 1934, in *Letters*, 160.

[115] To Irita Van Doren, June 9, 1934, to Alfred Harcourt, August 14, 1934, in *Letters*, 156, 163.

[116] Kelly, "Struggle for Recognition," 309.

[117] Ellen Glasgow to Anne Virginia Bennett, September 30, 1935, in Glasgow Papers. Apparently the movie received little notice, and I have discovered no indication of the amount of money Ellen earned in the transaction. In 1918 she sold the film rights to *The Deliverance* for one thousand dollars, but apparently the movie was never produced; in 1937, after the invention of talking pictures, she considered trying to resell the film rights but abandoned the idea. Lillian A. Comstock to Ellen Glasgow, March 2, 1937, in Glasgow Papers.

no anchor in the transient era of the New South. "I have treated the past and the present as co-existent in time," she said, "and time itself as a subjective medium."[118] She struck out for a new home on Mount Olympus.

[118] *A Certain Measure,* 183.

# 10

## *Miss Ellen on Mount Olympus*

When Miss Ellen touched ground again, it was on Mount Olympus where she breathed the rarefied atmosphere of the gods, dispensed the truth of life, the truth of fiction and the truth of history, and with all the disdain of a goddess she accepted the laurels that came her way. The undeveloped thesis of her address before the Southern Writers Conference now became her theme wherever she had the opportunity to comment upon life, art, or history; what she was unable to do in a single speech she accomplished in a decade of speaking and writing. She was cautious and intensely personal when talking about life, confident about the art of writing, often vitriolic about the junior members of her profession, and remarkably perceptive about the interrelations of art and history.

For reasons more practical than philosophical, namely a check for sixty dollars in a year when she considered her financial situation to be desperate, she wrote an article entitled "What I Believe" for the *Nation* in 1933.[1] The article was half-baked, contained statements apparently calculated to be shocking, and was often trite. In the tradition of a good social Darwinist, she said that "the two useless extremes of society, the thriftless rich and the thriftless poor, should be mercifully eliminated by education or eugenics" and that private ownership of wealth should be curbed. There is reason to doubt the sincerity of her statement, because surely she did not intend to include the wealth of her brother, but the article

---

1 Ellen Glasgow, "What I Believe," *Nation*, CXXXVI (April 12, 1933), 404–406; Henry Hazlitt to Ellen Glasgow, February 15, 1933, in Glasgow Papers.

did contain the embryo of her credo, which she revised and elaborated upon five years later and published in a more subdued and sophisticated form in a volume of essays entitled *I Believe*.[2]

With a rare touch of humility, she claimed that she had no illusions about the philosophic importance of her "unimportant theories of life and death," but did enjoy indulging in some metaphysical speculation. Since she thought that a person's religion or philosophy was a natural expression of his identity, she began with her childhood experiences and traced the development of her thought much as she had done in the secret autobiography. From her mother she claimed to have inherited a hatred of cruelty and a sympathetic understanding of the helpless, including animals and even trees. From her father, of course, she had learned of and rejected "the kind of God who had once savored the smoke of burnt offerings, and to whose ghost, in churches everywhere, good people were still chanting hymns of immelodious praise." God was replaced in her philosophy by "a distant trust in some spirit, or divine essence, which many poets and a few philosophers have called the Good." She traced her flirtation with the teachings of Christ, Buddha, St. Francis of Assisi, and mysticism, which left her, she said, with "a broader tolerance of the unseen and the unknown" and the belief in "philosophy as an expression of man's relation to the mystery around him."[3] Only Charles Darwin's *The Origin of Species* provided her with a lifelong creed and a perspective from which to explore the truth of life.

Her philosophic quest became a part of her imagination and expressed itself in her work as a novelist. Through her work she discovered "more steadfast serenity in fortitude than in any dubious faith" and explored more deeply the vagaries of human nature. The First World War, she thought, proved that man has a great destructive instinct which expresses itself through wars and other cruelties and makes the truly civilized man the real victim of modern society. Evolution does not necessarily mean progress,

[2] Clifton Fadiman (ed.), *I Believe: The Personal Philosophies of Certain Eminent Men and Women of Our Time* (New York: Simon and Schuster, 1938), 93–110.
[3] *Ibid.*, 93, 94, 96, 101.

and change does not necessarily mean growth; but in a moral order "slowly evolving from the mind of man," humanity "has collected a few sublime virtues, or ideas of sublime virtue, which are called truth, justice, courage, loyalty, compassion." In spite of her disdain for "that erratic quantity we know as human nature," and with utter disregard for her long-standing Barren Ground philosophy, she thought that the two most enduring satisfactions in life were the associations with one's fellow beings in friendship and love and the faithful pursuit of an art or profession.[4] Materialism she saw as the greatest impediment to the development of art and satisfactory social relationships,[5] inhumanity as the only sin, and benign laughter as the best tonic for life. On a note of other-worldly optimism she concluded "that the true value of life can be measured only, as it borrows meaning, from the things that are valued above and beyond life."[6] In life, "in spite of all the miracles of science and religion," she despaired of humanity, but she never ceased to hope that some transcendental force beyond human life would someday make life better. This was what she had been trying to say in her novels, even in *Barren Ground*. Hers was a critical and questioning mind that never accepted any answer as final to the question, what is the truth of life?

The writing of novels, to which she had devoted her life, was Miss Ellen's way of continuing her eternal quest for truth. Her technique of writing was intensely personal and buried in the secret autobiography, but in letters to her friends and an article in the *Saturday Review of Literature* she shared her insights into the art of fiction as she practiced it. The true novel, she said, was an act of birth, not a device or invention, and it required a long brooding season.[7] It was something that came to her naturally, or to which she had been "dedicated or doomed, by some malicious godmother who hung over [her] cradle."[8] Even as a child when she

[4] *Ibid.*, 104, 107, 108–109.

[5] To Allen Tate, March 11, 1933, in *Letters*, 129–30.

[6] Fadiman (ed.), *I Believe*, 110.

[7] Ellen Glasgow, "One Way to Write Novels," *Saturday Review of Literature*, XI (December 8, 1934), 335.

[8] Ellen Glasgow, "Elder and Younger Brother," *Saturday Review of Literature*, XV (January 23, 1937), 3.

lived with "Little Willie," the creature of her imagination, she knew that she must write. Ideas came to her not when she searched for them, but by sheer chance or intuition, perhaps caused, she said, by the lack of harmony between her inner life and early environment. Writing those ideas down in the form of fiction was an inescapable occupation and the hardest work in the world, which involved attempting the impossible task of reconciling the truth of life with the truth of fiction.[9] Actual places and events must be sifted through the imagination before they came alive in print, and it usually took three drafts and three years to make them do so. The experiences of her childhood were most real and transferred most easily into her fiction, but the book always had a life of its own with characters who were more real to her than live people and who seemed to dictate to the author their words and actions. The world of the novel in which she was often totally immersed at the time she was writing was more real to her than her own life, but it was a world whose creator saw the beginning and the end before she entered it. It was a world in which she lived for several years with the conflicting emotions of eager anticipation and neurotic dread of its conclusion.

The completion of a novel was an emotional shock for Ellen, because she was obliged to change suddenly from one world to another and usually found some things that were both good and evil in the transition. "I dread to finish a novel," she once said, "for you know when one is writing the world of the book seems almost more real than the other. When you are done, life is a blind alley for a while. I don't mean I'm happy when I'm working, but I'm less happy when I'm not."[10] To the question, is it worth the cost?, she answered: "Well, the writing of fiction is worth, I imagine, exactly what digging a ditch or charting the heavens may be worth to the worker, and that is not a penny more or less than the release of mind that it brings." Though she enjoyed both, she shunned fame and money as the goal of the artist and insisted that the

9 "One Way to Write Novels," 344.
10 "Ellen Glasgow Doubts if Life Is So Terrible," New York *Herald Tribune,* April 26, 1935, p. 15.

novelist must "touch life on every side" and keep an "untouched and untouchable" inmost vision as the guide to good writing.[11] Her vision sprang from her desire to put her best into her books in an effort to compensate for the "long tragedy" of her life. Indeed, there were moments when she felt that if it were not for her work she would find some way to end her life.[12] Her work was her life, and the end of a novel approached her as her own death.[13] She enjoyed the actual writing and began a new novel with enthusiasm. She told her publisher that even though she had vowed after the completion of *Vein of Iron* that she would "never, never commit another novel," she had launched upon a new adventure that was growing bigger and better. And she added in a postscript: "And shan't we have a good time with the new novel!"[14] Her dread of the completion of a book caused her to lose no time in getting started on a new one, and she was apparently never without an idea for a novel.

In collecting the tools of her trade, she omitted nothing that might help her with her work. The reference section of her library contained a vast collection relating to the craft of writing, and she admitted that she spent a great deal of time studying different methods of fiction and problems of technique.[15] Fowler's *Modern English Usage* was apparently her favorite tool, but she had a wide range of dictionaries and style manuals.[16] A set of *Studies in the Psychology of Sex* provided her with insights into that subject if she needed it, and she did not hesitate to speculate concerning the effect of marriage on one's art. She inquired of Amélie Rives Troubetskoy if her marriage to Pierre had lessened her creativity and received an instant negative response![17]

Theories and literary formulas, however, were discarded when she actually began to write; she allowed "life and life alone" to

11 "One Way to Write Novels," 350.
12 To Stark Young, July 12, 1932, July 28, 1934, in *Letters*, 112, 159.
13 To Bessie Zaban Jones, January 8, 1935, *ibid.*, 171–72.
14 To Alfred Harcourt, August 21, 1937, *ibid.*, 223–24.
15 *A Certain Measure*, 222.
16 Tutwiler, "The Writer as Reader," in *De Graffenried Family Scrapbook*, 216–21.
17 Amélie Rives Troubetskoy to Ellen Glasgow, September 9, 1931, in Glasgow Papers.

control "the slowly evolving situation."[18] She wrote at odd hours, with "sudden spurts" and often stayed up all night in her earlier years.[19] With the passage of time she became more disciplined, but she could never create a novel according to a schedule and refused to promise anyone that she would have it ready by a certain date.[20] "The power to write anything," she wrote to Douglas Freeman, "comes and goes like the winds of doctrine, and I am scarcely more than a medium."[21] She delayed the moment of actual writing as long as possible by wandering around the house and turning off the water faucets, sharpening pencils, and rearranging small items just for the sake of procrastination.[22] There were months when she did not touch the typewriter as she brooded over ideas. Then she would fill pages with trial titles, sentences, and phrases that may not have had any relationship to each other. She herself usually made only one copy of a novel, using her typewriter and then making corrections by hand with one of the four dozen sharpened pencils that Anne Virginia kept nearby. Anne Virginia then retyped the manuscript and the original, crude copy was often destroyed.

Whatever followed was in the hands of the publishers, or almost in the hands of the publishers, because Ellen Glasgow never completely let a novel go. She developed the art of manipulating critics as assiduously as she did the technique of writing. A trip to New York City usually coincided with the publication of a new novel, and Miss Ellen invited various critics to her hotel suite, explained to them what she intended in the novel, and then sent them out with instructions to write a good review. She made friends with the editors of the *New York Times Book Review*, the *Saturday Review of Literature*, *New York Herald Tribune Books*, and the book critic for the *New Republic* and thus assured a favorable treatment in those periodicals. She more than made friends with them; in some cases she actually wrote her own reviews. Stark Young of

18 *A Certain Measure*, 222.
19 To Mary Johnston, March 22, 1904, in *Letters*, 44.
20 To Alfred Harcourt, October 26, 1934, *ibid.*, 169–70.
21 July 8, 1937, *ibid.*, 220.
22 Interview with Mrs. William R. Trigg, Jr., January 10, 1969.

the *New Republic* asked her in advance what she wanted him to say about a novel and never failed to say it.[23] By the time *Vein of Iron* was published, she did not wait for him to ask; she just went ahead and told him what he must say.[24] And she urged her brother Arthur to speak to any editors or reviewers he knew in London concerning the British edition of the novel.[25] She had learned that she could count on Allen Tate, and she plied her friendship with Howard Mumford and Bessie Zaban Jones to the hilt in order to get good reviews into print.[26]

Even Douglas Freeman, editor of the Richmond *News Leader*, became a pawn in her hands. She had contributed her name and influence to the advertisement of Freeman's biography of Robert E. Lee, which won the Pulitzer Prize in 1935. Freeman, a Virginia gentleman who was sensitive to Ellen's feelings about the prize, immediately sent her a telegram in which he gave her the credit for the good reception of his biography of Lee.[27] To reinforce his sincerity Freeman wrote a laudatory article about Ellen Glasgow for the *Saturday Review of Literature*, in which he called her an idealist and which he allowed her to read and comment upon before submitting for publication.[28] The article did not express his honest opinion about her, and although he did not say it in print, he knew that her cynicism in her novels was Miss Ellen laughing at herself.[29] He knew also that perhaps there were more people who were afraid of her or depressed by her than there were who considered her an idealist.

But Ellen was grateful for favors granted to her in reviews and

23 Stark Young to Ellen Glasgow, August 21 and 26, 1932, in Glasgow Papers; Ellen Glasgow to Allen Tate, September 22, 1932, in *Letters*, 123.
24 To Stark Young, May 11, 1935, and n.d., in *Letters*, 177–78, 190–91.
25 To Arthur Glasgow, December 10, 1935, in *Letters*, 204.
26 Ellen Glasgow to Allen Tate, September 22, 1932, to Bessie Zaban Jones, May 9, 1938, to Howard Mumford Jones, July 22, 1938, all in *Letters*, pp. 125, 239, 242; to Howard Mumford Jones, June 14, 1935, in Howard Mumford Jones Papers; to Bessie Zaban Jones, March 5, 1938, July 19, 1938, July 28, 1938, in Bessie Zaban Jones Papers.
27 May 7, 1935, in Glasgow Papers.
28 Ellen Glasgow to Douglas S. Freeman, July 22, 1935, in Freeman Papers; n.d., in *Letters*, 195.
29 Douglas S. Freeman to MKR, in Rawlings Papers.

reciprocated whenever she got the opportunity. She hated to review books and rarely did so, but she expressed her appreciation to the *New York Herald Tribune Books* by reviewing two of her favorite books for it, and she rewarded Stark Young with a published complimentary critique of his novel, *So Red the Rose.*[30] For James Southall Wilson, Poe Professor of English at the University of Virginia, she gave a lecture to his class at the Breadloaf School of English in Vermont in the summer of 1936, and at the end of the year she paid tribute to the whole profession by entertaining members of the Modern Language Association at One West Main Street.[31]

Critics, especially young critics, might be manipulated by an aging lady and indomitable novelist who did not mind telling them precisely what she expected of them, but fellow writers were not so easily intimidated. The people who looked to Miss Ellen for wisdom were usually those who aspired toward greatness in literary achievement but had to settle for some lesser fate. Those who had talent of their own went their own way and did not heed the oracles of Miss Ellen. The result was an increasing agitated aversion for the very generation of young American writers who were eventually to take their places as far more enduring figures than she in the literature of the world. Sinclair Lewis, America's first winner of the Nobel Prize, had never been one of her favorites,[32] and neither Ernest Hemingway nor William Faulkner merited her

[30] Ellen Glasgow, "Portrait of a Famous and Much Loved Dog," review of Virginia Woolf's *Flush: A Biography*, in *New York Herald Tribune Books* (October 8, 1933), 3, 21; "George Santayana Writes a 'Novel,' " review of Santayana's *The Last Puritan*, (February 2, 1936), *ibid.*, 1–2; "A Memorable Novel of the Old Deep South," review of *So Red the Rose*, (July 22, 1934), *ibid.*, 1–2.

[31] James Southall Wilson to Ellen Glasgow, August 15, 1936, in Glasgow Papers; Ellen Glasgow to Bessie Zaban Jones, December 10, 1936, in Bessie Zaban Jones Papers.

[32] Luther Y. Gore (ed.), " 'Literary Realism on Nominalism' by Ellen Glasgow: An Unpublished Essay," *American Literature*, XXXIV (March, 1962), 72–79. Professor Gore suggests that this essay was written in 1921 and indicates perhaps that Ellen Glasgow's criticism of Hemingway and Faulkner is not inconsistent with her earlier criticisms of American literature. Perhaps this essay, which is in the Glasgow Papers, indicates more than anything else a lifelong inability to appreciate the literary merit of novelists who took a different approach to their task than she did.

praise. Apparently she resented the fact that so many of America's best known writers in the early part of the twentieth century came from the Midwest; and when writers from her own region began to be recognized, she thought that their recognition was for the wrong reasons. Her views were not secret, but neither were they widely publicized until April, 1935, when the Friends of the Princeton Library invited her to address their gathering in New York City.[33]

She accepted the invitation only on the condition that she might say what she pleased "and not merely pay after-dinner compliments."[34] In her address, entitled "Heroes and Monsters,"[35] she objected to aimless violence and said that its use in Southern letters was a sure sign that there was no school of realism in the South. "Raw-Head-and-Bloody-Bones" was the name she assigned to Southern fiction represented by William Faulkner and to a lesser extent by Erskine Caldwell, though she never read the complete works of either and made her judgment in reaction to Faulkner's *Sanctuary*. Perhaps she was too much a Virginia lady to accept the unsavory aspect of life which Faulkner chose to write about, but if she had taken the time to explore beneath the surface of his plots, no doubt she would have found many ideas that she herself had been expressing in a different way. "We remain incurably romantic," she said. "Only a puff of smoke separates the fabulous Southern hero of the past from the fabulous Southern monster of the present—or the tender dreams of James Lane Allen from the fantastic nightmares of William Faulkner."[36] Perhaps she was correct in that statement, but she revealed her lack of understanding of her junior craftsmen when she condemned their work as an attempt to run away from the past and from life. In a sequel to *Sanctuary*, written some years later, Faulkner himself wrote: "The past is never dead. It's not even past."[37] The "evasive idealism" of which Ellen Glasgow had accused the generation of Southern writers that came be-

33 New York *Times*, April 26, 1935, p. 17.
34 To Alfred Harcourt, March 31, 1935, in *Letters*, 176.
35 "Heroes and Monsters," *Saturday Review of Literature*, XII (May 4, 1935), 3, 4.
36 *Ibid.*, 3.
37 William Faulkner, *Requiem for a Nun* (New York: American Library, 1954), 229.

fore her, she broadened to include that generation which came after her.[38]

Unaware that she might not be a wholly competent literary critic, she continued to explain to the Friends of the Princeton Library that it "takes more than spoilt meat to make realism" and that the only permanent law of art is the law of change. Either "as a laborer in the vineyard or as a raven croaking on a bust of Pallas" she had taken part in the American literary scene, she said, and therefore knew whereof she spoke. She would not deny a place for Gothic literature, but she did wish that the younger Southern writers would deal as honestly with living tissues as they did with decay and remind themselves "that the colors of putrescence have no greater validity for our age, or for any age, than have—let us say to be very daring—the cardinal virtues. . . . The literature that crawls too long in the mire," she warned, "will lose at last the power of standing erect. On the farther side of deterioration lies the death of a culture."[39]

Of the 450 persons who heard her address, there must have been many who disagreed with her, but it was a rare treat to hear her speak because she usually avoided such engagements. The bust of Pallas, she discovered with more realism than even she wished to savor, is an uneasy pedestal, for when she returned to her seat after her speech she missed her chair and sat on the floor. Stark Young, who had coaxed her to give the speech in the first place, wrote her that she need not worry about the event, for she looked as if she had merely decided to sit on the floor, hat and all, real stylish.[40]

Unseated, but not dethroned, she continued her argument the next day in an interview with a reporter from the New York *Herald Tribune.* "If the human race is really what it appeared to be in the last novels of some Southern writers," she said, "it is high time for us to begin chanting the battle hymn of the grasshoppers. Exterminate them, I say. Let the grasshoppers win. . . . I don't care to

[38] For Ellen Glasgow's most extensive discussion of "evasive idealism," see Joyce Kilmer, *Literature in the Making* (New York: Harper and Brothers, 1917), 229–40.
[39] "Heroes and Monsters," 4.
[40] May 1, 1935, in Glasgow Papers.

be anyone's fellow maggot." Nevertheless, she did not want to be accused of being an optimist, so she added for good measure: "I'm not going to defend human nature, but if it's become so unutterably unappetizing, it's time to stop. I don't believe in reform. I believe in destruction."[41]

Miss Ellen had finally said in public what she had said and would continue to say in private for a long time. The revolution which she so bravely had started had misfired, and she became a rebel against the very cause for which she had fought in her youth. "Just as there is the one perfect time for revolt," she said, "so it follows, inevitably, that there is the one perfect time to revolt from a revolt."[42] She simply did not like "modern" writers, especially those who threatened her reputation. She dubbed them "Sewer-Realists" and complained, "You don't have to kick the chamber-pot under the bed to know you are in a bedroom, do you?"[43] Yet to her friend and kindred spirit Allen Tate, she admitted that "literature must be free to feed in strange pastures, and must remain alive to the world even when it draws inspiration from dying and death."[44] The dying to whom she was referring, however, were not those who died violently and sometimes grotesquely in the dust of Faulkner's Yoknapatawpha County, but the soldiers in gray who had died upon the field of battle and subsequently were celebrated by Allen Tate in his "Ode to the Confederate Dead."

The pastures in which William Faulkner and Ernest Hemingway grazed were a bit too strange. Faulkner's "school of Raw-Head-and-Bloody-Bones," she said, sent her back not to realism but to the "Weird Tales of Hoffmann." "Gothic tales have their place; but, after all, why do all mushrooms have to be toadstools?"[45] Time and again she disapproved of "the sodden futilitarians and the corncob cavaliers of Mr. Faulkner," and, without trying to discover

[41] April 26, 1953, p. 15.

[42] "An Inadequate Comment on Primary Literature and Coterie-Literature by Van Wyck Brooks," MS copy of Ellen Glasgow's critique of a paper written by Brooks, in Van Wyck Brooks Papers, University of Pennsylvania Library. See also Ellen Glasgow to Van Wyck Brooks, August 23, 1941, in *Letters*, 288.

[43] Miss Frances Williams to MKR, in Rawlings Papers.

[44] April 3, 1933, in *Letters*, 133.

[45] To Irita Van Doren, September 8, 1933, *ibid.*, 143–44.

any real meaning in Faulkner, protested that his characters of "inhibited peasants" were not indigenous to the soil.[46] A group she identified as "Young Intellectuals" and which no doubt included Ernest Hemingway, she said were actually morons.[47] Hemingway belonged to a "school of sophisticated barbarians" who "couldn't have been much worse even if [Gertrude Stein] had let them alone."[48] They reminded her of "spiteful children who feel, after they have been slapped, that they must run out and pull the cat's tail."[49] Concerning such people as Douglas Freeman, Stark Young, Allen Tate, and lesser Southern writers, she could be gracious and speak kindly, but the authors who were becoming the giants of American literature seemed to call forth her professional jealousy. "I go on writing better and better," she complained, "in an age when no one cares any longer for the standard of perfection—not even as an unattainable excellence."[50]

Although it is true that she was producing her best works, they were a generation too late, and the main stream of American literature was leaving her behind. For comfort she turned back to literary scholars and friends in the publishing business whom she had tamed, and with their help she sought to advertise herself as a leader of the forces of decency and sophistication in literature. But her public and private comments about her junior colleagues were so severe that her opinions became suspect before they were even uttered, and she herself was cast in the role of the spiteful child. That role was to a large degree self-imposed and unfortunate, because from her long life and work she had gained wisdom that might not have been wasted had it flowed from a less temperamental fount. Fortunately, individual temperament has a way of yielding to the ravages of time, and her intellectual contributions can be judged apart from her personality. In her own life she tried

---

[46] To J. Donald Adams, November 2, 1933, to Bessie Zaban Jones, February 7, 1934, to Irita van Doren, May 23, 1934, to Lewis Gannett, July 12, 1935, all in *Letters*, 149, 150, 154, 188–89.

[47] To Daniel Longwell, May 24, 1934, *ibid*, 155.

[48] To Irita Van Doren, n.d., to Carl Van Vechten, January 30, 1935, in *Letters*, 144, 172–73.

[49] To Carl Van Vechten, *ibid*.

[50] To Edwin Mims, March 28, 1936, *ibid.*, 208.

and tried hard to make some significant contributions and did rise to a certain level of success when she agreed to address the session of the Modern Language Association which she entertained in her home in December, 1936. Her audience was made up primarily of scholars, a few lesser writers—but none of the leading writers whom she had criticized—and certain members of the publishing world. It was the kind of audience she liked and one which she addressed with a greater degree of gentility than the Friends of the Princeton Library. Reading a paper in her private drawing room placed restraints upon her that she apparently did not feel when speaking to a large gathering in New York City. An attack of laryngitis, or so she said, prevented her from reading the paper herself, and Allen Tate read it for her.[51]

Her subject was the relationship between the scholar and the creative writer, and under the title "Elder and Younger Brother" it was revised slightly and published in the *Saturday Review of Literature*. The work of the scholar, she thought, should be "as "sensitive to the promise of tomorrow as to the fulfillment that has been dead and buried and safely turned to dust for a thousand years. The relation it bears to the creative impulse is that of the elder to the younger brother." Both the scholar and the novelist function as preservers of truth and are "united in the fundamental service of life." Scholarship has preserved the ancient treasures of literature, and the "will that creates has combined with the will that defends, restrains, selects, eliminates, safeguards, and keeps alive for the future."[52] She made no claim to scholarship for herself, but she said she was a reader who did not like any idea unless it was "attached by indestructible ties to the living." The law of change she touched upon again in its relation to ideas: "No idea is so antiquated that it was not once modern. No idea is so modern that it will not some day be antiquated. The intellect will outlive the assault on intellectualism. The Revolution will outlive revolutionaries. To seize the flying thought before it escapes us is our only

---

51 Ellen Glasgow to Bessie Zaban Jones, December 10, 1936, in Bessie Zaban Jones Papers; to Allen Tate, January 2, 1937, in Tate Papers.
52 Glasgow, "Elder and Younger Brother," 3–5.

touch with reality. The one thing needful, it would seem, is not to be consistent."[53] Consistent she was not, and she reviewed her own career to prove what she called the value of inconsistency.

More than thirty years ago I began my literary work as a rebel against conventions. I am still a rebel, but the conventions are different. Although I have not lost the heart of a revolutionary, I like now to be firmly convinced that I am standing on the right—by which I mean the humane—barricade. No longer would I make a revolution for the melancholy privilege of calling things by their worst names. Nevertheless, the mood of my earliest work was the rebel mood of today. In the stern school of neglect and misrepresentation I was taught that being the only rebel in one's world is very nearly as futile, and quite as tragic, as being the only Christian. At that age, I was fond of saying: Nothing but the inevitable is worth fighting. Now, after an ineffectual revolt, I have come to realize that the inevitable is a poor adversary—that it does not obey the rules of civilized warfare and has no true sporting instinct. Yet I still believe that the mood, if not the manner, of revolution is the most fertile soil for ideas.[54]

The conventions against which she had originally rebelled had changed, but she could scarcely be called a "lost rebel" in the light of the timeless quality of her statement about the revolution itself. Though some scholars have fallen into the habit of "discovering" that Ellen Glasgow rebelled in old age against the very things she had advocated in her youth, Ellen herself had the wisdom to realize and defend her intellectual pilgrimage from an undisciplined and ineffectual revolt into a mature analysis of the possible value of revolution itself. Never, however, did she grant any concession to the genre of writers whom she had condemned before the Friends of the Princeton Library. She approved the "dark labyrinth of human psychology" as an appropriate background for fiction, but she warned of the novelist's danger of drowning in that very labyrinth. And she appealed to the scholars for a "strong, clear note of authority in the midst of the excessive exaltation of the inferior, in the midst of the endless tumult over the cheap, the immature, the

[53] *Ibid.*, 4.
[54] *Ibid.*

rowdy, even the obviously defective." She urged the scholar to keep
an open mind and to hold fast to standards of excellence, no matter
what the cost, for it is "only by changing as the world changes," she
said, that "we shall be able to protect our rich inheritances and our
vested intellectual interests in any future."[55]

Ellen Glasgow was aware, obviously, that she was speaking to a
group of people, some of whom were going to write about her work,
but her personal interest in the relation between the scholar and
the artist merely heightens the significance of her statement upon
that relationship. There is a rare touch of humility in "Elder and
Younger Brother," because she gave her primary attention to the
contribution which the scholar makes to the creative writer, not
that which the writer makes to the scholar. She must have been
aware that she had reached a point in her own career, the end of
which was already in sight, when the preservation of her art would
depend primarily upon the treatment it received from scholars. For
the time being, she left it to the scholar to discover for himself a
vital source of knowledge in the work of the creative artist.

Among scholars, historians came late to the appreciation of literature, but have found there much to be learned from the younger
brother. Wherever the deposits of the human heart are found, there
are the materials for the historian as well as for the artist. The social historian especially wants to attempt to reconstruct the lives
and manners of those who did not write letters or keep diaries; he
wants to know what the people said and thought and believed as
they whittled and spat around the Courthouse Square.[56] If the ideas
of the past are to be "attached by indestructible ties to the living,"
as Ellen Glasgow said that they must be, then the social historian
must write so that his readers may empathize with the people about
whom they read, noting human actions, passions, motivations, relationships, and conduct.

The work of the creative artist often contains materials of value
to the historian that are unobtainable elsewhere. The data of social
history are innumerable, and literature acts as an emulsion that

55 *Ibid.*, 4, 5.
56 Fishwick, *Virginia: A New Look*, 169.

holds in relationship much of the material of social history, while at the same time providing "a record of social experience, an embodiment of social myths and ideals and aims, and an organization of social beliefs and sanctions."[57] In her earliest distinction between the truth of life and the truth of fiction before the Southern Writers Conference, Ellen Glasgow was conscious of the possibilities and limitations of the novelist as a historian, though she wisely refrained from rushing prematurely into too elaborate an explanation of her idea about the relation between the novel and history. The view of the novelist is clouded by his own temperament, taste, talent, literary tradition, and often by the demands of book buyers, all of which must be adjusted for before a novel can even be considered as a historical source.[58] But literary history is a branch of cultural history, and writers are deeply affected by the spirit of the age in which they live.[59] Novelists, especially Southern novelists, "have enriched our consciousness of the past in the present" and "given history meaning and value and significance as events never do merely because they happen."[60] The formal historian who margins his pages with notes and pads his footnotes with remote and perhaps questionable authorities is generally regarded as the true keeper of the records of his country, but the records of the spirit are often kept well and in far more accessible shape by the novelist. Ellen Glasgow believed that there is a point where the truth of life and the truth of fiction are one, but she probably never planned to say as much unless some accidental opportunity forced her into additional comment upon the subject.

That opportunity came in the most unexpected way early in 1937 when Maxwell Perkins, the famous editor for the publishing firm of Charles Scribner's Sons, asked permission to bring out a

[57] Bernard DeVoto, "Interrelations of History and Literature," in William E. Lingelbach (ed.), *Approaches to American Social History* (New York: D. Appleton-Century Co., 1937), 54.

[58] Jay B. Hubbell, *Southern Life in Fiction* (Athens: University of Georgia Press, 1960), 7.

[59] Arthur M. Schlesinger, "Social History in American Literature," *Yale Review*, XVIII (September, 1928), 137, 140.

[60] C. Vann Woodward, *The Burden of Southern History* (Rev. ed., Baton Rouge: Louisiana State University Press, 1968), 39.

collected edition of her works and for her to write a preface to each
volume. Ellen accepted immediately, but she delayed beginning
her work because she dreaded to write the prefaces and yearned
for a vacation in Europe before undertaking what seemed to her
to be an unpleasant task. Seven years had passed since she had been
to Europe, and Europe, especially England, had become to her a
place where she could refresh the springs of her mind and spirit
after completing a novel. The Depression had prevented her from
returning as frequently as she might have, and her summer vacations had consisted of a few weeks on the coast of New Jersey or in
a rented house in New England. She would never see old England
again, but in the spring of 1937 she and Carrie Duke sailed for Italy
where they were invited to be guests of friends from Richmond
who had bought a villa at Fiesole.[61]

Colonel Henry Anderson saw them off from New York with a
luncheon and champagne. The normally amiable and happy Carrie
became ill on board the ship, and Ellen was so uncomfortable during the voyage that she told Anne Virginia she hoped it would be
her last trip. Once in Italy, her outlook improved marvelously and
she wrote to Anne Virginia that it was the most restful break she
had had in years.[62] Ellen relaxed on the terrace of the villa, took
occasional trips to view the art treasures of Florence, and on one
happy day ate soup with the friars at one of the Little Poor Man's
monasteries in the Appennines. She and Carrie Duke sat alone in a
deserted church and listened to a friar play the organ, while she
turned back the centuries and thought of St. Francis, the friend of
the helpless and on many occasions her friend.[63] Late in June her
time was up, and she wrote "Dear Billy and Pat" to meet her at the
early train on July 3.[64] Apparently they passed her message on to
Anne Virginia or the chauffeur, and Ellen arrived back in Richmond to face the midsummer heat and the dreaded task of writing
the prefaces.

61 Ellen Glasgow to Mr. and Mrs. Carl Van Vechten, April 22, 1937, in Van Vechten
Papers, Yale.
62 Ellen Glasgow to Anne Virginia Bennett, May 19, June 1, 1937, in Glasgow Papers.
63 *Woman Within*, 264–66.
64 June 21, 1937, in Glasgow Papers.

Simply for the sake of writing the prefaces themselves, she would never have done it, but Scribners insisted, and James Branch Cabell offered his assistance. A handsome collector's edition of her works was an honor too great for her to turn down. The *Old Dominion Edition* of her works, which had been published by her former publishers between 1929 and 1933, contained only eight volumes with a very brief preface for each novel. Maxwell Perkins suggested that the Scribners' set contain twelve volumes, be called the *Virginia Edition*, and each volume have an extensive new preface to be written by the novelist.[65] There would be 790 sets printed, and the twelve volumes would sell by subscription for ten dollars each. Ellen frankly doubted that the edition, at this luxury price, could be sold in the economy of 1937; but she left that problem to the publisher and went to her friend James Branch Cabell for counsel on how to write the prefaces.

Cabell encouraged her to continue and even did a great deal of the work himself. He had reviewed the *Old Dominion Edition* of her works in 1930 and had made several casual suggestions then as to what volumes should be included.[66] He had even promised earlier to give her "a simple formula by which you can do a 2,000 word preface without the least mental strain." In 1937, at her request, he gave her the formula. It called for a description of the place of the book in the social history of Virginia, the author's personal view of it, the circumstances under which the book was written, and something about the history of its publication; and Ellen followed that formula precisely.[67] Cabell did much more than offer Ellen his formula. He did her proofreading, gave his opinion on what volumes should be included in the set and how they should be arranged, and even wrote some sections of the prefaces himself.[68] When the prefaces had been finished and all volumes of the sets

[65] Eighteen letters from Maxwell Perkins to Ellen Glasgow, dated May 6, 1937 through July 12, 1938, trace their business relationship during the preparation of the set, but are concerned almost entirely with insignificant details. In Glasgow Papers.

[66] James Branch Cabell to Ellen Glasgow, February 23, 1930, *ibid.*

[67] To Ellen Glasgow, January 18, 1930, September 16, 1937, *ibid.*

[68] A number of undated notes from Ellen Glasgow to James Branch Cabell, which are concerned with the prefaces, are preserved in the Cabell Papers.

published in 1938, Ellen never publicly gave Cabell any credit for his work. She did thank him privately: "I wonder why you are always so good to me. I know I do not deserve half of it. Still, I wish to encourage such generosity wherever I find it, and especially in high places. Thank God the final preface has gone!"[69]

The final product was well worth the agony required to produce it, because the nature and content of the prefaces brought Ellen Glasgow far more honor than the existence of the collected edition itself.[70] She eventually denied that they were prefaces at all, but insisted that they were essays in literary self-criticism, as indeed they were. She gave brief autobiographical sketches of her life at the time she was working on a particular novel, told something of her research for each novel and often the meaning she had intended to convey. She took the content of all of her recent speeches or essays —"The Novel in the South," "What I Believe," "One Way to Write Novels," "Heroes and Monsters," and "Elder and Younger Brother"—and dropped it into her prefaces. With almost no changes her article entitled "One Way to Write Novels" became the preface for *The Sheltered Life*. And, no doubt, strongly under the influence of James Branch Cabell, she advertised herself once and for all as a social historian of Virginia, a term that sells short the full range of her achievement as an artist but appropriately describes much of the lasting value of her work. The prefaces were her final and most comprehensive statement on the relationship of the artist to the historian.

Miss Ellen believed that the province of the novel, like that of the social historian, "is the entire range of human experience and that vast area of moral destiny."[71] With only the exception of *The Battle-Ground* her novels deal with events that were contemporary with her own life, with people and things she had ample opportunity to observe. *The Battle-Ground* draws heavily from stories told to her by her mother and from the complete files of three newspapers that cover the era. Her data were innumerable; she visited

69 To James Branch Cabell, Thursday, [1938] *ibid.*

70 In 1943 the prefaces were collected and published in a separate volume entitled *A Certain Measure.*

71 "Empty Novels Hit by Ellen Glasgow," New York *Times*, January 1, 1937, p. 21.

every town and hamlet about which she wrote, and most of her characters are people whom she had known or observed. Her novels are eyewitness accounts of her Virginia. The external events, the great political and economic developments that forged and were forged by the course of history, are always in the background, and she did not choose to fictionalize any of the great figures of Virginia's past; she created fictional characters whom she believed realistically displayed human nature and the impact of situations and values upon human personality. Fiction should, she said, "in a measure at least, reflect the movement and tone of its age"; and she vowed that this was her purpose in her "undocumented chronicle of human nature and the conditions under which it developed, or by which it was modified, in related periods of time." Her novels were the "authentic rendering of unwritten history,"[72] she claimed a little presumptuously but with justification, for by taking seriously the history of Virginia she provided the possibility for her readers to grasp the *feel* as well as the *fact* of history and thereby strengthened the bonds between the novelist and the historian. She explored the past—Virginia's past and her past—to give force to the realism she thought her readers should have; at the same time she was searching for an understanding of a world in which she was never wholly at ease. Her interest in the life around her was intensely personal. She wanted characters of flesh and blood, acting naturally as they struggled with fate and themselves. She lacked the imagination and the sympathy necessary to find assurance in the remote and medieval-like structures of James Branch Cabell. She had a taste for blood and irony even though she was too much a Virginia lady to savor it unrestrainedly. For her the facts of life could be better understood through imaginary characters who were real than through historical characters who were fictional. She did her job well and earned for herself the right to speak from Mount Olympus.

Her recognition came late and was often surrounded by bitter feelings and unfortunate accidents. In 1932 she was elected to membership in the National Institute of Arts and Letters, and in

[72] *A Certain Measure*, 24, 72.

1938 she became a member of the prestigous American Academy of Arts and Letters.[73] She claimed that "all such honors are entirely empty and not worth a straw," but she obviously enjoyed the prestige and attention it afforded her.[74] Several months before her official election to the Academy, a dinner was held in New York in her honor. A kindly secretary who looked upon Ellen Glasgow as a partially deaf, aging woman who must be carefully attended at such a gathering, offered to sit next to her at the dinner and render any assistance that she could. She drastically underestimated Miss Ellen, who hated to be dependent on anyone and whose personality had not mellowed in the least with the advancement of age or fame. Miss Ellen replied: "Much as I should enjoy being beside you, I think it would be better for me to have two of the men seated next me. There are so many men, and so few women. Do not worry about that. I get on perfectly well, and I like to meet new people."[75]

Meeting new people could be a chore, however, and she soon learned that a quiet dinner of twenty-one invited guests is a far cry from the bustle of a university commencement. Only the University of North Carolina had distinguished itself by actually conferring upon her an honorary degree in 1930 at a time when she had just begun to produce her best novels and was most interested in making contacts with literary scholars. She refused subsequent offers of honorary degrees from other schools, but when Douglas Freeman in his capacity as chairman of the board of trustees for the University of Richmond initiated that institution's offer to her of an honorary degree, she felt that she could not refuse.[76] Yet it took a considerable amount of reassurance from Freeman to make her appear at the ceremony. She dreaded public appearances, went to great extremes to prevent her picture from being taken, and was very sensitive about her deafness. She wrote Freeman that there

---

[73] Walter Prichard Eaton to Ellen Glasgow, November 15, 1932, Nicholas Murray Butler to Ellen Glasgow, February 10, 1939, in Glasgow Papers.

[74] To Douglas S. Freeman, October 15, 1936, in Freeman Papers.

[75] To Mrs. Grace Vanamee, September, [1938] in Glasgow File, American Academy of Arts and Letters, 633 W. 155th St., New York.

[76] F. W. Boatwright to Ellen Glasgow, February 4, 1938, in Glasgow Papers.

must be no cameras, loudspeakers, or photographs, and that she dreaded the ceremony on account of her "damnable deafness."[77] Freeman promised that he would do his best to see that she was subjected to a minimum of discomfort and publicity.[78] As the day of the ceremony approached, she became increasingly nervous, demanded from Freeman details about the academic gown, requested permission not to have to march in the procession, and reiterated her anxiety about being photographed.[79] Freeman reassured her again and even promised to get her a longer cord for her ear phone so that she could leave the receiver permanently attached to the lectern and hear everything that was said without difficulty.[80] The ceremony apparently was successful as far as Ellen was concerned, because thereafter she acknowledged that it was her duty to accept degrees from universities who desired to honor her. She was also vain enough to cherish such awards.

Five weeks after the ceremony in Richmond, she journeyed to Durham, North Carolina, to accept a degree from Duke University. For three consecutive years, Duke had offered her a degree and she had declined because of ill health or because the cermony conflicted with her vacation plans.[81] At Duke she and her companion were the guests of Dean Alice Baldwin of the Woman's College, who was responsible for entertaining her and sitting with her on the stage during the ceremony. In Miss Baldwin's home, Ellen Glasgow was a good conversationalist and a perfect guest, but the ceremony itself was a minor disaster.[82] She had agreed to accept the degree only on the conditions that no photographs would be taken and the degree would be that of Doctor of Laws, not Doctor of Letters. And she probably did not know that she would be sharing the stage with

[77] February 5 and March 22, 1938, in *Letters*, 234, 235.
[78] To Ellen Glasgow, March 24, 1938, in Freeman Papers.
[79] April 14, 1938, in *Letters*, 237.
[80] April 16, 1938, in Freeman Papers.
[81] William P. Few to Ellen Glasgow, May 8, 1936, April 19, 1937, April 2, 1938, Ellen Glasgow to William P. Few, May 10, 1936, all in Glasgow Papers.
[82] Alice M. Baldwin, "Ellen Glasgow," *South Atlantic Quarterly*, LIV (July, 1955), 403. The article is primarily a review of Ellen Glasgow's autobiography and does not mention the episode at the commencement exercises.

Norman Vincent Peale who was to receive an honorary degree at the same time. As she was accepting her degree someone took her picture. She was infuriated and turned her back to the audience and kept it turned for the remainder of the ceremony. Still on the stage with her back turned, she opened her degree. It was a Doctorate of Letters. After the ceremony Dean Baldwin tried to calm her nerves by letting her play with her pet Scottie and promising that she would approach President William P. Few and get the degree changed. Ellen went home with her Doctorate of Letters, and a few days later she received a bouquet of roses from Dean Baldwin as an additional peace offering.[83]

President Few of Duke University was intensely embarrassed, however, and took immediate steps to amend the error. He asked Douglas Freeman to serve as an intermediary for Duke and to present Ellen Glasgow with the proper degree at a time agreeable to her. Freeman urged her to accept the offer, and she replied graciously and no doubt sincerely that she was sorry to have caused President Few such anxiety and that the incident had passed from her mind. She accepted the offer and urged Freeman to convey her regrets to President Few and tell him how much she had admired the Gothic buildings at Duke. It was the end of the summer before the new degree was ready, and it remained in Freeman's custody for more than four months before Ellen decided to select a time when she would receive it. Finally, Dr. and Mrs. Freeman offered to give a tea for her in their home and invite her friends to see her receive the degree.[84] Ellen accepted readily, saying that she had been shy about asking guests to attend the ceremony in her own drawing room and asking if it would be necessary for her to wear her cap and gown.[85] She did wear the cap and gown, spent some time primping beforehand, and seemed relieved when the ceremony was over.[86] Dr. Freeman also wore his academic costume, and the witnesses included only three of Ellen's closest friends and

83 Interviews with Professors Mattie Russell, Robert H. Woody, and Jay B. Hubbell, Duke University.
84 Douglas S. Freeman to Ellen Glasgow, June 29, 1938, in Freeman Papers.
85 June 30, December 31, 1938, January 5, 1939, *ibid*.
86 Mrs. Douglas S. Freeman to MKR, in Rawlings Papers.

the presidents of the University of Richmond and the College of William and Mary.

It was well that John Stewart Bryan, president of the College of William and Mary, had the opportunity to witness her investiture and learn of her idiosyncrasies concerning such matters, because his college was about to offer her a degree the next spring. He immediately offered her a Doctorate of Laws, sensing perhaps that she preferred that degree to the Doctorate of Letters because she fancied herself to be as much a philosopher as a novelist. He recalled her maternal ancestry which related her to an early president of the College of William and Mary and flattered her by saying that she was "most sure and certain proof that genius has not run out in Virginia."[87] Ellen accepted for the last time.[88] She considered John Stewart Bryan to be a personal friend, and a trip to Williamsburg would be like a return home for her. It had been the scene of her third novel and was the major attraction to which she took many of the guests who visited her at One West Main. The College of William and Mary may have been the one school whose honorary degree Ellen most appreciated, and certainly the plans and even the citation were so well made as to guarantee that the event itself would be a happy one.

The universities and organizations who honored Ellen Glasgow were honoring far more than a woman who was troubled by the necessity to make public appearances and sometimes reacted with unusual behavior. They were honoring her achievement, her art that was timeless, her ability to create out of the materials of the human heart something that did not exist before and to utilize the traditions of the past in a social history that portrays "the ever-changing human drama." The words of the citation from the College of William and Mary captured both the ambition and her achievement of Ellen Glasgow: "To you, inheritor of a great tradi-

[87] March 8, 1939, in Glasgow Papers.
[88] The other colleges and universities which offered Ellen Glasgow honorary degrees which she declined, are the following: Rollins College, Sarasota, Florida, 1935; the University of Wisconsin, 1937; Goucher College, Baltimore, 1938; the University of Rochester, 1939; Middlebury College, 1940; and Smith College, 1944. Letters from the presidents or other officials of these institutions are in the Glasgow Papers.

tion, the world and its vast reaches of unplumbed reality beckon. With high intellectual courage as a philosopher and as an explorer you ventured into the fields of the new knowledge.

"Your own Virginia furnished rich and rugged background for your portrayal of the ever-changing human drama, and the life of your times has been perceived and revealed by your genius, to which has been added the skill and mastery born of unflagging search for perfection."[89]

The words of the citation, as truthful and calculated to please as they may have been, told Ellen nothing about herself that she did not already firmly believe. That search for perfection which she employed in the creation of her novels, she sometimes abandoned in her relationships with her fellow human beings. So much a part of that human drama which she had portrayed, as she sat under the old elm trees at the outdoor ceremony at the College of William and Mary, she was still very much the woman with a troubled mind who had created the untenable Barren Ground philosophy. Later she admitted that she paid more attention to the singing of the birds than to the speeches of the humans.[90]

[89] Glasgow Papers.
[90] To Van Wyck Brooks, July 4, 1939, in *Letters*, 253.

# 11

## *Historical Revelations*

Once James Branch Cabell had suggested that she was a social historian, Ellen favored the role. Isolated by actual physical deafness and by a philosophy of life which preached that one could live detached from one's fellows, she gladly accepted her role as one ideally suited to be an objective observer of human life in Virginia. The publication of the *Virginia Edition* of her novels gave her the opportunity to prove that the label of "social historian" was justly deserved. Collected and arranged chronologically according to the periods in the history of Virginia which they cover, her novels do provide a fairly comprehensive coverage of the history of Virginia from 1850 through 1942. Certain omissions are noticeable. The Reconstruction years, 1865 through 1870, are not dealt with per se, but the impact of those years upon the subsequent development of Virginia is readily accounted for in the development of characters in the novels that deal specifically with the post-Reconstruction years. Certain groups and areas in Virginia are passed over or touched only tangentially, but such omissions do not devalue Ellen Glasgow's extraordinary contribution to the understanding of the history of her state.

As a historian, she did not directly chronicle or analyze the political, economic, and military events in her state. She had neither the desire nor the training for such a task. Yet she knew, and made plain to the readers of her novels, that Virginia had fought on the losing side of a great civil war. She knew many years before Margaret Mitchell was old enough to say it, that the old life in the South had "gone with the wind." She knew also that after the society of the Old South, an entire way of life, had been smashed, there followed a long period of reconstruction, only part of which took place under Northern arms. This part she does not even mention, and indeed it hardly deserves mention when compared with reconstruction by the people themselves as they persisted to battle with life, to struggle, to lose, to hate, sometimes to win, and occasionally to love. Ellen Glasgow made a determined effort to tell this long story, and to tell it honestly, realistically. This is the sense in which she was a historian.

As a historian, she thought of the people of Virginia as being divided into three groups that corresponded to the stratification of the society of the Old South. Such a conception came naturally to an aristocrat, imbued with a strong feeling of class-consciousness, who yearned for the ways of the Old South, even though she knew all too well and attempted to make clear to her readers that those ways were gone forever. The first of her groups includes all Negroes. At the other end of the spectrum are the aristocrats, those whites who had owned land and slaves before the war and their descendants after the war. In the middle are all other whites, including small farmers and businessmen, tradesmen and laborers, and even the most shiftless element of white society called white trash. As novelist or historian Ellen Glasgow saw all of her characters as members of one of these three groups. At the same time she saw almost every character, no matter to which group he belonged, as a human being, and thus added an important dimension to her social history. The theme of her social history, then, is not merely that the history of Virginia from 1850 through 1942 can be explained through an analysis of her class structure; it is that the history of Virginia involves the sometimes tragic, sometimes comic, but always human, story of how all people of whatever class grappled with the complexities of human existence as they found it in the state of Virginia during the years from 1850 through 1942. To tell that story, Ellen Glasgow divided her Virginians into three groups whose changing roles in society, she felt, can be explained in the innumerable facets of human nature.

The first group, which includes all Negroes, she saw as neither a threat nor a phenomenon begging for thorough investigation. No major character in her novels is a Negro. Yet, she was aware that their presence made up a significant part of Virginia life, and she dealt with that presence in each of her novels. Her treatment of black people in fiction is always sympathetic and true to her own experience in dealing with and observing them. James, her Negro cook, was a vital part of her life. When asked if he had any children, he once replied, "Yes suh, seven chillen and Miss Ellen Glasgow."[1] Ellen made annual Christmas visits to the Afro-American Old Folks Home to carry food and gifts, and she made periodic visits to the black Y.W.C.A. to hear the Sabbath Glee Club perform. She maintained contact with the descendants of her mother's mammy, as well as some former servants, and gave them money, food, and even copies of her books.[2] Negro servants were always a part of her household and a normal part of her life. Her treatment of black servants in her novels is not unrealistic, because as late as 1930 one-half of all unskilled Negro wage earners in Virginia were domestic servants.[3] "In my Negroes," she wrote, "I have come very near to actual portraits."[4] She recognized the worth of Southern Negroes, never used them for low comedy, and sought to understand them as persons of significance with inner feelings that should be preserved in her creative history.

As her social chronicle opens in 1850, Negro characters are pictured as faithful slaves, treated well by their masters. The more inhumane aspects of slavery, however, are not omitted. In one scene in *The Battle-Ground* a low-class white man viciously whips a slave and is promptly reprimanded by his aristocratic neighbors. At the

---

[1] "Notes for a Biography of Ellen Glasgow," in Rawlings Papers.

[2] Agnes B. Reese to Ellen Glasgow, November 1, 1937, November 14, 1938, December 27, 1941, in Glasgow Papers. Mrs. Reese was the granddaughter of Ellen Glasgow's mother's mammy.

[3] *The Negro in Virginia*, Writers' Program of the Works Projects Administration (New York: Hastings House, 1940), 319.

[4] *A Certain Measure*, 257.

beginning of the novel the reader is given a glimpse of a wagon-load of slaves on their way to be sold because their master had died. Although the stereotype of the faithful and well-treated slave is evident, a stereotype that was so much a part of Ellen's white aristocratic heritage and environment, the novelist never condones either the whipping of human beings or the reduction of them to the status of property.

Negro characters during the Civil War are presented as people who love their masters and take pride in occupying the higher social levels within slavery. Big Abel, the faithful slave of Dan Montjoy in *The Battle-Ground*, is amiable and obedient, but he has his own pride and feelings. His pride is in his position as a body servant and in the clothes which his master hands down to him, and his feelings are for Saphiry, a Negro slave whom he persuaded his master to buy so that he might marry her. When the war came, he deserted wife and plantation to go into battle with his master, and when his master was wounded Big Abel took care of him with as much devotion as if they had been blood relatives. Big Abel was very conscious of his social position as a body servant, as was true of most of the house servants. "I ain' mix wid no fiel' han's," grunted Cupid, the butler, to his white masters. When house servants did mix with field hands, their lives became more complicated. Uncle Levi, "Marse Bolling's body sarvent," married a field hand only to have her sold up the river when he was set free at his master's death.[5] Tender and compassionate moments between whites and blacks in their peculiar relationship are duly recorded, but never is there any indication that Negroes were happy as slaves. Ellen Glasgow once commented that if she had lived before the war she would have been an abolitionist.[6] The novelist knew that even the best treated slaves welcomed their freedom.[7] In *The Voice of the People*, Uncle Ish, though still dependent upon his former master for his livelihood, commented that "freedom it are er moughty good thing."[8]

[5] *The Battle-Ground*, 322, 174, 128.
[6] Speech before the Southern Writers Conference, in Glasgow Papers.
[7] *The Negro in Virginia*, Writers' Program, 209.
[8] *Voice of the People*, 60.

Negroes who were younger than Uncle Ish at the end of the war often remained on the plantations to work for former masters or simply because they had no other place to go. Some few managed to set up small farms or open small businesses of their own, but all developed a kind of subculture in which religion, superstition, and irregular family life were their primary preoccupations. In a bizarre drama of devotion, mistrust, and fear, Negroes learned to manipulate whites, whose own anxieties and frustrations about changing race relations in an uncertain era forced them to allow themselves to be manipulated and eventually to become masters of manipulation themselves. Aunt Verbeny, the Negro cook for the Battle family in *The Voice of the People*, felt that it was her privilege as cook to help herself to as many chickens as she wanted. The chicken was not stolen, she explained; it was merely "misplaced," and "Hit don't becomst de quality ter fluster demse'ves over de gwines on uv er low-lifeted fowl." Yet, she was very dependent upon "her white folks" when it came to matters beyond her education, such as "ca'lations." "When I wants countin,' I want white folks' countin'," she said. Her trust in the white folks was transcended only by her faith in the Lord. "Ef you can't do a little shoutin' on de ea'th," she said, "you're gwineter have er po' sho' ter keep de Lawd f'om overlookin' you at Kingdom Come." Her religion, however, was tinged with superstition and carried its own moral code. Stealing from white people was certainly no sin, and the birth of an illegitimate child was "des' an accident."[9]

Delphy, another of the Battle servants, explained that some lies "is er long ways sweeter ter de tas' den Gospel trufe." Abraham had lied, she said, "en it ain't discountenance him wid de Lord." Her young master had fibbed as a boy to spare himself a whipping, so she naturally concluded that "hit's er plum fool ez won't spar' dere own hinder parts on er 'count uv er few words."[10] Delphy also looked out for herself. By the close of the century Negroes had begun a steady migration from the old plantations to the towns where

9 *Ibid.*, 55, 104, 275, 176.
10 *Ibid.*, 103.

they sometimes managed to open up barber shops, beauty parlors, and undertaking establishments.[11] In the novel, Delphy moved to Richmond where she "was doing a thriving trade as a shampooer."[12] She worked mostly on the heads of women whom she had known when she was a servant and who had also moved to Richmond, and she still recommended a generous application of kerosene oil as the cure for grayness, but in her own small way she was in business for herself.

The century changed, and with it the status of Negroes in Virginia. Writing at the end of the century, Ellen Glasgow sensed that change and incorporated it into *The Voice of the People*. Through disfranchisement and miscegenation Negroes continued to be victims of the society of which they were so much a part. Perhaps the blacks were just lucky that the advent of the Readjuster movement in Virginia in 1879 gave them limited political freedom and opportunities. The Readjuster movement was a coalition of Negroes, small farmers, and those of modest means against the Bourbon aristocrats. Its leader was William Mahone, the hero of the Battle of the Crater, and its impetus was the issue of the interest rate on Virginia's state debt. The Readjusters wanted to pay the full amount of the debt and a part of the interest, whereas the Funders wanted to pay the full amount of the debt and the full amount of the interest. William Mahone went to the United States Senate for one term, and his followers back in Virginia appointed a few Negroes to minor public offices and allowed many Negroes to vote freely.[13] By 1890, however, the Readjuster movement was dead, the Negro vote was managed by those who sought power, and there was widespread popular support for disfranchisement of black people.

This transition is captured in *The Voice of the People*. During the Readjuster era when black men were voting freely, one servant went to the polls with his former master, voted the Democratic ticket and was cheered by white bystanders, but another voted for the Readjusters much to the dismay of his former master. In the

---

11 *Negro in Virginia*, Writers' Program, 302.
12 *Voice of the People*, 401.
13 Buni, *Negro in Virginia Politics*, 3–5.

1890's, election frauds were common, and corrupt politicians in the novel discuss ways to dispose of ballot boxes in areas where there is a black majority.[14] Honest elections are only possible, the corrupt politicians suggested, after Negroes have stopped voting in large numbers. There were predictable outbreaks of violence, and Ellen Glasgow touched upon lynchings, both politically and socially motivated, in *The Voice of the People* and *Virginia*. But in *The Voice of the People*, the novel about the rise of a man from the lower classes to the governorship of Virginia, she demonstrated graphically what the historian C. Vann Woodward later observed as the direct increase in the barriers of racial discrimination with the rising tide of political democracy among whites.[15]

Ellen was more interested in the social, rather than the political, implications of the changing relationships between the races. Miscegenation had touched her own family, causing a great deal of suffering, and inevitably it became a major theme in her treatment of race relations. The mulatto to her was "the degenerate descendant of two races that mix only to decay," but her sympathy was always on the side of the wronged Negro woman.[16] "I've never seen any sense in trying to put the blame on the coloured women," one of the white female characters remarked, "when they are so nearly white."[17] The Negro wash-woman, Memoria, in *The Sheltered Life*, submitted with stoic resignation to George Birdsong because she felt obligated to him for rescuing her from a fire when she was a child. Part of old Cyrus Treadwell's villainy in *Virginia* was his fatherhood of a number of mulatto children, even though he had no feeling for anyone white or black. When his former black mistress and mother of his son confronted him with "savage coquetry" to remind him of their relationship in order to obtain money, he

---

14 *Voice of the People*, 272–73, 400. See also Buni, *Negro in Virginia Politics*, 11–12; Raymond H. Pulley, *Old Virginia Restored: An Interpretation of the Progressive Impulse, 1870–1930* (Charlottesville: University Press of Virginia, 1968), 50; and Allen W. Moger, *Virginia: Bourbonism to Byrd, 1870–1925* (Charlottesville: University Press of Virginia, 1968), 98.

15 *Origins of the New South, 1877–1913*, (Baton Rouge: Louisiana State University Press, 1951), 211.

16 *Voice of the People*, 309.

17 *The Sheltered Life*, 29.

looked at her with utter contempt and closed the door in her face. According to the novelist, if he could have read human nature as well as he read finance, he would have read this in her face: "I don't understand, but I submit without understanding. Am I not what you have made me? Have I not been what you wanted? And yet you despise me for being the thing you made."[18]

The increasing unsettledness about the roles the races were expected to assume in society widened the gulf between whites and blacks. Even Negro house servants seemed to live in private worlds where whites were unwelcome. Docia, the servant in *Virginia* who had been in the Pendleton family for years, was something of a tyrant. Yet Mrs. Pendleton, tormented by "the servant question" in general and intimidated by Docia personally, would not ask her to leave. Aunt Mehitable Green did her job well and was much loved by the whole family as a friend and counselor, but she seemed to move in her own mysterious world. Gabriel Pendleton, who had lived beside her all his life, felt that "a quality at once alien and enigmatical separated her not only from himself, but from every other man or woman who was born white instead of black." No white man could tell whether the laws made by white people ever penetrated that "surface of imitation of the superior race and reached the innate differences of thought, feeling, and memory which constituted her being."[19] Aunt Mehitable is a transitional figure from the generation which had been born in slavery and knew little except obedience to a white master, to the generation which was reared after the war and was much less friendly to the whites.[20] She commanded respect among both whites and blacks as a "conjure woman" and brewer of herbs to cure almost any malady, but her son became a thrifty, intelligent, and industrious tenant farmer who was a better manager than many of his poor white neighbors.[21] Her granddaughter, Fluvanna, also a servant to a white

18 *Virginia*, 157.
19 *Ibid.*, 341.
20 Charles E. Wynes, *Race Relations in Virginia, 1870–1902* (Charlottesville: University Press of Virginia, 1961), 112.
21 *Barren Ground*, 31, 75, 76.

family, was far less subservient than her grandmother and often did not speak the dialect that was characteristic of Negroes in Ellen Glasgow's earlier novels.

Independence did not mean equality; the novelist stated clearly that Negroes lived as inferiors "who often still attached themselves instinctively to the superior powers."[22] They were an "immature but not ungenerous race," careless in their work if not watched, a grave responsibility for white people, and a picturesque "peasantry."[23] Ellen Glasgow never believed in social equality among whites and blacks, her charities toward blacks were condescending and paternalistic, and her quasi-liberal statements were only theories which she did not follow up with action. Courageous individual blacks such as Dorothy Maynor, Ella Fitzgerald, Bill Robinson, and even Booker T. Washington, who rose to prominence in their professions despite the odds, are not mentioned.[24] John Mitchell, Jr., black editor of the Richmond *Planet*, outspoken civil rights advocate, and candidate for governor of Virginia in 1921, was certainly not a typical black man of his era, but the kind of thinking which motivated him and which he attempted to generate in other blacks is ignored in the Glasgow novels.[25]

Although Ellen Glasgow did convey some useful insights into the lives of Negro servants and the general black masses, she had a tendency to evade some of the issues. The two decades immediately after the turn of the century, which were her most prolific years, are commonly referred to as the Progressive Era, an era which in the South was dedicated to progress for whites only. "To liberals the Negro problem posed a challenge," one historian of the era wrote, "but a challenge that might be rationalized and explained away or evaded."[26] Ellen Glasgow was a part of this kind of Progres-

22 *Ibid.*, 276.
23 *Virginia*, 341.
24 Fishwick, *Virginia: A New Look*, 227.
25 For the story of John Mitchell, Jr., see Field, "Negro Protest in the New South: John Mitchell, Jr., 1863–1902."
26 Dewey W. Grantham, Jr., "The Progressive Movement and the Negro," in Charles E. Wynes (ed.), *The Negro in the South Since 1865* (University, Alabama: University of Alabama Press, 1965), 63.

sivism, because the novels she wrote during this era do not advocate any change in the status quo.

It was not until 1941 that she took a bold and progressive attitude toward black people. In the last novel that was published during her lifetime, *In This Our Life*, she created Parry Clay, a young Negro who was almost white and who wanted to get a college education and become a lawyer. Yet, she makes it clear that Parry is an exception, not a typical black youth. His mother is a servant who possesses more dignity than the white women for whom she works, and Parry works as a chauffeur for a wealthy young white woman. The young woman's father, Asa Timberlake, wanted to befriend the boy but was always embarrassed in his presence and could think of no way to offer friendship. He simply did not understand the more educated Negroes as he had understood "the older Negroes of servitude." Opportunities for Parry's advancement were limited in Richmond, and eventually he became the victim of a grave injustice. He was arrested and imprisoned for a hit-and-run accident in which he was not involved. Eventually he was cleared, but his spirit was broken: "His attitude appeared to be beyond rage, beyond resentfulness, beyond everything but bewilderment." In Ellen Glasgow's pessimistic view of the world, there was nothing he could do but accept his tragic fate. "A raw deal," thought Asa Timberlake, "but, like so many raw deals of an unfinished world, there was nothing that he could see to be done about it."[27]

With insight and sympathy, but always without commitment to their cause or hope for their future, Ellen Glasgow drew her portraits of Negroes in Virginia with sufficient honesty for her readers to grasp some appreciation of the problems of race relations in Virginia for almost a century. Not the struggles of Negroes, however, but "the rise of the middle class as the dominant force in Southern democracy" is the central theme of her social chronicle of Virginia.[28] "Broomsage ain't jest wild stuff. It's a kind of fate," said old Matthew Fairlamb in *Barren Ground*. Like the broomsedge

[27] *In This Our Life*, 281, 463, 431.
[28] *A Certain Measure*, 4.

that crept across Virginia's land, individuals from the middle and lower classes moved into more and more positions of political and social leadership to control the fate of the South.

Ellen Glasgow used the term "middle class" loosely to include almost everyone except Negroes and aristocrats. Her middle class includes small farmers, persons of aristocratic ancestry who repudiated their heritage, the offspring of marriages between one aristocratic parent and one from some lower strata of society, an occasional Presbyterian minister, lawyers, and politicians. It includes the country folk from the mountains, the Valley, Southside, and Tidewater Virginia. As a class they are neither good nor bad, but among individuals vice and virtue abound. As opposed to "good families," they are merely "good people" who have preserved nothing from their past except themselves and are consequently better prepared than the "good families" to live in the present.[29]

The genesis of such a large middle class, the novelist believed, is to be found in the mixing of persons during the Civil War. "Dis yer wah ain' de kin' I'se use ter," said Big Abel in *The Battle-Ground*, "caze hit jumbles de quality en de trash tergedder jes' like dey wuz bo'n blood kin."[30] Miss Ellen herself explained that she became intrigued with the democratic feeling which she discovered in the Army of Northern Virginia. "Here, in the rank and file," she wrote, "men who considered themselves aristocrats marched on a level with men who did not care whether or not they were plebeians."[31] Among the Confederate soldiers in *The Battle-Ground* are a gentleman who wore his aristocratic heritage proudly into battle, an aristocrat who refused to become an officer even though his class entitled him to the rank, and an illiterate mountaineer who went to war purely out of devotion to his native state. Not the need to defend slavery, but "the instinct of every free man to defend the soil," the novelist said, had brought men of all classes into the army of the South.[32] After the war, she suggests in *The Deliverance*, some members of aristocratic families of reduced

[29] *Barren Ground*, 5.
[30] *The Battle-Ground*, 342.
[31] *A Certain Measure*, 21–22.
[32] *The Battle-Ground*, 385.

means were willing to marry into plain families and accept a new position in society. The traditional social order was upset and forever. *The Voice of the People* and *The Romance of a Plain Man*, which taken together cover the period from about 1870 through 1910, deal specifically with the rise of the middle class in politics and business.

*The Voice of the People* is set against the background of the agrarian revolt in the 1890's and is the story of the son of a poor farmer who rose in spite of his heritage to become governor of Virginia. Nick Burr told his father: "I—I don't want to be like you, pa! . . . I want to be different." And he managed to become different by studying law under a sympathetic judge, assuming an air of uncompromising honesty, and eventually becoming governor. By securing the Democratic nomination in the wake of the defunct Readjuster movement, his election was guaranteed regardless of his class origin. "The few Republicans and Populists were lost in the ruling faction," but Nick proved to be a disappointment to his party when he bucked the party machine in the interest of racial and economic justice.[33] On the eve of his final day as governor, he died while trying to prevent the lynching of a Negro, an event which the author might have based on the riot in Roanoke, Virginia, in the early 1890's that resulted in the use of the militia to prevent a lynching.[34] The death of Nick Burr reflects the failure in Virginia of both Populism and the democratic principles for which he stood, a failure that was manifested in the Virginia constitution of 1902, which denied the vote to most blacks and to many whites.

In business, as in politics, a new kind of person was rising to prominence in Virginia. By 1890 business had taken the place of the plantation as the center of economic life, and a new aristocracy of "merchant princes" was coming to power.[35] Railroads were the most important business in the South; the men in the 1890's who

[33] *Voice of the People,* 35, 324.

[34] William DuBose Sheldon, *Populism in the Old Dominion: Virginia Farm Politics, 1885–1900* (Princeton: Princeton University Press, 1935), 101.

[35] Lewis Mattison, "Life of the Town," in H. J. Eckenrode (advisory ed.), *Richmond: Capital of Virginia* (Richmond: Whittet and Shepperson, 1938), 57.

controlled them exercised extensive economic and political power.[36] Therefore, for the hero of *The Romance of a Plain Man,* Ellen Glasgow chose Ben Starr, who was born in poverty in Richmond, but who worked his way up from paper boy to tobacco factory employee, to banker, to part owner of a small railroad, and finally to the presidency of the Great South Midland and Atlantic Railroad. From the point of view of power he was now an aristocrat, yet his background was not and never could be that of the entrenched aristocracy. He married into an aristocratic family, but many of his in-laws always looked upon him as common. Ben Starr, wealthy and powerful according to the standards of the New South, lived out his days feeling inferior to people whose era of wealth and power had ended.

Ben Starr was a good man among the new aristocrats, but Ellen Glasgow, the realist, clearly saw that villains, too, were among those rising to the top. In *Virginia,* Cyrus Treadwell, an industrial leader of poor character, used his economic power to control the town of Petersburg. He was both destroyer and builder, hated by the very people who took their bread from his hands. He, too, married an aristocrat, but her importance "dwindled to insignificance beside the rebuilding of the tobacco industry and his immediate elevation to the vacant presidency of one of the Machlin railroads." Involved in Petersburg's two most important industries, tobacco and railroads, his financial success did not move him toward benevolence; "his ambition was not so much to relieve the oppressed as to become in his turn the oppressor." Industrial progress led to tedium in the life of Petersburg; horse racing and the theatre became forms of diversion, even for members of Cyrus' family, but, unlike his Yankee counterpart, Cyrus looked askance at any human occupation that was not calculated to amass wealth.[37]

Industrialization changed the manner of life in the cities of Virginia. The urbanite became one who had no sense of his impor-

---

[36] Pulley, *Old Virginia Restored,* 95; Moger, *Virginia: Bourbonism to Byrd,* 95.
[37] *Virginia,* 67, 68, 69. See also James G. Scott and Edward A. Wyatt IV, *Petersburg's Story* (Petersburg: Titmus Optical Company, 1960), 289, 294, 144.

tance in the community; he merely turned his bolt and spent his pay, a carbon copy of many of his neighbors.[38] Consequently, in her last novel, Ellen Glasgow's middle-class urbanite has no sense of tradition and little ambition; he simply goes daily to his job in a tobacco factory and is virtually oblivious to what goes on around him. He has few close ties with neighbors, the past, or even his family. His house is "like a house on the stage, unreal, insubstantial, two-dimensional, and utterly without character. It might have stood anywhere in the world."[39]

The rise of the middle class caused the most radical changes in social structure in the cities, but the rumblings of class-consciousness were heard throughout the country and even into the mountains of Virginia. *The Miller of Old Church* (1898–1902), *Barren Ground* (1894–1924), and *Vein of Iron* (1902–33) explore the theme in the rural and mountainous sections of the state. The rural folk were somewhat startled at first by their new freedom and opportunities. The aged, such as Reuben Merryweather in *The Miller of Old Church*, simply endured quietly and made no effort to adapt to the times. The young, such as the miller Abel Revercomb, seized the transition as an opportunity to rise above their fathers. Such men, with such determination, Ellen Glasgow believed, would inherit the South.[40]

And she showed how that determination succeeded in *Barren Ground*, the novel that one critic said was an allegory of the South "rising from its own barren ground to fruitfulness and beauty." Dorinda Oakley, through incredible fortitude and determination, endured and prevailed despite her many problems of love and livelihood. While her lazy neighbors complained about the corrupt practices of railroads, the government, and monopolies, Dorinda experimented with the latest methods of farming and transformed her father's acres of broomsedge into a productive dairy farm. The description of Dorinda's agricultural success is remarkably close to that of one Frank Walker, a young man who was graduated from

38 Mattison, "Life of the Town," 57.
39 *In This Our Life*, 32.
40 *Miller of Old Church*, 34, 89, 85.

the Virginia Polytechnic Institute toward the end of the nineteenth century and who determined to apply his knowledge to farming.[41] He bought out the interests of his brothers in their grandfather's farm in Madison County, Virginia, much as Dorinda Oakley bought out some of her neighbors in that same piedmont section of Virginia. He used lime, rotated crops, and built up a well-equipped dairy farm exactly as Dorinda Oakley did. If Ellen Glasgow did not know the story of Frank Walker when she created her novel, her observations were so accurate that she wrote a realistic story of agriculture in Virginia in the first decades of the twentieth century and showed how the "good people" of the country sometimes utilized the opportunities that were afforded their class.

For the novelist, however, the "good people" of the middle class who made the most of life were preeminently the sturdy Scotch-Irish of the Great Valley of Virginia. They were her ancestors and the folk whom she chose to celebrate in *Vein of Iron*, the chronicle of the Fincastle family during the first three decades of the twentieth century. A hardy lot, they managed to overcome with grace and dignity such misfortunes as loss of job, pregnancy out of wedlock, death in the family, and the Great Depression of 1929. Thrifty, religious, and independent, the Fincastle family is a perfect literary portrait of the real Scotch-Irish settlers in the Valley.[42] Their most significant quality is their religion, orthodox Calvinism, which was based upon an almost fanatical devotion to "God's law," and which was the secret of their enduring vein of iron. "Even to meet Mrs. McBride in the road," noted the novelist, "was like facing the grim doctrine of predestination." John Fincastle refused to accept the "grim doctrine" and at the expense of his job and reputation, philosophized about the possibilities of life without Calvin; but even he was faithful to his family tradition as represented by his mother, who was as sturdy as an oak until her death at the age of eighty-seven. Her children and grandchildren moved

[41] Edwin Mims, *The Advancing South* (Garden City, New York: Doubleday, Page and Co., 1927), 50, 54–55.
[42] Roscoe D. Hughes and Henry Leidheiser, Jr. (eds.), *Exploring Virginia's Human Resources* (Charlottesville: University Press of Virginia, 1966), 22.

to Richmond where even the Great Depression could not break their spirits. Eventually they returned to the Valley to live and to die, and where they "could recover that lost certainty of a continuing tradition."[43]

From her ancestors Ellen Glasgow moved to her contemporaries and achieved her greatest success, as a social historian, in depicting the fall of the aristocrats, the third and top-most group into which she divided the population of Virginia. In depicting Negro characters, she never entirely escaped the "Old South" way of looking at them. In the case of the middle-class characters and their rise to dominance, she tried to make their struggles seem heroic but perhaps never succeeded to the degree that even she thought she should. Possibly, their rise to power was simply of itself too prosaic, even gross or sordid, for anyone to cast in an heroic style. But when she turned to her own group, the aristocrats, she was writing about people she knew best. With wit and wisdom and sometimes unladylike scorn, she probed their public and private lives, exploding the romantic aura that had traditionally surrounded them, and tugging the ladies and gentlemen of Old Virginia away from their moonlit retreats under the magnolia trees and into the light of a new day's blistering reality.

Her social chronicle of Virginia examines the story of the decline and fall of the aristocracy in three parts. During the Civil War and Reconstruction, the foundations of the aristocracy are shaken and their majestic Greek columns begin to crumble around their feet. From around 1880 to 1912 they grasp desperately and sometimes successfully for new political and economic straws; and finally, from 1912 to 1942, they are restless fossils, plagued by the unsolvable problem of how to reconcile their reverence for their ancestors with the bizarre social relationships in which their remaining human juices entangle them. In her very first novel, Ellen Glasgow had written that an aristocrat is "a man who sits down to think about what his grandfather had done while other men are doing something themselves."[44]

43 *Vein of Iron*, 112, 461.
44 *The Descendant*, 43.

Few Virginia aristocrats were transplanted English gentlemen. Most were descendants of immigrants who had acquired, by hook or by crook, large land holdings and slaves in the New World.[45] By 1850, the year with which Ellen Glasgow began her social history, those who had amassed wealth were regarded as aristocrats in the eyes of their fellow Virginians. Although such individuals actually composed only a small percentage of the population, their way of life was the ideal, never realized, but eagerly sought by the rest of the state. They were known by their attachment to a plantation that was run by slave labor, their participation in politics, and their imitation of English gentlemen. They had a strong sense of pride, a spirit of chivalry, a rigid code of honor, the ability to command men, reverence for their ancestors, scorn of competition, and a determination that their offspring should be educated to be gentlemen in either England or Virginia.[46] Like feudal lords, who made the laws for the isolated plantations over which they ruled, they looked to England for political and economic directions as well as for patterns in which to shape their everyday lives. Romantic they were, as Ellen Glasgow made plain in the first volume of her social history.

*The Battle-Ground* opens with majors, colonels, beautiful belles, and faithful slaves wandering through columned mansions, but before the novel ends all these illusions are stripped away because the novelist decided that "it might be interesting to look beneath the costume into the character of a civilization."[47] She saw much in that character to substantiate the legend. Generosity, elegance, tact, the gentleman's pride and code of honor are all there. Gentlemen discuss the pros and cons of slavery and agree that it is an institution for gentlemen, the very foundation of their society. All feared a slave insurrection, and at least one man thought that "there was some wild justice in the thing he dreaded, in the revolt of an enslaved and ignorant people." Nevertheless, he greeted the

[45] Thomas J. Wertenbaker, *Patrician and Plebeian in Virginia* (Charlottesville: The Michie Co., 1910), v, 28.
[46] *Ibid.*, 1, 54, 67, 103, 104, 108.
[47] *The Battle-Ground (Old Dominion Edition)*, viii.

beginning of the war with merriment. "There's nothing like a few weeks of war to give one an appetite," Major Lightfoot said to his grandson, who "had an odd feeling that it was all a great fox hunt they were soon to start upon."[48] But the battle dragged on, and the young gentleman learned the hard way that death and destruction and starvation accompanied it. He could have written what one who actually lived through the war did write: "I wanted to see a great war, saw it, and pray God I may never see another."[49] Ellen Glasgow accomplished the remarkable feat of treating the most romantic episode in the history of Virginia with ironic realism in an era when realism was still not wholly desired.

The intention of the novelist in *The Battle-Ground* was "to portray the last stand in Virginia of the aristocratic tradition,"[50] and she followed it immediately with *The Deliverance* to show, for one thing, what a single decade of war and reconstruction by military force had done to turn the aristocrat's life upside down. The Blakes, in *The Deliverance*, had once owned the plantation and lived in the "big house." Bill Fletcher had been their overseer. But at the beginning of this story, in 1870, Fletcher owns most of the plantation and lives in the "big house." Christopher Blake, about twenty-five, his two unmarried sisters, and their old, blind mother still own a little of the land and, ironically, live in what had been the overseer's house. The Negroes, though lazy, remain faithful to the Blakes. Christopher is compelled to work in the tobacco fields himself, one of the sisters sacrificed her life to the drudgery of the housework, and the other married beneath her class. Mrs. Blake, blind for twenty years, was never told that the South lost the war. She lectures her children upon the graces and duties of the aristocrat and listens to them pretend in her presence that they still have plenty of money and servants and that the Confederacy is an independent and thriving nation. "I saw in her [Mrs. Blake]," Ellen wrote, "not one old woman groping, blind and nourished by il-

---

48 *The Battle-Ground*, 65, 261, 227, 132, 56, 78, 214, 242, 258.
49 George W. Bagby, *The Old Virginia Gentleman and Other Sketches* (New York: Charles Scribner's Sons, 1911), 164.
50 *A Certain Measure*, 13.

lusions, through a memorable epoch in history, but Virginia and the entire South, unaware of the changes about them, clinging, with passionate fidelity, to the ceremonial forms of tradition."[51]

But change did not come so suddenly to all aristocrats, nor so painfully as to the Blakes. Immediately following Reconstruction, aristocrats comprised a group called "Redeemers" who were instrumental in reinstituting conservative government in Virginia. They allied themselves with black people as their paternalistic champions against the upland and lower-class whites.[52] In the Glasgow novels, as in life, many of the aristocrats of the period earned their livelihood as judges or lawyers, but often they retained their farms to provide support for Negroes who were their former slaves, as well as for themselves. When they moved to town, they took their Negroes with them as hired servants and made every effort to encourage them to vote conservatively. Still confident in their position, they feared neither the Negro franchise nor the rising middle class and often extended a helping hand to both. Judge Bassett in *The Voice of the People*, a gentleman "secure in the inalienable affability of one who is not only a judge of man but a Bassett of Virginia," personally provided the livelihood of his black servants and at the same time paid for the education of Nick Burr, the son of a poor white farmer who was determined to get ahead. And in *The Romance of a Plain Man*, a man of the finest family who had invested his wealth in tobacco and railroads, used his position and financial stability to boost the lower-class Ben Starr into a position that eventually equalled his own.

But the role of the benevolent patriarch was challenged by the advent of the Readjuster movement in 1879. Aristrocrats were members of the Conservative party, which aligned itself rigidly against the rising tide for readjustment of the state's debts.[53] Not to pay the full amount of the interest on Virginia's debt, they felt, would be a violation of the gentlemen's code of honor. But their

[51] *Ibid.*, 27.
[52] Woodward, *Origins of the New South*, 209; Wynes, *Race Relations in Virginia*, 95; *Negro in Virginia*, Writers' Program, 300.
[53] Woodward, *Origins of the New South*, 92.

efforts were in vain, because the Readjusters were in power for
most of a decade and the Conservatives were temporarily reduced
to rhetoric. "Virginia is not dead but sleepeth," said the judge in
*The Voice of the People*, "as a prelude to denunciation of the Readjuster party then in power."[54] But it was the aristocrats who were
dozing. The Readjuster movement ended, but Virginia never
again belonged to the lords of old. By the end of the century Nick
Burr became governor of the state, and Ben Starr was offered the
presidency of the very railroad his benefactor had once controlled.
The aristocrats did not suspect that in return for their paternalistic
benevolence they would reap a gradual loss of power in politics
and in business. Nor did they dream that one day those whom they
had befriended would consider themselves their social equals.

The rising middle class charged across the lines of class separation,
and the old codes of the aristocracy crumbled before the onslaught.
Nick Burr tried to marry into the aristocracy, but was thwarted in
his effort. Ben Starr was successful where Nick had failed, but was
never quite accepted as a social equal by the elderly aunts of his
spouse. But in spite of the intransigency of their elders, the young
aristocrats, born after the Civil War, began to desert the old
ways. Whereas, fifty years earlier the youthful offspring of the blue-
blooded Battle family in *The Voice of the People* would have
fought a duel to protect the honor of his lady, in the late 1890's
he impregnated a girl he did not want to marry, connived to place
the blame on someone else, and became a murderer. A similar
fate awaited Jonathan Gay, the aristocrat in *The Miller of Old
Church*, who still controlled many acres of land, and was convinced that there had "never been a fairer distribution of property
and there's never going to be."[55] He forgot his honor, became intimately involved with a middle-class girl, and was eventually shot
by her irate uncle.

In the early twentieth century, aristocratic young gentlemen were
allowed to bypass the old code of honor, but young ladies still were
expected to endure a useless and unhappy life. The fate of the ladies

[54] *Voice of the People*, 162.
[55] *The Miller of Old Church*, 385.

was to Ellen Glasgow more tragic than the moral degeneration of the gentlemen. Virginia Pendleton, heroine of *Virginia*, received a proper upbringing as the daughter of an Episcopalian minister in Petersburg in the 1880's, only to discover later in life that she was ill-equipped to deal with either her family or her environment. Virginia's education was at the hands of Miss Priscilla Batte, an old maid who had turned to the education of the young less as a matter of choice than of necessity. The only surviving child of a Confederate general, Miss Priscilla was naturally esteemed in the eyes of her fellow citizens, even though "in later years memory had become so sacred to her that she rarely indulged in it."[56] Reading, penmanship, arithmetic, geography, the history of Virginia, deportment, and the fine arts were the disciplines she drilled into her charges. She told them that a lady was expected to be timid and shy, take care of children, servants, and guests, and do any manual house labor before day so that no one would see her doing it.[57] The novelist's description of Miss Priscilla's school is typical of several such schools that flourished in Petersburg at the end of the nineteenth century.[58] Ellen herself had attended such a school briefly as a child, and she was convinced that there was a fallacy in educating a young girl according to the simple theory that the less she knew about life, the better prepared she would be to contend with it.[59] So she created Gabriella Carr, heroine of *Life and Gabriella* and contemporary of Virginia Pendleton, who repudiated the tradition of her class and deserted her native state for New York City where she found happiness and fame as a dressmaker.

Few young ladies of her group followed the example of Gabriella Carr. Many of them, according to Ellen Glasgow, remained geographically and spiritually where they were and simply stagnated.

[56] *Virginia*, 11.
[57] For verification of the Southern lady's practice of doing her house work before day, see Bagby, *The Old Virginia Gentleman*, 20–21.
[58] In Petersburg a college for the education of white young ladies known as Southern Female College stayed open until 1938. Miss Liza Newsom's School operated from 1864 to 1908, Misses Muffie and Mollie Harrison taught at home from 1885 to 1910, and Miss Nora Davidson in the same era called her school The Confederate School. Scott and Wyatt, *Petersburg's Story*, 116, 268, 275.
[59] *A Certain Measure*, 90.

"After all, class consciousness," mused old General Archbald in *The Sheltered Life,* "like his arteries, was not all that it used to be. Like every other superstition, he supposed, it was doomed to decay." The Archbalds and the Birdsongs lived in a section of Richmond that was becoming a slum and was polluted by the foul odor from a nearby chemical factory. "Industrialism might conquer, but they would never surrender." Their personal lives were often as foul as the odor in the neighborhood. Theirs was a life of "Illusion" lived in an "Age of Make-Believe" and based on the worship of "The Deep Past." Murder, maddening disillusionment, and ridiculous pretense became their fate. Miss Abby Carter symbolized them all as she sat against a wall at a dance with pursed lips and an affected smile, saying over and over to herself: "I am having a lovely time, I am having a lovely time. Oh, I must tell everybody what a lovely time I am having!"[60] In the novel and in life, decay came to them "not so much through an even partial surrender to the demands made upon them as through the inevitable consequences of their failure and their refusal to surrender."[61]

The First World War came and went, but Ellen Glasgow's aristocrats refused to change. *The Romantic Comedians,* set in Richmond in 1923, is the story of Judge Gamaliel Bland Honeywell, "a great lawyer but a perfect fool" of sixty-five who had recently lost his wife and had a passing interest in his Negro maid, and who had decided to take a new wife who was only twenty-three. He believed that if there was "anything wrong with the Episcopal Church or the Democratic Party, [he] would rather die without knowing it,"[62] but he soon learned that there was something wrong with an old man trying to live with a woman two generations his junior. He could not see the ironies of his own life, but he could instantly spot those in the life of his twin sister, which he readily explained in terms of her sin against the code of behavior for a lady.

Less daring than Judge Honeywell, Mr. Virginius Littlepage of *They Stooped to Folly* only dreamed about the joys of a young

60 *The Sheltered Life,* 101, 6, 111.
61 W. J. Cash, *The Mind of the South* (New York: Alfred A. Knopf, 1941), 154.
62 *The Romantic Comedians,* 9.

wife and an affair with an older woman who had forgotten her virtue. Surrounded by three generations of fallen women, he wondered if "the decadence of Europe was slowly undermining Virginia tradition, and even the Southern gentleman, he told himself, was beginning to suspect that the ruined woman is an invention of man." His wife tried to bind herself to the old by concentrating her energies on charities, particularly the home for unwed mothers, but even she had to loosen up to the point of changing the name of her institution from the "Home for Unfortunates" to the "House of Hope." Mr. Littlepage feared, and even hoped, that there was something wrong with the past, that there was a fatal flaw even in the Episcopal Church, that the ideal of pure womanhood was infested with moth and decay.[63]

The aristocrats of *In This Our Life*, set in Richmond just before the Second World War, discover that indeed there is something wrong with the past. They are festering lilies who have moved into "a new house, with rooms like closets, and with doors and windows that stuck fast in damp weather," and which looks like every other house on the block. The head of the family, Asa Timberlake, learns reluctantly that "one must, of necessity, live in one's age." As an employee of the Standard Tobacco Company, his income is low, but his brother-in-law is wealthy and generous with his family. The Timberlake daughters, even though they had the best blue-blooded ancestry, dye their hair, smoke cigarettes, indulge heavily in the use of alcohol, and even have the family names of Roy and Stanley. Stanley runs over a small child in her sports car, seduces her sister's husband, and eventually drives him to suicide. Roy becomes pregnant by a man whose name she never bothered to learn. The girls finally go their own way, and Asa, disgusted, leaves home to live with a widow on a farm.[64]

Only Asa's wife, Lavinia Fitzroy Timberlake, remains, a fossilized aristocrat living alone in a suburb of Richmond. As the last symbol of the old aristocracy, she uses the departure of her husband as a kind of consolation, just as the South had used the Civil War

[63] *They Stooped to Folly*, 21, 190.
[64] *In This Our Life*, 14, 20.

and Reconstruction as its Great Excuse.[65] "What has helped her
is having a just grievance," recorded the novelist. "It wasn't enough
for her to feel ill-used. She wanted something solid to complain of,
and now she has her real wrongs, and, what is more consoling,
everybody knows she has them." The death of Lavinia in 1942 is
symbolic of the end of the whole aristocratic tradition: "Her death
had become, for the moment, if but for the moment alone, the
death of a tradition." Pondering the death of his wife without
emotion, Asa Timberlake believed "that an era, as well as a
tradition, was ending. And not an era alone, but a bright, lost
vision, a long adventure, an inaccessible hope."[66] The aristocratic
tradition survived only as an archaic memorial, Ellen Glasgow
noted. "It was condemned to stand alone because it had been forsaken by time."[67]

The tragedy of the aristocracy in Virginia is the tragedy of every
man who cannot adjust to the passage of time, a weakness of human
nature that dooms man to writhe under what Ellen Glasgow called
the "predetermined conditions." Thus she added a fourth dimension to her social history, the dimension of the mystery of human life. Every aristocrat, every member of the middle class,
every Negro in her novels is a living, feeling, thinking human
being with emotions and experiences similar to every other human being. The chronicle of social stratification in Virginia is
good history, but the novelist's ability to give life to her characters elevated her history to the level of art. The professional
historian may be equipped to chronicle as well, or perhaps even
better, the social stratification in a state, but the professional novelist is uniquely prepared to add this fourth dimension, this human
element that must transcend statistics and details if history is to
become alive. The novel, no matter how firmly rooted in a particular soil, Ellen Glasgow said, "must draw nourishment from the

65 Robert Penn Warren, *The Legacy of the Civil War* (New York: Random House,
1961), 54.
66 *Beyond Defeat: An Epilogue to an Era* (Charlottesville: University Press of Virginia, 1966), 42, 132, 133. A sequel to *In This Our Life*, this novel was left in manuscript form and published many years after Ellen Glasgow's death.
67 *A Certain Measure*, 13.

ancient instincts, the blood and tears, which are the common heritage."[68] This quality in a good novel is also characteristic of good
history.

The myriad problems of human existence stalk through Ellen
Glasgow's novels and occasionally come alive in the mind of the
reader who resonates with them. Expectancy and disillusionment,
loneliness and despair, revenge and hatred, death and violence,
ambition and hope, passion and pity, love and the vagaries of sexual
relationships are paraded before the reader as the complex ingredi-
ents of what Miss Ellen loved to describe as human nature. The un-
forgettable experience of little Ada Fincastle visualizing, for page
after page in *Vein of Iron,* her father bringing her a doll with real
hair and her disappointment upon his arrival with a doll with
china hair, and the description of Nick Burr, in *The Voice of the
People,* strolling through Williamsburg only minutes before his
death, capture as only a successful novelist can the intense drama
of human emotions. Human nature, to Ellen, was something universal and unchangeable, something tragically limited by the struggle between the flesh and the spirit. Social orders are but mirrors
of man's favorite imperfections.[69] "Why are we always doing things
we didn't mean to do and didn't want to do?" Ada Fincastle asked
her father in *Vein of Iron.*[70] All of his life, another character in
another novel "had done the things that he condemned, condemn-
ing himself because he did them."[71]

The reason for that paradox of human nature, the novelist said,
is that man is trapped between dreams that are in conflict with the
realities of life. " 'Tis al'ays that way in my experience of life,"
said a character in *The Miller of Old Church,* "—when you glance
back or glance befo' 'tis pleasant enough to the eye, but at the
moment while you're livin' it that's al'ays the damn shoe that
pinches."[72] In her own interpretation of Virginia, Ellen said that
the larger conflict was not with tradition but "the eternal warfare

68 *Ibid.,* 142.
69 *Ibid.*
70 *Vein of Iron,* 125.
71 *Miller of Old Church,* 381.
72 *Ibid.,* 108.

of the dream with the reality."[73] A disillusioned husband in *The Ancient Law* discovered "that the thing you get doesn't ever seem to be the same as the thing you wanted."[74] And the displaced aristocrats in *They Stooped to Folly* learned that "Life, even at its best, was never what you had dreamed, was seldom what you had expected."[75] Ellen knew all too well that unhappiness is a particular malady of the young when they first tremble before the threatening insecurities to their livelihood and companionship. "Why is it," Jenny Blair Archbald asked herself with tragic intensity in *The Sheltered Life*, "that only young people are ever really unhappy?" When Mrs. Birdsong later told Jenny Blair that she was too young to know what trouble was, Jenny Blair replied, "I do understand. Oh, I do."[76] Jenny Blair's grandfather, though old himself, remembered when he was young, and understood.

General Archbald is the most enduring character in any of Ellen's novels and the one into whose lonely spirit she distilled much of her ultimate feeling about life.[77] At eighty-three the General remembered his youth and the woman he had loved but did not marry. As a boy he had wanted to be a poet, but he was called a milksop by his athletic father. His grandfather rubbed the blood of a freshly killed deer on his face, his girl friends made curlers out of his poems, and he was reprimanded for helping a hungry slave to escape—all experiences which he could not forget at the age of eighty-three, even though he had forgotten almost everything else. Remembered, or recorded, events and the eternal quest to marshal them into some meaningful form is the real task of both the novelist and the historian. The measure of Ellen Glasgow's understanding of this is the measure of her achievement as a social historian.

General Archbald at the end of his life knew that "within time, and within time alone, there was life—the gleam, the quiver, the heart-beat, the immeasurable joy and anguish of being."[78] Faced

---

[73] *A Certain Measure*, 89.
[74] *The Ancient Law*, 393.
[75] *They Stooped to Folly*, 151.
[76] *The Sheltered Life*, 321, 366.
[77] *A Certain Measure*, 204.
[78] *The Sheltered Life*, 148.

with the nearness of death, the complexities of human personality were still a mystery to him. His life spanned the history of Virginia from before the Civil War until after the First World War, but he knew, as all men and any good novelist must, that the spirit of humanity is capable of transcending the historical events that encompass an individual's narrow lifetime. Ellen Glasgow "knows that man is the captive of this earth," noted one of her critics. "But she knows also that he is not."[79]

[79] Howard Mumford Jones, "A Review of *In This Our Life*," *Saturday Review of Literature*, XXIII (March 29, 1941), 6.

# 12

## *Fresh Woods and Pastures New*

*"A Certain Measure* was my swan song," Ellen later wrote to James
Branch Cabell, referring to the book into which her prefaces for
the *Virginia Edition* of her novels were collected.[1] In many ways
she was right. The label "social historian" which she, and Cabell,
had given to herself was readily accepted by both literary critics
and historians as an adequate summary of her career. From the
time of the completion of the prefaces in 1938, Ellen's life began
to drift toward its inevitable conclusion. At times she was willing
to whimper and acquiesce, but more often she struggled valiantly,
sometimes savagely, to maintain a steady course.

Fate, that inescapable demon, seemed to prevent her from writing a new novel. After completing the prefaces, she resumed work
on *In This Our Life,* a novel scarcely begun when she had had to
put it aside to write the prefaces. Soon after she took it up again,
she fell and injured her back and had to spend three weeks in a
hospital in New York.[2] Even then she made the best of a bad situation. Her hospital room was filled with flowers, she had a private
nurse, her own pillowcases of Italian cutwork, and the regular attention of a manicurist and a beautician. One afternoon her friend
Carl Van Vechten visited her just after she had had her hair done.
"Why, Ellen," he said, "I've never seen you look so lovely." "But

---

1 September 25, 1944. A copy of this letter is in the Rawlings Papers; the original
is in the possession of Mrs. Cabell.

2 Ellen Glasgow to Bessie Zaban Jones, November 21, 1938, in Bessie Zaban Jones
Papers; to Hudson Strode, October 30, 1938, and to H. L. Mencken, January 10, 1939,
in *Letters,* 246, 248.

Carl," she responded with a twinkle, "you've never seen me in bed before!"[3] She was not too sick to laugh, and the visit to the hospital actually relaxed her nerves.

A greater misfortune, however, awaited her in Richmond. Shortly after she returned home, Billy died. His body was treated much as Jeremy's had been and was buried in the backyard garden at One West Main Street. In 1934 Ellen had bought a six-grave plot in Richmond's new Pet Memorial Park, and eventually some of her dogs were buried there, but it was not good enough for Jeremy and Billy.[4] No doubt the death of Billy, as much as the slow recovery from her accident, caused her to feel as if she had "fought through a war on the wrong side." What was worse, her novel broke up in her mind, and at times she felt that it had evaporated.[5]

Her election to the American Academy of Arts and Letters in December, 1938, did little to cheer her, but when she acquired a new dog, Bonnie, from the SPCA shelter in 1939 she began to regain her equilibrium and return to her novel. Though Bonnie was cared for primarily by Anne Virginia, the new dog became an important part of Ellen's life. James, her cook, once commented that Miss Ellen would not take a thousand dollars for that dog, and a group of enterprising little boys put up a sign urging their friends to pay one cent to see the thousand-dollar dog.[6] Human friends, too, steered her toward recovery and return to her work. She had long admired the work of the literary historian, Van Wyck Brooks, and he was the one who had nominated her for membership in the Academy. In the spring of 1939 she invited him and his wife Eleanor to visit her in Richmond. They came in April, just as spring was bringing new life to Richmond, traveled with Ellen to the points of historical interest between Richmond and Williamsburg, and established a warm friendship that was one of the chief

[3] Irita Van Doren to MKR, in Rawlings Papers. Van Vechten told the story to Mrs. Van Doren.

[4] The markers from the graves of Jeremy and Billy were moved to Pet Memorial Park, probably after Ellen Glasgow's death.

[5] Ellen Glasgow to Bessie Zaban Jones, November 21, 1938, in Bessie Zaban Jones Papers.

[6] "The Thousand Dollar Dog," clipping from an unidentified paper, dated May 6, 1952, in Rawlings Papers.

consolations of Ellen's older years.[7] Ellen was rejuvenated by their
visit, returned to her manuscript with enthusiasm, and determined
that the novel that was so persistently forcing itself up in her mind
should not be lost. In the summer she went to Maine to escape the
heat in Richmond and to search for a quiet place to finish *In This
Our Life*.

As early as 1916, she discovered the coast of Maine as an ideal
spot for a summer vacation. Every summer from 1935 through 1945
she went to Castine, a quiet coastal village just south of Bar Harbor.
Castine was a town with a history, a village with a heart. Gleaming
white houses lined quiet dusty streets that were shaded by towering
elm trees. No house was far from a sparkling bay or inlet and many
had been decorated by sea captains who brought strange notions
about architecture back from their voyages to the East. Place names,
markers, and legends enshrined the successive struggles of the In-
dians, French, British, and Americans for mastery of the area. For
beauty, isolation, and friendliness, a more perfect spot could not
be imagined, and Ellen loved it. In the summer of 1939 she rented
a house named "Littleplace" on Battle Avenue, and there in a
small studio that had once belonged to an artist she continued to
work on her manuscript. Anne Virginia went with her and attended
to the details of running the house. Every day they went for long
walks in the woods along Indian trails where Ellen almost wor-
shipped the trees, flowers, and birds. Her appreciation of nature
was shared by Miss Dorothy T. Blake, a local artist, a pillar of the
Episcopal church, and a lady whose enthusiasm for life is as refreshing as the crisp atmosphere of the village in which she lives.
One summer Miss Blake sold her home, and the new owner cut
down a willow tree that was in the yard. Shortly thereafter, when
Ellen passed Miss Blake in the street, Ellen said: "You needn't say
a word. I'm grieving as much as you."[8]

The local citizens of Castine regarded Ellen with amusement and

7 Ellen Glasgow to Van Wyck Brooks, March 27 and July 4, 1939, in *Letters*, 251,
253; May 15, 1939, in Brooks Papers.
8 Interview with Miss Dorothy T. Blake, Castine, Maine, October 4, 1968.

friendliness. They were accustomed to an influx of summer residents that usually included a celebrity or two. On very rare occasions Ellen mingled with them at a tea or a party, but usually she kept to herself. The natives smiled when the short, chubby woman walked down the street wearing a bright red cartwheel hat and followed by a bouncing, shaggy white dog.[9] She gave the impression of being a happy, gracious person, and everyone noticed that she always wore bright colors. The local doctor observed that she went about "strutting like a little partridge" as if she had many very important things to accomplish in a limited amount of time.[10] At one party she met a professor who engaged her in conversation about writers she had known. Speaking of her fellow artists, she concluded crisply: "Most of us are fat. All of us are tired. Have another drink, Mr. Thomas. Drink always helps."[11]

More intriguing to the citizens of Maine than her wit or her bright clothes, however, were the Negro servants whom she took with her. Nathaniel, her chauffeur, of course was indispensable. In Castine he was boarded with a white family where he quietly endured the summer and counted the days until he could return to Virginia. He refused to associate with the few other Negroes in the area, and when asked why, he replied with disdain, "Portuguese! Portuguese!"[12] A Negro cook, about whom Ellen had known very little before she took her to Castine in the summer of 1940, proved to be a particular source of excitement. "I smile," Ellen wrote, "whenever I hear that she is known in Castine, among the people who fought to set her free, as 'the old devil.' Up here, at least, they understand a little better that the white people of the South were set free when slavery was ended." Among the advantages of the "sturdy Maine folk" Ellen listed "the inestimable blessing

9 *Ibid.*

10 Interviews with Mrs. R. S. Wardwell and with Dr. Harold S. Babcock, Castine, Maine, October 4, 1968.

11 Francis W. Hatch, "On the Trail of a Lady Novelist," published during the summer of 1968 in *North Shore '68*, the weekly magazine section of the North Shore newspapers. Used by the courtesy of Mr. Hatch.

12 Information obtained from a person who wishes to remain anonymous.

of belonging to a single race." That was the crowning condition of life for the people who were thrifty, independent, and self-respecting in their clean little villages located in an extraordinarily beautiful country.[13] Ellen's appreciation of them was as generous as their acceptance was of her.

The summer of 1939 wore on, and more and more pages of the first draft of the novel piled up. By the first week in October it was finished, but Ellen dreaded to start South again.[14] The autumn in Maine was "so glorious that it hurts," she said, and in Castine she had found "perfect peace in a troubled world."[15] The war raging in Europe haunted her; she was certain that there would be no victors, and she wished to stay in Maine and try to forget about it.[16] If mere scenery could enable one to forget, she should have enjoyed at least the one day of mid-October as she traveled toward home through the White Mountains. The array of colored leaves on mountain slopes and the glistening white bark of the birches beside still rivers were the very picture of peace and serenity in a world that Ellen said had gone mad.

Before the end of October she was home. Although she knew it would take her two more years to revise the novel, she already dreaded reaching the end of the work and the "dark isolation" it would bring to her. And she yearned for her private Walden Pond where she would not even have to hear about the tragedies of the world.[17] She busied herself with small matters, including a private diatribe against the American Academy of Arts and Letters, which she believed to be governed by hostile political factions, journalistic standards, and too many writers from the Dust Bowl.[18]

Small matters as well as large receded for the time being, how-

13 To Van Wyck Brooks, August 5, 1940, in Brooks Papers; to Brooks, September 2, 1939, to Edwin Mims, October 4, 1939, in *Letters*, 255, 259.
14 To Bessie Zaban Jones, October 2, 1939, in Bessie Zaban Jones Papers.
15 To Hamilton Basso, October 6, 1939, in Hamilton Basso Papers, Yale University Library; to Mrs. Margaret May Dashiell, September 4, 1939, in Southern Historical Collection, University of North Carolina Library.
16 To Edwin Mims, October 4, 1939, in *Letters*, 259.
17 To Hamilton Basso, October 6, 1939, in Basso Papers.
18 To Van Wyck Brooks, November 21, 1939, in Brooks Papers.

ever, because during the first week of December she suffered a severe heart attack.[19] Her long-time personal physician, Dr. Mc. C. Tompkins, invited in a colleague, and they discovered that her heart condition was quite serious and was accompanied by arteriosclerosis.[20] But Ellen began to recover, even if slowly. Within two weeks she was sitting up, and by the end of the month she was able to stay up most of the day. For much of her life she had looked upon death as a friend; now it was the friend come near. At Christmastime so many people sent her flowers that she said it would be "a good time to die, surrounded by roses."[21] As a young woman she had written: "Though beggared to the tryst I go, / Death waits to woo me to her will. / I will press my spurs, I ride alone, / I laugh and journey to my own."[22] Now that the tryst seemed near, her attitude did not change.

But death did not come, and Ellen entered the new year as a semi-invalid who could continue her work only for very brief periods of time and who felt that "everything in the world seems too much." Besides the faithful Anne Virginia, only Carrie Duke and Lizzie Patterson were allowed to visit her. James Branch Cabell wrote letters of encouragement from his winter vacation in St. Augustine, Florida. Ellen appreciated his efforts, praised his most recent book, and called him her "beloved friend." By the end of January she had a relapse, because as she explained to Cabell, even a hard heart like hers could not stand too much wear and tear. She began to write to him frequently, and she complained bitterly of having to work as an invalid.[23] In her letters she cried out pathetically for love and sympathy from her literary friends, many of whom she would never see again.[24]

In the spring she nominated both James Branch Cabell and

19 To Bessie Z. Jones, January 4, 1940, in Bessie Zaban Jones Papers.
20 Dr. Alexander Brown, Jr., to MKR, in Rawlings Papers.
21 Copy of a letter to Rebe Tutwiler, December 30, 1939, in Rawlings Papers.
22 *The Freeman and Other Poems*, 17.
23 To James Branch Cabell, January 7 and 16, February 22, 1940, in Cabell Papers; to Van Wyck Brooks, January 6, 1940, in *Letters*, 261.
24 To Bessie Zaban Jones, April 24, 1940, in Bessie Zaban Jones Papers.

Douglas S. Freeman for membership in the American Academy of
Arts and Letters, an honor which she insisted was not worth much,
but she saw no reason why the Academy should remain exclusively
Northern.[25] She accepted and then withdrew from an offer made to
her by the Academy to serve on their committee to select the recipient of the Howells Medal, an award made once every five years
to a novelist in recognition for distinguished service to American
literature.[26] Her overriding concern was that she should be able
to finish her novel, and she dared not expend her energy on anything else. She assured her publisher that her work was going well
and that she could write even better when she was not in "bounding
physical health."[27] With her doctor's permission she planned to
leave in June for another summer in Castine.

On June 20, 1940, she and Carrie Duke left for Castine by train,
planning to stop for several days in New York City. But the trip
was too strenuous for her; a heart specialist ordered her to go to a
hospital immediately, and she spent a month in Doctors' Hospital
in New York. Her friends again banked her room with flowers,
and Ellen feared death less than she feared leaving "a piece of fine
work unfinished."[28] James Branch Cabell urged her to get well so
that she could finish her novel and autobiography and "in due
course, lift the present status of the Pulitzer Prize by accepting it."
He reminded her that she had "achieved more than any living
American woman" and had overcome far more handicaps, and he
urged her to consider this last illness as no more than "a spur to your
dear indomitableness." She replied that "life seems to be woven
with misfortunes, dramatic or tedious," and that her only reason for
wanting to continue to live was that she did not like to leave un-

25 To Mrs. Grace Vanamee, April 30 and May 7, 1940, in Glasgow File, American
Academy of Arts and Letters; to Stephen Vincent Benét, May 2, 1940, in Stephen
Vincent Benét Papers, Yale University Library; To Douglas S. Freeman, May 2, 1940,
in Freeman Papers; to James Branch Cabell, May 2, 1940, in Cabell Papers. Freeman
became a member of the Academy in 1945.
26 Mrs. Grace Vanamee to Ellen Glasgow, May 15, 1940, Ellen Glasgow to Mrs.
Vanamee, May 19 and May 30, 1940, in Glasgow File, American Academy of Arts
and Letters.
27 To Alfred Harcourt, May 8, 1940, in Letters, 264.
28 To Bessie Zaban Jones, June 12 and 30, 1940, in Bessie Zaban Jones Papers.

finished a fine piece of work.[29] She improved, and on the 24th of July continued her journey to Castine.

A different house awaited her in Maine, rented from Mr. R. S. Wardwell and carefully prepared for her arrival by Anne Virginia. Surrounded by old apple trees, it was on the corner of Perkins and Madockawando streets and commanded a fine view of the harbor and Nautillus Island beyond. Ellen named it "Appledoor," and it became the favorite of her Castine homes. A brick walkway and stone steps led down to the street. The house was a two-story white frame structure with four gables and lattice windows on the up-stairs rooms. A hedge of cedar trees in back and wild roses in front gave it privacy, and a porch on two sides was an ideal place to relax and enjoy the Maine air and scenery. Ellen arrived optimistic, was refreshed by walks in the woods, and wrote to a friend that nothing short of an act of God could kill her.[30] "Life has taught me," she wrote, "that the greatest tragedy is not to die too soon but to live too long."[31] On August 5 she wrote Van Wyck Brooks that she was firmly convinced that she would "outlive every form of life but that of the insect."[32]

Four days later she had a second severe heart attack. Dr. Harold S. Babcock, a man who had ruled over the health of Castine with extraordinary dedication, skill, and good humor, immediately came to her side. As a young man Dr. Babcock had come to Castine with a Nova Scotia lass as his nurse, companion, and bride; he had devoted his life to the community and was rewarded by their love and esteem. His eyes had a sparkle that defied disease and misfortune even more than his medical skill, and Ellen was fortunate that he was there. She described him exactly when she said that he had the "features of a kindly Roman senator."[33] When he arrived at her bedside on August 9, Dr. Babcock thought that she would die. He gave her a small hypodermic and waited, fearing to give her another shot lest the shock of the needle might carry her off. But she rallied

[29] July 15, 1940, in Glasgow Papers; July 20, 1940, in Cabell Papers.
[30] To Charles H. Towne, July 30, 1940, in *Letters*, 266.
[31] To James S. Wilson, August 2, 1940, *ibid.*, 267.
[32] In Brooks Papers.
[33] *Woman Within*, 289.

and began slowly to grow stronger. When the doctor visited her, she would begin a sentence and Anne Virginia would finish it for her, almost pulling the words from her mouth.[34] Ellen took Anne Virginia for granted, and she considered her only companion to be the tall, pointed fir tree that she could see from her bedroom window. For weeks the fir was all that she saw of Castine, and she began to feel a strange kinship with it.[35]

By the first of September she was sitting up, dictating to Anne Virginia, and philosophizing about her brush with death. She considered it a great moment of fulfillment and in time came to believe that she had been dead and had come back to life.[36] Every detail she described for James Branch Cabell as soon as she was strong enough to write letters. The thought of dying did not frighten her, she said, because she did not want to come back. Death, she discovered, held the ease and fulfillment she had never known in her life. "I really thought I was dying," she wrote Bessie Zaban Jones, "and I felt not the faintest fear or reluctance, or even a wish to hold back a moment."[37] Two years later she told a news reporter that she had been dead for ten minutes: "It was like being taken up and carried, like being enveloped in a great, surging slow tide—and it was bliss. Except for a half-minute I was fully conscious, my eyes open, all my life crowding into my mind, knowing my room and the people in it, and knowing what death was like— and it was bliss."[38] In private she modified her statement to say that she had come "as near death as one may come and return." Still she called it a "wonderful adventure" in which she was "lifted up, on the crest of a wave, and swept out into some perfect fulfill-

34 Hatch, "On the Trail of a Lady Novelist"; interview with Dr. Harold S. Babcock, Castine, Me.

35 To Van Wyck Brooks, August 24, 1940, in Brooks Papers; to Bessie Zazan Jones, September 25, 1940, in *Letters*, 268–69; to Van Wyck Brooks, October 7, 1940, in *Letters*, 170; *Woman Within*, 290.

36 *Woman Within*, 289; Berta Wellford to MKR, in Rawlings Papers.

37 To James Branch Cabell, September 14, 1940, in Cabell Papers; to Bessie Zaban Jones, September 25, 1940, in *Letters*, 268.

38 Robert van Gelder, "An Interview with Miss Ellen Glasgow," *New York Times Book Review* (October 18, 1942), 1.

ment."[39] Perfect fulfillment was not yet to be hers, however; life remained with her. As she grew stronger she was faced with the realities of a long trip back to Richmond, a manuscript that needed its third and final revising, and the necessity to accept her most distinguished award.

After she resigned from the Academy's committee to select the recipient of the Howells Medal, that committee decided to give the award to her. The decision was made early in August, but the award was not officially granted until the middle of November.[40] The Howells Medal, given only once every five years, was the most distinguished honor the Academy could present to one of its members and no doubt was to be valued even above the Pulitzer Prize. Since Ellen knew that she would be unable to go to New York to accept the award, she began to negotiate for someone to do it for her. Finally, J. Donald Adams, a book reviewer for the New York *Times*, agreed. But Ellen had to write a statement of acceptance, and she had not the slightest idea what to say. She wrote to the secretary of the Academy: "Will you tell me what kind of note I should write. How do I address my acceptance? I feel helpless about it." The secretary responded with the exact words she should use, and on November 14, 1940, Adams read Ellen's statement to the Academy: "A literary award confers a double honour when it is given, in the name of William Dean Howells, by the Academy of Arts and Letters. I accept this distinguished medal with the deepest appreciation."[41] Ellen had been at home for about three weeks and was lying in her bed in Richmond when the award was officially made. She received a bouquet of roses and a card of congratulations from the directors of the Academy. The next day Van Wyck Brooks wrote her that she was the only novelist even considered for the award, which was unprecedented. The medal is a heavy gold medallion, about three and one-half inches in diameter, with an engraving of

[39] To Signe Toksvig, August 15, 1943, *Letters*, 331–32.
[40] Booth Tarkington to Ellen Glasgow, August 7, 1940, William Lyon Phelps to Ellen Glasgow, August 27, 1940, in Glasgow Papers.
[41] Glasgow File, American Academy of Arts and Letters; see especially a letter to Mrs. Grace Vanamee, October 4, 1940.

William Dean Howells on one side and a quill and ink stand on the other. Inscribed around the edge are the words: "Awarded to Ellen Glasgow Nov. 14, 1940 for distinction in fiction."[42]

The Howells Medal may have been the greater honor, but the award for which Ellen had long hungered was the Pulitzer Prize. For ten years, ever since the publication of *The Sheltered Life,* there had been a considerable amount of agitation among novelists and critics because the Pulitzer Prize had not been awarded to Ellen Glasgow but had gone to lesser talents. Now it was widely rumored that the novel Ellen was writing, no matter what its quality, would receive the prize. James Branch Cabell, at least, was convinced of it. When she returned home in October, he went to her bedside and for the next four months spent hours there, reading her chapters, making minor corrections, and mostly just encouraging her not to give up. Cabell was undoubtedly one of her most devoted friends, and he undertook this work, he said, out of "love and friendship" and "honest sympathy," as well as "the derisive pleasure which [he] got from knowing that at long last [he] was completing a Pulitzer Prize winner."[43]

The task was finished, and early in 1941 Cabell departed for his winter vacation in St. Augustine, Florida. Ellen informed her publishers in no uncertain terms that the novel must receive top priority in advertising and must not be grouped with lesser works. Her theme, she said, was "an analysis of the modern mind and temperament in a single community," and her Negro characters were not merely "background" but a theme within themselves. If the publisher did not wish to advertise the novel as she wished, she threatened to break her contract.[44] Harcourt yielded to her demands without the slightest protest and published *In This Our Life* in March, 1941. Ellen lapsed into the inevitable and customary depression of the creator suddenly bereaved of her creation. The agony

42 November 15, 1940, in Glasgow Papers. The medal is in the Papers.
43 Cabell, *As I Remember It,* 219, 222. In *The Woman Within,* 291–92, Ellen Glasgow acknowledges his assistance but does not credit him with as much help as he claims to have given.
44 To Alfred Harcourt, November 27, 1940 and n.d., to Helen K. Taylor, December 17, 1940, to Alfred Harcourt, n.d., all in *Letters,* 271, 272, 273.

of reading the proof sheets caused her to moan that she "might as well, with far less trouble to [herself] and the world, have passed on in August." But she was proud of her accomplishment. "My heart has gone into it," she said, "and I know it is good."[45]

The book was good, but it was not her best. Set in Richmond in 1938, it is the story of the Timberlake family and their entire community engulfed in a moment of rapid change. Asa Timberlake led a boring life as a worker in a tobacco factory and as the husband to an aristocratic hypochondriac; he wanted only to escape to a peaceful existence on a farm. His daughter Stanley, spoiled by her uncle, ruined her own life and those of several around her by recklessly seeking happiness in sensual pleasures. Her sister Roy, Ellen's favorite character, searched with youthful optimism for happiness through perfection in an imperfect world.[46] Out of pity more than desire, she gave herself to a stranger in a compulsive determination not to be cheated by life. The scene scarcely seems to belong to the story, however, and the novelist left many loose ends in the development of Roy's character. Ellen drew her Negro characters from people she had known, and after she had written the description of Parry Clay in jail, she visited the Negro section of the local jail to make sure that her description was accurate.[47] The novel ends with Roy running out into a storm and crying out that she wants something good to hold on to. Her father assures her that she will find it, and Ellen thought she had ended the novel on an optimistic note.[48]

But her readers were understandably confused, and Ellen herself later admitted that the story "came to a pause, not to an end." Popular sales did not equal those of her previous books, but the critical acclaim was enthusiastic.[49] Many people who were her

45 To James Branch Cabell, January 15, February 25, 1941, in Cabell Papers; to Bessie Zaban Jones, February 25, 1941, to Charles Hanson Towne, December 30, 1940, in *Letters*, 279, 277.
46 *A Certain Measure*, 255.
47 To Bessie Zaban Jones, July 20, 1942, in *Letters*, 304; *A Certain Measure*, 257–58. Her notes on the visit to the jail are in the Glasgow Papers.
48 To Van Wyck Brooks, March 28, 1941, in *Letters*, 283; *A Certain Measure*, 257.
49 To Van Wyck Brooks, July 27, 1943, in *Letters*, 327–28; *A Certain Measure*, 263; Kelly, "Struggle for Recognition," 323–25.

friends and in positions to get their reviews in the best papers and journals, including H. L. Mencken, Charles Hanson Towne, Van Wyck Brooks, and Howard Mumford Jones, all praised the new novel. Henry Seidel Canby, editor of the *Saturday Review of Literature* and personal friend of Ellen Glasgow, had his magazine create the "*Saturday Review of Literature* Award for Distinguished Service to American Literature" and present it to her. Warner Brothers paid her forty thousand dollars for the film rights to the novel.[50]

Her greatest tributes, however, whether Ellen accepted them as such or not, were two unique fan letters. A Negro high school teacher from Washington, D.C., expressed her "profound appreciation" for Ellen's portrayal of black people as "respectable human beings with dignity, ideas and opinions." Three years passed before Ellen received the other letter; it was from a soldier stationed in a small town in North Africa. He praised her work and told of a midsummer afternoon in 1941 when he had stood across the street and gazed in reverence at the old gray house but had not the courage to knock on the door.[51] If he had knocked, no one would have been at home; and even if Ellen had been in town at the time, his welcome would have at best been uncertain. Surely, however, her heart was warmed by such private and sincere tributes, which must have enhanced the enthusiasm with which she revelled in the public reviews her friends had written for her.

Such public and private acclaim was all too tangible proof that the published novel was no longer her personal property, and in the spring and summer of 1941 she had already directed her mind toward other tasks. She felt that a sequel to *In This Our Life* might clarify the ambiguous ending, and she wanted to collect the prefaces she had written for the *Virginia Edition* of her novels into a single volume of self-criticism.

The idea to collect her prefaces into a single volume had been

---

[50] To Stanley Young, March 18, 1941; to Frank Morley, February 7, 1942; to Bessie Zaban Jones, June 26, 1942, in *Letters*, 281, 291, 302.
[51] Elaine J. Deane to Ellen Glasgow, June 26, 1941, Paul W. Donham to Ellen Glasgow, April 10, 1944, in Glasgow Papers.

with her from the time she first wrote them, and it was one which she had discussed frequently with James Branch Cabell. Cabell had been of inestimable assistance to her in writing the prefaces in 1937 and 1938, and naturally she sought his advice about the book. As soon as he received word that she had completed *In This Our Life,* he sent her his congratulations and suggested the order in which the prefaces should appear in the proposed volume. "After all, though," he added, "I tend to forget it is your book." But it was his book, too. Even the title that was eventually selected, *A Certain Measure,* was chosen by Cabell.[52] In the course of 1941 the book was finished, but its publication was delayed for two years; and for the time being the friendship between Ellen Glasgow and James Branch Cabell was not impaired.

After completing her preface for *In This Our Life* in the spring of 1941, Ellen returned to Castine for the summer. She arrived in June at her beloved "Appledoor" and stayed until the end of September. The vista of blue waters from her porch and the white and purple lilacs blooming around her door brought her only limited pleasure.[53] The war news depressed her, she felt lonely and isolated now that her novel was published. She had little to do but to wait for death and to write letters bemoaning her fate. In the spring, Marjorie Kinnan Rawlings, friend of James Branch Cabell and author of *The Yearling,* had visited her in Richmond to congratulate her upon the completion of *In This Our Life.*[54] Marjorie admired Ellen's work tremendously and told her so, and though they had never seen each other before, they established a warm and open friendship. While in Castine in July, Ellen received an unusual letter from Marjorie:

My very dear Ellen Glasgow:

I had such a vivid dream about you last night, that I must write you—which I have been meaning to do since our delightful brief

---

[52] To Ellen Glasgow, January 4, 1941, in Glasgow Papers. A letter from Ellen Glasgow to Cabell, dated July 3, 1941, confirms that he selected the title. A copy of the letter is in the Rawlings Papers; the original is in the possession of Mrs. Cabell.

[53] To Van Wyck Brooks, June 16, 1941, in *Letters,* 286.

[54] MKR to Ellen Glasgow, March 30, 1941, in Glasgow Papers.

visit together. The reality of a dream can never be conveyed to another, but you came to live with me. I was away when you came, and on my return, to one of those strange mansions that are part of the substance of dreams, you were outside in the bitter cold, cutting away ice from the roadway and piling it in geometric patterns. I was alarmed, remembering your heart trouble, and led you inside the mansion and brought you a cup of hot coffee. You had on blue silk gloves, and I laid my hand over yours, and was amazed, for my own hand is small, to have yours fit inside mine, much smaller. You chose your room and suggested draperies to supplement a valance. The valance was red chintz and you showed me a sample of a heavy red brocade of the same shade. I told you from now on I should take care of you, and you must not do strenuous things, such as cutting the ice in the roadway. James Cabell came into the room and asked what the two of us were up to. (As of course he would!)

My memory of my time with you is quite as vivid as the night's dream. I have thought of you oftener than I can tell you. So often a personality is detached from writings, and the two in fact seem to have nothing to do with each other. You as a person have the vitality, the wit and the irony of your work, but I was not prepared to find you so warm and so beautiful, in spite of the devotion of your friends, which would indicate those things to you.[55]

Ellen was touched and replied the very next day:

My very dear Marjorie:

I cannot tell you how much your letter meant to me—and still means. It came last night after a trying day, and it brought a thrilling sense of friendship and sympathy.

That was an extraordinary dream, and it was the more extraordinary because you have been so frequently in my mind since I have been at Castine. It was singular that the cold, and my cutting ice in geometrical patterns, should have come in. Ever since I finished *In This Our Life* I have felt as if I were drifting in an icy vacuum toward something—or nothing. I wonder whether other writers have this sense of being drained and lost and surrounded by emptiness whenever they have finished a book. Of course, my illness and five years of work that was like pushing against a physical obstacle may have intensified this feeling of being swallowed up in the void.

[55] July 19, 1942, *ibid.* The letter is also cited in *Woman Within*, 294.

But the dearest part of your dream was the way you brought me in and told me I must do no more cutting of ice in the roadway. And the warmth of the red curtains and the valance! Even the way James popped in and asked what we were up to had the accent of reality. I am so glad you wrote me about it.

My love to you, dear Marjorie,

Ellen.[56]

Ellen liked to pride herself on being independent, but she was the most dependent of persons. Her daily life was regulated by Anne Virginia Bennett, and in late years her professional activities owed much to the assistance of James Branch Cabell. The idea that Marjorie Rawlings could protect her from an icy world appealed to Ellen immensely, a phenomenon that increased in significance almost eight years after Ellen's death when Marjorie Rawlings began to write her biography. Marjorie died before she could complete the work, but she left a note concerning her later reflection upon the dream: "It was obvious that it was I who was to attend on her. It was my feeling at the end of the dream that her original humanity and gratitude turned suddenly to self-assured arrogance."[57] As Marjorie Rawlings discerned, Ellen had an increasing tendency to cry out for sympathy and affection from literary personalities whom she hardly knew.

Those whom she knew well she subjected to even more desperate whimperings about her fate. Time and the nearness of death had healed the old riff between Ellen and her sister Rebe. They had been childhood playmates, and now they began to relive the experiences they had enjoyed together. Much of their attention centered upon the family plot in Hollywood Cemetery, and they seemed to thrive upon a morbid exchange of attitudes toward death. James Branch Cabell was the only literary person within Ellen's easy grasp, and she reached out for him. She began to lament her reputation as a spinster and attempted to brief him on her love affairs,

---

[56] July 24, 1941, in *Letters*, 286–87.
[57] "Notes for a Biography of Ellen Glasgow," in Rawlings Papers. In 1953 Marjorie Rawlings was commissioned by Ellen Glasgow's literary executors to write the biography, but she died before she had finished collecting her notes.

but he would not listen.[58] From Castine she wrote ostensibly to thank him for his help with the prefaces, but really to inform him of her sad fate: "As for me, I have not broken away from that icy vacuum, which, if nothingness has a superlative, grows deeper and deeper. I know that I am over and done with, and I cannot reconcile myself to being merely a shell with an inadequate heart. . . . May you never know the horror of coming to the end of your work before your life is finished."[59]

Since the beginning of her illness, Cabell had worked overtime to cheer her, and his patience was beginning to wear thin. With disarming wit and benevolent sincerity, he responded to her note immediately:

Dear Ellen:

Are you not lovely! You are truly beautiful, and the sacred fire burns in you so visibly. With your great zest for life, it is dreadful to think of you as a virgin, but your books offer almost irrefutable testimony to the fact, unless indeed, your Virginian ladihood stepped in and caused you to become reticent—

End quote. You may or may not guess its origin, but when people write to me as an authority upon your maidenhood, I become, as befits an aging grandfather, embarrassed. What I really meant, though, is that your last letter was simply silly. Your theme song was The Old Gray Mare She Ain't What She Used to Be, whereas the correct melody is There's Life in the Old Girl Yet. What more do you want, you—so to speak—swine? You have a recognition more wide than Shakespeare ever received during his lifetime, or for that matter, Homer. Should you not ever publish another line, your fame is none the less secure and opulent. . . . I simply have not any patience with you, when you talk about being merely a shell with an inadequate heart. You are to the contrary the possessor of an, at least, mild amount of genius, which stays undiminished. If you were but also a Christian you would forthwith address your Maker in contrition.

James.[60]

Ellen took the hint, relented somewhat on her self-pity, and in her

---

58 Cabell, *As I Remember It*, 227.
59 August 1, 1941, in Cabell Papers.
60 August 6, 1941, in Glasgow Papers.

next letter announced that it would take "more than one little heart" to make an end of her. A mistress of irony, within a month she wrote Howard Mumford Jones that self-pity was the last vice she would encourage![61]

Since, as she said, the Almighty overlooked her, she descended from Maine by train on October 13, and after a brief stop in New York arrived back at One West Main Street by the end of the month. Her self-pity she confined for the moment to the secret autobiography which she still worked on at intervals. As her life ebbed, the movement of time became her preoccupation; it was a phenomenon with which she had wrestled in the creation of each of her novels and the nemisis for characters who had been too weak to survive change. In December, she scrawled another "miscellaneous pungency": "December 7, 1941, Sunday night. Clear and rather cold. War has come. Japan bombed Hawaii, without warning, early this morning. Many were killed. . . . Another Age of Disenchantment is ending. Another age of illusion is beginning."[62] Even the Second World War fitted neatly into the cycles to which she had consigned life. The unknown future, however, always troubled her. Still disturbed that the readers of *In This Our Life* did not discern that she looked to the future with optimism, she began work on a short sequel to that novel. She called it *Beyond Defeat: An Epilogue to an Era*. She completed a draft of the manuscript during 1942 and 1943, but she never allowed it to be published in her lifetime.[63]

The briefest of her novels, *Beyond Defeat* is set in Richmond in 1942, and the entire story takes place on the day Roy Timberlake returns home from a tuberculosis sanitarium. The result of her liaison with the stranger was an illegitimate baby named Timothy. Her sister Stanley has run off to California to marry a film producer, her rich Uncle William Fitzroy is dead, and her father has left her mother to go live with a widow on a farm that he had always wanted. Roy alone has the strength to survive dying traditions, and her child

---

[61] August 30, 1941, in Cabell Papers; September 24, 1941, in Howard Mumford Jones Papers.

[62] September 21, 1941, in Howard Mumford Jones Papers. See also, Glasgow Papers.

[63] Edited with an introduction by Luther Y. Gore, *Beyond Defeat* was published by the University Press of Virginia in 1966.

by an unknown father, Ellen said, is a living symbol of Roy's ability to accept an unknown future.[64] "But Timothy is the future," Asa Timberlake told Roy at the end of the story, "and for the future, the unknown is the heart of life."[65]

Indeed, for Ellen, stalked by death, the unknown was the heart of life, but she could never quite escape her present no matter how diligently she tried to disdain it. Marjorie Rawlings and Ellen continued their friendship by correspondence. Marjorie poured out the details of her own private life to Ellen and regretted that during their brief visit they had not had time to discuss "the man question," a subject still dear to Ellen's heart. Flattery was the order of the day, and Ellen responded with praise for Marjorie's *Cross Creek*, taking exception to a single scene in which rocks were thrown into the face of a dog. Early in 1942 the Southern Women's National Democratic Organization awarded Ellen a one-hundred-dollar prize for the most distinguished book of the previous year by a Southern-born writer on a Southern subject.[66]

Finally, on May 4, 1942, came the long awaited telegram: "Take pleasure in advising you award to 'In This Our Life' by Trustees of Columbia University of Pulitzer Novel Prize." In four days the telegram was followed by a check for five hundred dollars, and the Pulitzer Prize Committee had done its duty. Ellen's immediate reaction was to instruct her publisher to print and sell more copies, since she understood that the prize was excellent for advertising purposes. Privately, she said that it was "too little and too late"; publicly, she sniffed that it was "very nice."[67]

On May 5, 6, and 7, she was deluged with telegrams of congrat-

---

[64] To Frank Morley, December 7, 1943, in *Letters*, 340. See also Alfred Harcourt to Ellen Glasgow, February 26, 1942, in Glasgow Papers.

[65] *Beyond Defeat*, 134.

[66] MKR to Ellen Glasgow, January 17, 1942, in Glasgow Papers; to MKR, April 20, 1942, in *Letters*, 293–94; "Ellen Glasgow Given Award for Novel," Richmond *Times-Dispatch*, February 1, 1942.

[67] Frank D. Fackenthal to Ellen Glasgow, May 4, 1942, in Glasgow Papers; to Donald C. Brace, May 4, 1942, in *Letters*, 295; copy of a letter from Ellen Glasgow to Rebe Tutwiler, May 6, 1942, in Rawlings Papers; editorial clipped from the Norfolk *Ledger-Dispatch*, May 6, 1942, in Glasgow Papers.

ulations from friends and acquaintances and people she did not even know, ranging from Margaret Mitchell to Wendell Wilkie.[68] On May 6, her publisher informed her that the novel sold seven hundred copies on the day the prize was announced and was still doing well. The brief spurt in sales did not boost it to the best-seller list, however, and Ellen had to be content with her congratulations. Though she could not hide her cynicism, she was very proud and wrote to some of her friends that their warm response made her feel that the award was not "too little and too late."[69]

In the very month that the Pulitzer Prize was announced, Warner Brothers released the film version of *In This Our Life*. The première was in Richmond, the star was Bette Davis, and large crowds flocked to see it.[70] But Ellen was not in the crowds; she said that she could tell from the advertisement that the book Hollywood had filmed was not the one she had written, and she stayed at home.[71]

Summer was coming and the annual trip to Castine had become almost an obsession with her. Since gasoline was rationed because of the war, she used her automobile very little during the winter in order to save enough allowance for the trip. Appledoor was not available to her that summer, so she stayed in a four-story house on Battle Avenue "with the worst furniture and architecture of the period" and not a bed in it high enough for her dog Bonnie to hide under. Scarcely had she settled in Castine than she wrote to James Branch Cabell that she did not feel like writing. "What is the meaning of it?" she asked. "For more than forty years I was driven by some inner scourge to commit an act which appears to me, now, as useless as murder." She may have worked a little on *Beyond Defeat*, and her autobiography was certainly very much in her mind, but mostly she simply relaxed and enjoyed the view of the bay and the lilacs. Anne Virginia and Carrie Duke were with her; she was never alone. Much of the time she was in pain and simply waiting, wait-

[68] These telegrams are in the Glasgow Papers.
[69] Donald Brace to Ellen Glasgow, May 6, 1942, *ibid.*; to Van Wyck Brooks, May 7, 1942, to Margaret Mitchell, May 17, 1942, in *Letters*, 295, 297.
[70] Francis Earle Lutz, *Richmond in World War II* (Richmond: Dietz Press, 1951), 151.
[71] To Bessie Zaban Jones, June 26, 1942, in *Letters*, 302.

ing. "My weight this morning is 106," she wrote Cabell and his wife Percie. "But I love you both with all that is left of me, which is scarcely more than a bone and a bobbed head."[72]

The nearness of death did not drive her into the folds of orthodox Christianity. "I had a father who believed that to disbelieve in Hell was the Great Refusal," she wrote, "but his orthodoxy merely sent me off on a new departure of heresy."[73] Though she could never escape a subconscious belief in her father's dreadful doctrine of predestination, she had learned to worship beauty, especially the beauty of nature, and her brief walks in the Maine woods were like a religious experience. Cruelty she considered to be the only sin, and the stories of the war in Europe played desperately upon her nerves. Even in Castine she could not escape the war, but she would not allow it to obliterate her sense of humor. "The Village," she wrote, "seems to be inhabited entirely by old ladies, and I doubt whether I should recognize a man if I were to meet such a strange animal in the road. But the war fever burns. Old ladies are notoriously militant." At the end of the summer, after a two-hour escape from "a war-maddened world" into the peace and beauty of the Maine woods, she wrote, "If only man had never been created, what a glorious earth there might have been."[74]

But man had been created, she had been created, and even if she could not cope with her own personal suffering or that of the world, she at least had to endure it. The summer ended, and she was strong enough to stop for a few days in New York on her way home, but back in Richmond she drifted into "the more or less tedious struggle with the empty mechanism of living." On the last day of 1942 she had another heart attack and was confined to her bed for days. The winter was dreary and her letters to the friends whom she never saw were more depressing than the weather.[75] In the spring she acquired a new pen pal, Signe Toksvig, the Danish-born biographer of Hans Christian Andersen and Emanuel Swedenborg. The two

---

[72] June 27, 1942, and n.d., but probably in summer of 1942, both in Cabell Papers.
[73] To Bessie Zaban Jones, July 20, 1942, in *Letters*, 303.
[74] To Frank Morley, August 11 and 26, 1942, in *Letters*, 305, 306.
[75] To Van Wyck Brooks, November 5, 1942, March 22, 1943, *ibid.*, 309, 313–14.

women never met, but for more than two years they carried on a lively correspondence in which they bared their souls to one another. Ellen ranged over her entire life. She told of her interest in mysticism, her summers in Maine, and her attitudes toward her novels. She told of her childhood, her love for her mother and her dog, her hatred for her father's stern Calvinistic creed, and her antipathy to Christianity. And she told of the only two moments of freedom and peace in her life: that "golden afternoon in the Alps" with Gerald and that August day in Castine in 1940 when for a moment she savored the ecstasy of death.[76]

Those moments were to be hers no more except as she relived them in her autobiography and in her letters. June, 1943, came and with it the old urge to return to Castine. Henry Anderson, ever attentive and still her fiancé in theory at least, begged her not to attempt to make the trip. If she insisted, he offered to do anything he could to make her trip comfortable. She insisted, and she spent her summer in Castine working for only fifteen minutes a day over the second draft of *Beyond Defeat*, writing letters, and feeling so, so sorry for herself. She began to look at Anne Virginia suspiciously and without giving her reason begged James Branch Cabell never to mention her work in Anne Virginia's presence.[77] At the end of September she started home. Reclining in the back seat of her limousine, she commanded Nathaniel, her chauffeur, not to drive more than thirty miles per hour. The trip took five days and four nights, and she arrived in Richmond, she said, "barely more living than dead."[78]

But there was more life left in her than she was willing to admit, and the publication of *A Certain Measure* in October brought it all to the fore. In the "more freely interpretative form of fiction," Ellen said, she had written a complete social history of Virginia

[76] To Signe Toksvig, September 4, 1943, in *Letters*, 333. Thirteen letters of Ellen Glasgow to Signe Toksvig, dated May 21, 1943, through October 14, 1945, are published in *Letters*, 315–58. Sixteen letters of Signe Toksvig to Ellen Glasgow, dated June 1, 1943, through September 30, 1945, are in the Glasgow Papers.

[77] Henry Anderson to Ellen Glasgow, June 1, 1943, in Glasgow Papers; to James Branch Cabell, September 7, 1943, in Cabell Papers.

[78] To Frank Morley, October 24, 1943, in *Letters*, 336; to Charles Hanson Towne, September 28, 1943, in Charles Hanson Towne Papers, Yale University Library.

since the decade before the Confederacy.[79] The purpose of *A Certain Measure* was to reveal how it had been done. In her foreword she pointed out that humility was a hypocritical virtue she did not intend to indulge in while talking about her own work.[80] And that is one of the truest statements she made about herself in the entire book. Although the manuscript had been completed for more than a year, she had held up the publication allegedly because of the paper shortage during the war. But her reason probably ran much deeper. The book was actually a hodgepodge of many things: the revised prefaces to the *Virginia Edition* of her works, a new preface for *In This Our Life*, old speeches and articles, and a lot of the work of James Branch Cabell, who had tried to create some order out of her materials. She arranged six of her novels in chronological order according to the periods they covered from 1850 through 1912, and for some odd reason divided the other seven into novels of the country and novels of the city. She gave no reason for the abrupt change of organization, and the books actually fell more readily into the strict chronological arrangement and would have given more credence to her contention that it was a well-planned social history had she stuck faithfully to that arrangement. She insisted that the book should not be advertised as a book of prefaces, but as a volume of literary criticism, and to emphasize her point she gave it the subtitle "An Interpretation of Prose Fiction."[81] The manner in which the book was compiled made it a combination of both prefaces and criticism, spiced with a generous mingling of autobiography. The completed product was certainly a respectable achievement, and in private letters and public reviews, her friends poured out their praise. Howard Mumford Jones compared *A Certain Measure* to the prefaces of Henry James, and Stark Young called it "Beautiful Apologia."[82]

[79] *A Certain Measure*, 3.
[80] *Ibid.*, vii.
[81] To Donald C. Brace, May 9, 1942, in *Letters*, 297.
[82] Van Wyck Brooks to Ellen Glasgow, September 19, 1943, MKR to Ellen Glasgow, October 7, 1943, in Glasgow Papers; Ellen Glasgow to Charles Hanson Towne, September 28, 1943, in Towne Papers; Howard Mumford Jones, "The Regional Eminence of Ellen Glasgow," *Saturday Review of Literature*, XXVI (October 16, 1943), 20; Stark Young, "Beautiful Apologia," *New Republic*, CIX (October 25, 1943), 588.

Only James Branch Cabell was reticent. Ellen had sent him a copy of *A Certain Measure* from Maine with an inscription that gave not the slightest clue that he had ever seen the manuscript before its publication.[83] And Cabell could not help but notice that nowhere in the book was there any word of acknowledgement for his assistance. When Ellen arrived in Richmond in October, she called upon her anonymous collaborator and now asked him to write a review of the book. Cabell of course was decidedly under the impression that it was he who had first pointed out to her that her novels when taken collectively comprised a social history of Virginia, and he slyly asked her the loaded question, what did she mean by social history? The next day he received her reply in a letter:

> But what I tried to explain yesterday was only this: You asked the meaning of a social history, and my answer was, or would have been but for an interruption, that I meant by a social history the customs, habits, manners, and general outer envelope human nature had assumed in a special place and period. My place happened to be Virginia, and my period covered the years from 1850 to the present time. But the inner substance of my work has been universal human nature—or as I have always believed—and if the great Balzac had not been ahead of me, I should have called [my] books the Human Comedy.
>
> Blessings on you, dear James. I haven't had so merry an hour for a long time.
>
> Yours ever,<br>Ellen.[84]

Now, the lady who had not given him credit for his assistance and had asked him to write a review of a book he himself had partly written, was telling him what to say in the review.[85]

Cabell was equal to the occasion. His and Ellen's friendship had been partially founded upon a matching of ironic wits, a cautious

---

[83] Ellen Glasgow to James Branch Cabell, September 7, 1943, in Cabell Papers.

[84] October 28, 1943, *ibid.*

[85] Edgar E. MacDonald, "The Glasgow-Cabell Entente," *American Literature*, XLI (March, 1969), 76–91, gives a complete and penetrating discussion of the Glasgow-Cabell feud over *A Certain Measure*.

exchange of their sharpened senses of humor. Ignoring her advice, Cabell proceeded to write the review as he saw fit; and it was a bombshell.[86] Playing upon her self-advertisement as a "social historian," Cabell compared her to Edward Gibbon, sporting upon the fact that both had the initials "E.G." He announced that *A Certain Measure* was "zestfully phrased" and the best of her books.

Truly, in the production of an autobiography the historian has an advantage hitherto denied. It is the chief peril of an historian's work that his art must lead him to impersonate knowledge which he, or it may be even she, in mere point of fact and through no stint of endeavor, does not possess. Most precariously does this become true when the historian needs to make plain some special type of character or of emotion such as—perhaps on account of the involved artist's sex or race or rearing, or it may be through an unthrifty adhesion to continence and respectable living—the historian simply does not know anything whatever, except by report. I have heard mentioned hereabouts the word "intuition"; and I have made bold to regard the word as a quite possible synonym for "humbug." The historian, in his more vivid passages of impressive and subtle analysis, is compelled very often to fake his writing, through mere lack of omniscience.

Thus, during the composition of her social history of Virginia, "in the more freely interpretative form of fiction," Ellen Glasgow has been forced to depict, not only the actions, but the emotions, of several young men under the influence of love, and the retrospections, alike military and sociological and extra-marital, of a Confederate veteran—a passage which, quite rightly, she has chosen as containing some of her most representative prose. She has delineated also the resigned sentiment of a time-tamed husband toward his wife, the meditations of an illiterate Negress, and a father's partly impatient tenderness for his children. She, in brief, has needed (as a social historian) to deal introspectively with a large host of affairs which were no more comprehensible to Ellen Glasgow, through any vital experience, than was to Gibbon, let us say, the deplorably un-English temperament of the harlot-empress Theodora, or the moral standards of Mahomet, or the quaint zest

86 The review originally appeared in the New York *Evening Post*, December 2, 1943, and the Chicago *Sun*, December 5, 1943, and excerpts, under the title "Ellen Glasgow's Best Book," appeared in the Richmond *Times-Dispatch*, December 5, 1943, Sec. D, p. 2. Cited here from the Richmond *Times-Dispatch*.

with which quite a number of Early Christians appeared to enter the arena. And yet to depict these alien mentalities was, in each case, a part of the writer's job which had to be discharged, in one way or another, through the aid of industry and fancy, in default of knowledge. . . .

Her intellectual self-record is thus made an oddly chameleon-like volume by turns frank, or seductive, or arrogant, or self-contradictory, or rich with wisdom—being, when the need arises, as bare as Euclid, as diffuse as Mrs. Franklin D. Roosevelt, or as neatly burnished as a carved fragment from Pater—but at every moment the book remains pleasingly human. It is, in brief, all Ellen Glasgow. . . .

Ellen was not amused. She was furious, and she told her friends Carrie Duke and Berta Wellford why she was so angry.[87] To Cabell she said nothing for more than six months. In June, 1944, she mailed him a chilly note from her summer vacation in Maine:

> I was not unmindful of Percie and you this past winter, and indeed I did try to write. But (and this is the sad truth) I could think of nothing to say. Shut in, as I was for months, all the relative shapes and comparative values of things became strangely confused. In this life-giving air, lifted high above a blue rippling bay and a chain of hills, I find that only a war on the other side of the world, with mankind destroying itself and other more innocent animals, appears really important enough to bother about. Even the sharpened edge of what Berta Wellford felicitously called your 'all-time low' has become harmlessly blunted.
>
> You alone, I suppose, my dear James, know the reason for this abrupt change of front after thirty—or is it nearer forty—years? I am willing to grant you any number of reasons, though I cannot quite understand all the long endeavour to build up a charming appearance of sympathy and comprehension, if this were simply for the need of releasing, in the end, a sudden gust of inhibited malice. Literary smartness must depend, of course, for its best effects upon caricature and misrepresentation, and, as we both have learned, from the wise or witty, caricature demands the spicy flavour of malice or flippancy. And yet, even so . . . the only literary right I deny is the right of misrepresentation. . . . I find, as I grow older, that I cling more firmly to certain ancient beliefs or illusions:

[87] Carrie Duke to MKR, in Rawlings Papers; interview with Mrs. James Branch Cabell, November 14, 1968.

to steadfast loyalties, and to truths of the written or of the spoken word, and to the abiding sincerity of a long friendship. . . .[88]

Cabell ignored the touchy problem of their shaky relationship and replied promptly: "It was uncommonly good to be hearing from you at long last, my dear."[89]

Still miffed, Ellen maintained her silence for three months and sent another letter only slightly less harsh than her first one:

> Well, James, your letter was most agreeable, but its rightful place was in another summer. It told me everything, except the one thing I was rather curious about, and that is: Does the pleasure of releasing an inhibited gust of malice make the effort, or the satisfaction, worth more than it costs? . . . What you might care to say in a newspaper would certainly be no solemn matter, if only it had not denied everything you had said or written, and I had believed, for the past thirty or forty years. And this is true, even when, by minds less subtle or less literary than yours, what you said is misconstrued as cheap smartness. . . .
>
> A Certain Measure was my swan song; and though it has taken me forty years of benevolent neglect to win a place of my own, this valediction brought me (if I exclude your ingenious attack) only praise and a very cordial appreciation. But there were many years when I was pushed aside; and for all that your friendship meant to me in those earlier years, I shall never lose affection and gratitude, and even that discredited virtue loyalty, which remains a favorite of mine.
>
> After I reach home, perhaps you will both come down for an old-fashioned. We may still have a laugh together, for I think that ironic amusement will be the last pleasure we give up.[90]

Cabell was refusing to humor Ellen in the quarrel, and Ellen was beginning to relent somewhat. But she still had one powerful weapon which she was quite willing to use: the secret autobiography. Although there is no proof of it, it is quite likely that she wrote her chapter on Cabell at the height of her anger with him.

---

88 June 16, 1944. A copy of the letter is in the Rawlings Papers; the original is in the possession of Mrs. Cabell.

89 June 25, 1944, cited in MacDonald, "Glasgow-Cabell Entente."

90 September 25, 1944. A copy of the letter is in the Rawlings Papers; the original is in the possession of Mrs. Cabell.

Although she posed as the benevolent defender of his reputation, she delved deeply into alleged matters of Cabell's personal life that had absolutely no relationship to her autobiography, driven without doubt by that "inhibited gust of malice" of which she had accused him. And, Cabell said, she took a "grim enjoyment" in taunting him with what she had said about him in a book he would not be allowed to read until after her death. When the autobiography was published long after Ellen's death, Cabell quietly dismissed it as "containing her very best fiction" and proceeded to praise her with all of the courtesy that a gentleman of Virginia naturally afforded to a dead woman whom he had genuinely admired and respected.[91]

As long as Ellen lived, Cabell sought to make amends while persistently refusing to become entangled in any philosophical discussion of their uncertain friendship. By the time Ellen returned from Maine in the fall of 1944, he had already departed for his winter vacation in St. Augustine, and the quarrel lingered into the following year. In August, 1945, from Castine, Ellen cautiously offered an olive branch: "But I wish we could have again, on this perfect summer afternoon, one of our old talks on writing and the kind of writing that was worth while. Even if we did not agree, the talk would be better than the endless complaints about points and rationing I have had to hear for the past several years.

"With my love to the three of you, and with the old friendship and sympathy, Ellen."[92] Time was doing its work, and Cabell immediately accepted. "I must certainly see you in October," he replied. "There are so many things which may not be written about with profit, because a face to face quarrel, but not a letter, can end with a kiss."[93] Reportedly, that is the way it ended; Cabell called upon Ellen after she returned and they were reconciled.[94]

91 James Branch Cabell, *Let Me Lie* (New York: Farrar, Straus and Co., 1947), 263; Cabell, *As I Remember It*, 217–33.

92 August 22, 1945; cited in MacDonald, "Glasgow-Cabell Entente"; original in possession of Mrs. Cabell.

93 August 30, 1945, in Glasgow Papers.

94 "Notes for a Biography of Ellen Glasgow," in Rawlings Papers.

The quarrel came at an inopportune time for Ellen. Self-control in her relations with her fellows had never been one of her virtues, and the infelicities of age and more or less constant pain merely exaggerated the more tactless vagaries of her personality. But the quarrel was not Ellen's major preoccupation during the year and a half that it lasted, and the chances are that she and Cabell would have seen each other no more frequently had they not been feuding. Most of her attention in 1944 and 1945 was devoted to the matter of how to dispose of her personal and literary properties as she prepared to face the inevitable. Although, given plenty of time, it was certainly not out of character for her to forgive and forget, her final mellowing toward Cabell may have been a part of her preparation. However, the drawing up of her will and the selection of literary executors concerned her far more than the possibility of dying without being reconciled to her old friend and neighbor.

Ellen signed her will on April 15, 1944, but she added codicils on into the fall of 1945. She directed that her furniture, small amounts of money, and personal items should be distributed among her friends, sister, niece, and Anne Virginia Bennett. Her china dogs were to go to the Valentine Museum in memory of Cary. Each of the servants in her employ at the time of her death was to receive $100; Nathaniel, her chauffeur, was to receive an additional $200. She established a trust fund of $100,000 to be administered by the First and Merchants National Bank of Richmond. Of the income from the trust fund, $50 per month was to be paid to James Anderson, her cook for forty years, and the remainder of the income was to go to Anne Virginia Bennett who was charged with the responsibility to care for any dogs that were left. Upon the death of Anne Virginia the balance of the trust estate was to be held by her trustees "for the benefit of the Richmond Society for the Prevention of Cruelty to Animals in memory of my beloved Sealyham terrier, Jeremy."[95]

Additional notes of instruction were addressed to Anne Virginia,

95 "Last Will and Testament of Ellen Glasgow, Deceased," recorded in the Chancery Court at Richmond, Va.

and one contained a strange request: *"Do not forget Jeremy.* Remind Dr. Tompkins of his promise."[96] Anne Virginia knew what she meant. Ellen left her literary materials in the hands of Irita Van Doren and an old friend and an associate of her publishing firm, Frank V. Morley, charging them with the responsibility to publish her autobiography when they saw fit and to deposit her papers where they would be accessible in "some happier age" long after her death, when an interest might revive "in the life of the solitary spirit."[97]

The remainder of the "life of the solitary spirit" was occupied with small matters, but matters which to the dying woman seemed to be quite important. The details of living seemed to be more than life was worth. She relinquished the presidency of the SPCA to Anne Virginia, and perhaps foreseeing that after her death the annual meetings would be gatherings of old ladies sitting around relict to relic in Carrie Duke's antique shop, at the final meeting in her home Ellen allowed only the younger members to come in to speak to her.[98] She was almost constantly in pain, and the trips to Maine in the summers of 1944 and 1945 were more of an ordeal than a pleasure. She suffered terribly in the winter and spring of 1945, and spent weeks in a hospital where she was kept alive by artificial feeding.[99] Her old friend Dr. Joseph Collins urged her to come to New York where she could get the best medical care and offered to pay all of her expenses if necessary. Arthur sent her a check for one thousand dollars in March and another for three thousand in April to help with the medical expenses. A friend wrote her: "Fight, Ellen, fight!"[100]

[96] To Rebe Tutwiler and Anne Virginia Bennett, October 31, 1944, in Rawlings Papers.

[97] To Literary Executors, January 6 and 8, 1945. See also Frank Morley to Ellen Glasgow, February 13 and 14, 1944, March 21 and May 22, 1945, Irita Van Doren to Ellen Glasgow, March 21, 1944, all in Glasgow Papers.

[98] Margaret Dashiell to MKR, in Rawlings Papers.

[99] James Branch Cabell to MKR, May 27, 1945, copy of a letter in the Glasgow Papers.

[100] Collins to Ellen Glasgow, April 8, 1945, to Ellen Glasgow, April 14, 1945, *ibid.,* Arthur Glasgow to MKR, April 14, 1945, in Rawlings Papers; J. Donald Adams to Ellen Glasgow, April 21, 1945, in Glasgow Papers.

Ellen did, and she recovered enough to make the trip to Castine. But even the scenery could not cheer her. She was bored, suffered from insomnia, and told her sister that life was so terrible she hoped she would never have to make the trip to Castine again.[101] In Maine, perhaps on a bright morning when she had returned from a walk in the woods, she selected her epitaph, a line from John Milton's "Lycidas": "Tomorrow to fresh woods and pastures new."[102]

Ellen was struggling valiantly to show that kind of courage in the face of the unknown that she had given to Roy in *Beyond Defeat*, but in dealing with the temporal ties that yet bound her, her courage failed. "I dread the return to the place where I suffered so much," she wrote Van Wyck Brooks as she prepared to return to One West Main Street in October, 1945. Once at home, she seemed chipper and wrote Henry Anderson that she felt like walking a mile. To James Branch Cabell, however, she seemed to be in an advanced state of melancholia and talked morbidly about being starved both physically and mentally. Cabell urged Marjorie Rawlings to write Ellen and cheer her up by telling her how wonderful she was, and Marjorie gladly did so.[103] Eight days later, on November 11, Ellen had another mild heart attack. She was in the beauty parlor at the Jefferson Hotel, less than a block from her home. Anne Virginia was with her, sent the chauffeur home for a bottle of Scotch, and gave Ellen half a glass straight. Ellen revived, and Anne Virginia told the male operator to finish the permanent and hurry. Ellen dreaded the thought of dying in public, and once they were home, she asked Anne Virginia, "What would you have done if I had died there?"

"We would have gotten you right into the car," Anne Virginia replied. "No one would have known."[104]

101 "Notes for a Biography of Ellen Glasgow," in Rawlings Papers. See also Ellen Glasgow to Mrs. Van Wyck Brooks, August 14, 1945, in Brooks Papers.
102 Anne Virginia Bennett to MKR, in Rawlings Papers.
103 Ellen Glasgow to Van Wyck Brooks, October 10, 1945, in Brooks Papers; Henry Anderson to Ellen Glasgow, October 27, 1945, in Glasgow Papers; copy of a letter of James Branch Cabell to MKR, November 3, 1945; MKR to Ellen Glasgow, November 19, 1945; in Glasgow Papers.
104 Anne Virginia Bennett to MKR, in Rawlings Papers.

Ellen was not bedridden, and on the night of November 20, she was able to entertain a meeting of the SPCA. She came down in a red dress, chatted on her favorite subject, and later went to bed, locking the door behind her as was her custom. The next morning, November 21, 1945, signed by Anne Virginia Bennett and Carrie Duke, the telegrams went out: "Ellen Glasgow died this morning."[105] The following day, the editor of the Richmond *Times-Dispatch* proclaimed: "The greatest woman Virginia has produced is dead."[106]

At 6:30 in the morning Anne Virginia had unlocked Ellen's bedroom. The thermos of coffee by her bedside had not been touched. Ellen was dressed in a pink gown and bed jacket, her head half-turned on her pillow, one hand by her face, the trace of a smile on her lips. Anne Virginia called James the cook, Dr. Tompkins, and Carrie Duke. Dr. Tompkins said that there was nothing he could do; she had been dead for hours. "You remember your promise to her?" Anne Virginia asked, recalling the urgent letter Ellen had addressed to her. "I do," he said. The doctor went into the bathroom to make his preparations, or to pretend to make his preparations, returned to the bedside and made an injection into the body. Ellen had had a horror of being buried alive and had made the doctor promise her that if and when he found her dead he would inject strychnine.[107]

Neither did Anne Virginia forget Ellen's other request: *"Do not forget Jeremy."* She contacted the same funeral home that had handled the burial of Jeremy, because she was sure they would be willing to comply with Ellen's wish that the remains of Jeremy and Billy be exhumed and placed in the casket with her.

For two days the body lay in state on Ellen's own bed in her own bedroom. A white fishnet canopy that Ellen had had especially made was supported by the four posts of the bed, and a large candle stood guard on either side. An Episcopal clergyman was called. In a private moment he gathered Rebe, Anne Virginia, Carrie Duke,

105 Van Vechten Papers; Glasgow File, American Academy of Arts and Letters; Brooks Papers.
106 Virginius Dabney, "A Great Virginian Passes," November 22, 1945.
107 Anne Virginia Bennett to MKR, in Rawlings Papers.

James Anderson, and the other servants around the bed. They held hands and formed a circle while the clergyman prayed,[108] a ceremony which Ellen no doubt would have chosen to miss.

The funeral service was conducted downstairs at One West Main at 3:30 in the afternoon of November 23, 1945. A high church Episcopalian service, it was an elaborate imitation of her mother's funeral in the same room more than fifty years earlier. Soft coal fires crackled in all four downstairs grates. A spray of yellow roses was on the door, and the house was banked with flowers. The pall was, as Ellen had directed, another arrangement of yellow roses, and great candelabra stood at the head and foot of the casket, each with seven large candles. There was no music.[109] About seventy-five relatives and friends attended. Henry Anderson was not invited, but he came anyway and stood in the doorway, tall and proud, half defiant and half crushed.[110] James Branch Cabell had already gone to St. Augustine, Florida, for his winter vacation and did not return for the services. Arthur Glasgow, suffering from a cold, explained that more of his friends caught their deaths of cold at funerals than anywhere else, and he stayed away.[111]

The word spread that Miss Ellen's dogs had been placed in the casket with her; and as the procession made its way to Hollywood Cemetery, Negro maids came out and stood on their front porches and gazed with silent amazement at the final passage of Miss Ellen and Jeremy and Billy. In Hollywood the creed was again recited, and the vast array of flowers covered the family plot and overflowed to the nearby resting place of General J. E. B. Stuart. Placed on the casket along with the canopy of yellow roses was a purple heart of pansies sent anonymously on behalf "of the homeless cats and dogs of Richmond."[112] At the head of the grave was a great wreath of

108 Margaret Dashiell to MKR, *ibid.*
109 A typewritten description of the funeral is in the Glasgow materials in the Yale University Library. Handwritten in the margin is "Mr. Munford of Richmond to [name illegible]." Mr. Munford identifies himself as one of Ellen Glasgow's friends who attended the funeral and wrote this description the following day.
110 Douglas S. Freeman, to MKR, Rawlings Papers.
111 Interviews with Mrs. James Branch Cabell and Mr. Glasgow Clark, November 14, 1968.
112 Editorial, "A Purple Heart for Her," Richmond *News Leader*, November 24, 1945.

magnolia leaves that had been sent by the American Academy of Arts and Letters. Clouds were in the sky, and it was a cold and windy November day. Ironically, there was no sun to sparkle on the River James where it splashed over the falls at the foot of the hill and flowed on one hundred and twenty miles to the sea. Ellen had already ordered the Christmas cards which she intended to use for 1945. On the front was a bright painting of a sunrise over a landscape that looked like the coast of Maine. It had been painted by her friend Stark Young and was entitled "The Dawning of the Day." They were never mailed.

# Selected Bibliography

MANUSCRIPTS

Edwin A. Alderman Papers. University of Virginia Library.
Bagby Family Papers. Library of the Virginia Historical Society.
Hamilton Basso Papers. Yale University Library.
Eleanor Robson Belmont Papers. Columbia University Library.
Stephen Vincent Benét Papers. Yale University Library.
Van Wyck Brooks Papers. University of Pennsylvania Library.
John Stewart Bryan Papers. Library of the Virginia Historical Society.
James Branch Cabell Papers. University of Virginia Library.
Henry Seidel Canby Papers. Yale University Library.
The Century Collection. New York Public Library.
Margaret May Dashiell Papers. Southern Historical Collection, University of North Carolina Library.
De Graffenried Family Papers. Southern Historical Collection, University of North Carolina Library.
George T. Delacorte, Jr., Papers. Columbia University Library.
Douglas S. Freeman Papers. Library of Congress.
Ellen Glasgow File. American Academy of Arts and Letters, 633 W. 155th St., New York, N.Y.
Ellen Glasgow Papers. University of Virginia Library.
Joseph Hergesheimer Papers. University of Virginia Library.
Sophia Bledsoe Herrick Papers. University of Virginia Library.
Mary Johnston Papers. University of Virginia Library.
Bessie Zaban Jones Papers. Smith College Library.
Howard Mumford Jones Papers. Harvard University Library.
Elizabeth Jordan Papers. New York Public Library.
Amy Loveman Papers. Columbia University Library.

Macmillan Authors. New York Public Library.

Anna Katharine Markham Papers. Wagner College Library.

Sara Haardt Mencken Papers. Goucher College Library.

Fred B. Millet Papers. Yale University Library.

Silas Weir Mitchell Papers. Harvard University Library.

Robert C. Ogden Papers. Library of Congress.

Walter Hines Page Papers. Harvard University Library.

William Lyon Phelps Papers. Yale University Library.

Burton Rascoe Papers. University of Pennsylvania Library.

Marjorie Kinnan Rawlings Papers. University of Florida Library.

Eugene Saxton Papers. University of Virginia Library.

Scribners Papers. Princeton University Library.

Florence D. Stearns Papers. University of Virginia Library.

Gertrude Stein Papers. Yale University Library.

Allen Tate Papers. Princeton University Library.

Charles Hanson Towne Papers. New York Public Library.

Virginia Hunter Tunstall Papers. University of Virginia Library.

Carl Van Vechten Papers. New York Public Library.

Carl Van Vechten Papers. Yale University Library.

Sir Hugh Walpole Papers. Berg Collection, New York Public Library.

James Southall Wilson Papers. University of Virginia Library.

John Cook Wyllie Papers. University of Virginia Library.

### BOOKS BY ELLEN GLASGOW

*The Descendant.* New York: Harper and Brothers, 1897.

*Phases of an Inferior Planet.* New York: Harper and Brothers, 1898.

*The Voice of the People.* New York: Doubleday, Page and Co., 1900.

*The Freeman and Other Poems.* New York: Doubleday, Page and Co., 1902.

*The Battle-Ground.* New York: Doubleday, Page and Co., 1902.

*The Deliverance.* New York: Doubleday, Page and Co., 1904.

*The Wheel of Life.* New York: Doubleday, Page and Co., 1906.

*The Ancient Law.* New York: Doubleday, Page and Co., 1908.

*The Romance of a Plain Man.* New York: The Macmillan Co., 1909.

*The Miller of Old Church.* New York: Doubleday, Page and Co., 1911.

*Virginia.* New York: Doubleday, Page and Co., 1913.

*Life and Gabriella.* Garden City, N.Y.: Doubleday, Page and Co., 1916.

*The Builders.* Garden City, N.Y.: Doubleday, Page and Co., 1919.

*One Man in His Time.* Garden City, N.Y.: Doubleday, Page and Co., 1922.

*The Shadowy Third and Other Stories.* Garden City, N.Y.: Doubleday, Page and Co., 1923.

*Barren Ground.* Garden City, N.Y.: Grosset and Dunlap by arrangement with Doubleday, Page and Co., 1925.

*The Romantic Comedians.* Garden City, N.Y.: Doubleday, Page and Co., 1926.

*They Stooped to Folly.* Garden City, N.Y.: Doubleday, Doran and Co., Inc., 1929.

*The Old Dominion Edition of the Works of Ellen Glasgow.* 8 vols. Garden City, N.Y.: Doubleday, Doran and Co., 1929–33.

*The Sheltered Life.* Garden City, N.Y.: Doubleday, Doran and Co., 1932.

*Vein of Iron.* New York: Harcourt, Brace and Co., 1935.

*The Virginia Edition of the Works of Ellen Glasgow.* 12 vols. New York: Charles Scribner's Sons, 1938.

*In This Our Life.* New York: Harcourt, Brace and Co., 1941.

*A Certain Measure.* New York: Harcourt, Brace and Co., 1943.

*The Woman Within.* New York: Harcourt, Brace and Co., 1954.

*Letters of Ellen Glasgow.* Edited by Blair Rouse. New York: Harcourt, Brace and Co., 1958.

*The Collected Stories of Ellen Glasgow.* Edited by Richard K. Meeker. Baton Rouge: Louisiana State University Press, 1963.

*Beyond Defeat: An Epilogue to an Era.* Edited with an introduction by Luther Y. Gore. Charlottesville: The University Press of Virginia, 1966.

### ARTICLES AND UNCOLLECTED STORIES BY ELLEN GLASGOW

"A Woman of Tomorrow," *Short Stories,* XXIX (May/August, 1895), 415–27.

"Feminism," *New York Times Review of Books* (November 30, 1913), 656–57.

"Ellen Glasgow on Censorship and Sinclair Lewis," *American Library Association Bulletin,* XVI (July, 1962), 618.

"The Novel in the South," *Harper's Magazine,* CLVIII (December, 1928), 93–100.

"The Biography of Manuel," *Saturday Review of Literature,* VI (June 7, 1930), 1108–109.

"What I Believe," *Nation,* CXXXVI (April 12, 1933), 404–406.

"Portrait of a Famous and Much Loved Dog," *New York Herald Tribune Books* (October 8, 1933), Sec. 3, p. 21.

"A Memorable Novel of the Old Deep South," *New York Herald Tribune Books* (July 22, 1934), 1–2.

"One Way to Write Novels," *Saturday Review of Literature,* XI (December 8, 1934), 335.

"Heroes and Monsters," *Saturday Review of Literature,* XII (May 4, 1935), 3–4.

"George Santayana Writes a 'Novel,' " *New York Herald Tribune Books* (February 2, 1936), 1–2.

"Elder and Younger Brother," *Saturday Review of Literature,* XV (January 23, 1937), 3–5.

" 'Nominalism and Realism' by Ellen Glasgow: An Unpublished Essay." Edited by Luther Y. Gore. *American Literature,* XXXIV (March, 1962), 72–79.

BOOKS

Alderman, Edwin Anderson, Joel Chandler Harris, and William Kent, eds. *Library of Southern Literature*. Vol. IV. Atlanta: Martin and Hoyt Co., 1909.

Andrews, Matthew Page. *Virginia: The Old Dominion*. Garden City, N.Y.: Doubleday, Doran and Co., 1937.

Auchincloss, Louis. *Ellen Glasgow*. University of Minnesota Pamphlets on American Writers, No. 33. Minneapolis: University of Minnesota Press, 1964.

Bagby, George W. *The Old Virginia Gentleman and Other Sketches*. Edited with an introduction by Thomas Nelson Page. New York: Charles Scribner's Sons, 1911 [1884].

Beveridge, Albert J. *The Life of John Marshall*. Vol. III. Boston and New York: Houghton Mifflin Co., 1919.

Blankenship, Russell. *American Literature as an Expression of the National Mind*. New York: Henry Holt and Co., 1931.

Brenner, Robert H., ed., *Essays on History and Literature*. Columbus: Ohio State University Press, 1966.

Brooks, Van Wyck. *The Confident Years: 1885–1915*. New York: E. P. Dutton and Co., 1952.

————. *The Writer in America*. New York: E. P. Dutton and Co., 1953.

Buni, Andrew. *The Negro in Virginia Politics, 1902–1965*. Charlottesville: University Press of Virginia, 1967.

Butcher, Margaret Just. *The Negro in American Culture*. New York: Alfred A. Knopf, 1956.

Cabell, James Branch. *As I Remember It*. New York: McBride Co., 1955.

————. *Let Me Lie*. New York: Farrar, Straus and Co., 1947.

————. *Some of Us*. New York: Robert M. McBride and Co., 1930.

Cabell, Margaret Freeman and Padraic Colum, eds., *Between Friends: Letters of James Branch Cabell and Others*. Introduction by Carl Van Vechten. New York: Harcourt, Brace and World, 1962.

Cash, W. J. *The Mind of the South*. New York: Alfred A. Knopf, 1941.

Christian, W. Asbury. *Richmond: Her Past and Present*. Richmond: L. H. Jenkins, 1912.

Clark, Emily. *Innocence Abroad*. New York: Alfred A. Knopf, 1931.

Collins, Joseph. *The Doctor Looks at Life and Death*. New York: Farrar and Rinehart, 1931.

————. *The Doctor Looks at Literature*. New York: George H. Doran Co., 1923.

————. *The Doctor Looks at Love and Life*. Garden City, N.Y.: Garden City Publishing Co., 1926.

————. *The Doctor Looks at Marriage and Medicine*. Garden City, N.Y.: Doubleday, Doran and Co., 1928.

————. *Taking the Literary Pulse*. New York: George H. Doran Co., 1924.

Cooke, John Esten. *Virginia: A History of the People.* Boston and New York: Houghton Mifflin Co., 1893.

Daggett, Mabel Potter. *Marie of Roumania: The Intimate Story of the Radiant Queen.* New York: George H. Doran Co., 1926.

Dew, Charles B. *Ironmaker of the Confederacy: Joseph R. Anderson and the Tredegar Iron Works.* New Haven and London: Yale University Press, 1966.

Eckenrode, H. J., advisory ed. *Richmond: Capital of Virginia.* Richmond: Whittet and Shepperson, 1938.

Fadiman, Clifton, ed. *I Believe: The Personal Philosophies of Certain Eminent Men and Women of Our Time.* New York: Simon and Schuster, 1938.

Faulkner, William. *Sanctuary.* New York: New American Library, 1954 [1931].

———. *The Unvanquished.* New York: New American Library, 1959 [1938].

Fishwick, Marshall W. *Gentlemen of Virginia.* New York: Dodd, Mead and Co., 1961.

———. *Virginia: A New Look at the Old Dominion.* New York: Harper and Brothers, 1959.

———. *The Virginia Tradition.* Washington, D.C.: Public Affairs Press, 1956.

Gaines, Francis Pendleton. *The Southern Plantation: A Study in the Development and Accuracy of a Tradition.* New York: Columbia University Press, 1925.

Garland, Hamlin. *Roadside Meetings.* New York: Macmillan Co., 1930.

Geismar, Maxwell. *Rebels and Ancestors: The American Novel, 1890–1915.* Boston: Houghton Mifflin Co., 1953.

De Graffenried, Thomas P. *The De Graffenried Family Scrapbook.* Charlottesville: University Press of Virginia, 1958. Uncopyrighted.

Hart-Davis, Rupert. *Hugh Walpole: A Biography.* New York: Macmillan Co., 1952.

Hendrick, Burton J. *The Training of An American: The Earlier Life and Letters of Walter H. Page, 1855–1913.* Boston and New York: Houghton Mifflin Co., 1928.

Hicks, Granville. *The Great Tradition: An Interpretation of American Literature Since the Civil War.* New York: Macmillan Co., 1933.

Holman, C. Hugh. *Three Modes of Southern Fiction.* The Lamar Memorial Lectures, Mercer University, 1965. Athens: University of Georgia Press, 1966.

Hubbell, Jay B. *South and Southwest.* Durham: Duke University Press, 1965.

———. *Southern Life in Fiction.* The Lamar Memorial Lectures, Mercer University, 1959. Athens: University of Georgia Press, 1960.

———. *The South in American Literature, 1607–1900.* Durham: Duke University Press, 1954.

———. *Virginia Life in Fiction.* Dallas, 1922.

Hughes, Roscoe D. and Henry Leidheiser, Jr., eds. *Exploring Virginia's Human Resources.* Charlottesville: University Press of Virginia, 1965.

Jessup, Josephine Lurie. *The Faith of Our Feminists*. New York: Richard R. Smith, 1950.

Kazin, Alfred. *On Native Grounds*. New York: Harcourt, Brace and Co., 1942.

Kelly, William W. *Ellen Glasgow: A Bibliography*. Charlottesville: University Press of Virginia, 1964.

Knight, Grant C. *The Strenuous Age in American Literature*. Chapel Hill: University of North Carolina Press, 1954.

Knowles, Katharine and Thea Wheelwright. *Along the Maine Coast*. Barre, Mass.: Barre Publishers, 1967.

Larsen, William. *Montague of Virginia*. Baton Rouge: Louisiana State University Press, 1965.

Lehmann-Haupt, Hellmut. *The Book in America: A History of the Making and Selling of Books in the United States*. 2nd ed. In collaboration with Lawrence C. Wroth and Rollo G. Silver. New York: R. R. Bowker Co., 1951.

Lingelbach, William E., ed. *Approaches to American Social History*. New York: D. Appleton-Century Co., 1937.

Loggins, Vernon. *I Hear America . . . : Literature in the United States Since 1900*. New York: Thomas Y. Crowell Co., 1937.

Lutz, Francis Earle. *Richmond in World War II*. A Publication of the World War II History Committee. Richmond: Dietz Press, 1951.

Manarin, Louis H., ed. *Richmond at War: The Minutes of the City Council, 1861–1865*. Chapel Hill: University of North Carolina Press, 1966.

Mann, Dorothea Lawrence. *Ellen Glasgow*. Garden City, N.Y.: Doubleday, Doran and Co., 1928.

Marcosson, Isaac F. *Before I Forget*. New York: Dodd, Mead Co., 1959.

McDowell, Fredrick P. W. *Ellen Glasgow and the Ironic Art of Fiction*. Madison: University of Wisconsin Press, 1960.

Meade, Julian R. *I Live in Virginia*. New York: Longmans, Green and Co., 1935.

Meade, Robert Douthat. *Judah P. Benjamin: Confederate Statesman*. New York: Oxford University Press, 1943.

Meeker, Richard K., ed. *The Dilemma of the Southern Writer*. Institute of Southern Culture Lectures at Longwood College, 1961. Farmville, Va.: Longwood College, 1961.

Meyerhoff, Hans. *The Philosophy of History in Our Time*. Garden City, N.Y.: Doubleday, and Co., Inc., 1959.

Mims, Edwin. *The Advancing South*. Garden City, N.Y.: Doubleday, Page and Co., 1927.

Moger, Allen W. *Virginia: Bourbonism to Byrd, 1870–1925*. Charlottesville: University Press of Virginia, 1968.

Monroe, N. Elizabeth. *The Novel and Society*. Chapel Hill: University of North Carolina Press, 1941.

Moore, Virginia. *Virginia Is a State of Mind.* New York: E. P. Dutton and Co., 1943.

*The Negro in Virginia.* Compiled by Workers of the Writers' Program of the Work Projects Administration in the State of Virginia. Sponsored by the Hampton Institute. New York: Hastings House, 1940.

Overton, Grant. *The Women Who Make Our Novels.* New York: Dodd, Mead and Co., 1931.

Page, Thomas Nelson. *Red Rock: A Chronicle of Reconstruction.* New York: Charles Scribner's Sons, 1912 [1898].

Page, Walter Hines. *A Publisher's Confession.* Garden City, N.Y.: Doubleday, Page and Co., 1923.

Pulley, Raymond H. *Old Virginia Restored: An Interpretation of the Progressive Impulse, 1870–1930.* Charlottesville: University Press of Virginia, 1968.

Quinn, Arthur Hobson. *American Fiction: An Historical and Critical Survey.* New York: D. Appleton-Century Co., 1936.

Raper, J. R. *Without Shelter: The Early Career of Ellen Glasgow.* Baton Rouge: Louisiana State University Press, 1971.

Rothery, Agnes. *Virginia: The New Dominion.* New York: D. Appleton-Century Co., 1940.

Rouse, Blair. *Ellen Glasgow.* Twayne United States Authors Series. New York: Twayne Publishers, Inc., 1962.

Rubin, Louis D., Jr. *No Place on Earth.* Austin: University of Texas Press, 1959.

Rubin, Louis D., Jr., and Robert D. Jacobs, eds. *South: Modern Southern Literature in Its Cultural Setting.* Garden City, N.Y.: Doubleday and Co., 1961.

Santas, Joan Foster. *Ellen Glasgow's American Dream.* Charlottesville: University Press of Virginia, 1965.

Scott, James G. and Edward A. Wyatt IV. *Petersburg's Story.* Petersburg: Titmus Optical Co., 1960.

Sheldon, William DuBose. *Populism in the Old Dominion: Virginia Farm Politics, 1855–1900.* Princeton: Princeton University Press, 1935.

Sherman, Stuart P., and others. *Ellen Glasgow: Critical Essays.* Garden City, N.Y.: Doubleday, Doran and Co., 1929.

Simkins, Francis B. *A History of the South.* New York: Alfred A. Knopf, 1961.

Simonini, R. C., Jr., ed. *Virginia in History and Tradition.* Institute of Southern Culture Lectures at Longwood College, 1957. Farmville, Va.: Longwood College, 1958.

Sinclair, Upton. *My Lifetime in Letters.* Columbia, Mo.: University of Missouri Press, 1960.

Spiller, Robert E., and others. *Literary History of the United States.* 3 vols. New York: Macmillan Co., 1948.

Tarrant, Desmond. *James Branch Cabell: The Dream and the Reality.* Norman: University of Oklahoma Press, 1967.

Tindall, George B. *The Emergence of the New South, 1913–1945.* History of the South Series, Vol. X. Baton Rouge: Louisiana State University Press, 1967.

Torpey, Dorothy M. *Hallowed Heritage: The Life of Virginia.* Richmond: Whittet and Shepperson, 1961.

Tuck, Dorothy. *Crowell's Handbook of Faulkner.* New York: Thomas Y. Crowell Co., 1964.

Turner, Arlin. *George W. Cable: A Biography.* Baton Rouge: Louisiana State University Press, 1966 [1956].

Twelve Southerners, *I'll Take My Stand: The South and the Agrarian Tradition.* New York: Harper Torchbooks, 1962 [1930].

Wagenknecht, Edward. *Cavalcade of the American Novel.* New York: Henry Holt and Co., 1952.

Warren, Robert Penn. *The Legacy of the Civil War.* New York: Random House, 1961.

Wertenbaker, Thomas J. *Patrician and Plebeian in Virginia.* Charlottesville: Michie Co., 1910.

Wilson, Edmund. *Patriotic Gore: Studies in the Literature of the American Civil War.* New York: Oxford University Press, 1962.

Wilstach, Paul. *Tidewater Virginia.* Indianapolis: Bobbs-Merrill Co., 1929.

Woodward, C. Vann. *The Burden of Southern History.* Baton Rouge: Louisiana State University Press, 1968.

———. *Origins of the New South, 1877–1913.* History of the South Series, Vol. IX. Baton Rouge: Louisiana State University Press, 1951.

Wynes, Charles E., ed. *The Negro in the South Since 1865.* University, Alabama: University of Alabama Press, 1965.

———. *Race Relations in Virginia, 1870–1902.* Charlottesville: University Press of Virginia, 1961.

ARTICLES

Arnold, Aerol. "Why Structure in Fiction: A Note to Social Scientists," *American Quarterly,* X (Fall, 1958), 325–37.

Baldwin, Alice M. "Ellen Glasgow," *South Atlantic Quarterly,* LIV (July, 1955), 394–404.

"Blood and Irony," *Time* (March 31, 1941), 72–74.

Brock, H. I. "Southern Romance is Dead," *New York Times Book Review* (April 12, 1925), 2.

Buck, Paul H. "The Genesis of the Nation's Problem in the South," *Journal of Southern History,* VI (November, 1940), 458–69.

Cabell, James Branch. "The Last Cry of Romance," *Nation* CXX (May 6, 1925), 521–22.

————. "Two Sides of the Shielded," *New York Herald Tribune Books* (April 20, 1930), 1, 6.

Canby, Henry Seidel. "Ellen Glasgow," *Saturday Review of Literature*, XVIII (September 10, 1938), 3–4.

————. "Ellen Glasgow: A Personal Memory," *Saturday Review of Literature* XXVIII (December 22, 1945), 13.

————. "*SRL* Award to Ellen Glasgow," *Saturday Review of Literature*, XXIII (April 5, 1941), 10.

Cash, W. J. "Literature and the South," *Saturday Review of Literature*, XXIII (December 28, 1940), 3.

Clark, Emily. "A Weekend at Mr. Jefferson's University," *New York Herald Tribune Books* (November 8, 1931), 1–2.

Colvert, James B. "Agent and Author: Ellen Glasgow's Letters to Paul Revere Reynolds," in Fredson Bowers, ed., *Studies in Bibliography: Papers of the Bibliographical Society of the University of Virginia*. Vol. XIV. Charlottesville: Bibliographical Society of the University of Virginia, 1961, p. 177.

Cowley, Malcolm. "A Promise Paid," *New Republic*, CXIII (December 10, 1945), 805.

Davidson, Donald. "A Meeting of Southern Writers," *Bookman*, LXXI (February, 1932), 494–97.

Edel, Leon. "Miss Glasgow's Private World," *New Republic*, CXXXI (November 15, 1954), 20–21.

"Ellen Glasgow's Hobbies," *Hobbies*, LI (July, 1954), 34.

Farrar, John. "Publisher's Eye View," *Saturday Review of Literature*, XXX (August 9, 1947), 11.

Fishwick, Marshall W. "Ellen Glasgow and American Letters," *Commonwealth*, XVII (January, 1950), 13–14.

Freeman, Douglas Southall. "Ellen Glasgow: Idealist," *Saturday Review of Literature*, XII (August 31, 1935), 11–12.

Fremantle, Anne. "The Pursuit of Unhappiness," *Commonweal*, LXI (November 19, 1954), 194–95.

Gara, Larry, ed. "A New Englander's View of Plantation Life: Letters of Edwin Hall to Cyrus Woodman, 1837," *Journal of Southern History*, XVIII (August, 1952), 343–54.

Geismar, Maxwell. "Ellen Glasgow's Private History," *Nation*, CLXXIX (November 13, 1954), 425.

Haardt, Sara. "Ellen Glasgow and the South," *Bookman*, LXIX (April, 1929,) 133–39.

Herrick, Christine Terhune. "The Author of *The Descendant*," *Critic*, XXVII (June 5, 1897), 383.

Hoskins, Katharine. "The Time of Ellen Glasgow," *Nation*, CLXXXVI (February 15, 1958), 143–44.

Jones, Howard Mumford. *"In This Our Life*: A Review," *Saturday Review of Literature*, XXIII (March 29, 1941), 506.

———. "The Regional Eminence of Ellen Glasgow," *Saturday Review of Literature*, XXVI (October 16, 1943), 20.

Kazin, Alfred. "The Lost Rebel," *New Yorker*, XXX (October 30, 1954), 130.

Krutch, Joseph Wood. "A Novelist's Faith," *Nation*, CLVII (October 16, 1943), 442.

"Life of a Monkey against the Life of a Man," *World's Work*, XVI (July, 1908), 10417.

MacDonald, Edgar E. "The Glasgow-Cabell Entente," *American Literature*, XLI (March, 1969), 76–91.

Mann, Dorothea Lawrence. "Ellen Glasgow: Citizen of the World," *Bookman*, LXI (November, 1926), 265–71.

Marcossan, Isaac F. "The Personal Ellen Glasgow," *Bookman*, XXIX (August, 1909), 619–26.

Mencken, H. L. "New Fiction," *American Mercury*, V (July, 1925), 382–83.

———. "A Southern Skeptic," *American Mercury*," XXIX (August, 1933), 504–506.

———. "Two Southern Novels," *American Mercury*, XVIII (October, 1929), 251–53.

O'Connor, William Van. "The Novel as a Social Document," *American Quarterly*, IV (Summer, 1952), 169–75.

Reid, Jane Davenport. "The Ellen Glasgow Collection of Ceramic Dogs," *Commonwealth*, XVI (February, 1949), 13, 30–31.

Richardson, Eudora Ramsay. "Richmond and Its Writers," *Bookman*, LXVIII (December, 1928), 449–53.

Rouse, Blair. "Ellen Glasgow and the Old South," *Saturday Review of Literature*, XXXV (April 27, 1952), 27.

Rubin, Louis D., Jr. "The Road to Yoknapatawpha," *Virginia Quarterly Review*, XXXV (Winter, 1959), 118–32.

Schlesinger, Arthur M. "Social History in American Literature," *Yale Review*, XVIII (September, 1928), 135–47.

Simkins, Francis B. "The Everlasting South," *Journal of Southern History*, XIII (August, 1947), 307–22.

Trigg, Emma Gray. "Ellen Glasgow," *Woman's Club Bulletin*, Richmond, Va., XI (No. 2, 1946).

Van Auken, Sheldon. "The Southern Historical Novel in the Early Twentieth Century," *Journal of Southern History*, XIV (May, 1948), 157–91.

Van Doren, Carl. "Barren Ground," *The New Republic*, XLII (April 29, 1925), 271.

Willcox, Louise Collier. "Four Distinguished Novels," *Virginia Quarterly Review*, I (July, 1925), 261–71.

Wilson, James Southall. "Ellen Glasgow: Ironic Idealist," *Virginia Quarterly Review*, XV (January, 1939), 121–26.

———. "Ellen Glasgow's Novels," *Virginia Quarterly Review*, IX (October, 1933), 595–600.

———. "Ellen Glasgow: 1941," *Virginia Quarterly Review*, XVII (April, 1941), 317–20.

Young, Stark. "Beautiful Apologia," *New Republic*, CIX (October 25, 1943), 588–91.

———. "Prefaces to Distinction," *New Republic*, CXXV (June 7, 1933), 101–102.

NEWSPAPERS

New York *Herald Tribune*
New York *Times*
Richmond *Dispatch*
Richmond *News Leader*
Richmond *Times-Dispatch*
Newspaper clipping file on Ellen Glasgow, Valentine Museum, Richmond, Va.

UNPUBLISHED MATERIAL

Field, Ann B. "Negro Protest in the New South: John Mitchell, Jr., 1863–1902." M.A. thesis, Duke University, 1968.

Kelly, William W. "Struggle for Recognition: A Study of the Literary Reputation of Ellen Glasgow." Ph.D. dissertation, Duke University, 1957.

INTERVIEWS

Babcock, Dr. Harold S. Castine, Me., October 4, 1968.
Blake, Miss Dorothy T. Castine, Me., October 4, 1968.
Brockenbrough, Miss Frances. Richmond, Va., January 9, 1969.
Cabell, Mrs. James Branch. Richmond, Va., November 14, 1968.
Clark, Mr. Glasgow. Richmond, Va., November 14, 1968.
Freeman, Mrs. Douglas S. Richmond, Va., November 13, 1968.
Hatch, Mr. Francis W. Castine, Me., October 4, 1968.
Hubbell, Professor Jay B. Durham, N.C., March 16, 1967.
Longerbeam, Mr. H. L. Richmond, Va., November 15, 1968.
Perkins, Mrs. Arthur. Richmond, Va., November 15, 1968.
Shield, Mrs. James Asa. Richmond, Va., January 9, 1969.
Strout, Mrs. Regis. Castine, Me., October 4, 1968.
Sydnor, Mrs. Garland S., Jr. Richmond, Va., November 14, 1968.
Trigg, Mrs. William R., Jr. Richmond, Va., January 10, 1969.
Wardwell, Mrs. R. S. Castine, Me., October 4, 1968.

# Index